ROUTLEDGE LIBRARY EDITIONS: DEMOGRAPHY

Volume 11

POPULATION GROWTH IN LATIN AMERICA AND U.S. NATIONAL SECURITY

POPULATION GROWTH IN LATIN AMERICA AND U.S. NATIONAL SECURITY

Edited by
JOHN SAUNDERS

Routledge
Taylor & Francis Group
LONDON AND NEW YORK

First published in 1986 by Allen & Unwin Inc.

This edition first published in 2024
by Routledge
4 Park Square, Milton Park, Abingdon, Oxon OX14 4RN

and by Routledge
605 Third Avenue, New York, NY 10158

Routledge is an imprint of the Taylor & Francis Group, an informa business

British Library Cataloguing in Publication Data
A catalogue record for this book is available from the British Library

ISBN: 978-1-032-53819-8 (Set)
ISBN: 978-0-367-28388-9 (Volume 11) (hbk)
ISBN: 978-0-367-29934-7 (Volume 11) (pbk)
ISBN: 978-0-429-30263-3 (Volume 11) (ebk)

DOI: 10.4324/9780429302633

Publisher's Note
The publisher has gone to great lengths to ensure the quality of this reprint but points out that some imperfections in the original copies may be apparent.

POPULATION GROWTH IN LATIN AMERICA AND U.S. NATIONAL SECURITY

Edited by

JOHN SAUNDERS

Department of Sociology and Anthropology
Mississippi State University

Boston
Allen & Unwin, Inc.
London *Sydney*

Allen & Unwin, Inc.
8 Winchester Place, Winchester, MA 01890, USA

George Allen & Unwin (Publishers) Ltd.
40 Museum Street, London, WC1A 1LU, UK

George Allen & Unwin (Publishers) Ltd.
Park Lane, Hemel Hempstead, Herts HP2 4TE, UK

George Allen & Unwin Australia Pty Ltd.
8 Napier Street, North Sydney, NSW 2060, Australia

First Published in 1986

Library of Congress Cataloging-in-Publication Data

Population growth in Latin America and U.S. national security.

Includes index.
1. Latin America—Population. 2. United States—National security. I. Saunders, John V. D (John Van Dyke), 1930– .
HB3530.5P675 1986 304.6'2'098 86–7970
ISBN 0-04-497002-1 (alk. paper)

British Library Catalouging in Publication Data

Population growth in Latin America and U.S. national security.
1. United States—National security
2. Latin America—Population
I. Saunders, John
327.73 UA23

ISBN 0-04-497002-1

MANUFACTURED IN THE UNITED STATES OF AMERICA

Contents

List of Tables

PREFACE

CHAPTER 2

CHAPTER 3

CHAPTER 4

CHAPTER 5

CHAPTER 6

CHAPTER 7

Foreword

The Center for International Security and Strategic Studies (CISS) at Mississippi State University proudly presents this volume's findings on the critical and timely issues of *Population Growth in Latin America and U.S. National Security*.

The starting point of this project was the gloomy demographic projection that between 1981 and 2001, if present growth rates continue, the population of the Western Hemisphere will grow by 42%. This increase, translated into numbers, will be close to 263 million persons, of which 38 million will be added to North America (the United States and Canada) and the balance, 225 million, will be added to the Caribbean and Middle and South America. In other words, the population of North America will increase only 15%, but the population of the Caribbean and Middle and South America will grow by 61%. Thus, by the year 2001, North Americans will be outnumbered by 2 to 1 in this hemisphere.

This population surge in the Western Hemisphere would have serious political, economic, social, and strategic implications for the United States. Neither the Caribbean nor Middle and South American industries or local agriculture would be able to absorb the surplus manpower. Meanwhile, agricultural production would not meet demands, assuming the present model of economic superstructure remains constant. Increasing social tensions and economic inequalities in the hemisphere would offer the Soviet Union an opportunity to drive a political wedge between Latin America and the United States, and the Kremlin and its allies would be expected to establish as many pro-Moscow regimes as possible. Another serious consequence of the population surge in Latin America would be increased emigration (legal and illegal) to the United States and, to a lesser extent, to Canada.

America would face a situation in which immigrants by the millions would need not only social but also cultural emancipation. The evolving situation could be much more difficult for the nation than the emancipation process of blacks in the 1950s and 1960s, since social and cultural balances would be changed radically.

In the light of the developing demographic shift in hemispheric population and its far-reaching impact on the security and economic interests of the United States, the CISS gathered the best demographers and specialists in security affairs available in the United States. The specific issues they addressed included, on the demographic side, the prospect for fertility reduction, labor-force absorption, and food supply, as well as the impact of population growth on the economies of Latin America. The reflecting issues on the security side concentrated on the implications of this demographic transition for political stability, domestic and international conflicts in the region, and the impact of these trends for U.S. security.

The year-long work and consultation of the research group culminated in a nationwide research symposium held at Mississippi State University on February 21–22, 1985. There, the novel combination of demographers and specialists on international security affairs allowed both groups to reap the benefits of intellectual cross-fertilization.

The results of this innovative approach are presented in this volume. Dr. John Van Dyke Saunders, Senior Fellow of the CISS and professor of sociology, led the research work as project director with great competence. He carefully edited and blended the 12 manuscripts. His scholarly expertise, leadership, and organizational ability ensured the success of this undertaking. The contributing scholars helped immensely by completing their manuscripts on time and without compromising the highest scholarly standards. The project staff of the CISS also assisted in achieving professional excellence. The Tinker Foundation and the National Strategy Information Center provided generous financial support to the CISS, which made this important study possible. Last but not least, special recognition should be made of Allen & Unwin for publishing this volume and distributing it across the Atlantic and the Pacific from their facilities in London, Boston, and Sydney.

It is hoped that the findings of our research will benefit governments and laymen alike, as well as corporations interested in foreign trade, investment, and other economic activities in the Caribbean and in Middle and South America and nongovernmental organizations active in the region, and that they will find useful data and ideas in this book. We also hope our work will help to lay the foundation for intrahemispheric debate and planning for the tasks and problems that lie ahead of us.

JANOS RADVANYI
Director, CISS

Preface

With one exception, Latin America is the world region with the most rapidly growing population. A comparison of annual rates of natural increase (the excess of births over deaths) is instructive. Europe's population is expanding at a rate of .3% a year. That of North America (the United States and Canada) by .7% annually. The population of the USSR enlarges by 1% every 12 months and that of Asia by 1.8%. The comparable rate for Latin America is 2.3%, which is exceeded only by Africa, whose population is added to by 2.9% each year. The Latin American rate of 2.3% implies a doubling of the population in 30 years, whereas the rate in the United States of .7% implies a doubling in 100 years.

During the next 20 years, between 1985 and 2005, if present rates continue, the population of the Western Hemisphere will increase by 42% (Table 1). This increase, translated into numbers of persons, will be on the order of 284 million, substantially more than the present population of the United States. The number of inhabitants of the United States will grow, during this period, by only 15%; that of the Caribbean and Middle and South America will increase by 60%.

The most rapid increase is anticipated in Middle America, whose population will expand from 105 to 179 million in the next two decades, a 70% increase. Mexico, the most populous country in the region, will grow to encompass 133 million inhabitants by the year 2005. The population of South America, now barely larger than that of the northern portion of the hemisphere, will exceed the latter by 121 million in 2005. Brazil, the second-largest nation in the hemisphere in population and in territory, will be home for more than 200 million persons. It is probable that by 2005 North

TABLE 1
Estimated Population of the Americas, 1985, and Projection to the Year 2005

Geographical Area	1985 N (millions)	1985 %	2005 N (millions)	2005 %	Percent Change 1985–2005
The Americas	**670**	**100**	**952**	**100**	**42**
North America	*264*	*39*	*304*	*32*	*15*
United States	240	36	275	29	15
Canada	25	4	30	3	20
Caribbean, Middle and South America	*406*	*61*	*648*	*68*	*60*
Caribbean	31	5	44	5	42
Middle America	105	16	179	19	70
(Mexico)	(80)	(12)	(133)	(14)	(66)
South America	271	40	425	45	57
(Brazil)	(138)	(21)	(218)	(23)	(58)

Source: Compiled and computed from data in Population Reference Bureau (1985).

Americans will be outnumbered by more than 2 to 1 in this hemisphere. These dramatically different rates of population growth herald severe population pressures, even though growth rates may experience some decline.

The future growth of the population of Latin America cannot help but have political, economic, social, strategic, and other implications for the United States. The pace of economic development, for which rapid population growth is an impediment, is unlikely to create enough jobs to absorb a doubling of the size of the labor force in 20 years and effect a reduction of the unacceptably high rates of unemployment that prevail in many countries and are already causing widespread discontent. Young persons, many of whom will be migrants from rural areas, will flock to large cities to join others of their kind, augmenting the pool of the unemployed. They will face the options of engaging in illegal activities, among which must be counted terrorism and attempting to migrate illegally to a country that offers better economic opportunities. The growth of social and economic inequality and of social tensions to which rapid population growth will contribute in the absence of compensatory economic development will offer the Soviet Union new opportunities to drive a wedge between Latin America and the United States. Directly or though surrogates, the Soviets, through assistance to local radical insurgencies, will attempt to establish as many pro-Moscow regimes as possible. Recent history offers examples. If the choice is to migrate in search of employment, the United States will be the objective of the greatest number, most of whom will seek to enter illegally. The pressure now faced by the United States from illegal entrants along its southern border will be greatly magnified, leading to the adoption of draconian measures to stop the flow. These measures, which will be contrary to U.S. national ideals, will tend to create within the United States an underclass of less than equal residents and citizens, thus sowing new seeds of social discontent.

Argentina, Brazil, and Mexico are becoming increasingly important in international affairs. Argentina and Brazil have the resource base to build nuclear weapons. Mexico lacks only the capital to acquire it. Brazil may well become a major power in the next century, and crucial to the national interest of the United States. The existence of friendly governments in these countries, particularly in Brazil, will be of the utmost importance. Strategic natural resources, such as oil in Venezuela and Mexico and chromium and iron in Brazil, provide opportunities for expanded cooperation with the United States. Political instability caused, albeit indirectly, by rapid population growth could interrupt the flow of strategic materials from south to north and favor the establishment of Marxist regimes.

In the pages that follow, essays are presented that touch on these and other possible or probable consequences of rapid population growth in Latin America for the national interest and national security of the United States.

J.S.

About the Authors

JOHN DeWITT is Director, Office of Inter-American Affairs, Bureau of Intelligence and Research, Department of State. A career Foreign Service Officer since 1960, he has served abroad at posts in Monterrey, Brasilia, Cali, Guayaquil, Rio de Janeiro, and Paris. In his present position he supervises a staff of 13 responsible for preparing daily intelligence summaries and comments on developments in Latin America for the Secretary of State. In an earlier Washington assignment he was Deputy Assistant Secretary of State for Consular Affairs and served for 2 years as State Department representative on President Jimmy Carter's task force for reform of immigration legislation. He received an M.A. in Latin American area studies and a Ph.D. in geography from the University of Florida and a B.S. from the U.S. Naval Academy.

SERGIO DIAZ-BRIQUETS is Director of Research, Institute for World Concerns, Duquesne University. He was formerly associated with the Population Reference Bureau in Washington, D.C., and the International Development Research Center in Ottawa, Canada. A specialist in population and development issues, he holds an M.A. from Georgetown University and a Ph.D. in demography from the University of Pennsylvania. Dr. Diaz-Briquets has authored or coauthored several books, including *The Health Revolution in Cuba* (University of Texas Press, 1983), as well as a number of scholarly papers on population topics, among them international migration.

RICHARD CLINTON is Associate Professor, Department of Political Science, Oregon State University, where from 1977 until 1982 he was Associate Dean of the College of Liberal Arts. From 1971 to 1976 he was Assistant Professor of Political Science at the University of North Carolina at Chapel Hill and a research associate of the Carolina Population Center. He has been a consultant to a number of organizations including the Agency for International Development, Ford Foundation, International Planned Parenthood Federation, National Institute of Child Health and Human Development, Smithsonian Institution, and UNESCO. During 1982–1983 he was a senior Fulbright lecturer in Lima, Peru. He is the coeditor of *Political Science in Population Studies* (1972) and *Research in the Politics of Population* (1972), editor of *Population and Politics: New Directions in Political Science Research* (1973), and author of *Problems of Population Policy Formation in Peru* (1971) and *Poblacion y Desarrollo en el Peru* (forthcoming), in addition to some 30 journal articles and chapters in edited works.

MURRAY GENDELL is Professor of Demography, Chairman of the Department of Demography, and Director of the Center for Population Research at Georgetown University in Washington, D.C. He has been at Georgetown University since 1966, where he was first Associate Professor, then Professor, of Sociology until 1981. He has also taught at the City College of the City University of New York and Columbia University, from which he received the Ph.D. degree in sociology in 1963. He has held research positions at the University of California (Berkeley) in 1965–1966, the International Labor Office (Geneva) in 1963–1964, the New York City Department of Correction in 1957–1958, the U.S. Bureau of the Census in 1956, and Teachers College, Columbia University, in 1955. He has written about fertility trends in Brazil, women's labor-force participation in Latin America, and family and household structure in Guatemala. Recent publications include *Sweden Faces Zero Population Growth* (1980); "Projections of Non-English Language Background and Limited English Proficient Persons in the Year 2000: Educational Planning in the Demographic Context," *NABE* (National Association for Bilingual Education) *Journal* (1981); and *Factors Underlying Stalled Fertility in Four Less Developed Countries* (one of which is Costa Rica), a World Bank report (1983). He has served as consultant to the U.S. Agency for International Development, U.S. National Center for Health Statistics, U.S. Army Research Institute, and the World Bank, as well as private research organizations.

MARGARET DALY HAYES is Director of the Washington Office of the Council of the Americas, the senior private-sector organization involved in hemisphere relations. She served as senior Western Hemisphere staff person on the Senate Foreign Relations Committee before going to the Council of the Americas. Dr. Hayes has written and published widely in both scholarly and policy-related books and journals. She recently published *Latin America and the U.S. National Interest* (Westview Press, 1984). Dr. Hayes was lead consultant for security issues to the Bipartisan National Commission on Central America. She has also written extensively on Central American and Caribbean security questions.

Dr. Hayes was Associate Director of the Center of Brazilian Studies at the Johns Hopkins School of Advanced International Studies (1978–1980) and Executive Director of the Commission on United States–Brazil Relations (1979–1980). From 1974 to 1978 Dr. Hayes was principal investigator on several projects examining issues of the Panama Canal treaties. She has been a consultant to the Foreign Service Institute of the Department of State and has directed research for the U.S. Information Agency.

Dr. Hayes holds M.A. and Ph.D. degrees in political science from Indiana University and an M.A. degree in Spanish literature from New York University and the University of Madrid. She earned the bachelor's degree in journalism at Northwestern University.

JOHN J. MACISCO, JR. is Professor of Sociology at Fordham University in New York City. He worked for the Ford Foundation in Santiago, Chile at the United Nations Demographic Training Center, CELADE, and has taught at Georgetown and the University of Pennsylvania. His Ph.D. in Sociology is from Brown University. Dr. Macisco has authored and coauthored several books, including, *Migraciones Internas: Teoria, Metodo y Factores Sociologicos*, CELADE, Centro Latinoamericano de Demografia, Buenos Aires, Argentina, 1975, as well as papers on migration and adjustment of Latin American populations.

T. DAVID MASON is Assistant Professor of Political Science and Associate Director of the Center for International Security and Strategic Studies at Mississippi State University. He is a specialist in comparative politics (non-Western political systems) and security studies; his research has been concentrated on the development of theoretical models of civil violence and instability. He is the author of "Individual Participation in Collective Racial Violence," which appeared in the *American Political Science Review* (1984); China's Four Modernizations: Blueprint for Development or Prelude to Turmoil," which will appear in *Asian Affairs*; as well as several works on civil violence in the United States, El Salvador, and elsewhere.

PHILIP MUSGROVE is currently Advisor in Health Economics, Pan American Health Organization (PAHO). Before joining PAHO in 1982, he was a consultant to the World Bank's Living Standards Measurement Study; prior to that, from 1966 to 1968 and again from 1971 to 1980, technical coordinator in the ECIEL Program of Joint Studies of Latin American Economic

Integration and a member of the staff of the Brookings Institution. He has also been a research associate with Resources for the Future, and a consultant to the Inter-American Development Bank and to the Central Banks of Venezuela and the Dominican Republic. He has taught full-time (as Visiting Professor) at the University of Florida and part-time at George Washington University and American University, in the latter case in the Latin American Program in Applied Economics. He has also lectured, sometimes at the invitation of the U.S. State Department, at numerous Latin American universities and research institutions. He is the author of *Consumer Behavior in Latin America* (Brookings Institution, 1978), *The General Theory of Gerrymandering* (Sage, 1977), more than 20 articles in U.S. and Latin American economics journals, and chapters in 8 books. He is the coauthor of *Natural Resources in Latin American Economic Development* (with Joseph Grunwald; John Hopkins, 1970) and *Income and Demographic Effects on the Structure of Consumer Expenditure in the U.S., 1975–2025* (with Adele Shapanka; Resources for the Future, 1982); and editor and coauthor of *Ingreso, Disgualdad y Pobreza en America Latina* (ECIEL Program, 1983). He received the Ph.D. in economics from Massachusetts Institute of Technology in 1974, following studies at Haverford College and Princeton University.

DANIEL S. PAPP is Professor of International Affairs and Director of the School of Social Sciences at Georgia Tech. Papp came to Tech in 1973 after receiving his bachelor's degree from Dartmouth College in 1969 and his Ph.D. in international affairs from the University of Miami in 1973. During his time at Georgia Tech, Papp also served as Visiting Professor at Western Australia Institute of Technology in Perth (1977), as Research Professor at the Strategic Studies Institute of the U.S. Army War College (1977–1978), and as senior research associate at the Center for Aerospace Doctrine, Research, and Education at the Air War College (1983–1984). Dr. Papp's research centers on U.S. and Soviet foreign and defense policies. He has published over three dozen articles in journals such as *Soviet Union*, *International Journal*, *U.S. Naval War College Review*, Social Science Quarterly, *Parameters*, *Resources Policy*, *Current History*, and *Air University Review*, and in books such as *Soviet Armed Forces Review Annual*, *The Soviet Union in the Third World*, *The Defense of the West*, and *Military Strategy in Transition*. He is the author of *Vietnam: The View from Moscow, Peking and Washington* (McFarland, 1981), *Communist Nations' Military Assistance* (Westview, 1983), and *Contemporary International Relations* (Macmillan, 1984). In connection with his work, Papp has traveled widely in the Soviet Union, China, Eastern and Western Europe, Southeast Asia, and Africa. These travels have been variously sponsored by the U.S. Department of

Defense, the U.S. International Communication Agency, the Inter-University Centre for Post-Graduate Studies, the Georgia Tech Foundation, and the NATO Defense College. Honors and awards that Papp has received include Phi Beta Kappa, selection as the Outstanding Faculty Member at Georgia Tech by the Tech Student Government (1976), the U.S. Department of the Army Outstanding Civilian Medal (1979), selection for inclusion in *International Who's Who in Education* (1981), and *Who's Who in the South and Southwest* (1982).

JOHN SAUNDERS is Professor, Department of Sociology, Mississippi State University. He was formerly Head, Department of Sociology, Mississippi State University; Professor of Sociology at the University of Florida; Ford Foundation adviser in Lima, Peru; director of the Latin American Language and Area Center at the University of Florida; Associate Professor of Sociology and Chairman of the graduate program in Latin American Studies at Louisiana State University; Visiting Professor at Catholic University, Lima, Peru; Fulbright lecturer in Ecuador and Mexico; and has been on lecturing assignments for the Organization of American States in Mexico and elsewhere. He is a former member of the executive council of the Latin American Studies Association and of the Rural Sociological Society. He has been a consultant to the World Bank, the Agency for International Development, the Ford Foundation, and other organizations. He is the author of *Differential Fertility in Brazil; The Population of Ecuador: A Demographic Analysis; "Education and Modernization in Brazil,"* a chapter in *The Shaping of Modern Brazil*; translator with Alfred Hower from the Portuguese of *Marcore* by Antonio Olavo Pereira; editor and contributor, *Modern Brazil: New Patterns and Development*; and the author of "Race, Color, and Prejudice: A Brazilian Counterpoint," a chapter in *Racial Tensions and National Identity*; "The Population of the Brazilian Amazon Today," a chapter in *Man in the Amazon*; and senior author of *Rural Electrification and Development: Social and Economic Impact in Colombia and Costa Rica.* He also has published articles in Latin American and United States journals.

J. MAYONE STYCOS is Professor of Sociology and Director of the International Population Program at Cornell University, Ithaca, New York. He has been a consultant to the Population Council, International Planned Parenthood Federation, Population Reference Bureau, World Health Organization, and United Nations Fund for Population Activities. He has had research and consulting experience in most of Latin America and the Caribbean and is currently working on the evaluation of family planning programs in Egypt. He is the author of *Human Fertility in Latin America; Ideology, Faith, and*

Family Planning in Latin America; The Clinic and Information Flow; and *Putting Back the K and A in KAP.*

WILLIAM J. TAYLOR, JR. is Executive Director of the Georgetown University Center for Strategic and International Studies. Until retirement in 1981 as an army colonel, he served in Germany, Korea, and Vietnam, completing his final 10 years of professional military service as Director of National Security Studies at West Point and Visiting Professor at the U.S. National War College. He is a member of the Council on Foreign Relations and the International Institute for Strategic Studies. He is the author or coauthor of 7 books and more than 50 other publications. In 1983 Dr. Taylor was selected for *Who's Who in America, 1984–85.*

HOWARD J. WIARDA is Professor of Political Science and Adjunct Professor of Comparative Labor Relations at the University of Massachusetts in Amherst. He is on leave from his position as Resident Scholar and Director of the Center for Hemispheric Studies at the American Enterprise Institute for Public Policy Research in Washington, D.C. Before joining AEI, he was Visiting Scholar at the Center for International Affairs at Harvard University during 1979–1981 and Visiting Professor at the Massachusetts Institute of Technology.

Professor Wiarda has been the editor of the journal *Polity* and served previously as Director of the Center for Latin American Studies at the University of Massachusetts. He has served as a consultant and adviser to a variety of private foundations, business firms, and agencies of the U.S. government. He was a lead consultant to the National Bipartisan (Kissinger) Commission on Central America. He is a member of several honoraries and has held grants from the Rockefeller Foundation, Fulbright Program, Mershon Center, Social Science Research Council, American Philosophical Society, National Endowment for the Humanities, and National Institutes of Health.

Dr. Wiarda has published extensively on Latin America, southern Europe, the Third World, and U.S. foreign policy. His most recent books include *New Directions in Comparative Politics*; *In Search of Policy: The United States and Latin America*; *Rift and Change in Latin America*; *Human Rights and U.S. Human Rights Policy*; *The Dominican Republic*; *A Caribbean Crucible*; *The State, Organized Labor, and the Changing Industrial Relations System of Southern Europe*; *Corporatism and National Development in Latin America*; *The Brazilian Catholic Labor Movement*; *Latin American Politics and Development*; *The Continuing Struggle for Democracy in Latin America*; and *Corporatism and Development: The Portuguese Experience*. Professor

Wiarda has lectured extensively at leading universities in the United States, Latin America, and Europe; his writings have stimulated some fundamental reexaminations of the way we interpret Latin American politics and development.

I

INTRODUCTION

1

Population Growth, Population Pressure, and Political Stability in Latin America

JOHN W. DeWITT

The three aspects of Latin American population growth that I will discuss in the context of U.S. national security are

- Population growth in Mexico: its impact on immigration to the United States and its effect on Mexico's political stability
- Population pressures causing border tensions between neighboring states
- The effect of rural–urban migration on the political stability of Latin American nations

The goal of U.S. national security policy in Latin American is to *(a)* prevent intervention in the hemisphere by hostile powers; and *(b)* develop and maintain within the hemisphere a community of free, democratic, and independent nations. Population growth directly threatens the second goal and indirectly threatens the first.

POPULATION GROWTH IN MEXICO

I began my U.S. Foreign Service career as a visa officer at the Consulate General in Monterrey, Nuevo Leon, Mexico. The *bracero* program, one of a long series of programs, formal and informal, to bring Mexican laborers to the United States, was being phased out. Under this program, which lasted from 1942 to 1964, more than 4 million temporary agricultural workers came to the United States. The program lasted so long, and so many people participated in it, that it became institutionalized as a strategy of income maintenance in thousands of Mexican towns and villages.

As the program was phased out, former *braceros* applied for immigrant visas at our posts in Mexico. Our immigration law and administrative system was incapable of handling the demand. I spent my entire first year interviewing agricultural laborers seeking to continue their seasonal employment in the United States. The work was certainly not what I had in mind when I joined the Department of State, and it was a far cry from the tasks performed by my colleagues at glamorous European embassies, but in retrospect I doubt that I could have received better preparation for the pressing problems of the real world.

Fifteen years after leaving Monterrey, I was a deputy assistant secretary of state for consular affairs and the State Department's representative on President Jimmy Carter's governmental task force on immigration reform. On a trip to California in 1976, I visited the Border Patrol at San Ysidro, across from Tijuana. At sunset, looking across into Mexico, I could clearly see the groups starting to form for the nightly attempt to infiltrate into the United States. Even the most dedicated Border Patrol units, equipped with search light helicopters and the most sophisticated electronic sensing equipment developed in Vietnam, were incapable of stemming the tide. *Lines and Shadows* by Joseph Wambaugh describes the nightly drama of illegal entry in vivid and gruesome detail.

Two years before the inception of the *bracero* program in 1940, Mexico's population was about 20 million; today it is about 75 million. Even with falling fertility rates, Mexico's population is expected to rise to 174 million by 2025. The problems that I saw in Monterrey in the early 1960s when I observed the seemingly endless lines of visa applicants or the situation I observed 15 years later in San Ysidro will without doubt seem insignificant and completely inconsequential 40 years from now unless dramatic actions take place during the intervening years.

Mexico's population growth creates two national security problems: illegal aliens from Mexico form a group of second-class residents of the United States, and uncontrolled population growth threatens Mexico's political stability.

Second-Class Residents

The "numbers game" is inevitably a problem when dealing with how many illegal aliens are in the United States. When General Chapman was the head of the Immigration and Naturalization Service (INS) during Gerald Ford's administration, there was much talk of the "silent invasion," and figures of 10 to 12 million illegals were bandied about. Today we speak of 3 to 6 million illegals. In truth, we just do not know. But taking from 3 to 6 million as a rough estimate, we are talking about 3 to 6% of our total workforce and something like 4% of the total population in some of the states of major concentration—California, New York, Texas, Illinois, and Florida.

For a country based on the rule of law and dedicated to the proposition that all men are created equal, it is a serious problem for the maintenance of our most basic traditions and beliefs to have such a large, and growing, proportion of the population relegated to a clearly second-class status, subject to exploitation and abuse, and denied full access to due process of law, one of the most cherished possessions of the citizens and legal residents of this country. I strongly believe that our inability to reach even a partial legislated solution to this problem saps our inner strength and is indeed a national security problem.

The Senate has twice passed, by overwhelming margins—80 to 19 and 76 to 18—the Simpson–Mazzoli bill, which provided at least a step in the right direction to regulate immigration through interlocking provisions for employer sanctions, legalization of some illegal aliens, improved law enforcement and law adjudication procedures, and a modified temporary worker program. Unfortunately, an unholy alliance of a wide variety of special-interest groups has prevailed, and the House has not enacted the bill into law.

Imperfect though Simpson–Mazzoli may be, it represents a comprehensive effort to tackle an important issue recognized as a serious problem by the majority of the American people. Failure to enact this measure not only leaves us without an honest attempt to come to grips with the problem but also postpones the day of reckoning when, sooner or later, new legislation must be enacted. The saying that we are a nation of immigrants has almost become trite through constant use. Trite it may be; true it is without a doubt. The strength of our nation has derived in great measure from our willingness to welcome widely diverse immigrants to our shores in large numbers throughout our history. With antiforeign sentiment growing in the United States, I fear that when legislation is enacted, it will be in reaction to even larger numbers of illegals in our midst resulting in harsh and restrictive measures that will greatly curtail legal immigration to this country. We could end up with immigration legislation as harsh and restrictive as that enacted after World War I. The prospect of such legislation is another dimension of the national security concerns posed by our inability to pass legislation concerning illegal aliens.

Political Stability

Another aspect of Mexico's population growth is the threat it poses to that nation's political stability. The U.S.–Mexican border extends for 2597 km from San Ysidro/Tijuana to Brownsville/Matamoros. The threat of instability south of this long land border is definitely one of national security concern. Mexico's ability to maintain peaceful and orderly development in the coming years will be sorely tested.

The Mexican government admits to a current unemployment rate of 8–10%, but unofficial observers maintain that the combined unemployment and underemployment rate is between 35% and 50%. One of the six economic goals of the administration of Miguel de la Madrid is to create employment at the rate of 500,000 to 700,000 jobs per year. The near impossibility of this task is revealed by Wayne Cornelius's estimate that whereas 700,000 new jobs per year are required, an annual growth rate of the economy of 6–7% creates only about 300,000 jobs.

Wayne Cornelius estimates that there are about 2 million Mexicans working illegally in the United States. This number is about 13% of the Mexican workforce. It is estimated that they remit from $4 to $8 billion annually to Mexico and that approximately 21% of the Mexican population depends to some extent on illegal employment in the United States. Clearly, sound policy and effective legislation are required to regulate and control the flow of laborers from Mexico to the United States for the well-being of both countries.

BORDER PROBLEMS IN THE HEMISPHERE: PAST AND POTENTIAL

Cross-border tensions caused by illegal migration between neighboring states have caused serious problems in the past and have the potential for causing even more serious ones in the future. Past and present situations in the Dominican Republic, Honduras, Argentina, and Venezuela highlight the undesirable consequences of this phenomenon.

Dominican Republic

The desperate employment situation in the 1930s in Haiti resulted in some 200,000 Haitians residing in the Dominican Republic on the eve of one of the most gruesome massacres of modern times. Haiti—with about one-third the size and twice as many people as her neighbor to the west—had been infiltrating the border area for years, creating a mixed cultural zone whose inhabitants were known as *rayanos*.

President Rafael Trujillo, seeking popular support and stung by the rolling up of his spy network in Haiti, was in the border town of Dajaban on the evening of October 2, 1937, when he announced at the town church, "Yesterday 300 Haitians were killed at Banica. This must continue." And continue it did in an orgy of bloodletting. Some 5000 to 20,000 Haitian men, women, and children were hacked to death by machetes wielded by soldiers and rioting civilians; thousands more fled across the border to Haiti.

Secretary of State Cordell Hull, commenting on the incident on November 23, 1937, stated, "I have long considered President Trujillo as one of the biggest men in Central America and in most of South America, and being a big man, I feel we can only look to him to find ways to clear up such misunderstandings as exist between his country and Haiti." By the terms of an agreement signed on January 31, 1938, the Dominican Republic expressed regret and agreed to pay an indemnity of $750,000, of which only about $250,000 was actually paid.

Honduras

In 1969 Honduras had a population density of 57 people per square mile, while its neighbor to the west, El Salvador, had a population density of about 380 people per square mile. El Salvador, with a total population of about 3.3 million, a population growth rate of about 3.8% annually, and an archaic and feudal landholding system, had been exerting pressure along the Honduran border since the 1930s.

By 1969 about 300,000 Salvadorans were residing illegally in Honduras, some as squatters on small subsistence plots, others as workers on plantations. Pressure from Honduran peasants for land of their own and agitation by large landowners to crack down on land invasions led the government to take action against the illegal Salvadorans. On April 30, 1969, the Salvadorans were given 30 days to get off the land. By late May some 11,000 had returned to El Salvador, bearing with them atrocity stories of beatings, murder, and rape that splashed across the Salvadoran press.

With passions high on both sides of the border, a riot in San Salvador centering on a World Cup elimination match between the teams of the two countries pushed tensions beyond the breaking point. On July 14, 1969, the army of El Salvador invaded and from 2000 to 5000 were killed (mostly Hondurans) and about 100,000 became refugees (mostly Salvadorans returning home). The North American press had a snide-remark field day with the notion that two banana republics were so backward as to go to war over a soccer game. Yet the deep-seated problems caused by El Salvador's population pressure remain a critical element in the instability of Central America, an area in which our commitment to regional peace is an essential element of our national security concerns in this hemisphere. The continued border problems between the two countries make solid cooperation in military matters difficult today.

Argentina

Long after Sarmiento's proclamation "to govern is to populate," Argentina continues to encourage population growth with special emphasis on the border areas. Foreign workers are still required for the national economy, and there are an estimated 1.5 million foreigners in Argentina (14% of the workforce) from Chile, Bolivia, Paraguay, Uruguay, and Brazil.

There is a school of geopolitical thinkers and writers in Argentina that worries about, and writes about, demographic pressures from Brazil. Of special concern is the movement of Brazilians into Misiones Province, the panhandle of Argentina that thrusts up into Brazil, where population densities are twice as great on the Brazilian side of the border as on the Argentine side. Although the presence of foreign workers today is more a cause of concern for the geopoliticos than the policymakers, the potential for future serious confrontations is real.

Venezuela

Estimates of the number of illegals in Venezuela range from 1 to 4 million from Colombia, Ecuador, Bolivia, and the Caribbean. Venezuela's population is only 17 million, and the proportion of illegal immigrants in the workforce may be as high as 40%.

By far the largest number of illegals came from Colombia, which shares a 2291-km land border with Venezuela. A surge in illegal immigration along the *caminos verdes* took place in the early 1970s, when rising oil prices caused a boom in Venezuela. Salaries were about $324 per month, compared with $99 in Colombia. The welcome mat was yanked from under the illegals in 1976 when the visa requirement was imposed and deportations to Colombia rose to about 1000 per month. The campaign against the illegals has continued with varying degrees of intensity ever since. With Venezuela's own economic problems growing because of a $35 billion foreign debt, 20% unemployment, and a severely skewed distribution pattern of national wealth, xenophobia directed against unwanted foreign workers grew, and in 1984 they were blamed for everything from increased crime and health problems to the major economic ills besetting the country. This anti-Colombian feeling combined with a long-standing boundary dispute in the Gulf of Venezuela, where billions of barrels of oil may be at stake, provide the potential for future serious problems.

THE EFFECT OF RURAL–URBAN MIGRATION ON THE POLITICAL STABILITY OF LATIN AMERICAN NATIONS

One of the primary national security policies of the United States is to promote the development of a peaceful community of free and independent states within the hemisphere. The long-term national security interests of this country are clearly best served by the establishment of democratic governments throughout Latin America. The short-term benefits to national security provided by slavish adherence to U.S. policy lines by petty tyrants such as Fulgencio Batista or Anastasio Somoza who terrorize their own people bring only long-term policy disaster, as experience with Cuba and Nicaragua demonstrates only too clearly. Democracy is the best long-term guarantor of stability and the best guarantor of human rights. Democratic regimes are the best long-term guarantors that the national security interests of the United States will be met.

At the moment there seems to be an irresistible democratic tide sweeping the hemisphere. Over the past 5 years, elected civilian presidents have replaced military rulers in Argentina, Bolivia, Ecuador, El Salvador, Honduras, Panama, and Peru. On March 1, 1985, President Sanguetti took office in Uruguay; on March 15, Tancredo Neves assumed the presidency of Brazil. Not a single country that was democratic 4 years ago has lost its freedom.

All democrats should rejoice at this trend. None, however, should be complacent or believe that the shift is irreversible. Instead, there should be sober reflection on the magnitude of the problems faced by democratic leaders throughout the hemisphere as they attempt to keep their countries on a democratic path without being overwhelmed by the problems of political extremism and economic recession.

In my view, one of the most ominous portents weighing against the long-term continuation of the present democratic trend in Latin America is the massive movement from rural to urban areas throughout the hemisphere. The movement is transforming the region from the rural civilization that it was when the century began to the urban civilization it will be when it ends. By 1970, 57.3% of all Latin Americans were living in cities, a proportion expected to rise to 75.1% by the year 2000.

Mexico City presents the most staggering example of this super-urbanization process. In 1940 its population was 1.5 million; today it is at least 16 million, larger than 16 Latin American nations. By the year 2000 it will be the largest city in the world with an estimated population of 31 million. Most of the houses in Mexico City are self-built (65%); 30% have no drainage. The city is growing at the rate of 100,000 per month.

Saõ Paulo is projected to be the second-largest city with 25.8 million people in 2000; Rio de Janeiro, 19 million; Buenos Aires, 12.1 million; Bogota, 9.6 million; Lima-Callao, 8.6 million.

The situation of the great mass of urban poor is one of bare survival. In preparing this essay I reviewed a report I wrote in November 1980, when I was consul general in Rio de Janeiro, regarding an extended conversation with Dom Adriano Hipólito, bishop of Nova Igauçú, a man certainly as worthy of international acclaim, in my opinion, as Dom Helder Cãmara.

Dom Adriano had been bishop of Nova Igauçú for 12 years. His diocese included practically all major municipalities of the *Baixada Fluminense* and had a population of about 3.5 million. The *Baixada* consists of a string of municipalities that ring Rio to the north and west; it is squalid, violent, and poor. Dom Adriano, one of the leaders of the Progressive church of Brazil, is often called the "Red Bishop"; he has been kidnapped, beaten, sprayed with red paint, and left naked on the roadside; his church was bombed. The Vanguard of Communist Hunters *(Vanguarda de Casa aos Communistas—VCC)* claimed credit for these acts.

Nova Igauçú, the seat of the bishop's diocese, is typical of the *Baixada Fluminense*. With a population of about 1.5 million, it is the second-largest city in the state of Rio and the eighth-largest city in Brazil. Only 20% of the homes are served by municipal water and sewage systems. Unemployment is from 30 to 40%. About 70% of the employed work in Rio and journey to work by bus and train for as long as 3 hours one way at a monthly cost of as much as 20% of monthly wages. Violence is rampant. The neighboring municipality of Bedford Roxo has the highest homicide rate in the world, according to United Nations' statistics. So much for the peaceful Carioca who cares for nothing but beach, carnival, and soccer.

Butterworth and Chance write in *Latin American Urbanization*: "Speculations concerning the political involvement of the urban poor in Latin America range from the assessments of the poor as disorganized and apathetic or apolitical to assumptions that they constitute a huge frustrated and angry mass, a potential revolutionary force." That a large percentage of the urban poor is angry and frustrated seems to be without doubt. During my tour in Rio there were several *linchamentos*—literally stonings to death by mob action of petty thieves, destruction of commuter trains, and food riots. Recent riots in the Dominican Republic and in Jamaica demonstrate the explosive nature of the poor when driven to desperation by price increases.

On the political side, recent urban arrivals from rural areas probably retain the conservative outlook formed in the countryside. Second- and third-generation urbanites, however, are not as likely to accept fatalistically the deprivations of urban life as do those who remember from personal experience the harshness of a rural existence. The threat to democratic civilian rule from the mass of urban poor comes not from their potential as a revolutionary force but from the logical assumption that in a free and open democratic process they will vote for the candidate that offers them the best deal. This candidate may be an extremist or demagogue whose election would be so unacceptable to the power brokers and the military that an authoritarian regime would be imposed rather than permit the victor to take office. In relatively prosperous times it is difficult enough for moderate and prudent candidates to wage a successful campaign to gain the electoral support of the urban poor; in the exceptionally tight economic straits that will prevail in Latin America for the foreseeable future, it may be impossible.

2

Population, National Power, and Security: The United States and Latin America

JOHN SAUNDERS

Population has long been recognized as influencing national security and power. At the simplest level, the larger the population, the larger the army that it can raise and, other things being equal, the greater its armed might. For these reasons, imperialist nations have often adopted policies intended to encourage reproduction, and many nations have viewed with alarm population growth rates among their rivals that have exceeded their own.

The demographic history of the United States is instructive. The population of the United States, which in 1824 numbered 11 million, by 1924 had grown to 114 million, an increase of 936% in only a century.[1] This phenomenal increase was largely the result of an unrestricted influx of immigrants, predominantly of European origin. Consequently, in 1937, on the eve of World War II, the population of the United States numbered 128,825,000 and exceeded the combined populations of Italy and Germany by 18.6 million and that of Japan by 59 million (United Nations, 1948:Table 1). Between the end of unrestricted immigration in 1924 and 1984, the U.S. population increased by only 107% to 236 million. Had it not been for unrestricted immigration and the contribution to national growth and development made by immigrants and their descendants, the population of the United States on the eve of World War II would have been less than half as large as it actually was and American national power significantly smaller. The consequences that this condition would have had for the history of Western civilization are incalculable. On the eve of World War II, however, American military power was small, for American military forces were few in number and ill equipped. The United States and its allies were able to prevail

[1]Estimated from data in United Nations (1971:5).

because they drew on national power potential, a function of population, industrial might, and resources, not because they were more powerful militarily at the beginning. The national power of the United States, in particular, was large in relation to that of her soon-to-be enemies, as events demonstrated.

It is therefore pertinent to review one of these elements, the changes in relative population size between the United States and Latin America that have occurred in the past and may occur in the future.

In 1850 the population of the United States was smaller than that of Latin America, and the U.S. share of the combined population of both was but 43.2% (Table 1). More rapid population growth rates in the United States than in Latin America for the remainder of the century increased the U.S. share of the total population to 55.8% in 1900. This share remained above 50% until about 1948. Thereafter the trend was reversed. As massive efforts to reduce mortality in Latin America met with success, the population growth rates in that region increased, and the U.S. share of the total declined to 37.7% in 1984. Continuation of present rates of natural increase in the United States and in Latin America will result in the U.S. share dropping to 30.4% in 2004 and to 23.8% in 2024.

Viewed from a different perspective (Figure 1), the population of Latin America, which was only .8 as large as that of the United States in 1900, will be 2.3 times larger in 2004. The population of South America alone will be one and one-half times the size of that of the United States and the population of Brazil nearly 80% as large as that of the United States. Although population growth rates in Latin America may decline during the next two decades, it is unlikely that they will decline enough to alter these trends to any great extent.

If projections are extended 40 years into the future, to 2024, based on current rates of natural increase, the Latin American population will reach 1 billion, while the population of the United States will number 312 million. The prospect of 1000 million Latin Americans, although it may in fact be off the mark on either the up or the down side, cannot but cause one to take notice. Of these, one-third will be Brazilians, one-fifth Mexican, and two-thirds South American. The population of Brazil will exceed that of the United States. Latin Americans will outnumber U.S. citizens by more than 3 to 1 (Table 1).

In the pages that follow, some of the implications of population growth rates in Latin America for the national security of the United States, as these operate through the contribution they make to national power potential, are examined.

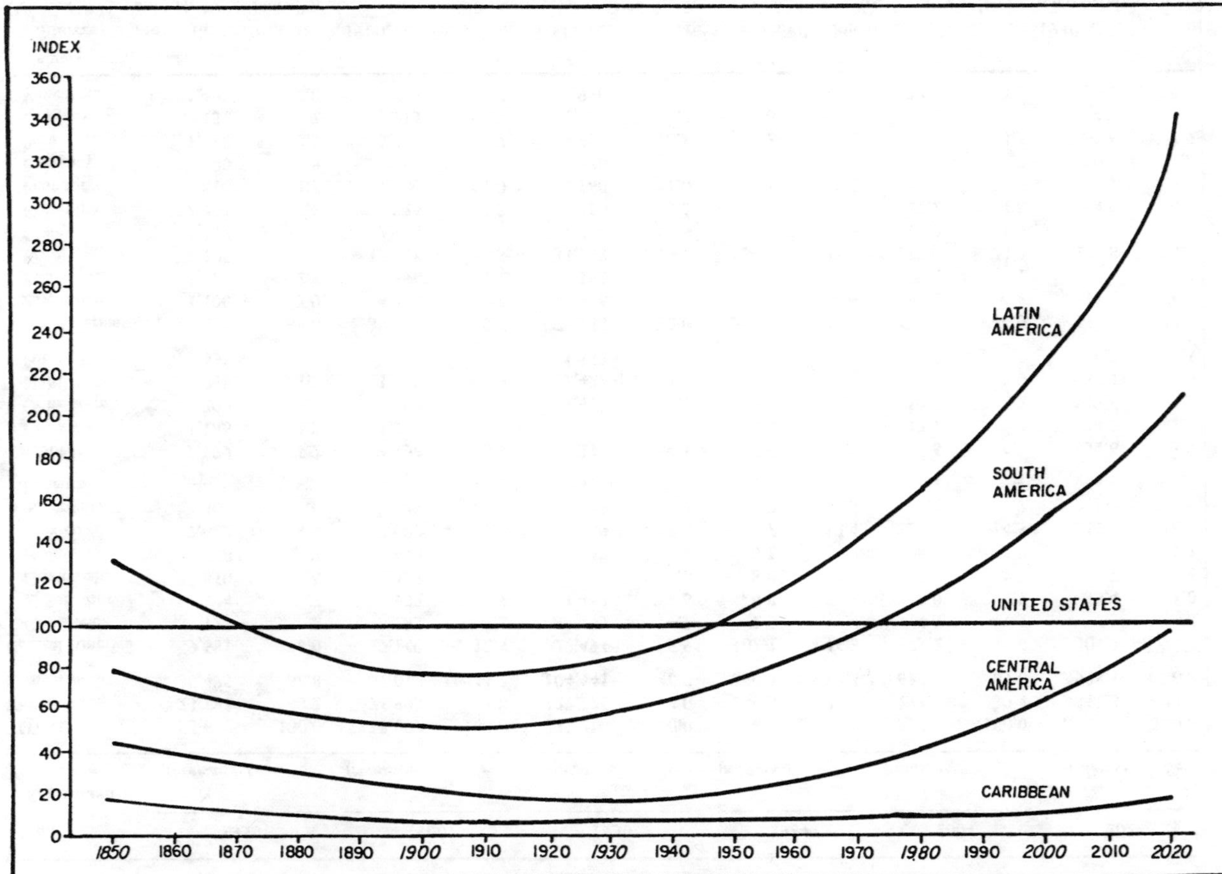

FIGURE 1. **The population of Latin America, South America, Central America, and the Caribbean compared to that of the United States, 1850–2020, by decade. United States = 100. (Source: Sanchez Albornoz, 1974; Population Reference Bureau, 1980.)**

TABLE 1

The Population of the United States and of Latin America by Region and Nation, 1850, 1900, 1930, 1984, and Projected to 2004 and 2024: Number and Percent Distribution

Region and Nation	1850 N (thousands)	1850 %	1900 N (thousands)	1900 %	1930 N (thousands)	1930 %	1984 N (millions)	1984 %	2004 N (millions)	2004 %	2024 N (millions)	2024 %
TOTAL	53,677	100.0	138,007	100.0	227,216	100.0	626.6	100.0	894.0	100.0	1,310.4	100.0
United States	23,182	43.2	76,995	55.8	122,775	54.0	236.3	37.7	271.7	30.4	312.3	23.8
Latin America	30,495	56.8	61,012	44.2	104,441	46.0	390.3	62.3	622.3	69.6	998.1	76.2
Central America	9,681	18.0	17,140	12.4	22,494	9.9	102.2	16.3	175.2	19.6	301.8	23.0
Costa Rica	125	.2	285	.2	499	.2	2.5	.4	4.3	.5	7.3	.6
El Salvador	394	.7	932	.7	1,443	.6	4.8	.8	8.0	.9	13.4	1.0
Guatemala	850	1.6	1,425	1.0	1,771	.8	8.0	1.3	15.9	1.8	31.7	2.4
Honduras	350	.7	443	.3	948	.4	4.2	.7	8.2	.9	16.0	1.2
Mexico	7,662	14.3	13,607	9.9	16,589	7.3	77.7	12.4	129.8	14.5	216.9	16.6
Nicaragua	300	.6	448	.3	742	.3	2.9	.5	5.9	.7	11.9	.9
Panama	—[a]	—	—[a]	—	502	.2	2.1	.3	3.1	.3	4.6	.4
Caribbean	2,779	5.2	4,496	3.3	9,211	4.1	25.0	3.9	35.6	4.0	51.6	3.9
Cuba	1,186	2.2	1,573	1.1	3,837	1.7	9.9	1.6	12.1	1.4	14.7	1.1
Dom. Rep.	200	.4	700	.5	1,400	.6	6.3	1.0	10.5	1.2	17.6	1.3
Haiti	938	1.7	1,270	.9	2,422	1.1	5.5	.9	8.5	1.0	13.1	1.0
Puerto Rico	455	.8	953	.7	1,552	.7	3.3	.5	4.5	.5	6.2	.5
South America	18,035	33.6	39,376	28.5	72,736	32.0	263.1	42.0	411.5	46.0	644.7	49.2
Argentina	1,100	2.0	4,743	3.4	11,896	5.2	29.1	4.6	39.2	4.4	52.8	4.0
Bolivia	1,374	2.6	1,696	1.2	2,153	.9	6.0	1.0	10.2	1.1	17.4	1.3
Brazil	7,205	13.4	17,318	12.5	33,568	14.8	134.4	21.4	211.8	23.7	333.8	25.5
Chile	1,287	2.4	2,904	2.1	4,424	1.9	11.9	1.9	17.0	1.9	24.3	1.9
Colombia	2,243	4.2	3,825	2.8	7,350	3.2	28.2	4.5	42.7	4.8	64.8	4.9
Ecuador	816	1.5	1,400	1.0	2,160	1.0	9.1	1.5	17.1	1.9	32.1	2.4
Paraguay	500	.9	440	.3	880	.4	3.6	.6	6.1	.7	10.5	.8
Peru	1,888	3.5	3,791	2.7	5,651	2.5	19.2	3.1	31.5	3.5	51.6	3.9
Uruguay	132	.2	915	.7	1,704	.7	3.0	.5	3.6	.4	4.3	.3
Venezuela	1,490	2.8	2,344	1.7	2,950	1.3	18.6	3.0	32.3	3.6	56.1	4.3

[a] Part of Colombia.

Source: Data for Latin America, 1850, 1900, and 1930: Sanchez-Albornoz (1974:169). Data for the United States, 1850, 1900, 1930: U.S. Bureau of the Census (1971:Table 1). 1984 data: Population Reference Bureau, (1984). Data for 2004 and 2024 estimated from Population Reference Bureau (1984)

DETERMINANTS OF NATIONAL POWER POTENTIAL

The military power of a nation can best be measured using factors such as the number of men under arms and the number and kinds of armaments at their disposal. Armies and armaments, however, are only expressions of policy decisions. Consequently, the military power of a nation can vary substantially from time to time. The nation's power potential, which represents the nation's capacity to arm itself, is more stable. A nation's power potential establishes an upper limit to its ability to use force.

Power potential is determined by the size of the population, the use of technology, and access to natural resources.[2] If a nation ranks high on each of these characteristics, then it either will be powerful or will have the potential to become powerful militarily. A nation of 10 million cannot place 1 million under arms, a nation of paupers cannot build or buy a modern military establishment regardless of the number of its inhabitants, nor can a nation of a few hundred square miles support the population or provide the resources that make for great power.

Population Size

Population size alone is an inadequate measure of national power potential. Total population is less relevant than the size of the population in the productive years of life. It is this fraction of a nation's population that contributes to its power potential.

More specifically, power is related to the size of the population aged from about 15 to 64, the ages that are responsible for the production of goods and services and that provide and provision men to be placed under arms. It is members of this age group—who work in factories, manage corporations, operate transportation and communication systems, grow food, mine, fish, and supply armies—who are the contributors.

Populations that by virtue of their age structure contain a large proportion of children will contain a small proportion of adults. Nations whose populations have a very young age structure have a reduced power potential thereby. The young will demand a large share of resources for their care and feeding, and these must be provided by a relatively small adult population. Such is the

[2] I am indebted to Organski and Organski (1961:27) for an early and partial statement of this theory: "There are three major determinants of power, the size of a nation's population, the level of economic development and the skill and efficiency of its government." See also Ray (1979: 102) and Morgenthau (1978:130–132). Ferris (1973:31–54) developed, with a view to studying what he terms power capabilities and conflicts, a "power capability score" derived from an elaborate procedure based on a factor analysis incorporating land area, size of armed forces, size of population, total and per capita government revenues, total and per capita defense expenditures, and net value of international trade.

case with India, which has the world's second-largest population, 40% of whom have not yet reached their fifteenth birthday, leaving India no alternative but to divert to the young a large portion of its resources, which otherwise could be applied toward the development of national power. Although India is the second-most-populous nation in the world, it is not the second-most powerful.

Technology

The extent to which the members of a population make use of modern technologies for production, transportation, and communication determines the degree to which they are equipped to exploit resources and contribute to the nation's power. Modern means of production, transportation, and communication rely almost exclusively on hydro- and nuclear-generated electric energy or on energy extracted from fossil fuels and on the machines built to employ it. The more modernized and industrialized a society becomes, the greater its consumption of these modern sources of energy and the lesser its reliance on traditional sources of energy such as wind, water, and animal power. Modernization is both cause and consequence of the use of ever more efficient devices for the conversion of inanimate sources of energy (Cottrell, 1955; Levy, 1966; Sofranko, Noland, and Bealer, 1975). Sofranko, Noland, and Bealer, after examining data on energy consumption, conclude that it is "the best gauge of societal modernization and of the status of societies relative to other societies" (1975:213). Energy consumption and technological development go hand in hand.

Data on per capita energy consumption are a useful index of the technological level and industrial might of a society. The United Nations provides information on energy consumption expressed as equivalents of the energy contained in a kilogram of coal. Entering into this computation are the consumption of coal, lignite, petroleum, gas and hydro, and nuclear-generated electricity. These data, which are relatively easy to compile, are preferable to income or other monetary statistics, which are more difficult to assemble and whose conversion to a standard unit of value is often problematic, as is comparison between different times because of differences in purchasing power and changes in value caused by inflation (Ferris, 1973: 36–37; Saunders and Reinhart, 1967:773–774).

Access to Natural Resources

The greater the area of a nation, the greater its probable access to natural resources, whether they be farmland, hydroelectric potential, minerals, or others. Some nations have gained access to natural resources beyond their borders, but in time of conflict this access has often been eliminated or reduced and should not be counted as contributing to a nation's power potential.

Natural resources other than those that are coextensive with land or water tend to occur over small geographic areas. Small areas may contain a large share of the world's resources of a given mineral. A nation that has twice the area of another does not necessarily possess double the natural resources. Thus a large nation may have little or no access within its borders to an important natural resource, as is the case with Brazil, which has a very large area but little access to petroleum. A large area, however, will be more likely to contain a greater diversity of resources than a small area. Although Brazil's petroleum reserves are small, it contains vast quantities of a large number of other important resources. Kuwait, a minuscule country, is estimated to have one-fifth of the world's petroleum reserves (Westerman and Bacheller, 1977: 563), but due to its small size, it has no other resources of consequence. Although a large area does not assure access to a given resource, it greatly enhances access to resources in general. Although a small area does not preclude accesses to a given resource, it greatly limits access to resources in general. Although the relationship of area to resources is imperfect, it is positive and real.

In considering the use of land area in a calculus of national power potential the square root of the area (in square kilometers) is used rather than the raw number. Thus, for example, while Australia's area (7,686,810 km^2) is 17.1 times larger than that of Sweden (449,750 km^2), the square root of the first (2772) is only 4.1 times larger than the square root of the second (670). This device enhances uniformly the numerical expression of a small area in relation to that of a large area. It is not to be supposed that Australia necessarily has 17 times more natural resources than Sweden. A factor of 4 seems, intuitively at least, to be more reasonable.

THE NATIONAL POWER POTENTIAL SCORE

I propose to quantify national power potential through the use of the indices discussed above. A nation's power potential is the product of the size of its population in the productive ages, here defined as 15–64, its consumption of energy per capita in the production of goods and services, and its area. To consume energy is also to produce energy or the wealth with which to acquire it. Energy consumption is also, therefore, a measure of production and productive capacity. The more powerful the economy, the greater will be the quantity of energy consumed. It is evident that economic power is substantially reflected by the product of population in the productive ages and energy consumption per capita. The greater the population and the higher the quantity of energy consumed by each of its members, the more powerful will be the economy.

The presence of a relatively large dependent population affects the power potential score in two ways. First, it means a smaller number of contributors (population age 15–64) than would otherwise be the case, and, second, it tends to depress energy consumption per capita by retarding development.

The case for land area is not as clear-cut. Although land area is a factor in national power, there is no firm theoretical basis for assigning it a weight in an equation of national power. The selection of the square root of the area in square kilometers is not, however, entirely without foundation. It denies a one-to-one relationship between area and resources but recognizes area as a limiting factor for small nations and as an enabling factor for large ones. The following formula for a national power potential score is proposed:

$$\text{NPP} = \frac{P_{15-64}}{1000} \times \frac{E_{\text{pc}}}{1000} \times \frac{\sqrt{\text{area}}}{1000},$$

in which power potential equals the product of the population in the productive ages, energy consumption per capita, and the square root of the area in square kilometers. Each is divided by 1000 to facilitate computation and to avoid the astronomical product that otherwise would result.

Power potential is not proposed as a concept that will predict armed conflict. The decision to engage in armed conflict is too individual and too conditioned by the unanticipated consequences of unforeseen events to be very predictable. Instead, it is indicative of influence in the international arena and of a nation's capacity to arm itself and to wage war if it so decides. It is suggestive of the outcome of a conflict rather than of the likelihood of its initiation. The following considerations are apropos: A nation that attacks another with an equal or greater power potential must win a quick and decisive victory or face the prospect of a protracted conflict or even defeat. A nation that attacks another with a greatly inferior power potential stands an excellent chance of victory. An adversary can greatly expand the power potential on which it draws through alliances that pool the power potential of more than one nation. Recent examples come to mind.[3]

[3]Of course, other factors influence the outcome of armed conflicts. Among these are the distance over which armed power must be projected. In this regard, for instance, Russia has a decisive advantage in Afghanistan in comparison to the U.S. intervention in Vietnam. There are also intangible factors, such as the willingness to accept a level of casualties that exceeds the enemy's, national character, and national morale.

When Iraq attacked Iran in 1980, its power potential was exceeded by that of Iran by a factor of 8.8. Failing to secure a quick and decisive victory, it now faces a war of attrition. At the time of the Six-Day War between Israel and Egypt in 1967, Egypt's power potential was greater than that of Israel by a factor of 9. Israel was able, nonetheless, to obtain a quick victory by destroying Egyptian military equipment. When, in 1982, Libya invaded Chad, its power potential was 68 times greater, and it did much as it wished except insofar as it was deterred by other nations with larger power potentials.

NATIONAL POWER POTENTIAL DISTRIBUTION AND CHANGE

Data that permit the calculation of national power potential scores for the United States and for the nations of Latin America are presented in Table 2, as are the scores for 1970 and 1980 and the percentage change in scores occurring between 1970 and 1980. Two features of these data are immediately apparent. The U.S. power potential score was greater than that of its closest rival, Brazil, by a wide margin in both 1970 and 1980. Brazil was followed by Argentina in 1970 and then by Mexico, which was in third place; in 1980 Argentina and Mexico had exchanged positions, Argentina being in third place.

Mexico was clearly preeminent in Central America in both 1970 and 1980, as was Cuba among her Latin Caribbean neighbors. In South America, in 1970, Brazil and Argentina were not very far apart, although Brazil was ahead. In 1980, however, Brazil's power potential was more than three times the size of Argentina's. During the intervening years Brazil's power potential had increased by 143%, while Argentina's had increased by only 28% (Table 2).

With the exception of Ecuador, the premier nations in Central and South America—Mexico and Brazil—experienced the largest percentage increases in national power potential from 1970 to 1980, establishing more firmly than ever their lead among the nations in these regions. Percentage increases of the national power potential score ranged from 9.8 in Nicaragua to 219.7 in Ecuador.[4] The United States was near the bottom of this range with an increase of 14.3%, a rate exceeded by every nation in the region except for Nicaragua.

Two factors are at work that help explain the slower rate of growth of the power potential of the United States and its decline in relation to Latin

[4]Ecuadorean energy consumption was given a powerful boost by the development of oilfields in the *Oriente* during the 1970s. Production soared from 308,000 metric tons of coal equivalent in 1970 to 15,270,000 tons in 1980.

TABLE 2

Population 15–64, Energy Consumption per Capita, Square Root of Area, and Power Potential Score, 1970 and 1980, United States and Latin American Nations

Region and Nation	*Population 15–64 (thousands)*		*Energy per Capita (thousands)*		$\sqrt{area\ (km^2)}$ *(thousands)*	*Power Potential*		*Percentage Change*
	1970	*1980*	*1970*	*1980*		*1970*	*1980*	
United States	128,203	149,075	10.811	10.628	3.060	4,241,168	4,848,169	14.3
Central America								
Costa Rica	931	1,188	.387	.552	.225	81	148	82.7
El Salvador	1,872	2,488	.194	.206	.146	53	75	41.5
Guatemala	2,703	3,640	.194	.267	.330	173	321	85.5
Honduras	1,400	1,862	.227	.225	.335	106	140	32.1
Mexico	26,775	34,782	1.048	1.629	1.404	39,937	79,550	99.2
Nicaragua	1,029	1,274	.358	.319	.360	133	146	9.8
Panama	795	468	.629	1.604	.275	138	206	49.3
Caribbean								
Cuba	5,418	5,700	.997	1.404	.338	1,826	2,705	48.2
Dom. Republic	2,156	2,646	.335	.484	.220	159	282	77.4
Haiti	2,862	3,190	.040	.065	.167	19	35	84.2
Puerto Rico	1,624	2,030	3.445	3.728	.094	526	711	35.2
South America								
Argentina	15,561	17,344	1.595	1.824	1.666	41,350	52,705	27.5
Bolivia	2,640	2,862	.227	.382	1.048	628	1,146	82.5
Brazil	51,678	71,120	.450	.793	2.917	67,835	164,513	142.5
Chile	5,600	6,780	1.152	1.035	.870	5,613	6,105	8.8
Colombia	10,829	13,844	.586	.768	1.067	6,771	11,345	67.5
Ecuador	3,087	4,160	.282	.669	.533	464	1,483	219.7
Paraguay	1,275	1,716	.142	.186	.638	116	204	75.9
Peru	7,280	9,328	.596	.626	1.137	4,933	6,639	34.6
Uruguay	1,580[a]	1,827	.907	.907	.421	603	698	15.8
Venezuela	5,550	7,506	2,392	3,520	.955	12,678	25,232	99.0

[a] Author's estimate.

Sources: Population Reference Bureau (1971, 1980): *United Nations* (1971, 1981).

America. First and less important, energy consumption per capita declined by 1.7% because of efforts at energy conservation. More important, the United States is suffering from what Thorstein Veblen called the penalty of taking the lead (Coser, 1977:273). An industrialized nation, while taking the lead, commits itself to technologies that at the time are advanced and efficient relative to others, and although new technologies are adopted with the passage of time, old technologies are not readily discarded, so new and obsolescent technologies exist side by side, reflecting a "fatal reluctance or inability to overcome this all pervading depreciation by obsolescence" (Veblen, quoted in Coser, 1977:274). The plight of the steel industry in the United States immediately comes to mind.

Rather than reflect a temporary condition, the relatively poor showing of the United States is the consequence of structural features of the society and the economy that will be difficult to overcome.

The nations of Latin America and, indeed, of the developing world have what Veblen might have called the advantage of starting late: the opportunity to skip development stages and invest at the outset in highly sophisticated technology. It is not surprising that the relative increase in Brazil's power potential score was 10 times greater than that of the United States nor that 11 of the region's 21 countries experienced increases of this measure 4 or more times larger than that of the United States.

In 1980 the power potential score of the United States was 29 times larger than that of Brazil and 61 times that of Mexico. It should not be supposed that differences of this magnitude will necessarily persist. If the annual percentage growth rates of power potential that prevailed from 1970 to 1980 are projected for 20 years, to 2000, the ratio between the United States and Mexico will be reduced to 20:1, and if projected for 40 years, to 2020, to 6.6:1 (Table 3). The ratio between the United States and Brazil will be reduced to 6.5:1 in 2000 and to close to parity (1.5:1) in 2020. Argentina, once the major power in South America, began an incomplete process of modernization early in this century and was well ahead of Brazil until about 1940, but has since declined relative to Brazil. Argentina suffers, perhaps, from the penalty of taking the lead and not holding it. It will be difficult for Argentina to catch up.

When data for a series of years are compared (Table 4), trends become clear. Small countries, although they may have phenomenal rates of growth of power potential, as is the case with Ecuador (Table 3), are destined to relative insignificance. Large nations, as occurred with Mexico and Brazil, have the opportunity to increase their power potential significantly in relation to other powerful nations. Both Mexico and Brazil reduced the difference that separates them from the United States. Adding data for another

TABLE 3
Annual Rate of Growth of Power Potential Scores, 1970 to 1980, and Projected Power Potential Scores, 2000 and 2020, United States and Latin American Nations

Region and Nation	*Annual Rate of Growth (%) of Power Potential, 1970–1980*	*Projected Power Potential 2000*	*Projected Power Potential 2020*
United States	1.347	6,335,716	8,279,682
Central America			
Costa Rica	6.213	494	1,649
El Salvador	3.533	150	301
Guatemala	6.377	1,105	3,805
Honduras	2.821	244	426
Mexico	7.134	315,636	1,252,371
Nicaragua	.937	176	212
Panama	4.088	459	1,023
Caribbean			
Cuba	4.010	6,040	13,490
Dom. Republic	5.897	887	2,790
Haiti	6.300	119	403
Puerto Rico	3.060	1,299	2,374
South America			
Argentina	2.456	85,623	139,103
Bolivia	6.200	3,817	12,711
Brazil	9.263	967,526	5,690,168
Chile	.844	7,222	8,545
Colombia	5.296	31,842	89,380
Ecuador	12.231	15,148	154,732
Paraguay	5.808	631	1,951
Peru	3.015	12,026	21,783
Uruguay	1.474	935	1,253
Venezuela	7.125	99,909	395,604

Source: See Table 2.

decade (Table 5) does not alter conclusions. The trend in the rate of growth in power potential has been downward for Argentina and the United States and upward for Brazil and Mexico since 1960.

In the modern world, superpower status can be achieved only by nations that are large in area and population and employ technology at a high level. At present, only the United States and the Soviet Union meet these requirements. Several other nations may do so in the future. Australia and Canada have large land areas and a high level of technology, but small populations.

TABLE 4

Power Potential Scores of Latin American Nations as a Percentage of the U.S. Score 1970, 1980, 2000, and 2020

Region and Nation	*1970*	*1980*	*2000*	*2020*
United States	100.0	100.0	100.0	100.0
Central America				
Costa Rica	*	*	*	*
El Salvador	*	*	*	*
Guatemala	*	*	*	*
Honduras	*	*	*	*
Mexico	.9	1.6	5.0	15.1
Nicaragua	*	*	*	*
Panama	*	*	*	*
Caribbean				
Cuba	*	*	*	1.6
Dom. Republic	*	*	*	*
Haiti	*	*	*	*
Puerto Rico	*	*	*	*
South America				
Argentina	1.0	1.1	1.4	1.7
Bolivia	*	*	*	*
Brazil	1.6	3.4	15.3	68.7
Chile	.1	.1	.1	.1
Colombia	.2	.2	.5	1.1
Ecuador	*	*	.2	1.9
Paraguay	*	*	*	*
Peru	.1	.1	.2	.3
Uruguay	*	*	*	*
Venezuela	.3	.5	1.6	4.8

Source: See Table 2.
*Less than .1 percent.

TABLE 5

Annual Rate of Growth (Percent) of Power Potential for Selected American Nations, 1960–1970, 1960–1980, and 1970–1980

Nation	*1960–1970*	*1960–1980*	*1970–1980*
United States	4.759	3.039	1.347
Mexico	2.333	6.292	7.134
Argentina	5.460	3.947	2.456
Brazil	5.965	7.601	9.263

Source: United Nations (1964, 1965). See also Tables 1 and 2.

India and China have large populations and land areas, but low levels of technology. In these instances, population size is so great that it constitutes a barrier to the achievement of high levels of technology use. Brazil has a large area, the sixth-largest population, and a low level of technology use.

Of the variables contributing to power potential, technology is the most susceptible to policy and the most readily increased. Very rapid gains in the level of technology use and application have taken place in a number of countries in recent decades, the most visible being Japan and Taiwan. Japan, it will be remembered, moved from a medieval level of technology maintained by centuries of self-imposed hermetic isolationism to major-power status during the relatively brief period between the opening of Japanese ports to world commerce in 1854 and the mid 1930s.

Population size cannot be easily altered by the implementation of policy, and territorial size can be increased only at great risk. Therefore, of the countries named, it is those that have low technology levels that are the prime candidates for superpower status in the next century. They are Brazil, India, and China. Although Canada and Australia have high levels of technology use, they are unlikely to develop populations large enough to enable them to contend on an equal footing with first-order powers unless population growth is substantially stimulated through immigration. Excessive population will be a handicap difficult although not impossible to overcome and requiring a long-term effort for India and for China. Brazil stands the best chance of evolving into a superpower during the next century. Indeed, this seems probable.

IMPLICATIONS FOR U.S. SECURITY

These developments constitute security concerns for the United States, first, because of reduced American influence and, second, because of conflict potential within the region that would provide openings for the Soviet Union or other rivals.

The increasingly greater power potential of Mexico and Brazil foreshadows a continuation of the decrease in American influence in Latin America that has been occurring since the end of World War II. Both Mexico and Brazil have pursued increasingly independent foreign policies over the last two decades. Recent examples are the declaration of recognition of Salvadoran guerrillas as representing the Salvadoran people issued jointly by Mexico and France in 1982. Brazil severed its military cooperation treaty with the United States in response to accusations of human rights violations made by the Carter administration.

Conversely, both countries are becoming more influential in their respective regions. Brazil has converted Paraguay and Bolivia into client states and gained concessions regarding transportation, trade, and electricity generation that are detrimental to the interests of Argentina. It has become an important supplier of arms on the international market. By the mid twenty-first century Brazil may rival the United States on the world scene. Mexico has become the leading arbiter of the current Central American conflict. The future course of these two nations is of vital importance to the security of the United States as its influence slips while that of Mexico and Brazil soar.

In the event that Ecuadoran national power develops as projected, it may be tempted to recapture the one-half of its national territory lost to Peru in an invasion in 1941 (Pareja Diezcanseco, 1958:432–437). If Bolivia achieves parity with Chile, it may seek to recapture territories lost to Chile in the War of the Pacific (Herring, 1967:585–586). If Venezuelan national power grows to exceed that of Colombia by a factor of four or more, the potential for conflict between them will increase. The eruption of such conflicts would provide extrahemispheric powers with opportunities to establish positions of political and/or military influence and compromise sources of strategic raw materials to the detriment of the United States.

REFERENCES

Coser, Lewis W.
1977 *Masters of Sociological Thought: Ideas in Historical and Social Context.* 2nd ed. New York: Harcourt Brace Jovanovich.

Cottrell, Fred.
1955 *Energy and Society.* New York: McGraw-Hill.

Ferris, Wayne H.
1973 *The Power Capabilities of Nation States: International Conflicts and War.* Lexington, Mass.: Heath.

Herring, Hubert.
1967 *A History of Latin America from the Beginning to the Present.* New York: Knopf.

Levy, Marion J.
1966 *Modernization and the Structure of Societies.* Princeton: Princeton University Press

Morgenthau, Hans J.
1978 *Politics among Nations: The Struggle for Power and Peace.* 5th ed. rev. New York Knopf.

Pareja Diezcanseco, Alfredo.
1958 *Historia del Ecuador*, (Vol. 2). 2nd ed. Quito: Casa de la Cultura Ecuatoriana.

Population Reference Bureau.
1971 *World Population Data Sheet.* Washington, D.C.: Population Reference Bureau.
1980 *World Population Data Sheet.* Washington, D.C.: Population Reference Bureau.
1984 *World Population Data Sheet.* Washington, D.C.: Population Reference Bureau.

Ray, James Lee.
1979 *Global Politics*. Boston: Houghton Mifflin.
Sanchez-Albornoz, Nicolás.
1974 *The Population of Latin America: A History*. Berkeley: University of California Press.
Saunders, John V.D. and George R. Reinhart.
1967 *Demographic and Economic Correlates of Energy Consumption in Demography* 4(2).
Sofranko, Andrew F., Michael Noland and Robert C. Bealer.
1975 *Energy Use and Alternate Measures of Societal Modernity in Sociology and Social Research* 39(4).
United Nations.
1948 *Demographic Yearbook*. New York.
1964 *Statistical Yearbook*. New York.
1965 *Demographic Yearbook*. New York.
1971 *Statistical Yearbook*. New York.
1981 *Statistical Yearbook*. New York.
U.S. Bureau of the Census
1971 *Statistical Abstract of the United States*, Washington, D.C.
Westerman, Sylvia and Martin A. Bacheller.
1977 *The CBS News Almanac*. Maplewood, N.J.: Hammond Almanac.

II

DEMOGRAPHIC DIMENSIONS

3

Medium-Range Prospects for Fertility Reduction in Latin America

J. MAYONE STYCOS

If there was any doubt by the mid 1970s that rapid population growth in the less developed countries (LDCs) was of concern for American national security interests, it was dispelled by Memorandum 200 of the U.S. National Security Council, issued on December 10, 1974. Entitled *Implications of World-Wide Population Growth for U.S. Security and Overseas Interest*, it detailed the threat posed by population growth to food supplies, energy, and economic development; it also highlighted political consequences, maintaining that "rapid growth, internal migration, high percentages of young people, slow improvements in living standards, urban concentrations, and pressures for foreign migration—are damaging to internal stability and international relations of countries in whose advancement the U.S. is interested, thus creating political or even national security problems for the U.S." (Anonymous, 1982:427).

Six year later, an Ad-Hoc Group on Population Policy composed of 18 U.S. departments and agencies prepared a document for the Fourth Annual Report of the National Security Council entitled *U.S. International Population Policy*. It maintained that rapid population growth threatened "U.S. foreign policy objectives of peace and stability, economic and social progress, and enhancement of human rights and dignity." Specifically, it expressed concern that by exacerbating problems of unemployment, urbanization, and economic discontent, population growth would increase the chances for "social unrest, political instability, mass migrations and possible international conflicts" (Anonymous, 1980:509–510). Subsequent statements of concern about the threat to U.S. interests have been voiced by other high-ranking officials in the administration[1] and Congress (Benedick, 1984).

If it is true that population growth in LDCs as a whole is crucial to U.S. security interests, it can only be all the more true with respect to Latin America. This is so not only because of the geopolitical position of most Latin American nations—that is, close and friendly neighbors—but because in a world of fast-growing regions, Latin America, at least until recently, has been growing the fastest.

Between 1920 and 1960, while the populations of the developed nations increased by 40% and those of the less developed by 70%, Latin American population grew by 138% (Stycos, 1978:407). Although African birthrates are currently higher than those of Latin America, African death rates are much higher, leaving Latin America with slightly higher rates of natural increase—2.8% per year for 1975 – 1980. By the year 2000, expected growth for the region (55%) exceeds all other regions except Africa (United Nations, 1981). In view of this enormous potential for growth, it is of some interest to ascertain the most likely course of that growth, as a first step in determining what actions would be appropriate for the United States.

LONG-RANGE PROJECTIONS

Latin America, which included fewer than 90 million inhabitants in 1920, now has a population of 364 million. This fourfold increase in only 60 years gives us some notion of the extraordinary velocity of growth in the hemisphere. Figure 1 shows that the population of the United States and Canada exceeded that of Latin America into the 1940s, but now Latin American growth is almost two-thirds larger than that of the United States. In Figure 2, an extrapolation of 2.4% annual growth rate projected by the United Nations for 1980 – 1985 results in a population in excess of 1 billion by the year 2025 and is nearly 2 billion by the middle of the next century. Several observations on Figure 2 can be made.

1. Although the United Nations clearly explains that its three variants "are intended to present plausible but not exhaustive ranges within which future population would likely grow" (United Nations, 1982:31), there is a tendency to regard the "high" estimate as the "maximum." In fact, the huge

[1]The Reagan administration spokesman took a different line at the 1984 World Population Conference and has subsequently seemed little concerned about population problems. However, the abortion controversy has confused the issue. It is still not clear whether or not a fundamental change in attitude toward population growth has occurred.

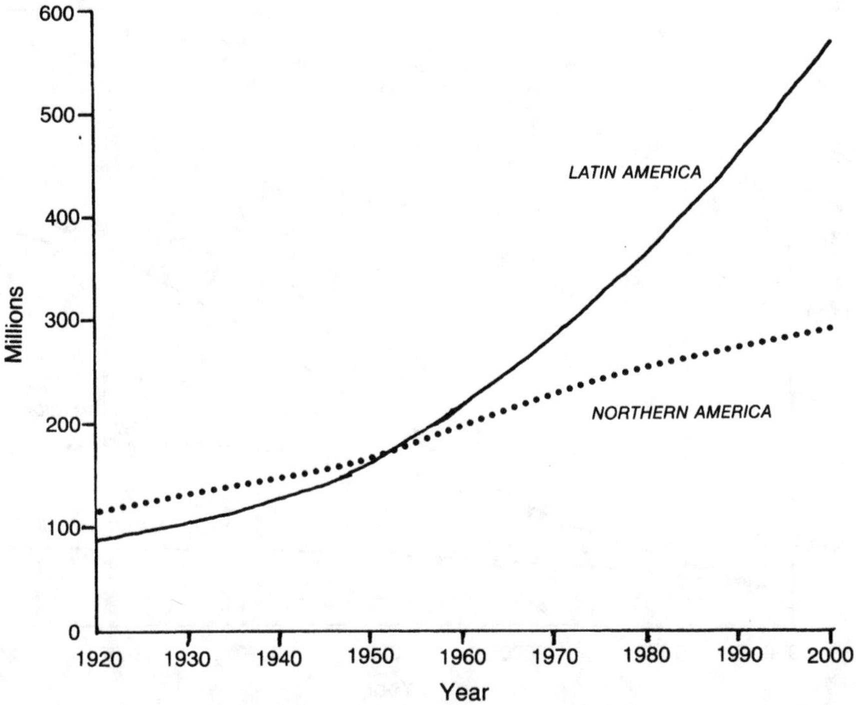

FIGURE 1. **Population of Latin America and Northern America (United States and Canada), 1920–2000. (*Sources:* Miró, 1966; United Nations, 1982, medium projections; *Statistical Abstract of the United States,* 100th ed.)**

difference between an extrapolation of the current growth rate and that implied by the United Nations' projection shows that even the latter is based on considerable optimism concerning future declines in natural increase.

2. Even assuming the lowest projection, there will be two Latins for every Northern American (United States and Canada) early in the next century. The higher estimate suggests the ratio could be 4 to 1 around the middle of the next century and 5 to 1 by its end. The shift from the parity in population sizes that held true well into this century to a ratio of several Latins to every Northern American in the next century would represent a profound change in the demographic balance of the hemisphere.

3. Although differences among the projections occur as early as the turn of the century, the differences accelerate in the next century: By the year 2075, the high United Nations' estimate produces a population twice that of

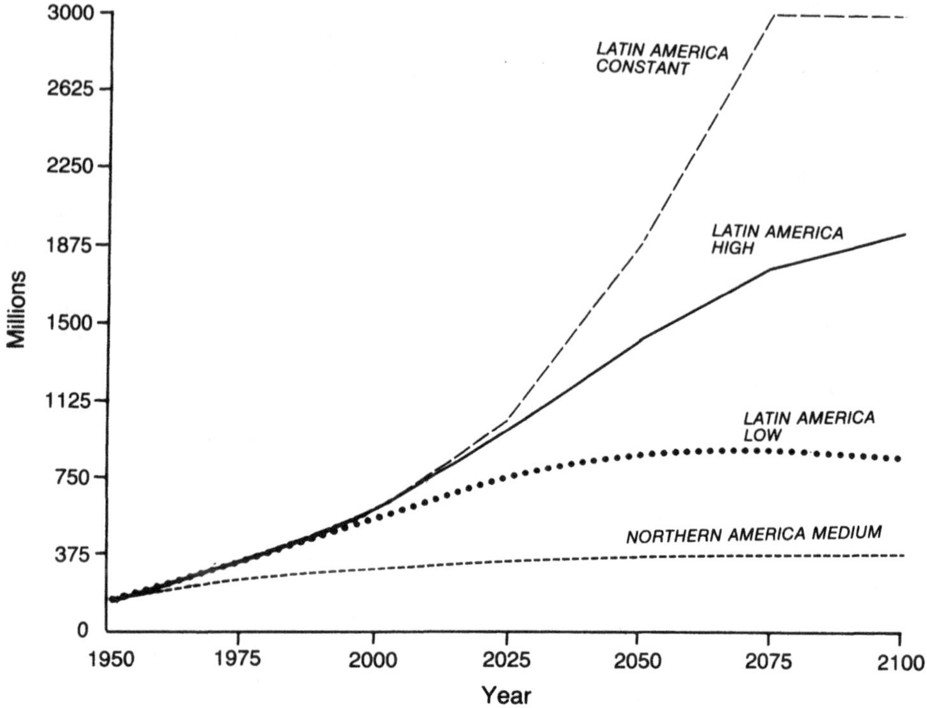

FIGURE 2. **Population projections for Latin America and Northern America (United States and Canada), 1950–2100, at various rates of growth. (*Source:* United Nations, 1982, high and low projections. Constant projection at 2.38%.)**

the low estimate, and the extrapolation of the constant rate is almost four times as high as the low estimate. This is another way of showing that any changes introduced in the rates now will have profound impacts in the next century; or, no matter what is done now, there will be major increases in population that will have to be dealt with in the next century.

MEDIUM-RANGE PROJECTIONS

Medium-range projections (15–35 years) are aimed at periods close enough in time to interest long-range planners; they are subject to smaller error than are long-range predictions. Despite this fact, there is a surprising degree of variation in the level and accuracy of projections among different experts, and among the same experts or agencies over time. Population projections for the year 1980, released by the United Nations in the mid 1950s, underestimated the 1980 populations of 12 of 17 Latin American nations. In 8 of these, the population was underestimated by at least 20%. For Central America alone, the estimate was under by 19 million, or 26% of the 1950 population[2] (Kayani, 1980).

While both data and measurement techniques have been improving, the pattern of more recent projections for the year 2000 are not less disquieting. Around the mid 1960s CELADE was projecting a Latin American population of 612 million for the year 2000 (Miró, 1966), while the United Nations was projecting 624 million. Five years later, the United Nations raised the figure to 652 million, and subsequently consistently lowered it: 620 million in 1973, 608 million in 1978, and 566 million in 1980 (United Nations, 1964, 1973, 1977, 1981). CELADE's 1983 medium projection of 554 million is lower still. Lowest of all is the World Bank's projection of 543 million. The latter figure is virtually identical with the United Nation's low estimate of 544 million.

At the other extreme are U.S. Bureau of the Census (1979) projections. Its medium estimate of 636 million by the year 2000 is surprisingly similar to the United Nations' 1963 estimate (638 million), but 12% higher than the United Nations' 1980 medium estimate and 17% higher than the World Bank's. The Census Bureau's high estimate (677 million) is 24% above the United Nations' low estimate of 544 million.

Thomas Frejka, whose projections in the early 1970s gave a high of 626 million for Latin America in the year 2000 (1972:86), has updated his projections and added evaluations termed "plausible high" and "plausible low." If replacement fertility was achieved by about 2040, then the Latin American population would be 619 million by 2000. Although this is somewhat below Frejka's earlier high, it still implies a fertility decline "similar to that experienced by several European countries and countries with populations of European origin in the nineteenth and early twentieth centuries" (1981:493). Although this would not therefore appear to be an implausible rate for Latin America, Frejka selects as his "plausible high" a population of only 587 million for the year 2000, which is based on achieving replacement

[2]More recent errors seem to be in the opposite direction. Comparison of Centro Latinoamericano de Demografia (CELADE) projections for age-specific fertility rates made in 1973 for 1970–1975 with data derived from World Fertility Survey (WFS) data gathered in the mid 1970s show that the projections overestimated fertility in Colombia, Costa Rica, Panama, and Peru. This was also true, although to a lesser extent, for projections made in 1977 (Taucher, 1984).

fertility by 2010, or only 25 years from now. Indeed, this is only 10 years later than the date at which replacement fertility would have been reached in order to achieve the "plausible low" of 559 million. Frejka's plausible low, however, is 16 million higher than the World Bank's medium (only) projection.

I conclude that although there has been a drift toward "optimism," there is still significant variation among projections. First, are the variations important? Even by the year 2000, the differences are substantial in absolute numbers: The difference between the Census Bureau's high and the United Nations' low for the year 2000 is nearly twice the population of Central America around 1970; the difference between the World Bank and the Census Bureau's medium projection (93 million) is roughly the size of Latin America's population in 1920; and the difference between the United Nations' medium projections made in 1968 and 1980 (72 million) is almost the population of Mexico. In one of the more dramatic shifts, the U.S. Census Bureau has recently revised its projections for Latin America, dropping the 1979 estimate of 636 million by the year 2000 to 560 million (unpublished data), a difference equivalent to the population of Mexico.

The magnitude of these differences becomes much clearer as the next century unfolds: Thus the difference between the CELADE and the United Nations medium projections for the year 2025 is 61 million; the difference in medium estimates between the World Bank and the United Nations for that year is 117 million; and the difference between the current high and low estimates of the United Nations is 104 million.

THE DRIFT TOWARD OPTIMISM

Virtually all the projections we have discussed exercise judgments about future trends in fertility, and most have recently revised their projections downward to reflect contemporary declines in fertility. Moreover, all projections are based on the assumption that replacement fertility will be achieved in a "reasonable" amount of time. Thus, the United Nations states that "irrespective of whether the country is developed with very low fertility . . . or developing with high fertility . . . it is assumed that fertility will arrive at replacement levels in the not too distant future" (United Nations Secretariat, 1984:31–32). The World Bank assumes that some Latin American countries will reach the replacement level as early as 1995, but none later than 2035; Frejka's use of "plausible" high and low ranges assumes it would be reached between 2000 and 2010.

Thus, all projections are founded on the faith that the demographic transition that characterized Europe will also hold for Latin America—

except that it will occur much faster, once it begins. In deciding on the pace for individual countries, the United Nations works with at least three basic assumptions: *(a)* "Fertility will decline as economic and social development takes place"; *(b)* "existing or anticipated government policies and programs . . . will expedite the process of fertility decline"; and *(c)* "once the decline begins, it will begin slowly, gain momentum, and then slow down its speed again" (United Nations, 1981:3).

The state of knowledge concerning all three points is such as to make population projection in 1980 nearly as hazardous as in 1950. The problems are succinctly put by Paul Demeny (1984:18), who believes that the projections of fertility decline in high-fertility nations reflect "a more sanguine view than is warranted by history about the efficacy of future socioeconomic development in inducing rapid fertility decline, or the assumption that policy intervention aimed at rapidly reducing fertility will become far more pervasive and effective than has been the case thus far."

Similar doubts are expressed in an article by Kingsley Davis (1984:62), who reminds us that "the subject of population is fraught with self-deception and frustration. If the present euphoria over falling birth rates leads to complacency, to a continuation of the same policies, it will be cruel and tragic. . . ." Davis argues that apparent fertility declines may reflect measurement error; regards as unwarranted the assumption that birthrate declines will "continue into the future until something like a replacement rate is reached"; and doubts that family planning programs are primarily responsible for fertility declines.

HAS FERTILITY REALLY DECLINED?

There is little doubt that significant reductions in fertility in Latin American have occurred recently; indeed, the decline seemed well under way at least a decade ago. Comparing crude rates reported for 1955–1960 by CELADE with rates reported by the United Nations in the early 1970s, Stycos (1978: 408) found declines of about one-third in Costa Rica and Barbados; of about one-quarter in Puerto Rico, Chile, and Trinidad; and between 12% and 20% in Jamaica, Panama, El Salvador, Guatemala, and Venezuela. Using age-specific data, Conning (1973) concluded that there were true declines throughout the 1960s in 11 countries. "History may prove," according to Stycos (1978:408), "that a turn in Latin American fertility took place . . . toward the close of the 1950s."

A more recent analysis found that all of the 21 LDCs in the Americas showed declines in crude rates between 1965 and 1980; the mean decline was 24%. Total Fertility Rates (TFRs), which averaged 6.1 in these countries in 1965, averaged 4.4 in 1980. The average decline was 28.5%; only 6 countries had declines of less than 20% (Bolivia, Ecuador, El Salvador, Guatemala, Haiti, and Nicaragua); of these, all but Haiti and Bolivia declined by 10 to 19% (Mauldin and Lapham, 1984:Table 5).

In addition to the remarkable consistency of the data—all countries show some declines—it is notable that the smallest declines have been in countries with the poorest data, such as Haiti, Bolivia, and Ecuador. The larger declines have occurred in countries that have had better statistics throughout the period, and whose quality we would least expect to deteriorate. Moreover, declines have been substantial in the three largest countries—Brazil, Mexico, and Colombia—that constitute 60% of the region's population. Between 1960 and 1980, Brazil's TFR declined by 31%, Colombia's by 44% and Mexico's by 37%. In each case a trend is apparent (Table 1).

In Mexico and Colombia, Contraceptive Prevalence Surveys were taken 2 years after World Fertility Surveys were conducted. In both instances, the later survey evidenced a lower TFR, dropping from 4.4 to 3.7 in Colombia and from 5.7 to 5.1 in Mexico (Anderson and Clelland, 1984:3). While there are problems involved in comparing two such samples, the trend data that can be implied from evidence internal to the WFSs also suggest declining fertility in all 12 countries covered by the WFS. Figure 3 shows that every age group has participated in the Mexican and Colombian declines, but, as is usually the case with the initial stage, the change is most pronounced among older women.

TABLE 1
Trends in Total Fertility Rates

Year	*Brazil*	*Colombia*	*Mexico*
Around 1960	6.2	6.8	6.5
1965	5.8	6.6	6.6
1970	5.3	5.7	6.7
1975	4.7	4.8	5.7
1980	4.3	3.8	4.1

Source: Merrick (1984:Table 2).

ARE FAMILY PLANNING PROGRAMS WORKING?

Assuming then that fertility is really declining, can family planning programs take the credit? If so, optimism about the future is more warranted, since such programs are more susceptible to public policies than are more general programs of development.

Population policies have been slow in evolving in Latin America because of religious, ideological, and geopolitical considerations. The presence of vast territories of low population density and the strong anti-Malthusian ideologies of the religious right and political left have led to strong resistance among leadership groups to the notion that rates of natural increase are excessive. In 1976, of 27 Economic Commission for Latin America (ECLA) region governments responding to a United Nations questionnaire, fewer than half (13) stated that lower rates of natural increase were desirable in their country (United Nations, 1977). A similar questionnaire 4 years later showed little net change in official attitudes. Five countries (Argentina, Paraguay, Bolivia, Uruguay, and Chile) expressed interest in having substantial increases to their populations; 11 others (including Peru, Brazil, Ecuador, Honduras, and Guatemala) considered inappropriate any programs to alter the rates of their growth. Only 3 countries (El Salvador, Mexico, and Trinidad) had demographic targets for slowing the rate of population increase (United Nations, 1981).

As distinct from population policies, family planning policies have moved faster, but have lagged about a decade behind those in Asia. Thus, by 1965 only 7% of the region's people were living in countries with such policies, compared with 98% in South and East Asia, and 46% in West Asia and North Africa; by 1973, however, the Latin American figure had reached 56%. By the mid 1970s, 20 countries representing 54% of the region's population were backing the policies with "real programmatic support" (Watson, 1977).[3]

The most rigorous attempt to quantify and compare national family planning programs was carried out by Mauldin and Berelson (1978) for the early 1970s and has been updated to reflect conditions in the early 1980s (Lapham and Mauldin, 1984; Mauldin and Lapham, 1984). In the later study, each of 93 countries was assigned a score on each of 30 items reflecting

[3]"Real programmatic support is defined as a national family planning program of sufficient scope to reach a number of new acceptors equivalent to one percent of the number of women aged 15–49 in 1975" (Watson, 1977:6).

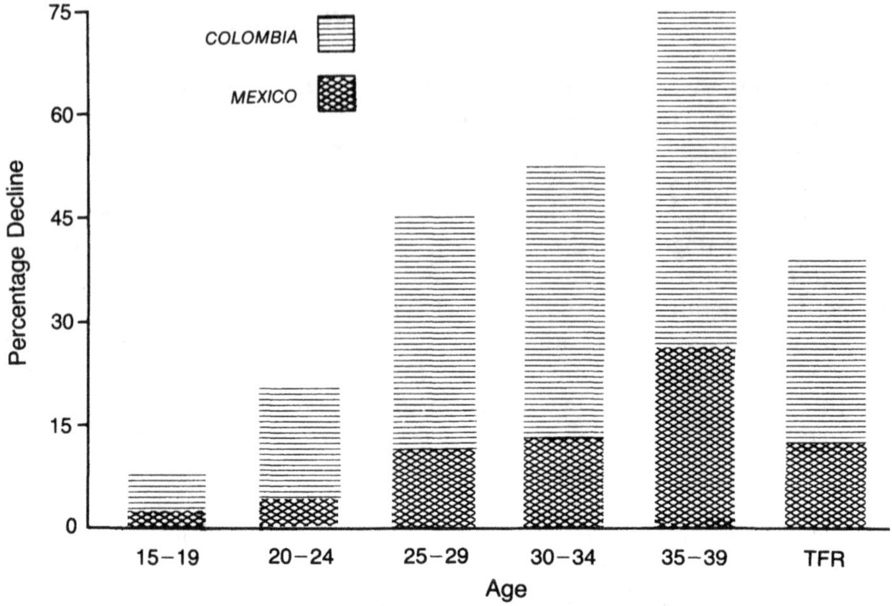

FIGURE 3. **Decline in age-specific fertility, Colombian and Mexican World Fertility Surveys. Percentage by which marital fertility in 5 years preceding survey was lower than 10–14 years prior to survey. (*Source:* United Nations, 1983:49–50.)**

four dimensions of family planning efforts: policy and stage-setting activities; service and service-related activities; recordkeeping and evaluation; and availability and accessibility.

In both years a majority of the Latin American countries were placed in the weak or very weak category (scoring less than 55 out of a maximum score of 120). In terms of numbers of countries there has been a slight deterioration in the region's program efforts (Table 2). Latin America does well vis-à-vis Africa and the Middle East, and is a close second to Asia, when each country is given an equal weight, but is far behind Asia when scores are weighted according to population size (Table 3). All in all, we would have to characterize the region's programs as in place but far from functioning with maximum effort. However, the trend in effort is upward, since the 2 largest countries (Brazil and Mexico) showed the largest improvement in scores between 1972 and 1982. Several other large countries (e.g., Colombia, Ecuador, and Peru)

TABLE 2
Program Effect Scores for Twenty Latin American Countries, 1972 and 1982

Score	*1972*	*1982*
Strong (80–120)	2	1
Moderate (55–79)	7	7
Weak (25–54)	10	9
Very weak or none (0–24)	1	3

Source: Compiled from Mauldin and Lapham (1984).

showed moderate improvement, while most of the 12 countries that showed no change or declines in effort were smaller countries (Mauldin and Lapham, 1984:Table 11).

Whether such programs are affecting the birthrates is difficult to ascertain, but data from Mauldin and Lapham (1984) show a reasonably strong impact of both program effort and social setting (based on such measures as life expectancy, gross national product (GNP) per capita, and urbanization). Thus, in the more advanced countries that have expended moderate efforts on family planning programs, the TFR has declined by 38% on the average between 1965 and 1980; for countries with weak family planning inputs and a lesser degree of modernization, the decline has been only 12%; and if one of the two ingredients is present, the decline is in between, at about 25% (Table 4).

TABLE 3
Mean Percentage of Maximum Program Effort Achieved, Weighted and Unweighted for Population Size, by Region

	Unweighted		*Weighted*	
Region	*Total Score*	*Service*	*Total Score*	*Service*
Latin America	39	33	47	41
South and East Asia	46	42	70	64
Middle East and North Africa	20	17	26	22
Sub-Saharan Africa	15	12	14	13
Total (N = 93)	29	25	59	53

Source: Mauldin and Lapham (1984:Table 4B).

TABLE 4
Mean Percentage Decline in Total Fertility Rates, 1965–1980, by Program Effort and Social Setting

	Program Effort	
Social Setting	*Moderate (N)*	*Weak or Very Weak (N)*
High	38%(7)[a]	28%(5)[c]
Middle	25%(2)[b]	12%(5)[d]

[a] Cuba, Costa Rica, Trinidad, Colombia, Chile, Panama, Jamaica.
[b] Dominican Republic, El Salvador.
[c] Paraguay, Peru, Brazil, Venezuela, Mexico.
[d] Nicaragua, Bolivia, Guatemala, Ecuador, Honduras.
Source: Calculated from Mauldin and Lapham (1984:Table 9).

Cutright (1983:107–108) has used the program effort data along with several critical modernization variables (literacy, urbanization, and life expectancy) in multiple regression analyses of Latin American 1980 crude birthrates and changes in these rates between 1960 and 1980. Family planning effort had large and independent effects on both measures. Net of the socioeconomic indicators, an increase of 10 points in the family planning effort was related to a decline of 3 to 4 points in the birthrate.

If programs seem to be having some effect despite the overall modesty of the effort, what could we expect from stepped-up efforts? Two kinds of efforts may be distinguished: those directed at better satisfying felt needs and those that create new demands.

Works by Hollerbach and Nortman (1984) and Nortman (1982) on the measurement of unmet needs for family planning have provided useful comparative data for several Latin American countries. Based on data from recent Contraceptive Prevalence Surveys, they found little variation in the proportions who want to stop or space childbearing (about 9 of every 10 women in Colombia, Mexico, Honduras and Costa Rica), but considerable variation in the ratio of users to nonusers of contraception among women with a desire to avoid pregnancy. The percentage of sexually active, fecund, ever-married women of reproductive age who did not want to get pregnant in the near future but who were not using contraceptives was 25% in Costa Rica, 41% in Colombia, 40% in Mexico, and 60% in Honduras (Hollerbach and Nortman, 1984:Table 1). Thus, even in countries with rapidly declining birthrates (the first three) there is still a very large unmet need for contraception.

There is some evidence, however, that in some countries supply may be catching up with demand. If true, this might suggest that birthrates will bottom out at higher levels than envisioned by projections that are assuming continuing declines until replacement levels are reached. Merrick (1983) has noted that after marked declines in the early 1970s, between 1977 and 1980 TFRs in both urban and rural Brazil scarcely changed and were still, at 4.33 in 1980, well above replacement levels. In Costa Rica a similar phenomenon may have occurred in the late 1970s. The TFR, which declined 16% between 1965–1970 and 1970–1975, and then by 26% in the next 5-year period, has shown little change between 1975–1979 (3.5) and 1980–1983 (3.3) (calculated from data in Bixby, 1983).

If we compare recent TFRs with the mean number of children desired by women interviewed in the WFS, we find a rough correspondence (Table 5).

If we consider, first, the preferences of women who have already completed their family size, it is evident that in half of the eight countries, women have had the same number or fewer children than they consider ideal. In the other four countries they have had, on the average, from one-half to one child more than they consider ideal. On the whole, then, older women in the Latin American countries represented here have had about or slightly more than the number of children they consider ideal, and this number is two to three times

TABLE 5
Mean Number of Living Children and Mean Number of Children Desired, 1975–1980

	All Women		*Women Age 40–44*	
	TFR[a]	*Desired Size*[b]	*Living Children*[b]	*Desired Number*[b]
Colombia	4.3	4.1	5.6	4.9
Costa Rica	3.6	4.7	6.0	6.1
Dominican Republic	4.8	4.6	5.5	5.6
Mexico	5.4	4.4	6.0	5.2
Panama	4.0	4.2	5.5	5.1
Paraguay	5.2	6.1	5.5	6.5
Peru	5.5	3.8	5.2	4.4
Venezuela	4.7	4.2	4.9	4.9

[a] CELADE (1983).
[b] Kent and Larson (1982).

the number required for replacement fertility. Such women may in part be rationalizing the number they have already had; the desired number of women of all ages (15–44) may provide a better comparison. For this group, the mean preferred number is lower, but in most countries by no more than one child. The TFR, which includes unmarried women, is already at or below the preferred number in Panama, Paraguay, Dominican Republic, Colombia, and Costa Rica. Even in Mexico, Peru, and Venezuela, where the TFRs are substantially higher, the desired size is around 4. If total *marital* fertility rates (TMFR) are used, the national averages for desired family size have already been reached in the metropolitan areas of six of the eight countries; and in three of the eight, TMFRs in "other urban areas" are already below the national averages for desired family size, though rural rates are much higher (Ashurst *et al.*, 1984).

The United Nations' latest projections suggest that Latin America's current TFR of 4.2 will decline to 3.2 by the beginning of the next century, and to 2.05 by year 2040. As we have noted, this projection is based on "observed past demographic trends, expected social and economic programs, on going government policies and prevailing public attitudes toward population issues" (United Nations, 1983:18). It seems, however, something of an act of faith to project such a decline in the face of current family-size preferences. In short, with fertility declines now reaching the point at which most women's family-size preferences are realized, it may be necessary in the future, if replacement fertility is to be achieved early in the next century, to change couples' preferences. This is creating rather than merely satisfying demand, and would require governments to step up programs of education, incentives, and disincentives.

CONCLUSIONS

If rapid population growth in LDCs is of concern for U.S. national security, then there is clearly cause for concern about Latin American population trends into the next century. Twenty years ago, Central America had about 50 million people; in another 20 years it will have over 150 million. By the year 2025, even using United Nations' medium estimates, Central America's population will be as large as that of the United States today.

We have seen that there have been real fertility declines in Latin America, but given the relatively modest program efforts and the possibility that achievement of family-size goals are now within sight, faith in continuing declines and the achievement of replacement fertility is not warranted.

If current fertility and mortality levels should be maintained, Latin America's population would cross the 1 billion mark toward the middle of the next century. Even the difference by the year 2000 between United Nations' high and low projections is impressive. If Mexico grows at the high rate, it will have as many people in 15 years as Brazil has now. If Brazil grows at the high rate, it will have as many people in 15 years as the United States has now. The difference between the high and low rate for these two countries alone amounts to 59 million by the end of the century—a difference amounting to the population of Mexico in 1975.

In the light of such considerations it would seem reasonable for the United States to step up assistance to those countries seeking to improve their family planning programs in order to accelerate the fertility declines already begun. It will also be necessary to plan for a different demographic balance in the hemisphere—one in which the scales are markedly tipped in the Latin American direction.

REFERENCES

Anderson, John and John G. Clelland

1984 "The World Fertility Survey and Contraceptive Prevalence Surveys: A comparison of substantive results." *Studies in Family Planning* 15(1).

Anonymous

1980 "United States International Population Policy." *Population and Development Review.*

1982 "United States international population policy." *Population and Development Review.*

Benedick, Richard

1984 "U.S. policy perspectives on International Conference on Population, 1984." Paper presented at the 1984 meetings of the Population Association of America, Minneapolis.

Bixby, Luis R.

1983 "Determinantes de la fecundidad en Costa Rica." *Notas de Poblacion* 11:32.

Centro Latinoamericano de Demografia (CELADE)

1983 *Boletin Demografico*, No. 31. Santiago.

Conning, Arthur

1973 "Latin American fertility trends and influencing factors." *Proceedings of the Liege IUSSP Conference* 2:125–147.

Cutright, Philips

1983 "The ingredients of recent fertility decline." *International Family Planning Perspectives* 9(4).

Davis, Kingsley

1984 "Declining birth rates and growing populations." *Population Research and Policy Review* 3(1).

Demeny, Paul
1984 *A Perspective on Long-Term Population Growth.* Working Paper No. 104. New York: Population Council, Center for Policy Studies.
Frejka, Tomas
1972 *The Future of Population Growth.* New York: Wiley.
1981 "Long-term prospects for world population growth." *Population and Development Review* 7(3).
Hollerbach, Paula E. and Dorothy Nortman
1984 "Cross-cultural estimates of the unmet need for family planning." Paper presented at the 1984 meetings of the Population Association of America, Minneapolis.
Kayani, Ashraf
1980 "Comparacion entre proyecciones de poblacion elaboradas por las Naciones Unidas para la America Latina y estimaciones Actuales, 1950–1980." *Notas de Poblacion,* CELADE, No. 22.
Kent, M.M. and A. Larson
1982 "Family size preferences: Evidence from the World Fertility Surveys." In *Reports on the World Fertility Survey.* Washington, D.C.: Population Reference Bureau.
Lapham, Robert and W. Parker Mauldin
1984 "Contraceptive prevalence: The influence of organized family planning programs." Paper presented at the 1984 meetings of the Population Association of America, Minneapolis.
Mauldin, Parker and B. Berelson
1978 "Conditions of fertility decline in developing countries, 1965–1975." *Studies in Family Planning* 9(5).
Mauldin, Parker and Robert Lapham
1984 "Conditions of fertility decline in LDCSs: 1965–1980." Paper presented at the 1984 Conference of the Population Association of America, Minneapolis.
Merrick, Thomas
1983 "Fertility and family planning in Brazil." *International Family Planning Perspectives* 9(4).
1984 *Recent Fertility Declines in Brazil, Colombia, and Mexico.* Working Papers in Demography. Washington, D.C.: Center for Population Research, Georgetown University.
Miró, Carmen
1966 "The population of twentieth century Latin America." In J. M. Stycos and J. Arias (eds.), *Population in Latin America.* Washington, D.C.: Potomac Books.
Nortman, D.
1982 "Measuring the unmet need for contraception to space and limit births." *International Family Planning Perspectives* 8(4).
Nortman, D. and E. Hofstatter
1978 *Population and Family Planning Programs.* New York: Population Council.
Stycos, J. Mayone
1978 "Recent trends in Latin American fertility." *Population Studies* 32(2).
Taucher, Erica
1984 "Family planning and population projections." In United Nations, *Population Projection: Methodology of the United Nations.* Population Studies No. 83. New York.

United Nations
1964 *Provisional Report on World Population Prospects as Assessed in 1963.* New York.
1973 *World Population Prospects as Assessed in 1968.* New York.
1977 *World Population Prospects as Assessed in 1973.* New York.
1979 *World Population Trends and Policies* (Vol. 1). New York.
1979 *World Population Trends and Policies: 1977 Monitoring Report* (Vol. 2). New York.
1981 *World Population Prospects as Assessed in 1980.* Population Studies No. 78. New York.
1982 *World Population Trends and Policies: 1981 Monitoring Report* (Vol. 2). New York.
1983 *Fertility Levels and Trends as Assessed from Twenty World Fertility Surveys.* New York.
1982 "Long range global population projections, as assessed in 1980." *Population Bulletin of the United Nations*, No. 14.
1984 "Current projection assumptions for the United Nations demographic projections." In United Nations, *Population Projections: Methodology of the United Nations.* Population Studies No. 83. New York.

U.S. Bureau of the Census
1979 *Illustrative Projections of World Population to the 21st Century.* Special Studies Series P-23, No. 79.

Watson, Walter
1977 *Family Planning in the Developing World.* New York: Population Council.

4

Population Growth and Labor Absorption in Latin America, 1970–2000

MURRAY GENDELL

The widespread poverty found in developing countries is the result of both low levels of per capita income and great inequality in its distribution. Even in the developing countries in which per capita income is relatively high, such as in Latin America, one finds a large proportion of people with very low incomes. One of the chief reasons for the low income is the difficulty they have finding employment or, if employed, working as much time or as productively as they are able and willing to do. It has been estimated that 29% of the labor force in all developing countries in 1973 were either unemployed or underemployed, up from 25% in 1960. In Latin America the increase was swifter, from 18% in 1960 to 25% in 1973 (Todaro, 1981:204).

The underutilization of labor has other alarming consequences than the impoverishment of millions of workers and their families. It represents a loss of potential output, keeping national income from rising more rapidly. It increases the risk of dissatisfaction with the existing social system, which could lead to political unrest and deviant behavior. And it increases the number of people who want to move to a country with better employment prospects, even if their entry has to be illegal. Illegal immigration to the United States, especially from Mexico, has been a political issue in the United States for some years now, and it seems likely to continue to be a domestic and foreign policy concern for many more years.

Given the serious consequences of substantial labor underutilization, it is important to estimate future prospects. Will there be any improvement, no change, or a deterioration in the next decade or two? This chapter tries to answer that question with respect to Latin America. Although a thorough analysis requires examining the situation in each country, this is infeasible. In order to provide some useful disaggregation, however, much of the data are presented for each of the four largest countries (Argentina, Brazil, Colombia, and Mexico) and for the rest of Latin America combined, as well as for all of Latin America. In addition, the data are presented separately for men and women and for the urban and rural sectors.

Because the degree to which labor is utilized is determined by labor demand and supply, the analysis proceeds by looking, first, at estimates of labor supply for the recent past and projections for 1980–2000. Then, estimates of labor demand in recent years and projections of future demand are examined. Population growth and changes in labor-force participation rates are the two direct determinants of labor supply. As is shown below, there has been and will continue to be (at least to the year 2000) little change in the participation rates, and so changes in labor supply in Latin America have been and will continue to be determined almost completely by population growth. For this reason, special attention is given in the analysis to the main determinant of changes in rates of growth, namely, the change in fertility. Finally, because of its size and proximity to the United States and the unusual rapidity of the growth of its population and labor force, special attention is given to Mexico. In the course of doing so, some comparisons with Argentina, Brazil, and Colombia are presented.

LABOR SUPPLY IN LATIN AMERICA

The growth of the labor force in Latin America has been exceptionally rapid in recent decades. Except for East Asia and the Pacific during the 1960s, the pace of labor-force growth has been swifter in Latin America during the 1960s and 1970s than in the other major world regions (see Table 1). Furthermore, it is anticipated that Latin America's unfortunate eminence in this respect will continue for the rest of the twentieth century.

TABLE 1
Growth Rates of the Labor Force in Major World Regions, 1960–2000

	Average Annual Percentage Increase			
	1960–1970	*1970–1980*	*1980–1990*	*1990–2000*
East Asia and Pacific	2.4	2.6	2.3	2.0
Low-income Asia	1.7	2.0	2.0	1.9
Middle East and North Africa	1.9	2.6	2.9	2.2
Sub-Saharan Africa	2.2	2.2	2.5	2.6
Southern Europe	.8	1.3	1.3	1.2
Latin America	2.4	2.7	3.0	2.7
All developing countries	1.8	2.2	2.2	2.1
Industrialized countries	1.2	1.2	.7	.5

Source: World Bank (1979:47).

To account for this swift growth of the labor force, we need to look at the pace of population growth and at the trend in the proportion of the population that is in the labor force, the two direct determinants of labor-force growth. But first it would be helpful to examine Latin America's labor-force growth in more detail. Tables 2, 3, and 4 present the growth of the labor force 10 years of age or older in the whole region, in the four largest countries (Argentina, Brazil, Columbia, and Mexico), and in the rest of Latin America, from 1970 to 2000, disaggregated by urban–rural residence and sex. For a number of reasons (especially the errors in the basic data and the inherent uncertainties involved in projections), the data presented in the tables in this report should not be taken as precise. It is therefore inadvisable to regard small differences as real. In addition, the results of the projections depend very much on the nature of the assumptions adopted. (See the Appendix for a brief description of the assumptions adopted in the projections presented here.) Moreover, subsequent projections may well produce significant changes. For example, as a result of declines in fertility during the past 10–20 years in Latin America, the projected size of the population has been successively lowered; the more recent the projection, the lower the size of the population and the growth rate.

This trend of declining growth is evident in the tables. The growth of the labor force in Latin America is projected to be lower in the 1990s (29%) than in the 1980s (32%), and the latter is smaller than the estimate for the 1970s (34%) (see Table 2). A similar pattern is evident for the four largest countries and the rest of Latin America. Except for Argentina, the proportional increases per decade, though expected to decline, are nevertheless large. Even in

TABLE 2
Labor Force Ten Years of Age or Older in Latin America, 1970–2000 (numbers in millions)

Year	*Latin America*	*Brazil*	*Colombia*	*Mexico*	*Argentina*	*Remainder of Latin America*
1970	86.2	30.0	6.4	13.7	9.4	26.7
1980	115.1	40.3	8.8	19.5	10.7	35.8
1990	152.3	52.8	11.6	28.0	12.0	47.9
2000	196.9	66.9	14.6	38.8	13.5	63.1
				Percentage Increase		
1970–1980	33.5	34.3	37.5	42.3	13.8	34.1
1980–1990	32.3	31.0	31.8	43.6	12.1	33.8
1990–2000	29.3	26.7	25.9	38.6	12.5	31.7
2000–1970	2.28	2.23	2.28	2.83	1.44	2.36
2000–1980	1.71	1.66	1.66	1.99	1.26	1.76

Source: CELADE (1982).

TABLE 3
Urban Labor Force Age Ten or Older in Latin America, by Sex (numbers in millions)

Sex and Year	*Latin America*	*Brazil*	*Colombia*	*Mexico*	*Argentina*	*Remainder of Latin America*
Males						
1970	36.7	12.3	2.7	6.3	5.4	10.0
1980	53.3	18.4	4.1	10.0	6.3	14.5
1990	76.1	26.6	5.9	15.5	7.2	20.9
2000	104.0	36.2	7.9	22.7	8.1	29.1
Females						
1970	13.5	4.5	1.2	1.7	2.1	4.0
1980	20.7	7.1	1.9	3.0	2.6	6.1
1990	30.8	10.7	2.7	5.0	3.1	9.3
2000	43.5	15.0	3.6	7.7	3.8	13.4
				Percentage increase		
Males						
1970–1980	45.2	49.6	51.9	58.7	16.7	45.0
1980–1990	42.8	44.6	43.9	55.0	14.3	44.1
1990–2000	36.7	36.1	33.8	46.5	12.5	39.2
2000–1970	2.83	2.94	2.93	3.60	1.50	2.91
2000–1980	1.95	1.97	1.93	2.27	1.29	2.01
Females						
1970–1980	53.3	57.8	58.3	76.5	23.8	52.5
1980–1990	48.8	50.7	42.1	66.7	19.2	52.5
1990–2000	41.2	40.2	33.3	54.0	22.6	44.1
2000–1970	3.22	3.33	3.00	4.53	1.81	3.35
2000–1980	2.10	2.11	1.89	2.57	1.46	2.20

Source: CELADE (1982).

Argentina, the anticipated growth (12–14%), though much slower than in all but a few of the other Latin American countries, is more than negligible. In contrast, particularly striking is the extremely rapid growth in Mexico, in excess of 40% per decade during the 1970s and 1980s and only slightly less than 40% projected for the 1990s.

As a result of these swift, even if moderating, rates of growth, the labor force in Latin America is projected to more than double between 1970 and 2000, and to increase by about 70% between 1980 and 2000. The range of variation is considerable, however, as indicated by the difference between Argentina and Mexico. For 1970–2000, the anticipated multiplication is a relatively modest (but hardly trivial) 44% in Argentina, but a nearly tremendous tripling in Mexico. In the latter case, a doubling is projected for just the

TABLE 4
Rural Labor Force Age Ten or Older in Latin America, by Sex (numbers in millions)

Sex and Year	*Latin America*	*Brazil*	*Colombia*	*Mexico*	*Argentina*	*Remainder of Latin America*
Males						
1970	30.7	11.6	2.2	4.8	1.6	10.5
1980	35.0	13.0	2.5	5.6	1.6	12.3
1990	38.8	13.7	2.7	6.4	1.5	14.5
2000	42.1	13.9	2.7	7.2	1.4	16.9
Females						
1970	5.3	1.6	.26	.9	.25	2.3
1980	6.0	1.8	.29	1.0	.24	2.7
1990	6.6	1.8	.30	1.1	.22	3.2
2000	7.2	1.8	.31	1.2	.21	3.7
			Percentage increase			
Males						
1970–1980	14.0	12.1	13.6	16.7	0	17.1
1980–1990	10.9	5.4	8.0	14.3	−6.3	17.9
1990–2000	8.5	1.5	0	12.5	−6.7	16.6
2000–1970	1.37	1.20	1.23	1.50	.88	1.61
2000–1980	1.20	1.07	1.08	1.29	.88	1.37
Females						
1970–1980	13.2	12.5	11.5	11.1	−4.0	17.4
1980–1990	10.0	0	3.4	10.0	−8.3	18.5
1990–2000	9.1	0	3.3	9.1	−4.5	15.6
2000–1970	1.36	1.13	1.19	1.33	.84	1.61
2000–1980	1.20	1.00	1.07	1.20	.88	1.37

Source: CELADE (1982).

last 20 years of this century, implying an average annual growth rate of about 3.5%. Clearly, the extreme rapidity of the growth of the labor force in Mexico deserves further examination. The size of this labor force and its proximity to the United States are additional reasons for a more detailed study of the situation in Mexico, which is presented later.

Before moving on to look at the large variations in the growth of the labor force in urban and rural areas and between men and women, a few words about the anticipated trends in Brazil and Colombia are in order. For one thing, the trends in the two countries are similar. For another, these trends are similar to that for all of Latin America. The projected decline in the growth rates in the two countries is more rapid than for the whole region or in Mexico and Argentina, reflecting rapid declines in fertility during the 1970s.

The projected increase in the labor force during the 1990s is "only" around 26%, a considerable drop from the gains of 34–38% during the 1970s. Nevertheless, the growth rates have been so high that, despite the decline, the labor force in each country is expected to be two-thirds larger in 2000 than it was in 1980.

Turning to variations by sex and residence, the most important point to note is that the rapid growth has been concentrated in the urban sector, and this will continue to be true in the future (see Tables 3 and 4). Given the high growth rates for whole countries and the whole region, this means that the growth rates have been even higher in the urban sector. Thus, during the 1970s, whereas the region's labor force grew by one-third, it increased by almost half in the urban sector. Conversely, the gain in the rural sector (13–14%) was much smaller. As in the whole region, the growth rate in each sector is projected to diminish over time. In the rural sector, by the 1990s, there is expected to be little or no growth in the rural labor force in Brazil and Colombia. In Argentina, the rural labor force may have declined during the 1970s, with further declines anticipated for the following two decades. The proportional changes in the rural sector are about the same for men and women and, except for Argentina, similar from one country to another (at least for those shown in Table 4).

In the urban sector, however, there is a definite tendency for the female labor force to grow somewhat more rapidly than the male labor force. Hence the growth rates of the female labor force are spectacular, around 50% in Latin America during the 1970s and 1980s, with an anticipated growth of approximately 40% during the 1990s. As before, there is a large range of variation, evidenced by the data for Mexico and Argentina, with gains of about 75% and 25% respectively during the 1970s. Even with a substantial projected decline in the growth rate in Mexico, the anticipated growth of women in the urban labor force is about 50% during the 1990s. However, because of low rates of female economic activity, the size of the female labor force has been much smaller than that of the male labor force; and while the rapid growth rates of the female labor force lead to a tripling (nearly a quintupling in Mexico) between 1970 and 2000 and a doubling between 1980 and 2000, there is little change in the percentage of the labor force that is female. For all of Latin America, only 15% of the rural labor force were women in 1970, and no change is anticipated by 2000. In the urban sector the percentage is projected to increase slightly, from 27 to 29%. This is because the growth rate of the male labor force, although less than that of the female labor force, is not *much* less.

Turning now to the reasons for this rapid growth in the urban and the total labor force, it is evident from Table 5 that the refined activity rates are expected to change very little, except for women in the urban sector and the

TABLE 5
Estimates for 1970 and Projections for 1980–2000 of the Refined Economic Activity Rates[a] in Latin America, by Residence and Sex

Sex and Year	*Whole Region*	*Urban*	*Rural*
Both sexes			
1970	45.1	43.8	47.0
1980	45.2	44.5	46.4
1990	46.2	46.1	46.4
2000	47.0	47.3	46.3
Males			
1970	70.4	66.2	76.3
1980	69.3	66.0	75.1
1990	69.7	67.4	74.9
2000	69.8	68.1	74.4
Females			
1970	19.7	22.8	14.6
1980	21.0	24.2	14.4
1990	22.7	25.9	14.4
2000	24.2	27.3	14.4

[a] A refined economic activity rate is the percentage of the population 10 years of age or older who are economically active.
Source: CELADE (1982).

whole region among whom an increase in activity rates of 20–25% is projected. For example, a rate of 24.2 for all women in 2000 is 23% greater than the rate of 19.7 estimated for 1970. (The intercountry variation around these regional averages is modest.) It follows, then, that the rapid growth of the labor force must be the result of rapid population growth, as Tables 6 and 7 confirm.

In the urban sector, the working-age population (defined here as those 10 years of age or older) increased by about 50% during the 1970s in Brazil, Colombia, and Mexico. There was a much slower but still significant gain of nearly 20% in Argentina. For all of Latin America, the increase is estimated at 46%. The pace is projected to decline during the following two decades, but still result in a hefty growth of over one-third during the 1990s. As noted for the growth of the labor force, Mexico's rate of population growth is at the high end of the range of variation, with about 40% growth in the urban sector and an increase of about one-third for the total working-age population projected for the 1990s.

Population growth was much slower in the rural sector during the 1970s (20%), but it was not inconsiderable. The projections for subsequent decades indicate a decline in the growth rate. Taking Argentina as an indicator, it appears that the rural population has already stopped growing and may have

TABLE 6
Population Ten Years of Age or Older in Latin America, 1970–2000 (in millions)

Region	*Total*	*Urban*	*Rural*
Latin America			
1970	191.2	114.6	76.5
1980	254.8	166.5	88.4
1990	329.7	231.8	97.9
2000	418.9	312.3	106.6
Brazil			
1970	66.4	38.7	27.7
1980	89.1	57.8	31.3
1990	114.7	81.5	33.2
2000	143.7	109.7	34.0
Colombia			
1970	14.1	8.7	5.4
1980	18.9	12.7	6.1
1990	23.8	17.6	6.2
2000	29.6	23.3	6.4
Mexico			
1970	34.0	20.4	13.6
1980	47.7	31.8	16.0
1990	65.7	47.5	18.2
2000	87.2	67.1	20.1
Argentina			
1970	19.1	15.2	3.8
1980	21.9	18.1	3.7
1990	24.7	21.1	3.6
2000	27.6	24.0	3.6
Rest of Latin America			
1970	57.6	31.6	26.0
1980	77.2	46.1	31.3
1990	100.8	64.1	36.7
2000	130.8	88.2	42.5

Source: Calculated from data presented in CELADE (1982).

even begun to decline in Latin America's low-fertility countries. Colombia's rural population is projected to get close to zero growth by the 1980s and Brazil's by the 1990s. In Mexico, however, a 10% rise is still projected for the 1990s. In the rest of Latin America, rural growth, though declining between 1970 and 2000, is anticipated to be a relatively high 16% during the 1990s. The rates are the same for males and females.

TABLE 7
Percentage Increase of the Population Ten Years of Age or Older in Latin America, 1970–2000, by Residence

Region	*Total*	*Urban*	*Rural*
Latin America			
1970–1980	33.3	45.3	15.6
1980–1990	29.4	39.2	10.7
1990–2000	27.1	34.7	8.9
Brazil			
1970–1980	34.2	49.4	13.0
1980–1990	28.7	41.0	6.1
1990–2000	25.3	34.6	2.4
Colombia			
1970–1980	34.0	46.0	13.0
1980–1990	25.9	38.6	1.6
1990–2000	24.4	32.4	3.2
Mexico			
1970–1980	40.3	55.9	17.6
1980–1990	37.7	49.4	13.8
1990–2000	32.7	41.3	10.4
Argentina			
1970–1980	14.7	19.1	−2.6
1980–1990	12.8	16.6	−2.7
1990–2000	11.7	13.7	0
Rest of Latin America			
1970–1980	34.0	45.9	20.4
1980–1990	30.6	39.0	17.3
1990–2000	29.8	37.6	15.8

Source: Calculated from Table 6.

By way of summarizing the description of the anticipated growth of the labor supply in Latin America, let us see how many additional job seekers are expected. The number of people to be added to the labor force in Latin America between 1970 and 2000 is about 111 million, with 82 million of them being added from 1980 to 2000. Ninety percent of these gains are anticipated in the urban sector (see Tables 8, 9, and 10). More than half of the projected growth is expected to occur in Brazil and Mexico, except in the rural sector, where most of the growth is anticipated in countries other than the four largest ones. In the rural sector, the increments become smaller in each succeeding decade, whereas they become larger in the urban sector. Since the latter is so much larger than the former, the result is that additions to

TABLE 8

Absolute Increase of the Labor Force Age Ten or Older in Latin America, 1970–2000 (in millions)

Year	*Latin America*	*Brazil*	*Colombia*	*Mexico*	*Argentina*	*Remainder of Latin America*
1970–1980	28.9	10.3	2.4	5.8	1.3	9.1
1980–1990	37.2	12.5	2.8	8.5	1.3	12.1
1990–2000	44.6	14.1	3.0	10.8	1.5	15.2
1970–2000	110.7	36.9	8.2	25.1	4.1	36.4
1980–2000	81.8	26.6	5.8	19.3	2.8	27.3

Source: CELADE (1982).

TABLE 9

Absolute Increase of the Urban Labor Force Age Ten or Older in Latin America, 1970–2000, by Sex (in millions)

Sex and Year	*Latin America*	*Brazil*	*Colombia*	*Mexico*	*Argentina*	*Remainder of Latin America*
Males						
1970–1980	16.6	6.1	1.4	3.7	.9	4.5
1980–1990	22.8	8.2	1.8	5.5	.9	6.4
1990–2000	27.9	9.6	2.0	7.2	.9	8.2
1970–2000	67.3	23.9	5.2	16.4	2.7	19.1
1980–2000	50.7	17.8	3.8	12.7	1.8	14.6
Females						
1970–1980	7.2	2.6	.7	1.3	.5	2.1
1980–1990	10.1	3.6	.8	2.0	.5	3.2
1990–2000	12.7	4.3	.9	2.7	.7	4.1
1970–2000	30.0	10.5	2.4	6.0	1.7	9.4
1980–2000	22.8	7.9	1.7	4.7	1.2	7.3
Both sexes						
1970–1980	23.8	8.7	2.1	5.0	1.4	6.6
1980–1990	32.9	11.8	2.6	7.5	1.4	9.6
1990–2000	40.6	13.9	2.9	9.9	1.6	12.3
1970–2000	97.3	34.4	7.6	22.4	4.4	28.5
1980–2000	73.5	25.7	4.5	17.4	3.0	21.9

Source: CELADE (1982).

TABLE 10
Absolute Increase of the Rural Labor Force Age Ten or Older in Latin America, 1970–2000, by Sex (in millions)

Sex and Year	*Latin America*	*Brazil*	*Colombia*	*Mexico*	*Argentina*	*Remainder of Latin America*
Males						
1970–1980	4.3	1.4	.3	.8	0	1.8
1980–1990	3.8	.7	.2	.8	–.1	2.2
1990–2000	3.3	.2	0	.8	–.1	2.4
1970–2000	11.4	2.3	.5	2.4	–.2	6.4
1980–2000	7.1	.9	.2	1.6	–.2	4.6
Females						
1970–1980	.7	.2	.03	.1	–.01	.4
1980–1990	.6	0	.01	.1	–.02	.5
1990–2000	.6	0	.01	.1	–.01	.5
1970–2000	1.9	.2	.05	.3	–.04	1.4
1980–2000	1.2	0	.02	.2	–.03	1.0
Both sexes						
1970–1980	5.0	1.6	.33	.9	–.01	2.2
1980–1990	4.4	.7	.21	.9	–.12	2.7
1990–2000	3.9	.2	.01	.9	–.11	2.9
1970–2000	13.3	2.5	.55	2.7	–.24	7.8
1980–2000	8.3	.9	.22	1.8	–.23	5.6

Source: CELADE (1982).

the total labor force between 1970 and 2000 are greater in each succeeding decade. Especially notable is that Brazil is projected to add almost 27 million people to the labor force between 1980 and 2000, virtually all (97%) of whom will be in the urban sector. Similarly, Mexico is expected to add 19 million people to its labor force from 1980 to 2000, with 90% of the gain in the urban sector.

Can these additional jobseekers find employment? To help answer this question, let us see what we know about the recent trend in the demand for labor and then consider what the trend may be in the future.

LABOR DEMAND IN LATIN AMERICA

The urbanization of the labor force noted above implies a large shift out of agriculture, as Table 11 indicates. According to PREALC's (1982) estimates, 55% of economically active persons (EAP) in Latin America were in agricul-

TABLE 11
Industrial Structure of the Labor Force in Latin America, 1950–1980 (in percent)

Industry	*1950*	*1960*	*1970*	*1980*
Agriculture	55.0	48.2	42.3	35.1
Mining	1.2	1.1	.9	.8
Manufacturing	14.1	15.4	16.3	18.3
Construction	3.5	4.2	5.5	6.7
Electricity	.5	.6	.8	.9
Commerce	7.9	9.2	10.7	12.2
Transport	3.7	4.5	4.4	4.2
Services	14.1	16.8	19.1	21.8
Total	100.0	100.0	100.0	100.0

Source: PREALC (1982:34).

ture in 1950. This percentage declined steadily to only 35% by 1980. Aside from a decline in the very small percentage of EAP in mining, all other major branches of industry grew, particularly services (from 14 to 22%). More modest, but still significant, gains occurred in manufacturing (14 to 18%) and commerce (8 to 12%).

As Table 12 shows, the decline in the percentage of EAP in agriculture was substantial in both the modern and traditional sectors. Labor productivity and remuneration is lower and labor underutilization is greater in the latter than the former. Thus, the amount of labor underutilization in agriculture as a percentage of all EAP declined considerably between 1950 and 1980. But given the decline in the modern sector also, as a percentage of EAP in agriculture the size of the low-productivity traditional sector increased somewhat, from 60% (33.1/55.3) in 1950 to 65% (22.8/35.3) in 1980.

Most of the decline of 20 percentage points in the percentage of the labor force in agriculture was absorbed by a large increase of 14.5 percentage points in the formal part of the urban sector, in which productivity, remuneration and labor utilization are relatively high. Offsetting to some extent this substantial gain in effective labor utilization were increases in domestic service and in the informal part of the urban sector, both areas of low productivity, remuneration and labor utilization. Thus, the 10 percentage-point decline in rural sectors characterized by labor underutilization between 1950 and 1980 was considerably offset by an increase of 6 percentage points in urban sectors of limited utilization of labor. Consequently, there was a net decline of 4 points in the percentage of the labor force in sectors of low labor utilization. Thus, the major change in underutilization of labor from 1950 to 1980 was a shift in this underutilization out of agriculture into urban economic activities.

Turning from underemployment to unemployment, there is a considerable

TABLE 12
Sectoral Distribution of the Labor Force in Latin America, 1950–1980 (in percent)

Sector	*1950*	*1960*	*1970*	*1980*
Urban	43.5	50.5	56.7	64.0
Formal	30.1	34.9	39.8	44.6
Informal	8.7	10.6	11.5	13.8
Domestic service	4.7	5.0	5.4	5.6
Agriculture	55.3	48.4	42.4	35.3
Modern	22.2	19.2	15.3	12.5
Traditional	33.1	29.2	27.1	22.8
Mining	1.2	1.1	.9	.7
Total	100.0	100.0	100.0	100.0

Source: PREALC (1982:34).

body of data on open unemployment in many Latin American countries between 1963 and 1980. It is limited, however, to the principal cities (Table 13). With some exceptions, rates of open urban unemployment have not been "particularly high" (PREALC, 1982:3), nor have they displayed a marked tendency to rise or fall. Unemployment affects mainly young men and women. It is comparatively low for adult men, most of whom are heads of households and hence cannot afford to be without any income for more than a brief period. Comparing the rates of open urban unemployment with the percentages of the labor force in the urban sectors of low labor utilization, the data indicate that *under*employment is a more important form of labor underutilization than *open un*employment.

To sum up, open unemployment has not been a large or growing problem in Latin America, whereas underemployment has affected a large fraction of the labor force. In 1980 42% of the labor force were in sectors of low labor utilization. Is this high degree of underutilization likely to change, and if so in what way?

PREALC (1976) projected the extent of labor utilization in Latin America from 1970 to 2000, using an economic model of the region developed by ECLA. Space constraints do not permit a description of the model, but some of the assumptions can be presented. The population is assumed to grow at a decreasing rate, from an average annual rate of 2.9% between 1970 and 1980 to 2.8% during the 1980s and 2.7 percent during the 1990s. The rural sector, growing at only 1% per year, declines from 50% of the total population in 1970 to 34% by the year 2000. The labor force grows at an average annual rate of 2.9%. GDP expands at an average annual rate of 6.5%, with the rate more rapid in the modern than in the traditional sectors. The assumed average annual growth rates of labor productivity are as follows:

TABLE 13

Rates of Open Unemployment in Urban Latin America, 1963–1980 (in percent)

Country	*1963*	*1964*	*1965*	*1966*	*1967*	*1968*	*1969*	*1970*	*1971*	*1972*	*1973*	*1974*	*1975*	*1976*	*1977*	*1978*	*1979*	*1980*
Argentina	—	6.1	5.4	5.9	6.3	5.1	4.2	4.9	5.8	6.5	5.3	3.7	3.1	4.6	3.0	2.9	2.1	2.2
	8.8	5.7	5.0	5.7	6.2	5.0	4.0	4.9	6.0	6.6	5.3	3.4	2.6	4.5	2.8	2.8	2.0	3.5
	—	—	—	—	—	—	—	—	—	—	—	4.2	2.4	4.8	3.4	3.9	2.0	2.3
Bolivia	—	—	—	—	—	—	—	—	—	—	—	—	—	7.7	7.3	4.5	6.0	...
Brazil	—	—	—	—	—	—	—	—	—	—	3.9	—	—	2.6	3.3	...	...	...
	—	—	—	—	—	3.2	3.0	3.7	—	2.8	3.6	—	—	2.3	3.0	...	...	...
	—	—	—	—	—	—	—	—	—	—	—	—	—	—	3.4	3.2	...	...
Colombia	—	—	—	—	—	—	—	10.0	—	11.5	—	—	10.4	—	—	7.6	...	...
	—	—	—	—	—	—	—	—	—	—	—	12.7	11.0	10.6	9.0	9.0	8.9	9.7
Costa Rica	—	—	—	—	5.4	4.6	3.5	—	—	—	—	—	—	5.4	5.1	5.8	5.3	6.0
Chile	—	—	—	7.2	6.1	6.0	5.3	3.9	4.4	3.6	—	—	16.6	14.6	13.6	—	14.6	11.4
	4.9	5.3	5.4	5.3	6.1	6.0	6.1	7.1	5.7	3.7	4.8	9.7	16.2	16.7	13.2	14.0	13.6	11.8
Ecuador	—	—	—	—	—	5.5	—	—	—	—	—	—	5.3	—	—	—	—	—
El Salvador	—	—	—	—	—	—	—	—	—	—	—	14.2	8.6	—	—	—	—	—
Guatemala	—	—	—	—	—	—	—	—	—	—	—	—	—	—	2.9	—	—	—
Mexico	—	—	—	—	—	—	—	—	—	—	7.2	7.0	7.0	6.7	8.1	7.0	5.7	...
Nicaragua	—	—	—	—	—	—	—	—	—	—	16.4	8.0	11.1	9.8	—	—	24.6	13.7
Panama	5.8	4.7	—	—	9.2	10.0	9.3	10.3	10.7	9.5	—	7.5	8.6	9.0	—	9.6	11.6	—
Paraguay	—	—	—	—	—	—	—	—	—	—	12.0	—	—	6.7	—	—	—	—
Peru	—	—	—	—	—	—	10.6	8.3	7.7	7.3	7.1	6.6	8.1	8.4	9.4	10.4	10.5	...
	—	—	—	—	—	—	—	6.9	7.5	7.6	5.0	4.1	7.5	6.9	8.7	8.0	6.5	7.1
Dominican Republic	—	—	—	—	—	—	13.2	—	—	—	20.0	—	—	—	8.6	—	—	—
Uruguay	—	—	—	—	7.2	8.4	8.7	7.5	7.6	7.7	8.9	8.1	—	12.7	11.8	10.1	8.3	7.4
Venezuela	—	—	—	—	9.5	7.4	8.4	7.8	7.1	—	—	7.6	8.3	6.8	5.5	5.1	5.8	6.6

Note: The surveys were generally conducted in the major urban areas. For identification of the specific places, consult the source.

Source: PREALC (1982:99 and 100).

	High-productivity areas	*Low-productivity areas*
Agriculture	4.6	2.5
Industry	3.9	3.2
Services	3.4	1.3

The main conclusion of the projection is that though the proportion of total production coming from the modern high-productivity areas rises from 55% in 1970 to 70% in 2000, the modern sectors are not able to absorb labor fast enough. Though the rate of employment growth in the urban areas is high, 3.8% per year (3.7% in the modern urban sector), it is not rapid enough to absorb the growth of the urban labor force. Total employment expands at a rate of 2.7%. As a result, open unemployment nearly doubles, and underemployment (expressed in terms of "equivalent unemployment") increases only slightly (see Table 14). Even with the much more rapid increase of the rate of open unemployment (to about 10%) than the rate of equivalent unemployment (to 35%) in the year 2000, the latter is still 3.5 times larger, reinforcing the observation that underutilization of labor in Latin America takes the form primarily of underemployment rather than open unemployment.

Thus, despite 30 years of economic growth, concentrated in the modern sectors, the underutilization of labor *increases* rather than decreases. Part of the reason is the growth of average labor productivity, which triples during the projection period (implying an average annual growth rate of about 3.7%), so that by 2000 it is at a level similar to that of West Germany in 1970. This effect is reinforced by the more rapid gains in productivity in the

TABLE 14
Projection of Labor Utilization in Latin America, 1970–2000

	Percentage of Labor Force	
Underutilization	*1970*	*2000*
Rate of open unemployment	5.3	9.9
Rate of equivalent unemployment[a]	33.5	35.0
Rate of total underemployment	38.8	44.9

[a] The estimates of underemployment expressed as equivalent unemployment were obtained using a productivity criterion. A norm of average national productivity was applied in the areas where underemployment was concentrated: traditional agriculture and low-productivity urban activities. Hence, in assessing the results for the year 2000, one must keep in mind the increases in productivity differentials implied by the style of development during the period.

Source: PREALC (1976:134).

(primarily urban) modern than in the traditional sectors of the economy, and the increasing urbanization of the labor force. A notable consequence of these trends is that whereas three-fourths of equivalent unemployment in 1970 was rural, by 2000 only two-fifths of it will be located there. The bulk of it will be located in "urban services of low productivity" (PREALC, 1976:135).

More favorable results are reached by a projection prepared by the United Nations Industrial Development Organization (United Nations, 1982:Chap. XIX). This model was developed not essentially as a projection of employment utilization, but rather as a "scenario of industrialization in which the goal . . . of 25 percent of world manufacturing arising from the developing countries in the year 2000 is achieved" (United Nations, 1982:244). It is assumed that Latin America will account for about half (13%) of the 25% goal. Given this objective, the assumed rates of average annual growth of GDP had to increase rapidly from the estimated rate of 4.6% during the late 1970s to 6.9% during the 1980s and a remarkable 10.9% during the 1990s. The latter is considerably greater than the rates assumed for other world regions, with the next largest rate being 8.9% for Asia during the 1990s (United Nations, 1982:Table 116). For 1975–2000, the average annual rate is a very high 8.0%.

Rates of population growth are assumed to fall from the annual average of 2.66 during the late 1970s to 2.61 during the 1980s and then 2.40 during the 1990s. (Larger declines are projected after 2000, up to 2025, than before 2000 in all world regions, with the rate in Latin America 1.54% per year during that interval.) The assumptions about *(a)* the ratio of the average annual percentage increase in labor productivity to the average annual percentage increase in value added and *(b)* the average annual percentage increase of value added imply an average annual percentage increase of labor productivity of about 4.5%.

As a result, the average annual growth rate of labor demand from 1975 to 2000 is 3.2%, considerably greater than the 2.7% estimated for 1960–1975. It is also greater than the 2.7% average growth of labor supply implied in CELADE's 1982 projection of the labor force in Latin America. And this is the case even though the rates of population growth used in the United Nations scenario are greater than those used by CELADE:

	United Nations	*CELADE*	*Difference*
1975–1980	2.66	2.54	0.12
1980–1990	2.61	2.33	0.28
1990–2000	2.40	2.08	0.32

Note: The increasing difference between the two projections probably reflects the clearer perception of the recent fertility declines in a number of Latin American countries, notably Brazil, Colombia, and Mexico, which the more recent projection (CELADE's) incorporates.

Unsurprisingly, we may conclude that a very rapid growth of GDP would enable Latin American countries to absorb the anticipated growth of their labor supply. The critical question is whether such a rapid rate of growth of GDP is likely. The characterization above of the 8% growth rate as "very high" itself implies that it is *not* likely. More explicit reasons may be cited, however.

As noted above, this growth rate is much greater than the rate estimated for the late 1970s (4.6% during 1975–1980). But since this period is short and follows the large increase in oil prices during the early 1970s, it may be wondered whether it is a good basis for comparison. During the longer and more favorable (to economic growth) period from 1960 to 1975, GDP grew on average 6% per year (United Nations, 1982:Table 110). Though considerably better than the 4.6% rate of the late 1970s, this rate is still well below that of the 8% average assumed in the United Nations projection from 1975 to 2000.

Furthermore, the 1980s have started poorly, with very low growth rates resulting from the adverse impact of the worldwide recession of 1980–1983, the longest in 50 years (World Bank, 1984:1). Estimates of the rates for 1980–1981 and 1981–1982 (Hopkins, 1983:462) are as follows:

	Percent	
Latin America	*1980–1981*	*1981–1982 (est.)*
Middle-income countries	1.0	−0.1
Low-income countries[a]	2.0	1.6

[a] Bolivia, Dominican Republic, El Salvador, Haiti, Honduras, Nicaragua, and Peru. The total population of these countries in 1980 was 45.6 million, which was 12.5% of the total population of Latin America (CELADE 1982:2).

The oil importers among the middle-income countries of the region (including Argentina, Brazil and Colombia, but excluding Mexico and Venezuela, which are oil exporters) had an even more difficult time, as the following World Bank (1984:11) data indicate:

	Average annual percentage change in GDP
1960–1973	5.6
1973–1979	5.0
1980	5.8
1981	−2.3
1982	−0.4
1983 (est.)	−2.2

The middle-income oil importers in Latin America had 241 million people in 1980, two-thirds of the region's total population.

Finally, as if the above were not sufficiently good grounds for skepticism about a very high rate of economic growth being achieved in Latin America during the 1980s and 1990s, one must add that the heavy debt burden of the largest countries in the region—Argentina, Brazil, and Mexico—will make it difficult for these countries to achieve attractive rates of economic growth for many years to come. Indeed, depending on the policies of the industrial countries with respect to debt servicing and repayment and terms of trade with debtor nations, and on the rate of economic growth in the industrial countries, the economic futures of these debtor countries vary from manageable to gloomy (World Bank, 1984:42–47).

Hopkins (1983:471) has estimated the impact of the recent recession on unemployment by estimating labor productivity (by regressing output per employed person on the economic growth rate per annum and GNP per capita, using 1970 and 1980 data for 15 countries) and applying this estimate to output. The productivity estimates for the middle- and low-income groups of Latin American countries were negative. Thus, even with very low estimated annual average growth rates for 1980–1982 of 0.5% for the middle-income countries and 1.8% for the low-income countries (apparently taken as estimates for 1980–1985), unemployment is estimated to increase only modestly between *(a)* 1980 and *(b)* 1982 and 1985 (Hopkins, 1983:471). His figures are as follows:

	Percent	
Latin America	*1980–1982*	*1980–1985*
Middle-income countries	0.9	2.5
Low-income countries	1.5	3.5

However, he also estimated what would be the result of assuming that productivity did not decline, setting it to zero, during 1980–1985, on the grounds that negative productivity growth could not likely continue "for long." As would be expected, larger increases in unemployment occur than with declines in productivity. The numbers are as follows:

	Percent	
Latin America	*1980–1982*	*1980–1985*
Middle-income countries	4.2	10.3
Low-income countries	2.2	5.2

The results are obviously considerably different in the two cases. Even allowing for the rough character of the estimates, it would appear that the very low rates of economic growth of the early 1980s is likely to result in at least some exacerbation during the first half of the 1980s of the already large underutilization of labor (as indicated by the PREALC data) and perhaps even a substantial worsening. There is certainly no reason to expect any improvement.

As for the PREALC projection, we can see now that the assumed regional average rate of GDP growth of 6.5% per year from 1970 to 2000 is significantly higher than the approximately 5.5% growth rate that is estimated to have occurred from 1970 to 1980, and is much higher than the rate of perhaps no more than 1% for 1980–1985, which the data presented by Hopkins and the World Bank suggest. The implied growth rate for 1970–1985 is about 4% per year. An average annual growth rate of about 9% for 1985–2000 would be required to raise the average annual growth rate for 1970–2000 to 6.5%, as PREALC postulated, given the estimate of about 4% for the first half of this 30-year interval. Since we concluded above that the assumption of an average annual growth rate of 8% (United Nations projection) for 1975–2000 was unlikely to be achieved, the achievement of a still higher average rate during the latter half of this period is even more unlikely.

Thus, the labor absorptive capacity of the Latin American economies is apt to be weaker than indicated by PREALC's projection, implying a greater increase in labor underutilization than indicated by this projection. This is offset, however, by the lower rate of growth of the labor force currently anticipated, 2.9% versus 2.75%. Since the currently projected rate is only modestly lower, however, the offset is probably only partial. If the rate of growth of labor productivity were not as rapid as the PREALC projection assumed, then there would be an additional offset to the deterioration of the labor absorptive capability of the Latin American economies during the last three decades of the twentieth century, resulting from slower economic growth than assumed.

The last point indicates a dilemma. On the one hand, raising labor productivity is desirable because it allows remuneration to rise, or production costs to decline, or both. On the other hand, it reduces the ability of an economy to absorb the growth in its labor supply. Where the existing utilization of labor is substantially deficient or the labor force grows rapidly, or both, such a reduction in labor absorptive capacity is painful. The dilemma can be overcome by a rate of economic growth great enough to absorb the growth in both labor supply and productivity. What we have seen is that it appears highly unlikely that the rate of economic growth in Latin America during the 1980s and probably during 1980–2000 will be great enough to absorb fully the currently anticipated growth in the labor force, while allowing at least some growth in labor productivity.

POPULATION TRENDS IN MEXICO

As noted above, the population and labor trends in Mexico deserve further examination because of the size of the population, the country's proximity to the United States, and the rapidity of the recent and anticipated growth of the population and labor force. These have been and will continue to be major determinants, along with Mexico's rate of economic growth, of the volume of migration from Mexico to the United States, which has become a political issue in the United States and a sore point in the relations between the two countries.

Mexico's population increased 150% between 1950 and 1980, from 27 to 69 million (Table 15). The average annual growth rate was 3.1%, at which pace a population doubles in a bit over 22 years. Thus, in a century, between four and five doublings would occur, multiplying the population between 16 and 32 times. Without any decline in this growth rate, Mexico's population

TABLE 15
Growth of Mexico's Population: Estimated, 1950–1980; Projected, 1985–2000

Year	*Number (in millions)*		*Index (1950 = 100)*		*Index (1980 = 100)*	
1950	27.4		100			
1955	31.7		116			
1960	37.1		135			
1965	43.5		159			
1970	51.2		187			
1975	60.2		220			
1980	69.4		253		100	
	A	*B*	*A*	*B*	*A*	*B*
1985	78.5	79.0	286	288	113	114
1990	86.2	89.0	315	325	124	128
1995	93.0	99.2	339	362	134	143
2000	99.6	109.2	364	399	144	157

Notes:
A—Fertility declines to a total fertility rate of 2.2 children per woman in 1995–2000.
B—Fertility declines to a total fertility rate of 3.0 children per woman in 1995–2000.
The assumptions regarding mortality and migration are the same in projections A and B.
Source: Mexico (1983:Tables 1, 20, 27).

would be 140 million a few years after the end of the twentieth century and over 1 billion well before the end of the twenty-first century. Such awesome growth is obviously unacceptable, and the growth rate has begun to decline as a result of a national effort to reduce the birthrate. As Table 15 shows, if the TFR falls to an average of 2.2 children per woman by the late 1990s, then the population is projected to grow to "only" about 100 million. The average annual growth rate between 1980 and 2000 would be 1.8%. If, however, fertility falls less rapidly, but still substantially, to a TFR of 3 children per woman by the late 1990s, then Mexico's population would be about 10 million greater, and the average annual growth rate would be 2.3%. On these assumptions, the anticipated population in the year 2000 would be 3.6–4.0 times that of 1950 and 44–57% greater than in 1980.

Obviously, considerable growth occurs even during a period of substantial deceleration. This is especially true when, as in Mexico's case, the deceleration of the growth rate starts from a very high level. Although this may be discouraging, one must recognize that it is nevertheless a large gain, for (as noted above) with no decline from the average annual rate of 3.1% between 1950 and 1980 the population would be about 130 million in the year 2000. Furthermore, a continuation of the decline in the growth rate, as compared with no decline, would have increasingly great effects. Thus, the gains in the twenty-first century would be more and more encouraging. In order to get a better understanding of the trends of population growth, let us take a closer look at the demographic components of growth in Mexico since 1950.

Table 16 presents the trends in fertility, mortality and migration. The crude rates—that is, the number of events per 1000 persons in the population—are directly related to the rate of population growth; hence they are indispensable to an examination of the components of population change. They are influenced, however, by the age structure of the population. A large proportion of elderly persons in a population, for instance, tends to raise the crude death rate, because age-specific death rates are much higher among the elderly than the among the rest of the population (except in populations with high infant mortality). To ascertain the trends in fertility and mortality themselves, the total fertility rate and life expectancy at birth are also presented in Table 16. These measures are not influenced by age structure. There is no comparable measure for migration.

Until the 1970s, fertility was very high, with women of reproductive age averaging almost seven children per woman and the (crude) birthrate at a very high level in the mid to upper 40s. By the 1950s, however, the death rate had declined to 16, resulting in a rate of natural increase of over 3%. Though net migration was negative, the rate was very low, so it offset the rate of natural increase only slightly. Consequently, the rate of population growth was just barely less than 3%. Thereafter, the rate of net migration fluctuated until the 1970s. The subsequent decline in the rate results from the assumption that the *amount* of net emigration (70,000 per year) estimated for the 1960s would be the same during the following decades.

Mexico (1983) does not describe the basis for this assumption. Readers should keep in mind, however, that net migration is the result of immigration as well as emigration. Though the volume of emigration to the United States may be large, much of it may be temporary, resulting in a substantial amount of return migration, immigration from the United States. In addition, there has been a significant volume of immigration from Central American countries, which has probably been scarcely offset by emigration to those countries.

Between the early 1950s and the late 1960s, the TFR remained constant at a high level. The birthrate, nevertheless, declined by 5% from 46.7 to 44.2 because the proportion in the population of women of reproductive age declined a little. The death rate, however, continued to drop by a larger amount that the birthrate. As a result, the rates of natural increase and population growth rose. By the late 1960s the latter was 3.25%. Fertility

TABLE 16
Components of Population Growth in Mexico: Estimated, 1950–1980; Projected, 1980–2000

	Number per 1000 persons						
Period	*Births*	*Deaths*	*Natural Increase*	*Net Migration*	*Population Growth*	*Total Fertility Rate*	*Life Expectancy At Birth*
1950–1955	46.7	16.2	30.5	−1.4	29.1	6.8	50.8
1955–1960	45.8	13.2	32.6	−1.2	31.5	6.8	55.4
1960–1965	44.9	11.3	33.7	−1.7	31.9	6.8	58.6
1965–1970	44.2	10.2	33.9	−1.5	32.5	6.7	60.3
1970–1975	42.7	9.2	33.5	−1.3	32.3	6.4	62.2
1975–1980	37.6	7.9	29.6	−1.1	28.5	5.4	64.1
Projection A							
1980–1985	32.7	7.0	25.7	−1.0	24.7	4.4	65.7
1985–1990	25.8	6.2	19.5	−.9	18.7	3.2	67.2
1990–1995	21.8	5.9	15.9	−.8	15.1	2.5	68.4
1995–2000	20.2	5.7	14.5	−.7	13.7	2.2	69.6
Projection B							
1980–1985	33.9	7.1	26.8	−.9	25.9	4.6	65.7
1985–1990	31.2	6.5	24.7	−.8	23.9	4.0	67.2
1990–1995	28.4	6.0	22.3	−.7	21.6	3.4	68.4
1995–2000	25.6	5.7	19.9	−.7	19.2	3.0	69.6

Note: Because of rounding, the sums of components sometimes deviate from totals by .1.
Source: Mexico (1983:Tables 4, 23, 30).

began to fall in the early 1970s, but the pace was slow. However, between the early 1970s and late 1970s, the tempo of fertility decline accelerated sharply, causing the rate of population growth to peak at around 3.2% and then fall to 2.85% by the late 1970s. The drop in the growth rate was not as large as that in the birthrate because the death rate continued to fall.

The projection of Mexico's population assumes that the birthrate will decline much more than the death rate. Given the negligible rate of net emigration, this differential is almost completely translated into a reduction of the growth rate between the late 1970s and the late 1990s of between (approximately) 1% and 1.5%. The variation reflects two different assumptions about the pace of fertility decline. The swifter decline assumes that a TFR of 2.2 is reached by the late 1990s. That would be a very impressive achievement. The slower fall assumes that TFR would drop to 3.0 by 1995–2000. Even if not as impressive as getting to a TFR of 2.2, it would still be a major achievement. But it is certainly feasible. The TFR has fallen in a number of developing countries to below 4, and in some of them to below 3. In 1982, in Latin America alone, Colombia had a TFR of 3.6 and Costa Rica 3.5. Chile was at 2.7 and Cuba at 2.0 (World Bank, 1984:Table 20).

The reader may note that the decline in the TFR is swifter than that in the birthrate. The reason is that the relative number of women of reproductive age in the population increases as the proportion of children declines as a result of the drop in fertility. This mechanism moderates the fall in the birthrate. Eventually, the increase in the proportion of women of reproductive age will peak and then decline. This would occur if fertility were to stop falling and start rising. But even without a rise in fertility, it would happen when the proportion of the population age 50 or older begins to increase substantially, while the decline in the proportion of children under age 15 slows down or levels off. Without an increase in fertility, it may take as long as 50 years for the increase in the proportion of women to top out. Fortunately, this age-structure effect is not nearly as great as the change in the rate at which women reproduce. But it does help explain why it would take at least several decades for a high fertility population to get its birthrate down to a very low level (under, say, 15).

The reader may have noted also that even on the assumption that the TFR reaches 2.2 by the late 1990s, the rate of population growth would still be close to 1.4%. Though about half of a rate of around 3%, such a rate would still result in considerable increments to the population. This is another manifestation of the difficulty of reducing population growth in a country with a history of high fertility and population growth to a manageable level in anything less than several decades. But there comes a time when the forces moderating the decline weaken and the pace may accelerate. For one thing, the death rate can hardly get much lower than the 5.7 projected for the late

1990s. (In 1982, very few countries had a death rate under 5: Costa Rica, 4; Kuwait and the United Arab Emirates, each with 3.) For another, as noted above, the proportion of women of reproductive age will eventually decline from some relatively high level. And the age-structure changes causing this decline may also exert an inflating effect, even if only a modest one, on the death rate. Some time during the next century, perhaps before 2025, these changes are likely to work to accelerate the decline in the rate of population growth in Mexico.

Offsetting these factors are likely to be further (though decelerating) increases in life expectancy and increasing difficulty in reducing TFR below the long-run replacement level (approximately 2.1–2.2 for a country with a life expectancy of around 70). The net result may well be a growth rate of at least 1% well into the twenty-first century. With a population exceeding 100 million by then, the annual population gain would exceed 1 million, and the growth of the labor force would also be considerable.

It is reasonable to expect, however, that the Mexican economy will be much larger then, and thus better able than today to provide jobs for the additions to the labor force. Moreover, given the changes in age structure that a large sustained fertility decline inevitably produces, Mexico is very likely to find its dependency burden considerably reduced. As a measure of this, we may use the ratio of those of dependent ages (say, under age 15 and over age 64) to those of productive age (in this example, those age 15 to 64). This ratio falls from 93 in 1980 (i.e., almost one person of dependent age to one person of productive age) to 63 (TFR = 3.0) or 49 (TFR = 2.2) in 2000. Though this is only a rough measure, the changes are so large that there seems little doubt the actual dependency burden will be reduced. As a result, a smaller fraction of available resources will need to be allocated to the support, health, and education of dependents. This may allow a larger fraction to be provided for productive investment, which may in turn increase the demand for labor.

Before looking at the trends in economic activity in Mexico, it would be useful to compare briefly the fertility decline in Mexico with the declines in Brazil and Colombia (Table 17). In all three countries the decline in the TFR exceeded 30% by around 1980. In Colombia it exceeded 40%. Although these declines are large, because the TFRs were initially high (well over 6), TFRs of about 4 around 1980 still leave much room for further decline.

Another significant point to note is that the decline began about a decade later (in the 1970s) in Mexico than in Brazil and Colombia (in the 1960s). As a result, the declines in the dependency ratio will begin about 10 years later in Mexico than in Brazil and Colombia. Similarly, the projected declines in the growth rates of the working-age populations (defined as 10 years of age or older in this study) from the 1970s to the 1980s are considerably greater in Brazil and Colombia than in Mexico. Not until the change between the 1980s

TABLE 17
Trends in the Total Fertility Rate (TFR) in Brazil, Colombia, and Mexico, 1960–1980

	Brazil		*Colombia*		*Mexico*	
Year	*TFR*	*Index*	*TFR*	*Index*	*TFR*	*Index*
Around 1960	6.2	100	6.8	100	6.5	100
1965	5.8	94	6.6	97	6.6	102
1970	5.3	85	5.7	84	6.7	103
1975	4.7	76	4.8	71	5.7	88
Around 1980	4.3	69	3.8	56	4.4	68

Source: Merrick (1983:Table 2).

and 1990s does the decline in Mexico exceed that of the other two countries (Table 7). As for the projected changes in the labor forces, while the growth rates decline between the 1970s and 1980s in Brazil and Colombia, there is, if anything, an *increase* (even if only a slight one) in Mexico (Table 2). Not until the 1990s is the growth rate of the Mexican labor force projected to slow down.

TRENDS IN ECONOMIC ACTIVITY IN MEXICO

As noted above, Mexico's labor force has been growing and is expected to continue growing, at least to the year 2000, more rapidly than the labor force in Latin America as a whole. As a result, the Mexican labor force as a percentage of the labor force in all of Latin America is projected to increase from 16% in 1970 to 20% in 2000 (Table 2). The proportional gain is projected to be even greater in the urban sector, from 17% of Latin America's urban labor force in 1970 to 22% in 2000 (Table 3). The swifter growth of the urban labor force in Mexico than in Latin America as a whole is evident also in the data on the sectoral distribution of the labor force (compare Tables 12 and 18). Whereas 55% of Latin America's labor force was in agriculture in 1950, in Mexico the percentage was 64. But by 1980, Mexico's percentage in agriculture (38) was much closer to the regional average (35). An even more striking difference is that within agriculture, virtually all of the decline in Mexico took place in the traditional sector, whereas in Latin America as a whole the decline occurred to about an equal extent in both the modern and the traditional sectors.

Similarly, there was a more rapid increase in the formal urban sector in Mexico than in the region as a whole. But there was a more rapid growth also in the informal urban sector in Mexico than in the region. Keeping in mind

TABLE 18
Sectoral Distribution of the Labor Force in Mexico, 1950–1980 (in percent)

Sector	*1950*	*1960*	*1970*	*1980*
Urban	34.5	45.7	52.1	61.5
Formal	21.6	32.2	33.9	39.5
Informal	9.7	10.0	14.5	18.3
Domestic service	3.2	3.5	3.7	3.7
Agriculture	64.4	53.0	46.8	37.6
Modern	20.4	25.4	21.9	19.2
Traditional	44.0	27.6	24.9	18.4
Mining	1.1	1.3	1.1	.9
Total	100.0	100.0	100.0	100.0

Source: PREALC (1982:64).

that traditional agriculture, domestic service, and the informal urban sectors are where productivity, remuneration, and labor utilization are low, these differentials indicate a markedly greater decline in underemployment in Mexico than in the region. Summing the percentages in these three sectors, we see a drop in Mexico of 16.5 percentage points, but only 4.3 points in the whole region:

	1950	*1980*	*Change in percentage points*
Mexico	56.9	40.4	−16.5
Latin America	46.5	42.2	−4.3

As the following figures indicate, the reason for this differential decline is that whereas in the whole region most of the decline in agricultural underemployment was shifted to urban underemployment, in Mexico only a minor part of the decline in agricultural underemployment was replaced by urban underemployment:

	1950	*1980*	*Change in percentage points*
Mexico			
Urban underemployment	12.9	22.0	9.1
Agricultural underemployment	44.0	18.4	−25.6
Latin America			
Urban underemployment	13.4	19.4	6.0
Agricultural underemployment	33.1	22.8	−10.3

As for unemployment, "relatively low unemployment seems to have been achieved in Mexico at the cost of low participation rates for women, widespread seasonal unemployment, and low incomes for large numbers of workers" (Keesing, 1977:9). There is evidence also of substantial displacement of workers because of mechanization. In general, the employment situation in 1970 was perhaps better than it had been during the 1930s, but there may have been a deterioration since 1950. The available data do not permit more definite conclusions (Keesing, 1977:9 and 19). Though Keesing (1977:19) argues that the employment problem in Mexico is not as serious as often contended, and that using low income as a criterion of underemployment tends to exaggerate the problem, he concludes that "Mexico does seem to have a chronic problem in the area of employment and job shortages, as distinct from low incomes."

Given this evidence of substantial underutilization of labor and of very rapid, though declining, rates of labor-force growth for at least the remainder of the twentieth century, one must wonder what are the prospects for a rate of economic growth in Mexico during 1980–2000 high enough to absorb the large projected increases in the labor force (on average, almost one million per year—see Table 8), let alone reduce the degree of labor underutilization? For reasons similar to those presented above in discussing the analogous prospects for all of Latin America, the answer is that the prospects are not promising, at least not during the 1980s. Indeed, given the considerably higher rate of labor-force growth in Mexico than in the region as a whole, it would appear that the prospects are worse. But the average annual growth rate of GDP was also greater in Mexico during the 1970s than in the region, 5.8% for Latin America (United Nations, 1983:Table 7) and 6.4% (1970–1982) for Mexico (World Bank, 1984:221).

Without also projecting the rate of change in labor productivity, however, one cannot estimate the degree of labor absorption only from data on the growth of the labor force and of production. Without labor productivity projections, one can conjecture whether its rates of change would differ appreciably from that of the whole region. The more rapid movement of the labor force between 1950 and 1980 from the low productivity to the high-productivity sectors in Mexico than in the region (compare Tables 12 and 18), noted above, suggests that the growth rate in labor productivity from 1950 to 1980 has been greater in Mexico. If such a differential were to continue in the future, Mexico's prospects for labor absorption would be poorer than that of the region as a whole because of more rapid growth in labor productivity, as well as its more rapid labor-force growth. If, on the other hand, Mexico's economy finds it harder in the future to increase its labor productivity than it has done during the past few decades, then it may find gains in labor productivity to be less of an obstacle to absorbing labor than does Latin America as a whole.

Declines in labor productivity, however, would make the achievement of a high rate of economic growth more difficult. Moreover, the heavy debt burden and the consequent austerity that the lenders have imposed as a condition for refinancing it may well limit the prospects for an average rate of growth of GDP as high as achieved during the 1970s, about 6.5%. The GDP grew by about 8% per year in 1980 and 1981. But in 1982 the GDP declined by about 0.5%, followed by a much larger drop (4.7%) in 1983 (*Washington Post*, 1984:A22). Growth resumed in 1984, but the rate was less than 4% (*Washington Post*, 1985: K3). Thus, for the first half of the 1980s, the annual growth rate would appear to average about 3%. It would take an average rate of about 10% for the rest of the 1980s for the decade average to approximate the average rate (6.5%) achieved during the 1970s.

The achievement of a 10% growth rate is obviously extremely unlikely even under conditions much more favorable than those existing in Mexico now. For one thing, the high growth rate of the 1970s was financed partly by foreign borrowing and growing government budget deficits. These, of course, have had to be cut back greatly. For another, private investors, who now have to supply a larger share of the financing needed for rapid growth than they did during the 1970s, are being deterred from doing so by the high rate of inflation, the weakness of the peso, and the extent of government controls on prices, foreign trade, and foreign investment (*Washington Post*, 1984:A22). Furthermore, the price of oil fell in 1985 and may continue to drop in 1986.

In sum, Mexico is unlikely to absorb all of the large increase in its labor force anticipated during the 1980s, thus adding to the considerable underutilization of labor that prevailed during previous decades. Whether that is the prospect for the 1990s also is more difficult to judge. Much depends on the success of the efforts to manage the debt during the remainder of the 1980s. If that is at least reasonably successful, rates of economic growth comparable to those of the 1960s and 1970s may be achieved during the 1990s. At the same time, the favorable effects of the onset of the rapid decline in fertility during the 1970s will become evident in the marked deceleration of labor-force growth projected for the 1990s (Table 2) and the reductions in the dependency burden noted above. Though the problem of labor underutilization is not likely to be overcome quickly, given rates of economic growth comparable to those of recent decades, progress may begin to be made during the 1990s.

SUMMARY AND CONCLUSION

Because of rapid population growth, the labor force in Latin America has been growing and will continue to grow at a rapid rate, especially in Mexico. Coupled with a decline in the relative size of the agricultural labor force, this rapid growth has been even swifter in the urban sector. As rapid as the rates of real economic growth have been, given the increases in labor productivity that have occurred, the economies of the Latin American countries have not been able to absorb all of the expansion in the supply of labor. Moreover, it appears likely that the underutilization of labor will increase during the 1980s. However, if the Latin American economies can grow during the 1990s at least as swiftly as they did during the 1960s and 1970s, then the employment situation may stop getting worse and may, in some countries, even begin to improve. This may happen if the projected declines in the rate of growth of the labor forces and in the ratio of dependents to economically active persons actually occur.

These declines would be the result of reductions in the birthrate, which began in some countries (notably Brazil and Colombia) during the 1960s and in others (notably Mexico) during the 1970s, and which have proceeded swiftly so far. To the extent the fertility declines continue, especially if rapidly, the prospects for improvements in labor absorption brighten. However, given the lag of about 15 years in the effect of a drop in the rate of population growth on the pace at which the supply of labor increases, and given the recency of fertility decline in Latin America, any such improvements are likely to be much greater after the turn of the century than before.

APPENDIX: INFORMATION ABOUT THE PROJECTIONS

CELADE (1982:XVII–XVIII and 165–166) provides a fuller account than is feasible here.

In collaboration with the national institutions of 12 of the 20 countries for which data are presented, CELADE prepared projections on population and the labor force for 1950–2025 (population) and 1970–2000 (labor force). Projections for the other 8 countries were prepared without the "direct participation of national institutions from these countries" (CELADE, 1982: 166). The population projections for 1970–2025 are based on a "medium fertility hypothesis, or recommended hypothesis for each country" (CELADE, 1982:166). "Medium fertility" is not further specified, but it implies that the course of fertility during the specified interval would be intermediate to a high and a low hypothesis. The high hypothesis implies little or no change in the level of fertility, and the low hypothesis a substantial decline.

Although CELADE (1982) presents projections only for the national population of the region and not the urban and rural populations, the latter must have been made. For the procedure described for projecting the urban and rural economically active populations indicates that they were obtained by multiplying the corresponding age and sex-specific economic activity rates and population. As for the projections of the activity rates by age and sex in the urban and rural sectors, CELADE (1982:XVII–XVIII) says that the historical trends and the "most plausible" future course of the activity rates were taken into account, keeping in mind the degree of urbanization reached and the "agro-industrial development perspectives of each country." CELADE (1982:166) provides a more detailed description.

REFERENCES

Centro Latinoamericano de Demografia (CELADE)

1982 *Boletin Demografico*, No. 29. Santiago. February.

Hopkins, Mark

1983 Employment trends in developing countries, 1960–1980 and beyond." *International Labor Review* 122(4) (July–August).

Keesing, Donald B.

1977 "Employment and lack of employment in Mexico, 1900–1970." In James W. Wilkie and Kenneth Ruddle (eds.), *Quantitative Latin American Studies: Methods and Findings*. Statistical Abstract of Latin America, Supplement 6. Los Angeles: UCLA Latin America Center Publications, University of California.

Merrick, Thomas W.

1983 *Recent Fertility Declines in Brazil, Colombia, and Mexico*. Working Papers in Demography, CPR 83–005. Washington, D.C.: Center for Population Research, Georgetown University.

Mexico. Direccion General de Estadistica

1983 *Mexico: Estimaciones y Proyecciones de Poblacion, 1950–2000*. Mexico City.

Programa Regional de Empleo en America Latina y Caribe (PREALC)

1976 *The Employment Problem in Latin America: Facts, Outlook and Policies*. Santiago: International Labour Office, Regional Employment Programme for Latin America and the Caribbean.

1982 *Mercado de Trabajo en Cifras, 1950–1980*. Santiago: International Labour Office, Regional Employment Programme for Latin America and the Caribbean.

Todaro, Michael P.

1981 *Economic Development in the Third World*. 2nd ed. New York: Longman.

United Nations

1982 *World Population Trends and Policies: 1981 Monitoring Report*. Vol. 1, *Population Trends*. New York.

1983 *Yearbook of National Account Statistics, 1981* (Vol. 2). New York.

Washington Post

1984 News story. July 15.

1985 News Story, September 29.

World Bank

1979 *World Development Report 1979*. Washington, D.C.

1984 *World Development Report 1984*. Washington, D.C.

5

Population Growth and Emigration in Latin America: What Is the Nature of the Relationship?

SERGIO DIAZ-BRIQUETS and JOHN J. MACISCO, JR.

Emigration from Latin America and the Caribbean to the United States is by no means a new development. Immigrants from this region have been arriving in the United States since at least 1820, when immigration statistics were first compiled. Between 1820 and 1980, 5.3 million Latin American and Caribbean immigrants were admitted as legal permanent residents. The number of Western Hemisphere immigrants (Canada excluded) has varied considerably over time (Table 1). The earliest migratory flows represent only a small fraction of the number of legally admitted migrants in recent decades. Between 1820 and 1900, for example, some 167,000 Latin American and Caribbean migrants reached American shores; in contrast, between 1971 and 1980, 1.8 million arrived. The immigrants' national origin has undergone noticeable changes during the period. In the 1880s a majority of the migrants were from the Caribbean; Mexico became the major source through much of the first half of this century. By the 1960s, as immigration from the region accelerated, a majority of the migrants again came from the Caribbean.

These figures convey only part of the immigration story. They do not reflect the arrival of temporary laborers that at different historical periods have been allowed to enter the United States legally, or the voluminous flows of undocumented entrants arriving in the country over much of its history. The quantitatively most important example of legally admitted temporary workers was the Mexican *bracero* program. The importation of Mexican workers, however, dates back to the nineteenth century. The institutionalized importation of laborers can be traced to World War I when, in order to cope with acute rural manpower shortages, and under special wartime exemptions, approximately 72,000 Mexican workers were brought to the United

TABLE 1
Latin American and Caribbean Immigration to the United States, by Country or Region of Origin and Decade, 1821–1830 and 1971–1980

Years	Mexico[a]	Caribbean	Central America	South America	Other America[b]	Total
1821–1830	4,817	3,834	105	531	—	9,287
1831–1840	6,599	12,301	44	856	—	19,800
1841–1850	3,271	13,528	368	3,579	—	20,746
1851–1860	3,078	10,660	449	1,224	—	15,411
1861–1870	2,191	9,046	95	1,397	—	12,729
1871–1880	5,162	13,957	157	1,128	—	20,404
1881–1890	1,913	29,042	404	2,304	—	33,663
1891–1900	971	33,066	549	1,075	—	35,661
1901–1910	49,642	107,548	8,192	17,280	—	182,662
1911–1920	219,004	123,424	17,159	41,899	—	401,486
1921–1930	459,287	74,899	15,769	42,215	31	592,201
1931–1940	22,319	15,502	5,861	7,803	25	51,510
1941–1950	60,589	49,725	21,665	21,831	29,276	183,086
1951–1960	299,811	123,091	44,751	91,628	59,711	618,992
1961–1970	453,937	470,213	101,330	257,954	19,630	1,303,064
1971–1980	640,294	741,126	134,640	295,741	789	1,812,590
Total	2,232,885	1,830,962	351,538	788,445	109,462	5,313,292

[a] No record of immigration from Mexico from 1886 to 1893.
[b] Included with countries not specified to 1925.
Source: U.S. Department of Justice (1983: Table 2).

States. With the implementation of the *bracero* program during World War II, extended in 1951 by Public Law 71, the annual number of seasonal Mexican migrants rose dramatically: from 53,000 in 1943 to 447,000 in 1959 (Corwin, 1973).

In 1964, temporary work programs were severely curtailed when the Johnson administration terminated the Mexican contract-labor program. Small legal flows of temporary labor, primarily from the English-speaking Caribbean, continue to this date; most of these laborers work during harvest time in Florida's sugarcane fields. These temporary labor flows date back to 1943; in 1945 some 40,000 West Indian workers were employed in agricultural and industrial activities. In 1980–1981, 8460 laborers were authorized to come to the United States to work in the sugarcane harvest (McCoy and Woods, 1982).

The biggest unknown regarding Latin American and Caribbean immigrants concerns the number of undocumented migrants. Estimating the size of the undocumented migrant population has become almost a national pastime. Estimates vary widely, ranging from about 2 to 12 million persons.

The most commonly accepted figures are between 3.5 and 6 million, most of whom are assumed to be of Western Hemisphere origin; of these, about half are believed to be Mexican (Davis, Haut, and Willette, 1983). While there is no agreement on how large is the stock of illegal migrants, and even less about the size of the yearly flows in and out of the United States, it is undeniable that illegal immigration has increased substantially since the 1960s. Part of the increase can be directly attributed to the termination of the *bracero* program. Many Mexican workers had come to depend on their earnings while in the United States; with the legal route closed, these workers, and others, often continued coming north, but this time clandestinely and often with the active encouragement of their employers.

There are other indications of the large-scale entry of many illegals. In recent years the number of illegal immigrants apprehended has risen to over 1 million a year; in 1983, along the Mexican border alone, this figure was surpassed. Some, however, have claimed that much of the increase can be attributed to more effective enforcement. The number of tourist and other temporary visas granted by U.S. consulates in Latin American and Caribbean countries has also increased during this period. It is known that many of the recipients of these visas use them to enter the country and then remain here after the visas have expired. There is also conclusive and highly visible evidence that in many major cities of the United States, particularly in California, Illinois, Florida, along the Eastern Seaboard and in the Southwest, major ethnic colonies of illegal immigrants have taken root in the last two decades.

In summary, it is unquestionable that Latin American and Caribbean immigration to the United States has experienced a sizable increase since World War II. The magnitude of the migratory flow, mainly because of its undocumented component, is difficult to estimate. The increase in immigration from the region has been noticeable since the 1960s, and it may have intensified during the 1970s and early 1980s.

POPULATION GROWTH AND EMIGRATION TRENDS

The onset of increased emigration from Latin America and the Caribbean to the United States closely coincides with the years 1960–1965, during which the region as a whole reached a population growth rate of 2.8% per year. Between 1950 and 1965, the regional population grew from 164 to 248 million (Table 2). More important, perhaps, the emigration increase also coincided with the arrival at working ages (roughly 15–19 years of age) of the earliest and much larger post–World War II birth cohorts. The postwar acceleration in population growth rates was indiced primarily by an unprece-

TABLE 2
Estimated and Projected[a] Population of Latin America and the Caribbean, 1950–2025 (in thousands)

Year	*Caribbean*	*Middle America*	*Temperate South America*	*Tropical South America*	*Total*
1950	16,886	36,101	25,437	85,628	164,053
1955	18,496	42,035	28,026	99,464	188,022 (24)[b]
1960	20,431	49,299	30,729	115,272	215,731 (27)
1965	22,884	57,937	33,384	133,955	248,160 (33)
1970	25,210	68,093	35,941	154,251	283,496 (35)
1975	27,948	79,723	38,419	175,764	321,854 (38)
1980	30,648	92,723	41,067	199,452	363,704 (42)
1985	33,565	106,848	43,801	225,530	409,743 (46)
1990	36,619	122,382	46,505	253,792	459,298 (50)
1995	39,888	138,747	49,109	283,689	511,433 (52)
2000	43,286	155,709	51,605	315,146	565,747 (54)
2005	46,891	173,193	53,983	348,602	622,669 (57)
2010	50,624	191,020	56,221	383,629	681,494 (59)
2015	54,451	208,755	58,320	420,409	741,935 (60)
2020	58,301	226,156	60,236	458,859	803,552 (62)
2025	61,887	242,909	61,925	498,476	865,198 (62)

[a] Medium variant.
[b] Numbers in parentheses represent millions of inhabitants added to the region's population during the quinquennium.
Source: United Nations (1981: Table 1).

dented mortality decline, unaccompanied by equally significant fertility declines. The widespread use of newly developed insecticides, drugs, and other medical advances brought about a substantial reduction in mortality from infectious causes.

While the regional population growth rate crested in 1960–1965, it is often not realized that in absolute terms the population of Latin America and the Caribbean will continue to increase at an accelerating pace well into the next century. For example, whereas between 1960 and 1965, 33 million people were added to the regional population, it is projected that by 1995–2000 the increase will amount to 54 million. This phenomenon is a result of the population momentum associated with the broad-based population pyramids characteristic of most countries in the region. Despite declines in the number of births by the average woman, the absolute number of women in childbearing ages rises continuously. Even during the 2020–2025 quinquennium, when the regional population growth rate is projected to decline to 1.48 per year, the regional population will increase by some 62 million.

This brief review of population growth trends suggests that population increases are related to the onset of high emigration rates from the region to the United States. It also suggests that population pressures will persist and intensify well into the future. But population growth is only part of a complex nexus of determining forces that act together to produce emigration from the region to the United States and other countries, some within the region itself.

DETERMINANTS OF EMIGRATION: A COMPLEX NEXUS

Given the close correlation between the acceleration in population growth rates and the onset of large-scale emigration from Latin America and the Caribbean to the United States, it is easy to conclude that a simple cause-and-effect relationship exists between the two. This is often the conclusion of casual observers who fail to consider that the relationship is vastly more complex. To derive a more comprehensive understanding of the variables at work it is necessary to delve deeper into the multiplicity of factors that in combination with rapid population growth promote emigration. The thesis of this chapter is that while rapid population growth may be a necessary condition for emigration to occur, it is not a sufficient condition. Just as crucial is the ability or inability of economic growth to keep pace with population increases. Venezuela is a case in point. Natural increase rates there have been high for several decades, but few Venezuelans have emigrated. Instead, the country became a magnet for large contingents of immigrants from other countries in the region. Venezuela's oil wealth provided the impetus for the expansion of the national economy and the absorption of a growing labor force, both domestic and foreign-born (Sassen-Koob, 1979).

What the Venezuelan example indicates is that emigration may be a consequence of low rates of economic growth. But even with rapid economic growth, it can be posited that other noneconomic and economic mechanisms shape the course and extent that emigration takes. In some instances, rapid economic growth is unable to reduce emigration and in fact may promote it. The Dominican Republic is a good illustration of the latter situation: Despite impressively high economic growth rates during the 1960s and most of the 1970s, the country recorded some of the highest emigration rates in the region during that period (Morrison and Sinkin, 1982)

Subjective conditions associated with the modern world and the development of country-specific cultural expectations must also be included in any explanation of emigration. These are related, in turn, to dynamic internal processes of social, economic, and political changes affecting all countries in Latin America and the Caribbean. These changes are often manifested as protracted political and revolutionary struggles. Emigration is in part a consequence of these changes, just as revolutions are; both can be regarded as adaptive responses of national polities and individuals. Population growth is the most notorious indication of change; the sheer increase in numbers contributes to intensify the pace of change. Below, we examine some of the principal developments that stand behind emigration from the region and through which population growth acquires the determining role it has.

EMPLOYMENT GENERATION AND LABOR-FORCE GROWTH

The most immediate link between population growth and emigration is the labor market. Labor markets in Latin America and the Caribbean are saturated; it is not uncommon in many of these countries for 30–40% of the economically active population to be either unemployed or underemployed. Rising numbers of new labor-force entrants make matters increasingly worse. The situation becomes chaotic during recessionary periods, such as in Mexico during the early 1980s, but is difficult even during prosperous times. Between 1978 and 1981, for instance, when Mexico's economic growth rates exceeded 8% per year, new jobs were created at an annual rate of 5.4%, a rate higher than the rate at which the labor force was growing. By 1982, with Mexico in the grip of one of its worst economic crises, economic growth rates became negative, and the rate at which jobs were created declined to .8% per year (Banco de Mexico, 1983). In country after country, prosperity has not necessarily contributed to the easing of the employment crisis. Throughout the region, the development strategies followed have emphasized the use of capital-intensive technologies in urban-based industrial activities. In rural areas, the substitution of traditional subsistence crops by export crops heavily reliant on modern agricultural practices (e.g., mechanization) has tended to displace labor (Macisco, 1975). These development strategies hinder the employment-generating capacity of local economies, although they may be capable of sustaining high economic growth rates.

SOCIAL CHANGE

The social changes experienced in Latin America and the Caribbean in the postwar period were enormous. In this regard, changes within the region reflect the winds of change sweeping humanity at large. Population growth is itself the product of a worldwide revolution in health and mortality-control technology. Associated with population growth is the rapid pace of urbanization that has transformed the region; the incipient emergence, and in some cases, consolidation, of a broad industrial base; sizable gains in educational attainment; major developments in means of mass communication; and dramatic expansions in transportation networks. These changes played a key role in opening the region to a broader world and have considerably reduced some of the cost associated with emigration. As a result, they have contributed to the intensification of emigration from Latin America and the Caribbean, and to international migrations within the region.

Urbanization

In 1950, about 40% of the regional population of approximately 165 million resided in urban areas (Davis, 1969). By 1985, with a population of almost 400 million, 66% was in urban places. In absolute terms, the urban population of the region increased from 65 million in 1950 to 264 million in 1985. Most of the total population growth in the intervening 35 years, 83%, accrued to cities and towns (Centro Latinoamericano de Demografia, 1981). The significance of these urbanization trends for emigration should not be taken lightly. Most Latin American emigrants, except perhaps those from Mexico, come from an urban background. The explanation for this phenomenon is relatively straightforward. Social scientists have established that migration entails a selectivity process, that is, migrants are not randomly drawn from the population at the place of origin. The decision to migrate entails the ability to recognize opportunities in places of destination, as well as the ability to overcome obstacles blocking the migratory path. These obstacles are more evident when migrating across national borders. Urban residents tend to be better informed and educated, have higher aspirations and more resources with which to finance transportation costs. In general, they are more likely to want to emigrate, and once they decide to do so, are more likely to carry out their decision successfully.

Industrialization

In the modern world, industrialization is almost synonymous with urbanization. In most parts of the developing world, and Latin America and the Caribbean are no exception, industrial activities are highly concentrated in large cities. Past development efforts have had an inherent urban bias at the expense of rural areas. The urban development bias has placed a marked emphasis on the production of consumer goods, and has exposed a growing proportion of the population to the advantages associated with the modern industrial world. The benefits of rapid industrial growth—and consumerism—however, have been insufficient to satisfy latent expectation or have not been distributed equitably. The emergence and growth of a middle class with high propensities to consume, and the "demonstration" effects of this consumerism, frustrate many individuals seeking to partake of the good life. Many of those who cannot satisfy their material aspirations domestically choose to emigrate. Limited opportunities within their own countries, and the prosperity and wealth of the United States, become irresistible. Many prospective migrants are aware of the comparatively much higher wages they can command in the American economy, even if engaged in menial work.

Education Improvements

Without exception, over the last several decades, all Latin American and Caribbean countries have made impressive strides forward in educational attainment. In many countries, attendance rates for the population of primary school age now exceed 80%, even 90%. Secondary school and higher education attendance rates, while not as high, have experienced higher relative increases. In Central American and Caribbean countries, for example, secondary school attendance rates are about 50%; in some cases, more than 60% and 70%. It is not uncommon for sizable percentages of the population 18–23 years of age to be enrolled in institutions of higher education. In Costa Rica, Cuba, El Salvador, Nicaragua, Panama, and the Dominican Republic, 20% or more of the population in this age group was attending school in 1980. In 1960, in contrast, only in Panama was over 10% of this age group pursuing studies (Economic Commission for Latin America, 1981). These changes in the education profile of the region have brought about a qualitative transformation of the employment picture. The issue today is not limited to creating new employment opportunities. It includes the need for creating jobs capable of satisfying the higher aspirations of a much better educated population that will not be content with poorly remunerated and unskilled employment. Since migrants tend to be disporportionately drawn from among the better educated, as the pool of better-educated individuals increases, so does the pool of prospective migrants.

Communication Improvements

The better-educated and more aspiring urban residents are constantly bombarded with visions of the good life that industrial and wealthy economies provide. This vision is in stark contrast with what many of these people can hope for in their homelands. Day in and day out they read magazines, tailored along the lines of U.S. publications, extolling the virtues of modern lifestyles. These magazines, plus newspapers, electronic media, and motion pictures, provide a Hollywood-like image of what life abroad could be. The contrast between this vision and the realities they face magnify the attractiveness of emigration, even if in actuality there is a great gulf between the image and the reality.

Transportation Improvements

Modern means of transportation, particularly air travel, have cut the distance between Latin America and the Caribbean to the United States to a matter of hours. Flying is no longer the exclusive privilege of the wealthy. The cost of a round-trip airfare from the region to the United States is well within the reach of many prospective migrants, especially those with friends and relatives working in the United States. In addition, air travel to the United States, allegedly for tourist purposes, is constantly promoted by the airlines and the tourist industry. Many individuals who eventually emigrate receive their first direct exposure to U.S. society through short-term travel. For many illegal migrants, entry to the United States is limited only by the cost of a place ticket and by their ability to convince U.S. consular officials of their bona fide intentions as they petition for a tourist visa.

ETHNIC COLONIES

There are other powerful factors that in years to come are apt to sustain high emigration rates from Latin America and the Caribbean to the United States. A key factor is the presence of large ethnic colonies of earlier migrants from the region. Some of these ethnic colonies and enclaves are of relatively recent origin (e.g., Cubans and immigrants from the Dominican Republic since the 1960s); others have a much earlier history (e.g., Mexicans and West Indians). The presence of ethnic colonies eases the process of integration into U.S. society and reduces some of the psychic, social, and other costs that immigrants initially have to pay. Friends and relatives residing in the United States can assist with transportation costs, provide financial and social support on arrival and during the initial period of adjustment, and be highly instrumental in facilitating the labor-market insertion of new arrivals. High-density ethnic enclaves further ease the integration process, since they acquire, to some extent at least, sociocultural characteristics similar to those of the countries the immigrants left behind.

U.S. IMMIGRATION REGULATIONS AND FAMILY REUNIFICATIONS

American immigration regulations play a pivotal role in ensuring that emigration from the region to the United States will continue, and at an accelerated pace. Whether under the current immigration legislation or that proposed by the pending bill to revise and reform the Immigration and Nationality Act (Simpson–Mazzoli or some such variant), a priority on the migrant selection process is family reunification. Parents, spouses, and children of U.S. citizens are admitted to the country exempt from the numerical limitations that apply to immigrants. Other close relatives of citizens and permanent residents (green card holders) are accorded preferential treatment under the numerical limitation system set by Congress to control the level of legal immigration. As more immigrants from the region are admitted and settle permanently in the country, and as more become naturalized citizens, the prospects for the further entry of Latin American and Caribbean immigrants rises. Prior immigration has, in this sense, the capacity to generate a momentum for additional immigration. This process is already in evidence. Between 1951 and 1960, the United States admitted 2.5 million immigrants. About 25% of these immigrants came from Latin America and the Caribbean. By 1971–1980, when the total number of immigrants admitted reached 4.5 million, approximately 40% came from the region (U.S. Department of Justice, 1983). If the Simpson–Mazzoli proposal calling for the regularization of the status of undocumented immigrants already in the country is approved, the potential number of new legal residents will escalate by at least a few hundred thousand to perhaps several million. As many as 90% of the potential beneficiaries of this provision are believed to be of Latin American and Caribbean origin.

None of these factors alone, or all in combination, explains the increase in emigration to the United States, however. The missing link is the overwhelming attraction that the United States has for immigrants, a familiar motivation for the masses of immigrants from all over the world that the country has received throughout its history. This attractiveness, of course, goes well beyond the obvious benefits that the American economy confers on the immigrants. It includes the many benefits that an open, liberal democracy offers to those seeking a more peaceful life, especially those fleeing persecution or civil strife at home. The Cuban refugees, many arrivals from South America and the Caribbean, and the recent influxes from Central America are the best testimony of this appeal. Regardless of how politicians, revolutionaries, or scholars, here and abroad, evaluate the impact of U.S. actions in the region, the individual seeking a new life is primarily concerned with his safety and well-being, and that of the people close to him.

Beyond these motivations and "push" forces are several mechanisms that directly explain the ability of American society to absorb millions of immigrants. The explanation can be found in the functioning of the American labor market and its ability to generate jobs, specifically a demand for certain kinds of workers that the domestic workforce, under current conditions, does not provide. To this we now turn our attention.

THE AMERICAN LABOR MARKET

In modern industrial, capitalist economies international labor migrations appear to be more responsive to demand than to supply factors. This is particularly true with undocumented migrants. It has been suggested that if immigration were to result exclusively from an oversupply of workers in developing countries, immigration levels would be far higher than they actually are. The reason behind this assertion is that the number of immigrants coming to the United States is regulated by the availability of jobs (Piore, 1979). In the case of legal immigrants, the United States, as well as every other country, exercises the right to limit and select the immigrants it is willing to admit and, indeed, would like to control the entry of undocumented immigrants. Since unemployment rates among immigrants tend to be lower than the average—immigrants can hardly afford to be unemployed—it follows that immigration flows are highly responsive to job availability. During the Great Depression, for example, legal immigration levels declined to a fraction of what they had been during prosperous years (Table 1).

What accounts for the seemingly never-ending demand for immigrant labor? Economic growth and certain demographic factors play an important role. Several characteristics of the American economy and society—if not of most capitalist, industrialized nations—also explain the demand for immigrant labor. All of these determinants are intertwined.

The first characteristic may be described, if in a simplified fashion, as the need, in certain segments of the American economy, for cheap and unskilled labor, that is, labor willing to take the poorly paid, low-status, dead-end service and agricultural jobs for which there is a perennial shortage of workers at prevailing wages and working conditions. Such is the low social status accorded to these occupations that it is unlikely that these jobs would attract native workers even with much higher pay and better working conditions. Many industrial jobs share many of these characteristics.

Largely on account of competition from recently industrialized, low-labor-cost countries, an increasing number of American industries remain economically viable only because they can rely on inexpensive immigrant labor. Although this has been true for some time now in many traditional, low-technology industries (e.g., apparel and shoe manufacturing), other American industries are being forced to reduce production costs by using nonunionized, cheaper labor. A clear indication of this development is the migration of industrial activities from the high-labor-cost regions in the North of the United States to the South. It is also exemplified by the opening of new manufacturing plants by American companies abroad, with the corresponding closing of domestic facilities. An alternative is the use of immigrant labor. This process is now evident even in basic, technologically advanced, heavily capitalized American industries, such as the manufacturing of automobile components. There has been a proliferation of small, independent firms that manufacture these components and supply them to major corporations on a contract basis. These new production facilities are increasingly operated by immigrant workers (Morales, 1983).

A second characteristic is rooted in the social history of the United States, and in the process of social mobility associated with the gradual integration and "assimilation" into the mainstream of American society of successive ethnic immigrant groups. Immigrants have always joined the bottom of the American socioeconomic hierarchy and have been more than willing to engage in occupations few native workers want. But the children and later descendants of the immigrants are not content with remaining at the bottom of the socioeconomic pyramid. As they become assimilated (i.e., better educated, fluent in English) the native-born descendants of immigrants gain access to better-paid, more skilled, and prestigious occupations; they join the professions and the business world. More recent immigrants occupy the slots so vacated; in this sense, immigration waves are instrumental in promoting social mobility.

The post–World War II years witnessed an intensification of this process. Partly fueled by an unprecedented period of economic prosperity, and by dramatic changes in human rights perceptions and legislation, the postwar era was marked by upward mobility for blacks and other minorities. To date this process has benefited a relatively small number of minorities, but it has definitely changed the collective and individual aspirations of these groups. They are no longer willing to pass their lives in the menial and poorly rewarding jobs held by their ancestors for generations. Social welfare and affirmative action programs further reinforce these tendencies, since the economic survival of the most disadvantaged members of these minorities is no longer necessarily limited to poorly paid employment. Recent immigrants from Latin America and the Caribbean take those jobs. They are instrumental and sustaining the functioning of the American economy and in facilitating the social mobility of native minorities, just as earlier immigrants did for the ethnic groups that preceded them.

The above discussion does not suggest that all new immigrants enter the job market at low levels of pay and skills. Regulations for the selection of migrants ensure that a given number of relatively skilled (as well as some highly skilled) newcomers gain access to the United States. Indeed, it is common for these migrants to hold high-status positions in the American economy. However, a familiar dichotomy is evident in this selectivity. Legal immigrants tend to have higher average levels of education and skill than the population of origin, but, in relation to the population of the United States, they compare much less favorably. Therefore, a substantial number of immigrants only have skill levels that qualify them to be employed as unskilled workers. At times, because they lack credentials, English fluency, or legal immigration documents, they hold jobs for which they are overqualified. For these migrants, however, the migration decision is a rational one, since in the United States they can earn substantially higher wages and face much better long-term prospects.

POPULATION GROWTH AND EMIGRATION: A COMPREHENSIVE VIEW

The preceding discussion underlined that it is an oversimplification to assume a direct cause-and-effect relationship between population growth and emigration. The relationship is vastly more complex, since it is mediated by a wide array of intervening factors. Some of these factors are of relevance within the specific socioeconomic context of emigration countries; others have explanatory power within the United States itself.

Our first conclusion is that emigration from Latin America and the Caribbean to the United States results primarily from a profound process of socioeconomic change that the region is undergoing. Population growth is a product of this process as much as it is an instrument for further change. It acquires its latter role by exacerbating existing structural problems within the region, some dating back centuries. Population growth is also the source of new problems. What is essential to realize is that large-scale emigration is the result of change, not of stagnation.

A second conclusion is that emigration on its present scale would not occur unless economic conditions in the United States, particularly in the American labor market, did not favor the absorption of immigrants. Structural transformations in the American economy play a role, as does the traditional demand for cheap and unskilled labor. A perennial shortage of these workers appears to be a pervasive characteristic of modern, wealthy, and industrialized capitalist societies. In the United States, it can be said that immigration has a necessary social role. In an immigrant nation, successive waves of new immigrants serve as a motor for economic growth and help facilitate the social mobility and successful integration of earlier immigrant groups (and minorities today).

Objective conditions and subjective perceptions can be regarded as distinct but interrelated determinants of emigration from the region. It is not far-fetched to state that, in the present Latin America and Caribbean context, subjective aspirations have outrun objective possibilities. Social and economic changes have brought to the people of the region a grasp of what a better life could be like. Economic realities have thwarted the fulfillment of those aspirations. At this point, population growth becomes a determinant of emigration. To the extent that it negates many of the fruits of economic growth, it becomes an element in the equation. Subjectively, an emigration mentality now pervades many countries in the region. A major avenue to advance one's prospects is emigration. Mexico, Guatemala, and El Salvador are typical of this situation. This mentality has repeatedly been described in many of the smaller Caribbean Island nations (Patterson, 1978).

For several reasons, economic growth per se is not enough to satisfy the aspirations held by many people in the region. It is obvious that given the region's accumulated needs, only decades of sustained economic growth will be able to lower the gap between wants and realities. The lofty goal of sustained economic growth obviously is a difficult one to achieve. The current economic crisis and the huge foreign debts these countries are facing are indicative of the perils of sustaining uninterrupted economic growth. The economic crisis has negated, in many countries severely negated, much of the progress made in nearly two decades of rapid growth.

No less crucial in the unfulfillment of aspirations are the socioeconomic structures typical of most countries in the region. The benefits of economic growth have been spread unevenly. Living standards have risen appreciably for a small but growing middle class and the wealthy; large segments of the population have profited only marginally and others not at all. These inequities and the hope for a more just social order partly explain the political instability and violent conflicts in the region. The present circumstances of Central America represent the culmination of decades of uneven economic growth and related social injustices. Nationals from El Salvador and Guatemala enter the United States, Mexico, and other countries in a desperate search for peace and a better life. As has been pointed out, it is often impossible in these migrations to discern economic motivations from an escape from persecution. Long before the situation became chaotic in El Salvador, migrants from that country were coming to the United States legally and illegally, the latter after an overland journey taking them across Guatemala and Mexico. There is a wealth of evidence indicating that a highly inequitable social system combined with high population growth rates is associated with these population flows (Durham, 1979).

Political instability and social, economic, and demographic changes have had similar effects in other countries. Over 700,000 Cubans have sought refuge in the United States. Many of the most recent newcomers came here as much for political as for economic reasons. The Cuban case is particularly instructive in several regards. The revolutionary path in which the country embarked had as one of its specific objectives the elimination of social inequities. While largely succeeding in wiping away some of the most glaring injustices, the country has produced, on a per capita basis, some of the highest emigration rates in the region. A closed political system and a stagnant economy have a lot to do with this emigration. There is evidence suggesting, further, that unemployment problems associated with a rapid expansion of the labor force in the late 1970s made the Cuban authorities opt for the emigration safety valve. The Mariel sea lift can partly be attributed to demographic reasons (Diaz-Briquets, 1983).

Two lessons can be drawn from the Cuban experience. Those who clamor for drastic change in the social, economic, and political structures of the region should consider that such changes alone may create more problems than they solve. While change is needed, it must be grounded in objectives of social justice; the creation of flexible, participatory, and democratic institutions; and an environment conducive to economic growth. Costa Rica and Panama, for example, offer alternative models in which goals of social equity, economic growth, and political participation have been largely met. Emigration rates from these two countries, not surprisingly, are among the lowest in Latin America and the Caribbean. The second lesson taught by the Cuban experience, perhaps more clearly than for any other country, it that rapid population growth in the presence of stagnant economic conditions and inflexible political systems is a major force behind emigration.

PROSPECTS FOR LATIN AMERICAN AND CARIBBEAN EMIGRATION

In view of past and future trends in population and labor-force growth, the uncertain future for smooth and peaceful social change, and the clouded economic picture, there is every reason to believe that emigration pressures in the region will persist and even intensify. Further, the American economy will likely continue to generate a demand for immigrant labor, even more so if the domestic economic situation continues to improve. The most likely situation that can be visualized at present is that legal immigration will remain at levels comparable to those observed during the 1970s, although they may increase somewhat. The immigration reform legislation under consideration by Congress calls for an increase in the annual immigration ceiling under the numerical limitation system. The presence of a growing number of Latin American and Caribbean immigrants guarantees that additional immigrants from the region will be admitted in years to come exempt from these ceilings, as earlier immigrants are naturalized. In contrast, the more vigorous enforcement of existing and proposed legislation to limit illegal immigration can have an impact on the number of undocumented immigrants. Temporary guest-worker programs, as called for in one of the latest versions of the immigration reform legislation, could prove to be instrumental in regularizing the temporary entry of many workers who now come to work in the United States clandestinely. However, there is a major debate over this provision of the bill.

POTENTIAL U.S. POLICY INITIATIVES TO REDUCE EMIGRATION PRESSURES

Aside from the domestic policies the United States can institute or strengthen to cope with rising numbers of potential immigrants, the nation is in a position of implementing various initiatives to reduce emigration propensities in Latin America and the Caribbean. Promoting economic growth in the region is one of them. This objective can be fostered by providing higher levels of foreign assistance, creating incentives to increase private investments, and redoubling efforts to augment trade. Many proposals along these lines are being discussed; one of them, the Caribbean Basin Initiative, is already under way. In pursuing these objectives the United States will be well served by seeking the close cooperation of multilateral development lending agencies, such as the World Bank and the Interamerican Development Bank. A reorientation of development activities by U.S. agencies to take into account the migration factor in their programs would also be helpful.

The United States should use its wherewithal and influence with Latin American and Caribbean governments to promote the restructuring and evolutionary transformation of existing inequitable social and economic systems. It should also allocate greater resources for strengthening existing family planning programs. It must be realized, however, that the payoff of these programs will not be evident for many years. In the interval, other actions, mainly of an economic nature, are necessary.

In conclusion, seeing population growth as the major factor in immigration is to miss the important intervening roles that social structure plays in population flows. Policymakers will be well advised not to assess issues in simplistic terms.

REFERENCES

Banco de Mexico
1983 *Informe Anual 1982*. Mexico City.
Centro Latinoamericano de Demografia (CELADE)
1981 *Boletin Demografico*, No. 28 (July).

Corwin, Arthur F.
1973 "Causes of Mexican emigration to the United States." *Perspectives in American History* 7:557–635.

Davis, Cary, Carl Haub and JoAnne Willette
1983 "U.S. Hispanics: Changing the Face of America." *Population Bulletin* 38(3) (June).

Davis, Kingsley
1969 *World Urbanization 1950–1970*, Vol. 1, *Basic Data for Cities, Countries and Regions*. Population Monograph Series, No. 4. Berkeley: University of California Press.

Diaz-Briquets, Sergio
1983 "Demographic and related determinants of recent Cuban emigration." *International Migration Review* 17 (Spring):95–119.

Durham, William H.
1979 *Scarcity and Survival in Central America: Ecological Origins of the Soccer War*. Stanford: Stanford University Press.

Economic Commission for Latin America (ECLA)
1981 *Statistical Yearbook for Latin America: 1980*. Santiago.

McCoy, Terry L. and Charles H. Wood
1982 "Caribbean workers in the Florida sugar cane industry." Occasional paper No. 2, Center for Latin American Studies, University of Florida, Gainesville.

Macisco, John J.
1975 "Algunas consideraciones sobre un marco analitico para las migraciones rurales–urbanas." Pp. 87–105 in *Migraciones Internas*. Santiago: CELADE.

Morales, Rebecca
1983 "Transitional labor: Undocumented workers in the Los Angeles automobile industry." *International Migration Review* 17(4):570–596.

Morrison, Thomas K. and Richard Sinkin
1982 "International migration in the Dominican Republic: Implications for development planning." *International Migration Review* 16(4): 819–836.

Patterson, Orlando
1978 "Migration in Caribbean societies: Socioeconomic and symbolic resource." Pp. 106–145 in William H. McNeill and Ruth S. Adams (eds.), *Human Migration: Patterns and Policies*. Bloomington: University of Indiana Press.

Piore, Michael J.
1979 *Birds of Passage: Migrant Labor and Industrial Societies*. Cambridge: Cambridge University Press.

Sassen-Koob, Saskia
1979 "Economic growth and immigration in Venezuela." *International Migration Review* 13(3):455–474.

United Nations
1981 *World Population Prospects as Assessed in 1980*. Population Studies No. 75. New York.

U.S. Department of Justice, Immigration and Naturalization Service
1983 *1980 Statistical Yearbook of the Immigration and Naturalization Service*. Washington, D.C.

6

Food Supply and Latin American Population Growth: Is This the Right Question?

PHILIP MUSGROVE

POPULATION, FOOD SUPPLY, AND SECURITY

The title of Population Growth in Latin America and U.S. National Security Conference expresses the presumption that demographic growth in the rest of the Western Hemisphere may threaten the security of the United States, now or in the future. Accepting that hypothesis for the moment, two major questions are left open. One is whether such dangers arise from too large a population or from too rapid a rate of growth; that is, whether the potential problems refer to some sort of carrying capacity or to the difficulty of "keeping up with" population growth in other respects, such as income and investment. The second question is how population growth actually does or would translate into a security problem; that is, What other variables are affected by demographic expansion in such a way as to constitute a threat?

As to the first question, it probably makes sense to worry about population levels only in the very long run. Over a few decades or less, the rate of growth has much more to do with the prospects for economic progress, quality of life, political stability, or any other factor than does the sheer number of human beings. This is so both because the notion of carrying capacity is so sensitive to technical progress as to be very elastic and because a high rate of population growth requires a high rate of saving and investment simply to keep income per person constant, whatever the initial size of population. As to the second question, one can imagine many different mechanisms by which population growth could give rise to a security problem; each mechanism corresponds to some failure of another variable or another process to keep up with or accommodate demographic increase. One of the simplest such failures, conceptually, is that of food supply to grow along with population, leading to a gradual erosion of living standards or to deprivation and even famine for some parts of the population. Since food is a biological necessity requiring real resources to produce, a shortage cannot easily be met by a change of tastes or lifestyle; it is intrinsically harder to adjust to a decline in food supplies than to some other possible consequences of population growth, such as reduction of wilderness, increased density, and greater pollution. Nevertheless, the fact that food is necessary and that conceptually food supply seems to provide a clear connection between population growth and problems of political instability or violence posing threats to national security does not mean that this is a helpful way to look at the food and population issue.

The next two sections of this chapter take up the aggregate relation between population and food supply, using a variety of data and projections for 22 countries, all south of the United States, with a population of 1 million or more. Two countries not normally considered part of Latin America (Jamaica and Trinidad–Tobago) are included in this group. The excluded countries are all quite small; all but four are islands rather than continental countries; and none are predominantly Spanish or Portuguese speaking, although Belize uses Spanish nearly as much as English. The section immediately following treats population and several variables related to food supply in the recent past, which for this purpose means since 1960. The subsequent section considers the prospects up to the end of the century. Projections beyond that date are considered too speculative to justify extending the exercise.

The third section of the chapter then considers whether this sort of aggregate treatment actually captures the essence of food and population problems, concluding that it does not. Simple quantitative comparisons need to be replaced by study of the distribution of command over food within the population, and of the factors that cause that control to be inadequate, to vary among groups in the population, or to change through time. The argument here is partly conceptual and partly an empirical illustration drawn from a more detailed examination of two countries, Brazil and Peru. The chapter's final section speculates on the connections, if any, between the food-supply problem in this sense and security. Questions of what forces create or reveal a food scarcity, whom it affects, and how rapidly it occurs all seem to be relevant here. Security issues may also be related to variables that help determine the supply and distribution of food, even when on any biological basis the latter is adequate. These closing speculations are meant only as a bridge to those contributions that take up national security matters directly.

POPULATION AND FOOD SUPPLY IN RECENT DECADES

The obvious first question to ask, before considering future prospects, is whether food supplies have kept up with population in the recent past. Because supplies can be formed partly by imports, it seems important to look not only at final availability but also at domestic production. And because food crops may not be the most profitable use for a parcel of land, it seems important to consider total agricultural output; production of nonfood crops may, if exported, contribute more to total food supply than the use of the same land to grow food directly. Table 1 assembles four indicators that together show how well population growth has been matched by agricultural performance and food supply. All are divided by population, without adjustment for age and sex composition, and all compare one or more years in 1980–1982 with one or more years in 1960–1962. One indicator is not available at all for Cuba, and in three cases estimates for 1965 are used in place of those for 1960–1962. The indicators are as follows:

Value Added in Agriculture includes nonfood products, and because it measures value rather than volume, it responds to price changes. (General price-level change is removed by expressing values in 1980 dollars.) This variable measures use of agricultural land and command over food rather than food output or supply.

Index of Food Production attempts to remove both price changes (by using a constant base price for each commodity, allowing only volume to vary) and nonfood crops. It measures quantity, but does not translate directly into food value since the nutritional content per kilogram varies widely among products.

Calories per Day is an estimate of the most important nutrient (energy) available from both domestic production and net imports of all foods. Allowances are made for food fed to animals or used as seed, and for changes in stocks.

Cereal Imports, measured in kilograms, is a measure of the extent to which supply was achieved through imports rather than by domestic production. Only cereal grains are considered, since they furnish the bulk of food imports in volume, value, and calories for most countries. (In some cases, imports of animals and meat may be comparably important.)

Of the four indicators, cereal imports are the most reliably measured, and calories per person per day are probably the least reliable. All the variables except imports include estimates of subsistence production, and the calorie

TABLE 1

Change in Agricultural and Food Output, Caloric Availability, and Cereal Imports, per Person, 1960–1982, Twenty-Two Countries

Country (in ascending order of est. 1982 income per person)	*Value Added in Agriculture, 1982/1960*	*Index of Food Production, 1980–1982/1961*	*Calories per Day, 1981/1960–1962*	*Cereal Imports (all grains), 1982/1960*
Haiti	84	77	99	543
Bolivia	116	115	109	147
Honduras	117	91	101	209
El Salvador	86	101	114	146
Nicaragua	130	93	95	200
Guatemala	128	130	100	1400
Costa Rica	124	118	111	192
Peru	101	88	97	238
Dominican Republic	98	97	101	480
Jamaica	92	85	119	194
Ecuador	117	98	106	475
Colombia	145	132	106	471
Paraguay	178	106	119	30
Cuba	[a]	97	104	458
Panama	124	126	94	196
Chile	104	94	113	1260
Brazil	138	140	93	124
Mexico	114	112	112	1500
Argentina	119	128	121	[b]
Uruguay	122	104	91	41
Venezuela	122	116	115	372
Trinidad and Tobago	81	82	114	198
Total, 22 countries	122	121	104	250

[a] Not available.

[b] No imports in either year.

Source: Table 2. In each column, the first year or years shown are the most recent for which data are available; the index for that period is calculated setting the index for the second year or years (ca. 1960) equal to 100.

availability estimate also requires assumptions about the nonfood end uses of output.

For the 22 countries taken together, Table 1 shows substantial progress in production over the two decades: Both the value of agricultural output and the quantum of food rose 20% faster than population. Calorie intake per person, however, seems not to have changed, suggesting that the gain in output per person went into exports, animal feeds, or foods of lower calorie value per kilogram. In total, these three factors actually had to increase somewhat faster than production, since cereal imports expanded rapidly during the period. At least in calorie terms, increased exports plus increased livestock feeding had to offset the growth in output plus imports for domestic human consumption to remain constant on average. This result is consistent with any of the following circumstances, singly or in combination: *(a)* adequate nutrition in 1960, so that demand for calories did not subsequently increase as agricultural (and other) incomes rose; *(b)* a shift in tastes or in the domestic distribution of income toward more consumption of meat (and perhaps low-calorie vegetable foods), requiring more agricultural output to yield the same final calorie availability; or *(c)* a domestic food demand that could not compete with foreign demand for the increased output despite domestic food deficits. Either *(a)* or *(b)* supposes that extra income was spent on commodities that are luxuries compared to basic foodstuffs, with no implication for changes in relative prices. Possibility *(c)* in contrast, suggests that food prices should have risen, largely offsetting the income effect of greater output per person. Either *(a)* or *(c)* would lead to increased exports, helping to finance the increased grain imports, but the implications for domestic sufficiency are different.

Any division of the countries into groups is somewhat arbitrary, but a simple classification may nonetheless be useful.

Four countries—Guatemala, Colombia, Panama, and Brazil—show roughly the same pattern as the total: output growth, including food, with no gain or even a decrease in calorie availability despite higher imports. These are countries in which agricultural success does not seem to have translated into greater self-sufficiency or greater food availability.

Another four countries—Honduras, Nicaragua, Ecuador, and Uruguay—also show a decline or no gain in food availability despite an increase in agricultural value added. Food output did not rise, however, so the extra value added came from higher prices or from nonfood crops. All except Uruguay also increased cereal imports.

In five countries—Bolivia, Costa Rica, Mexico, Argentina, and Venezuela—growth in both output value and food quantum did translate into more calories available, typically about 10% more. In every case except Argentina, imports also increased substantially.

Paraguay is a peculiar case: Output and food availability both rose, but food output did not change much (and imports declined from a low initial level).

Finally, there are eight countries—Haiti, El Salvador, Peru, Dominican Republic, Jamaica, Cuba, Chile, and Trinidad–Tobago—in which agricultural and food output at best kept up with population (declining sharply in Haiti, Jamaica, and Trinidad–Tobago), and calorie availability seems to have been maintained or even increased only because of increased imports. If there is a race between population and food production, these countries are the losers, but among them there are more cases of *increased* food availability than among the first two groups, where agricultural output successfully kept pace with population growth.

Given the imprecision of the data used here, both conceptually and statistically, and the arbitrariness of country groupings and even of country boundaries for large and heterogenous countries, it is hazardous to draw any conclusions about these two decades' experience. Still, here are four rough conclusions to consider.

First, agricultural output and food supply overall have not merely kept up with population growth but significantly outraced it. As the Inter-American Development Bank (1983) has concluded in a long survey of the Latin American primary sectors, agriculture has been a striking success on average. The agricultural sector has even weathered the current economic recession better, in many countries, than manufacturing.

Second, at least in comparisons among countries, there is essentially no relation between success in raising output and increased domestic food availability. The simple correlation between value added and calorie supply is −.09, and that between the food output index and calories is −.10 (with or without including Cuba). There are at least four reasons why the association is so weak. One is the initial level of calorie availability: The higher this is, the less reason there is to expect an increase, no matter what happens to output. Estimates of caloric adequacy in 1981 (supply as a percentage of requirements estimated from the climate and the age−sex distribution of the population) cluster just below 100% in five countries, below 95% in another three, and range up to 120−140% in five more countries. Another reason is the internal distribution of income and any changes in that distribution; the extra income represented by increased output may accrue to people of higher-than-average income and food consumption, or to the poor. A third reason is the different balance-of-payments situations of the countries; some are under greater pressure than others to export any increase in the agricultural surplus, and such pressure should be reflected in domestic relative prices and consumption. Finally, related to this export need is the availability of free or subsidized imports of food. Peru, Ecuador, Colombia, Paraguay, Panama, Chile, Brazil, Mexico, Uruguay, and Venezuela received 5% or less of their cereal imports in the form of food aid in 1982 (World Bank, 1984:Table 6) (aid in 1981−1982 relative to imports in 1982). At the other extreme, aid in some form supplied 38% of imports in Honduras, 41% to Costa Rica, 46% to Haiti, 74% to El Salvador, and essentially all of imports to Nicaragua.

The third conclusion is a matter not so much of what the numbers in Table 1 say as what they hide. Since they are all averages (as are the quantitative indicators in Table 2 from which they are derived), they say nothing about the distribution of income, food supply, or calorie intake, and therefore say little or nothing about welfare (Musgrove, 1984). Still less can they explain current or potential political unrest. At most, indicators such as these can detect grossly inadequate levels of some variable (average calorie availability so low as to suggest widespread hunger, for example) or sharp deterioration in one or more measures. Average calorie insufficiency may be a problem in such countries as Bolivia, El Salvador, and Guatemala, but in none of the "underfed" countries is there evidence of the average situation worsening up to 1981. (The current levels may be worse, of course, as the recession has deepened.) In general, the declines shown in Table 1 either refer to agricultural output—which probably *is* grounds for worry in the group of eight "unsuccessful" countries—or else occur in countries such as Nicaragua, Panama, Brazil, and Uruguay where *average* food availability still appeared to be adequate, calorically, in 1981. To learn anything more, it will be necessary to look at distribution within countries.

Finally, success in keeping food output or supply growing as fast as population does not seem to depend very much on the absolute rate of population growth over the two decades, and where there is an association, it is, surprisingly, positive. The index of food production per person shows a linear correlation of .28 (rank correlation of .26) with population growth, indicating that, on average, where population expanded most rapidly, food grew faster still. As indicated, however, greater production does not necessarily imply more calories available per person; in fact, caloric availability gives correlations of −.02 (linear) and .01 (rank) with population growth. A comparison among these countries certainly does not show that rapid population growth made it harder to expand food output per head, but neither does it suggest that demographic growth was any help in raising average intake of food. Again, the effect of population growth on welfare can only be judged by considering distribution among the population of a country. What seems clear at the aggregate level is simply that countries' experiences were very diverse.

POPULATION AND FOOD SUPPLY IN THE NEAR FUTURE

Just as few things are easier than predicting the number of 15-year-olds in a population 10 years from now, few are more difficult than predicting their number 20 years from now. And predicting population growth is an exact science compared to predicting the future production of any particular commodity or group of commodities. If one could assume no change in relative

TABLE 2

Indicators of Agricultural and Food Output, Calorie Intake, and Cereal Imports per Person, Twenty-Two Latin American Countries, 1960, 1970, and 1982 or Nearby Years

Countries (in ascending order of estimated income per person)	Population (millions)			Value Added in in Agriculture, per Person (1980 dollars)			Index of Food Production per Person (1969–1971 average = 100)			Calorie Availability per Person per Day (Net Supply)			Cereal Imports[d] (kg per Person)		
	1960 (1)	1970 (2)	1982 (3)	1960 (4)	1970 (5)	1982 (6)	1961 (7)	1969–1971 (8)	1980–1982 (9)	1960–1962 (10)	1969–1971 (11)	1981 (12)	1960 (13)	1970 (14)	1982 (15)
Haiti	3.6	4.2	5.2	100	95	84	110	100	85	1904[b]	1873	1879	7	15	38
Bolivia	3.3	4.9	5.9	85	75	99	87	100	100	1990	1976	2179	34	39	50
Honduras	2.0	2.6	3.9	156	200	182	87	100	79	2160[c]	2115	2171	11	23	23
El Salvador	2.7	3.5	5.1	163	181	140	96	100	97	1890[c]	1840	2146	24	17	35
Nicaragua	1.5	1.8	2.5	171	267	222	83	100	77	2300[c]	2470	2184	14	26	28
Guatemala	3.9	5.3	7.4	221	253	282	88	100	114	2050[c]	2049	2045	1	21	14
Costa Rica	1.3	1.7	2.3	218	275	271	85	100	100	2420[c]	2417	2686	37	26	71
Peru	10.4	13.4	17.4	153	178	154	99	100	87	2260	2254	2183	37	42	88
Dominican Republic	3.4	4.1	6.3	170	167	166	107	100	104	2180[c]	1952	2192	10	13	48
Jamaica	1.7	1.9	2.2	131	135	121	106	100	90	2230[c]	2473	2643	95	150	184
Ecuador	4.4	6.0	8.5	140	158	164	103	100	101	1990[c]	1987	2100	8	15	38
Colombia	17.2	20.5	27.2	147	176	213	94	100	124	2370[c]	2122	2521	7	15	33

Paraguay	2.0	2.3	3.4	210	239	373	105	100	111	2520	2752	3005	37	32	11
Cuba	6.9	8.6	9.8	N.A.	N.A.	N.A.	117	100	113	2665[b]	2379	2766	50	134	229
Panama	1.2	1.5	2.0	139	196	173	82	100	103	2420[c]	2499	2271	28	30	55
Chile	7.6	9.4	11.3	129	126	134	104	100	98	2480[c]	2694	2790	10	58	126
Brazil	72.3	92.5	125—	90	94	124	95	100	133	2720	2493	2529	29	22	36
Mexico	38.6	50.7	73.8	148	166	169	93	100	104	2500[c]	2701	2805	2	16	30
Argentina	20.3	23.7	28.5	213	233	253	95	100	122	2810	3358	3405	0	0	0
Uruguay	2.6	2.8	2.9	186	237	226	105	100	109	3200	3027	2912	102	0	42
Venezuela	7.6	10.3	14.7	130	167	159	82	100	95	2300	2389	2642	47	96	175
Trinidad and Tobago	.9	1.0	1.1	96	98	78	76	100	62	2361	2387	2694	128	150	253
Total or Mean	216—	273—	366—	134[a]	149[a]	164[a]	95	100	115	2523	2518	2614	20	28	50

Notes: Rounded to nearest million. N.A. = not available. Means are weighted by population for closest year (1960 in the case of data for 1961 or 1960–1962, etc.)

[a] Excluding Cuba.

[b] 1965.

[c] 1961–1962.

[d] Wheat, rice, maize, barley, oats, and flour made from them.

Sources: (1), (2), (3) except Cuba: InterAmerican Development Bank (1983:Table 1).

Cuba (2): Pan American Health Organization (1980:Table I-2); (1) and (3) calculated from population growth rates in World Bank (1984:Table 1).

(4), (5), (6): Total value added in agriculture, from InterAmerican Development Bank (1983:Table 9), divided by population.

(7): Food and Agriculture Organization (1972, 1981); index linked to 1969–1971 base as 1961 (base 1969–1971) = 1961 (base 1961–1965) × 1971 (base 1969–1971) ÷ 1971 (base 1961–1965).

(8), (9): World Bank (1984:Table 6).

(10) except Cuba, Haiti, and Trinidad and Tobago: Food and Agriculture Organization (1968). Those three countries, estimates for 1965, Reutlinger and Selowsky (1976: Table A.1).

(11): Food and Agriculture Organization (1982).

(12): World Bank (1984:Table 24).

(13), (14), (15): Total cereal imports in metric tons divided by population. Imports in 1982 from World Bank (1984:Table 6); in 1960 and 1970 from Food and Agriculture Organization (1964, 1973).

prices, it would be a relatively simple exercise to predict the overall demand for food as a function of population and incomes, but particularly in the case of food, that would be an unrealistic assumption. Relative food prices have changed a great deal in the recent past in Latin America; changes in food prices have large effects on the level and distribution of real incomes; and because these income effects are often large, particularly at low incomes, one cannot rely on the price inelasticity of food demand to guarantee that food *quantities* demanded will be relatively insensitive to price. Even assuming away price effects, there remains the difficulty that food demand, especially for basic foodstuffs supplying the bulk of calories, is quite sensitive to the distribution of income. This occurs because the income elasticity of demand for calories (and to a lesser degree for other nutrients) declines rapidly as income rises, as has been shown on an aggregate basis by Reutlinger and Selowsky (1976:Appendix C) and within individual countries by the World Bank (1979:Table B.5 and p. 72) for Brazil and Amat y Leon and Curonisy (1981:290–293) for Peru.

It is possible to make assumptions about how the distribution of income will evolve, as a function of growth in mean income, and on that basis project demand (Musgrove and Shapanka, 1982), but the exercise is likely to be mechanical, without its being possible to reconcile the projected demand with a structure of output and employment that would in fact generate that income distribution. Since the overall inequality of income appears to be fairly stable in the absence of really revolutionary changes—despite governmental efforts such as land reform, labor market interventions, and other attempts to redistribute income or wealth (Figueroa, 1984b)—much the easiest way to predict food demand is to assume that it will expand proportionally to population, reproducing the distribution of food consumption and (in) satisfaction of food needs in the population. Besides ignoring income and price effects, this extreme simplification ignores what may, in Latin America, be a major determinant of food demand, that is, the urban–rural distribution of the population, these segments sometimes having quite different consumption patterns and demand elasticities (World Bank, 1979:69–71).

How much food demand will grow, on these simplifying assumptions, then reduces to the question of how fast population can be expected to grow. The relevant question about supply then becomes, Can it grow equally fast? The World Bank (1984:192–193) has recently published population projections for the countries included in Table 1. The "standard" projection leads to a total population of 532 million in the year 2000; this is a 45% increase over the 1982 level, or a 2.08% per year growth rate. This is significantly slower than growth between 1960 and 1982, which averaged 2.40% per year (2.34% annually in the earlier decade, accelerating to 2.44% in the latter 12 years). Assuming a rapid decline in fertility such as has recently been occurring in several countries of the region (Merrick, 1984) leads to an end-of-the-century population of 490 million, or an average growth rate of 1.62% per year; assuming that mortality also drops more rapidly than is currently occurring increases the estimate only slightly.

Can food output in Latin America grow at 2% per year for the next two decades? There does not seem to be any reason why it cannot. A recent review of the region's agricultural potential (Inter-American Development Bank, 1983) suggests that continued growth is feasible and likely, but also that increased output in the future will come more from raising yields than from expanding the cultivated area. In some countries, expansion of area is still relatively easy, and in some cases improvements in the productivity of livestock raising will free pastureland for crops, but in other countries the extensive agricultural frontier has essentially disappeared. Clearing and setting new land, especially forest, would be expensive and ultimately not very productive, as it would probably increase erosion and soil destruction. This review also suggests that in many areas, water will be more of a scarce resource than land unless technological change reduces water requirements per unit of land or of output.

This moderately optimistic overall assessment does not, of course, answer two other questions. First, how much of the potential for increased agricultural production will be used for food, rather than nonfood, crops? And second, how will the increased output be distributed among countries? As is clear from Table 1, the food–nonfood shares of agricultural growth have differed a great deal among countries, and agricultural "success" has been quite unevenly distributed. In particular, there is no reason to expect that food output will increase most in those countries that have recently been least successful in this respect and therefore most "need" to raise domestic food supplies.

This last point serves to raise a much larger issue, which is that even a successful expansion of food output at a somewhat faster pace than population is unlikely to meet the nutritional needs of the whole population by the end of the century. Simply meeting demand, even without a change in relative food prices, carries no implication for satisfying needs, because the low incomes (and perhaps also the tastes and habits) of millions of consumers limit their effective demand to consumption at or below estimated minimum levels of nutrition. Even with assumptions about income growth more optimistic than now seem warranted, given the current economic recession, it seems most unlikely that malnutrition or inadequate consumption of food will be eliminated by the end of the century without some substantial redistribution of income or foodstuffs (World Bank, 1979:72). This conclusion for

TABLE 3

Percentage Increase in Food Supply, 1982–2000, Required to Offset Different Sources of Growth in Demand or in Need

Country	*(1) Population Growth*	*(2) Average Calorie Deficit*	*(3) Intracountry Deficit*	*(4) Income Growth per Person*	*(5) All Four Effects*	*(6) Per Capita Effect Only*
Haiti	38	10.0	4.7	6.5	69	23
Bolivia	54	9.9	3.5	5.6	85	20
Honduras	74	4.2	4.9	5.7	101	16
El Salvador	59	6.4	5.0	5.7	88	18
Nicaragua	72	1.0	6.1	5.6	95	13
Guatemala	59	7.5	5.0	6.0	90	20
Costa Rica	48	0	0.3	4.6	55	5
Peru	48	2.0	8.8	5.6	73	17
Dominican Republic	48	0	5.3	5.6	65	11
Jamaica	32	0	0.9	4.7	39	6
Ecuador	59	3.1	7.1	5.9	86	17
Colombia	40	0	3.1	4.9	51	8
Paraguay	47	0	2.6	4.1	57	7
Cuba	19	0	1.4	4.4	26	6
Panama	40	0	5.4	5.4	56	11
Chile	28	0	1.4	4.4	36	6
Brazil	45	0	6.5	4.9	62	12
Mexico	48	0	2.8	4.4	59	7
Argentina	26	0	1.2	3.6	32	5
Uruguay	14	0	1.4	4.2	20	6
Venezuela	77	0	3.0	4.7	91	8
Trinidad–Tobago	35	0	1.5	4.6	43	6
Total, 22 countries	45	0.7	4.3	4.7	58	9

Sources: (1) World Bank (1984:Table 1, pp. 192–193).
(2) World Bank (1984:Table 24, pp. 264–265). Percentage calculated as (100/percentage of requirement) for countries where requirement was not met in 1981.
(3) Brazil: World Bank (1979:Annex III, p. 50). Peru: Amat y Leon and Curonisy (1981:135). Other countries: estimated using the techniques of Selowsky (1980:Table A-2), described in the Technical Note.
(4) Assuming 2.0% annual growth in income per person, and a relation of calories to income described by $C = -146 + 345 \log Y$ (see Technical Note).
(5) Product of the growth rates in columns 1–4; see Technical Note.
(6) Product of the growth rates in columns 2–4 only.

Technical Note: Estimates of the internal calorie deficit in column 3 are available only for Brazil and Peru. In Brazil, the deficit was estimated for each of several income and location cells using the 1974–1975 ENDEF survey. For Peru, the deficit is estimated from the two estimates that 52.2% of the population is malnourished and that the average daily calorie shortfall of the underfed is 400 calories. For all other countries, Selowsky's 1980 estimates of calorie intake by income decile are used to derive decile-specific deficits as a function of the degree of income inequality and the average satisfaction of calorie requirements. (The deficits are adjusted to reflect a requirement of 2300 calories per day, to match the estimate used for Brazil and Peru, rather than the

Brazil—which was successful in raising both income and food output sharply between 1960 and 1980—probably applies with equal force to most of the other countries studied here (Reutlinger and Selowsky, 1976:29).

How much faster would food supply need to grow in order to eliminate the deficit of calories and keep up with population growth to the year 2000? The answer has two components: one is the elimination of the *average* calorie deficit in those countries where mean intake now appears to be less than needs, and the other is the elimination of the deficit for the malnourished population *within* each country. Since eliminating the average calorie deficit would presumably raise the consumption of the malnourished, the internal deficit is defined as the deficit that would presumably remain once the average shortfall was gone and mean intake was at least equal to recommended levels. Once malnutrition was eliminated, further growth in income would continue to raise demand for food, although insofar as calories are concerned, the growth would be slow.

Table 3 attempts to quantify these different sources of expansion. The "intracountry deficit" is estimated following a procedure described in the Technical Note to the Table, except that for Brazil in 1974–1975 and Peru in 1972 direct estimates are available. The effect of income growth on calorie demand may be overstated, since many countries start at incomes so low that there is significant undernourishment, and eliminating the internal deficit would presumably reduce the effect of income increases thereafter. The overall effect is, however, probably small.

The chief result of the calculations in Table 3 is that over the immediate future, population growth dominates income increase as a source of in-

---

2150 assumed by Selowsky.) The less-equal income distribution was applied to Haiti, Bolivia, El Salvador, Guatemala, Dominican Republic, Jamaica, Ecuador, Colombia, Paraguay, Mexico, and Venezuela, and the more-equal distribution—implying less malnourishment at any average income level—to the other nine countries. This method of estimating the internal deficit is independent of per capita income in the country; the effect of income level is presumed to be reflected in the degree of average satisfaction of calorie requirements, which may be .9, 1.0, or 1.1. The relation of caloric intake to income is based on comparison across countries rather than within populations, and is consistent with the method used to project calorie demand as a function of income growth in column 4. The function used is $C = -146 + 345 \log Y$, where Y is income per person in 1982 dollars and C is calorie intake per person per day. This is the functional form used by Reutlinger and Selowsky (1976), with the coefficients adjusted to yield an elasticity of .15 when $C = 2300$, or need is exactly satisfied. The percentage increase in C after T years of income growth at r per year is then just $345T \ln(1 + r)/C_0$ where C_0 is the base-year (1982) level. No allowance is made for a reduction in the income-elasticity of calorie demand due to the prior satisfaction of the intra-country deficit due to malnutrition.

If r_1, r_2, r_3, r_4 are the increases calculated separately in columns 1–4, the per capita effect r_6 is defined by $(1 + r_6) = (1 + r_2)(1 + r_3)(1 + r_4)$, and the total effect r_5 is defined by $(1 + r_5) = (1 + r_1)(1 + r_6)$ This is why the percentages are not additive; for all 22 countries, 58% exceeds the sum of 45 and 9%, but $1.58 = (1.45)(1.09)$, reflecting the interaction of the population and per capita effects.

In the total calculations for all 22 countries, each country is weighted by its total 1982 calorie intake, or 1982 population times per-person intake.

creased food demand. The sum of internal deficits and the effect of income growth (at 2% per year, which may be overly optimistic) each add less than 5% to current calorie intake, whereas population growth alone will, on the standard projection, raise needs by 45%. Taking all factors together leads to a requirement of a 58% increase for the 22 countries, with much variation among them. To eliminate malnutrition and keep up with demographic and income growth, calorie intakes would need to rise by 80% or more in Bolivia, Honduras, El Salvador, Nicaragua, Guatemala, Ecuador, and Venezuela, whereas increases of 30% or less would be adequate in Cuba and Uruguay (and probably also in Argentina, where the projections assume some continued growth, due to incomes, above the already very high level of 3400 calories). When all factors are considered together, the presumption that supply could expand enough probably remains valid (growth of 2.5% per year would be required), but the distribution of requirements among countries becomes more worrisome. This happens because the countries facing the highest population growth are generally also those with current low incomes, average calorie deficits, and substantial malnutrition. For Haiti, Bolivia, El Salvador, and Guatemala, for example, the per-person effects add about 30 percentage points to the requirement due to population growth alone.

GETTING ENOUGH TO EAT: ENTITLEMENTS, INCOMES, AND PRICES

The discussion so far has treated the "food supply problem" as though it were only, or principally, a matter of physical scarcity. The one exception to this treatment is the recognition that a country may have an internal deficit—some people not getting enough to eat—even though total supply is adequate. The fact that most countries import some part of their food supply, and often a substantial part, indicates that physical production alone does not determine whether there is enough to eat; there is no more reason to suppose that total supply, including imports, determines that. In fact, it makes more sense to regard supply as the result of the command people have over food, or their effective demand, than as the cause of dietary adequacy or inadequacy. To put the problem this way is to focus attention on incomes and food prices, to see it as an economic rather than a physical problem.

More generally, one can consider people's "entitlements" to food: These may consist of their own production of food for domestic consumption, their incomes earned in whatever activities (including the raising and selling of food), or their enrollment in programs that give away food or otherwise make it available outside of market channels. Sen (1982), whose term this is, argues convincingly that even famines are caused by the collapse or loss of entitlements, rather than, as is usually assumed, by "food availability decline." Analysis of famines in India, Bangladesh, Ethiopia, and the Sahelian countries of Africa shows that while famine can occur in a situation of reduced food output, it can also occur when production is higher than normal—that there can be "boom famines" as well as "slump famines." Even when there is some aggregate scarcity, it is usually much too small to explain the extent of hunger in a famine, or to explain why some people die while others get more than enough to eat.

The same arguments apply equally well to situations of chronic malnutrition or food inadequacy for part of the population, except that instead of a "collapse" of their entitlements, it may be appropriate to speak of entitlements that are chronically too small. Reductions in entitlements that stop short of outright famine can also occur, although the line where famine begins is more a social or political boundary than a biological one: Widespread infant mortality aggravated by malnutrition is only somewhat slower and less alarming than widespread death of adults from hunger.

It has been traditionally believed that while much of the population must buy its food and therefore is obviously susceptible to changes in prices and employment, the entitlement of peasant farmers, who produce food for their own use, is immune to such changes. Recent research has largely demolished that idea. Studying eight Peruvian villages, Figueroa (1984a) has found that only about half of peasant income derives from domestic production, and that that income is typically too low to guarantee an adequate diet; food is in fact the principal item bought with the monetary income earned by sale of own produce or wage income. Peasants do have, in their own land, an entitlement that is somewhat isolated from the market, but it is subject to two serious limitations: In land-poor areas, it is often too small even for subsistence; and it can be worked for the highest yield in income only if its produce can be sold. In the absence of markets for their output, farmers *must* grow food to eat, and this is often not the most economical use of their land. Because such peasant farmers are poor, often using three-quarters of their income for food, adverse changes in prices or employment opportunities may actually affect their food intake more severely than that of nonfarmers who grow none of their own food but who enjoy higher incomes and can therefore adjust more easily to a given absolute or proportional income loss.

Seeing both final food supply and its distribution among the population as functions of entitlements or effective demand explains why the overall increase in food production in Latin America has not translated into increased average consumption; more generally, it explains why, across countries and through time, there is so little association among output and intake. It does not yet explain, however, what exactly has happened to incomes and prices to give the observed results; as was remarked earlier, several different scenarios are possible, with different implications for these variables. As with the aggregate results, there is probably much diversity of experience; unfortunately, it is not easy to find enough detailed information to analyze many cases. The rest of this section therefore considers only two countries, Brazil and Peru, for which some relatively disaggregated data and analyses exist. In total, Brazil is an agricultural success, while Peru is a relative failure, over the last two decades; yet both countries show roughly constant calorie intake, substantial undernourishment, and growing imports of food grains. There appears also to be considerable similarity in the causes of these outcomes, despite great differences in other aspects.

Peru: Urban Price Bias and Increased Inequality

A nationwide survey of household incomes and food consumption was undertaken in Peru in 1971–1972 (Amat y Leon and Curonisy, 1981); a smaller survey, emphasizing poor households, was conducted in 1978. These detailed data, together with national or department-level estimates of food production and consumption over several decades, form the basis for a recent evaluation of the evolution of food consumption in the country (Leonard, Franklin, and Youngblood, 1984, and sources cited there). The nature and consequences of public policies concerning food prices have been examined by Ferroni (1980). The distribution of income and welfare revealed by the 1971–1972 survey have been studied extensively (Amat y Leon and Leon, 1983), and the evolution of income distribution since about 1960 has been analyzed by Webb (1977) and by Figueroa (1984b), with an emphasis on the impact of various government policies.

Together, these studies seem to show two major phenomena affecting the adequacy of food consumption and the share of it that is produced domestically. The first—which is repeatedly referred to by various authors but nowhere documented as thoroughly as one would like to see—is a systematic urban price bias, which has kept food cheap in the cities, especially Lima, discouraged domestic production, and encouraged imports, especially of foods such as wheat, whose consumption has been subsidized. This does not mean that food prices are much higher in the interior or in rural areas than on the coast and in the major cities: Leonard et al. (1984:42) found a surprising degree of price uniformity throughout the country, considering the difficulties of transport and the economic dualism distinguishing the coast from the interior. It does mean that only a small share—just over one-third—of what is spent on food by households in Lima represents income to rural food producers (Figueroa, 1984a:90–96). The remaining two-thirds are absorbed by imports and by processing and trade margins. The attempt to keep food cheap in the cities, even at the cost of steadily increasing imports and stagnation in the traditional food-producing sector, appears to be a long-standing policy, not a pronounced shift over the past few years; none of the students of the problem show *trends* in relative prices working against agriculture. This does not mean, of course, that such a policy is either completely uniform or entirely stable; it includes subsidies to *production* in the case of rice, and at intervals, balance-of-payments crises force sudden increases of food prices as the Peruvian sol is sharply devalued or subsidies are reduced. The most easily discernible effect of urban price bias is the steadily increasing imported share of basic foodstuffs, which is not confined to wheat or grains generally but also characterizes meat, milk, and edible oils, as Table 4 shows. Given Peru's shortage of arable land, however, and the evidence that its peasant farmers cannot produce appreciably more food without substantial technological change in the form of irrigation, fertilizers, and improved varieties, not all the increase in imports can be attributed to anti-agricultural policy. The country would probably have become less self-sufficient even under the best of policies, although less dramatically so.

An urban bias alone could discourage domestic food production and promote rural–urban migration, but neither of those effects would necessarily worsen anyone's intake of food, provided that jobs were created fast enough, and at adequate wages, to make up for the lost potential income from farming and to generate the exports needed to balance increased food imports. Unfortunately, that has clearly not happened. Overall income growth has been extremely slow, and many pieces of evidence indicate a deterioration in the distribution of income or an increasing inequality. The share of profits in income has risen, reducing labor's share; inequality among households or individuals has widened; and such policies as have attempted to redistribute income from capital to labor or from richer to poorer have mostly shifted incomes *within* the richest quartile of recipients. Poor people seem to have

TABLE 4
Imports as a Share of Total Consumption (Production Plus Imports) of Some Basic Foodstuffs, Peru, 1943–1975

Foodstuff	*1943*	*1960*	*1970*	*1975*
Wheat	33	41	46	46
Corn	N.A.	N.A.	1	34
Rice[a]	9	9	0	11
Edible Oils	4	26	44	44
Milk	3	18	26	29
Beef	2	4	22	10

[a] Domestic production subsidized.
Source: Adapted from Figueroa (1984a:Table 7.5).

benefited from the reforms of the late 1960s and early 1970s only insofar as they obtained land under the land reform; but the per-recipient transfers in the case of poor peasant farmers were much smaller than the transfers to less poor agricultural workers in modern coastal farming or the gains to favored industrial, mining, and fishing workers (Figueroa, 1984b). The evidence that income distribution has become worse over the last two decades is strikingly supported by evidence suggesting that the relatively well off eat better than they used to.

The urban poor appear to have maintained roughly constant calorie intake during the 1970s, at the cost of a qualitative deterioration of the diet (more calories from basic grains and tubers), while the diet of the rural poor appears to have declined in quantity as well as quality (Leonard et al., 1984:36; World Bank, 1981:32–33). The effects antedate the climatic disturbances of the last few years, which have reduced food output and rural incomes sharply in both the extreme north and the extreme south of the country. It is also to be noted that a worsening of the distribution of income would have led to a food-consumption problem in Peru, given the low average levels of income and food intake, even in the absence of any bias of public policy against agriculture.

Brazil: Export Bias and Increased Inequality

Like Peru, Brazil conducted a nationwide survey of incomes and food consumption in the 1970s, and there have been numerous studies of the information obtained in that survey and subsequent smaller surveys. Preliminary findings concerning food intake and nutrition were published by the World Bank (1979), and the nutritional situation of mothers and children was later examined in great detail (IBGE and UNICEF, 1982). The evolution of agriculture and food output has been studied by several authors, notably Homem de Melo (1983), while the evolution of the distribution of income since 1960 is the subject of a large and often contentious literature. Findings through the mid 1970s are surveyed by Pfeffermann and Webb (1979), and changes during the 1970s are treated by Denslow and Tyler (1983), among others. Pastore et al. (1983) have studied the distribution of income and welfare among *families* over the decade, with emphasis on the prevalence of poverty.

There is rather more detailed information available for Brazil than for Peru; perhaps partly in consequence, it is somewhat less clear what has happened over the last two decades to affect food supplies and intakes. Two trends nonetheless seem definite. One is a bias, in prices, credit, and other policies, in favor of exports as against production for the domestic market. It is important to note that this is not an anti-agricultural bias generally; in recent years, in fact, agriculture has been a relatively favored sector, which probably helps to account for its success in raising output faster than population growth. Instead, exports have been favored over domestic consumption, and a number of crops not consumed significantly by poor households have prospered relative to traditional basic foodstuffs. (The fact that food output, not only agricultural value, expanded shows that there was not a simple bias for nonfoods against foods either.)

Insofar as incomes are concerned, it is clear that their distribution became more unequal after 1960: The growth represented by the Brazilian "miracle" went predominantly to raise the incomes of the nonpoor. It does not follow, however, that the poor did not share at all in the miracle, and still less does it follow that they became absolutely worse off. It appears, rather—although here the evidence is not very conclusive—that between 1960 and the late 1970s the real incomes of the poor increased slightly, and that the number of families and of individuals living in poverty declined, or at least rose very little, leading to decline in the *share* of the population in poverty. (One reason it is hard to be sure what has happened to the poor is that the price index appropriate for deflating changes in average income does not represent the spending patterns of the poor, and there have been substantial changes in relative prices.)

If food output went up, and if no one was made any poorer in real terms, while income grew, then one should expect some increase in food intake. This would be slight if income increases went only to the nonpoor, and could be substantial if the income of the poor also rose. It may be that this is just what happened between 1960 and the late 1970s, although given the rather low income elasticity of calorie demand, total calorie consumption per person would have changed little. By 1982, however, the combination of world economic recession and the continued drought in northeastern Brazil would have wiped out much of the income gain of the preceding decade, with reductions in real incomes for the poor and especially for the poorest peasant farmers. The increases in agricultural output occurred largely in the center–south of the country, where all incomes (including farm incomes) are higher than the comparable national averages. This regional difference is important for what happened to particular crops and therefore for the food situation of particular population groups.

The most important traditional foodstuffs in the diet of the Brazilian poor are rice, beans, manioc, and corn; together with sugar, these foods provide the bulk of calories and a substantial share of protein. Sugar is also a major export crop, and in the last decade it has become a source of methanol to replace motor vehicle fuel. It is probably the only product for which the poor compete directly both with foreign consumers and with the domestic industrial sector. The other four crops all fell in price relative to the export crops between the late 1960s and the late 1970s. Output growth slowed or even became negative, so calorie availability per person declined from a peak in the late 1960s. Except in the case of corn, yields per hectare have stagnated or even declined, partly because the land diverted from these crops to export crops has usually been the best land in use. Total area in the traditional staples has expanded, but apparently onto poorer quality lands whose yield is lower.

These findings are summarized in Tables 5 and 6, adapted from Homem de Melo's 1983 detailed study and from Alves's (1978?) paper on "export promotion versus nutrition." Table 5 shows that since 1967, beans have had a high price relative to the prices of agricultural inputs, but that food crops generally and rice in particular have not; export crops have been much more profitable, leaving agriculture in total with an almost constant level of output

TABLE 5
Indexes of Agricultural Output Prices, 1960–1978 (1967 = 100), Relative to Agricultural Input Prices and Traditional Foodstuffs

Year	(1) Total agricultural Output	(2) Total Less Coffee	(3) Export Crops Only	(4) Food Crops Only[a]	(5) Rice	(6) Beans	(7) Col. 3 ÷ Col. 4	(8) Export Crops[b]	(9) Exports Less Coffee	(10) Beef
1960	95	94	112	86	74	162	130			
1961	100	100	120	83	68	99	145			
1962	104	103	113	123	120	214	92			
1963	103	100	123	112	127	136	110			
1964	117	109	164	101	91	100	162			
1965	94	92	112	77	51	86	145			
1966	100	102	90	109	93	159	83			
1967	100	100	100	100	100	100	100	100	100	100
1968	97	94	113	96	97	101	118	112	99	105
1969	105	98	136	115	80	197	118	132	103	111
1970	102	92	153	85	64	138	180	131	105	107
1971	101	96	128	94	95	131	136	141	113	111
1972	103	95	148	93	87	135	159	126	105	94
1973	109	101	153	109	74	271	140	134	111	116
1974	91	86	123	78	73	128	158	136	106	115
1975	105	96	154	89	97	135	173	193	117	114
1976	133	103	304	104	58	258	292	232	122	114
1977								237	134	122
1978								210	137	150

[a] Rice, beans, corn, manioc, potatoes, onions, tomatoes, and bananas.
[b] Coffee, sugarcane, soy, cotton, peanuts, and oranges.
Sources: (1)–(6) adapted from Alves (1978?:Tables 3 and 4); all indexes relative to IPI (index of input prices) adjusted to 1967 = 100.
(7), ratio of (3) to (4): approximation to the narrower index in (8).
(8)–(9), Homem de Melo (1983:Table 3).

TABLE 6

Indexes of Area Planted, Yield, Total Output, and Calorie Availability per Person, Four Traditional Foodstuffs, 1960–1964 to 1970–1974 (1960–1964 = 100)

Crop and Variable	*1960–1964 or 1961–1963*	*1965–1969*	*1970–1974*
Rice			
Area	100	138	150
Yield	100	94	92
Output	100	119	127
Calories	100	101	97
Beans			
Area	100	136	139
Yield	100	102	94
Output	100	128	130
Calories	100	111	82
Corn			
Area	100	125	140
Yield	100	105	114
Output	100	130	158
Calories	100	106	109
Manioc			
Area	100	126	138
Yield	100	106	101
Output	100	133	140
Calories	100	115	105

Sources: Area, yield, and output from Alves (1978?:Table 5). Calories per person from Homen de Melo (1983:Table 5), using 1961–1963 = 100 and 5-year averages for 1965–69 and 1970–74.

prices relative to the cost of inputs, at least once coffee is excluded. When export crops are compared directly either to all food crops or to an index of eight traditional foodstuffs, they are seen to have enjoyed systematically higher prices since 1967, again excluding coffee. (Coffee trees require several years to mature, so cultivation is not easily switched between them and annual crops; planting is undertaken only if prices are expected to stay high, and trees are not destroyed even if returns are negative for a few years.)

Table 6 shows that while the area planted increased around 40% for all four crops over the period, yields declined or grew so little that output did not keep up with population in the case of rice and beans, and in the case of manioc initially grew but then declined relative to population. By 1979, total calories per person available from these four crops was only 90% of the average 1961–1963 level. These results antedate the severe economic recession of recent years, and the long drought in the Northeast, which has reduced output of beans, corn, and manioc and left large numbers of peasant farmers with little or no agricultural income. They also antedate the expansion of public programs to subsidize basic foodstuffs in the urban Northeast and to distribute free food to the very poor in both urban and rural areas of that region (Musgrove, 1986), which may have reduced the unfavorable distributional effects of the bias toward exports and against traditional crops.

It can certainly be argued that Brazil needed, and still needs, to stimulate exports and that it has a great comparative advantage in agriculture, so some shift away from traditional food crops may have been necessary, at least in total output. It does not follow, however, that export promotion needed to follow the technological bias described by Homem de Melo (1983), which reduced employment opportunities in agriculture and so probably contributed to worsening the distribution of income. Neither does it follow that traditional agriculture should have been neglected because it offered little scope for expansion; Peliano et al. (1983) argue persuasively that there are substantial possibilities for expanding traditional food output, both through increased area and through restoring yields to their historic peaks or higher. What such a policy would require, however, is a redirection of credit and technical assistance to those crops and to peasant farmers, and probably a serious land reform as well. Unfortunately, the poor have not only not received such preferential treatment but in recent years they have not even continued to enjoy low prices for their traditional foodstuffs. As the supply of the latter has shrunk, food prices have risen much faster than the overall price level, and real incomes in terms of food have fallen sharply, especially in the Northeast where poverty is already most widespread.

CONCLUDING REFLECTIONS: IS THERE A LINK FROM POPULATION GROWTH TO SECURITY VIA FOOD?

The first section of this chapter showed that at the level of individual countries, population growth over the last two decades cannot be associated with decline in food production or in food supplies per person. In fact, across the 22 countries studied, there is a slight *positive* relation between population growth and agricultural success in raising food output. The third section, above, showed that in the two countries studied in more detail, the existence of malnutrition and even its possible worsening through time are better explained by low incomes and by price and trade policies than by demographic pressure. Food supply can be barely adequate, as in Peru, yet only part of the population goes hungry; or production can clearly outrun population, as in Brazil, yet the traditional foods of the poor may decline in availability and consumers may be too poor to switch to more available but higher-price foods. In both countries, the climatic problems of the last few years—drought in northeastern Brazil and southern Peru, excessive rainfall in northern Peru—have reduced food output below what it would have been, but the problems of hunger and inadequate effective demand for food existed earlier. In Brazil, and possibly also in Peru, the climatic disasters may actually have reduced effective demand for food even more than they reduced supply, by destroying incomes, including nonagricultural incomes. And at least in Brazil, the effects of the drought on total output were more than offset by the expansion of more productive farming in other parts of the country. (This probably did not occur in Peru.)

Do these findings mean that population growth has nothing to do with the issue of whether food consumption is adequate? More generally, do they mean that if there is any link from demographic growth to security problems, it does not operate via food? Almost surely, the answer to both these questions is no. But to see why there may be some important connections, it is appropriate to concentrate on demand for food rather than on production, and to consider distribution rather than aggregate amounts.

One possible connection is that faster population growth is likely because of the necessarily higher proportion of dependent children in the population to mean lower rates of saving. To the extent that an economy's growth is limited by inadequate domestic saving—that is, the principal constraint is not the capacity to import, and foreign savings do not compensate for domestic inability to finance investment—faster population growth will therefore mean slower growth in income per head, although not necessarily zero or negative growth. Since the rate of saving depends on a multitude of other factors, including the proportion of elderly dependents in the population—in which respect rapid demographic growth is an advantage—and since economic growth rates are only loosely associated with saving rates, there is still much debate whether empirically population growth does systemically retard economic growth (Leff, 1984; Ram, 1984; and earlier studies cited there). The likeliest result is that high dependency rates depress saving by *households*, but their saving may be a quite variable share of total saving, and yield different returns than the savings of businesses or the public sector. In any case, low saving rates do not imply a food problem unless they lead to negative economic growth or falling incomes. Their potential for generating problems of political stability or insecurity also seems to arise only in the long term, since changes in population growth rates are relatively slow, and it is presumably their cumulative impact that matters.

A more direct and rapid mechanism by which population growth can lead to malnutrition is through worsening the distribution of income. Ahluwalia (1976) found, in a cross-section of countries, that after controlling for income level and several other factors, rapid recent population growth is associated with greater income inequality, particularly with a smaller share of income going to the poorest households. In land-poor countries with few employment opportunities outside agriculture, the chief reason for this may be increasing population density, and lower income per person, on the land. Where alternative employment exists, however, the surplus agricultural population migrates permanently or seasonally, maintaining the right amount of labor on the land (Figueroa, 1984a). Where expansion of the agricultural frontier is possible, of course, that may absorb the excess population. More generally, with or without scarcity of land, rapid population growth means large families, which at low incomes means difficulty in creating human capital through adequate nutrition, schooling, and health care. The argument that high dependency means low savings is relevant here for individual households, and relevant for public investment in health and education. High population growth is not uniform in a population, but is concentrated among families with poor diets, low adult educational achievement, and high rates of failure or desertion in children's schooling. This is true even in urban areas, where land scarcity is irrelevant and human capital formation is the chief way of raising incomes (Musgrove, 1985).

It is at least plausible that rapid population growth helped account for the worsening distribution of income in both Brazil and Peru during recent decades. With slower growth, it would have been easier to create employment and improve the skills of the labor force, wages would have been somewhat higher, and so on. Many other factors contributed, of course, including biases in particular public policies; the most that can be argued is that rapid population growth exacerbates the tendency toward greater inequality. This argument is supported by evidence that a slowing of demographic growth, and a concomitant reduction in family size, offsets the worsening in the distribution of family incomes so that income per person is less unequally distributed. This clearly occurred in Caracas, Venezuela, during the income boom caused by the 1973–1974 oil price increase (Musgrove, 1981), and demographic factors were also important in reducing the impact of inequality in Brazil in the 1970s (Pastore et al., 1983). In both cases, the prevalence of poverty would have increased had there been no reduction in fertility and family size.

The connection of population growth to income inequality may be important for political stability because while overall inequality usually changes only very slowly, marginal changes can be quite rapid. For a particular population group, a small shift in the distribution of income can mean a large reduction in their relative incomes and even in their absolute incomes. When the latter occurs, and the group is not well off to start with, their effective demand for food will suffer, and hunger will result. Two points about this process deserve emphasis. First, food *supply* will be directly involved only if the group suffering an income loss consists of farmers, but even then the net marketable supply to the rest of the population may increase, although total output declines. Second, shifts in income distribution affecting the distribution of effective demand for food happen largely through changes in relative prices; changes in quantities may be the consequence rather than the cause.

This discussion emphasizes not the customary level or distribution of command over food, but *changes* in those variables, as being more likely to cause dissatisfaction, instability, or eventual security problems. If hunger translated directly into instability, most of Latin America should be in continuous turmoil, with the least problems in the richest countries; clearly that is not the case. (In fact, both great internal violence and foreign war characterized Argentina in 1976–1982, and in that country there is too much to eat on average and very little hunger by Latin American standards.) This does not mean that the static or background situation is irrelevant; in particular, the importance of landholding patterns in determining income distribution and of land reform as a political issue and even a motivation for civil war form an important exception to the idea that changes matter more than levels.

In relating food demand (and supply) to political questions, Sen's 1982 idea of "entitlement" may be valuable. The word suggests not only an objective situation—ability to produce or acquire food—but also the view that one has a right to that output or income. This may be simply because one becomes accustomed to a given level of income or consumption (including subsidized or free consumption in the case of clients of transfer programs), or because even if one does not have control over a resource, one believes one should, and does not recognize someone else's entitlement to it. Then a crude but useful generalization might be that political problems arise when an entitlement is lost, especially if quickly, or when an entitlement is disputed or not recognized in the first place. Since people's ideas of what they are entitled to differ much, and can change quite independently of their objective situation, casting the population–food–political connection in terms of entitlements does not make prediction easy; it does direct attention away from simple aggregate relations and toward the more important issues of how demographic change, food consumption, and political factors interact.

REFERENCES

Ahluwalia, Montek

1976 "Inequality, poverty and development." *Journal of Development Economics* 3 (December).

Alves, Denisard

1978? "Brazilian agriculture: Export promotion versus nutrition." Instituto de Pesquisas Econômicas, Universidade de São Paulo, São Paulo. Mimeographed.

Amat y León, Carlos and Dante Curonisy

1981 *La Alimentación en el Perú*. Lima: Centro de Investigación de la Universidad del Pacífico.

Amat y León, Carlos and Héctor León

1983 *Niveles de Vida y Grupos Sociales en él Perú*. Lima: Centro de Investigación de la Universidad del Pacífico and Fundación Friedrich Ebert.

Denslow, David and William Tyler

1983 *Perspectives on Poverty and Income Inequality in Brazil* Working Paper No. 601. Washington, D.C.: World Bank, July.

Ferroni, Marcos

1980 "The urban bias of Peruvian food policy: Consequences and alternatives." Ph.D. dissertation, Cornell University, Ithaca.

Fundação Instituto Brasileiro de Geografía e Estatística (IBGE) and UNICEF

1982 *Perfil Estatístico de Crianças e Mães no Brasil*. Rio de Janeiro: IBGE.

Figueroa, Adolfo

1984a *Capitalist Development and the Peasant Economy in Peru*. Cambridge: Cambridge University Press.

1984b "The distribution problem in different sociopolitical and economic contexts: Peru, 1950–1980." In Seymour Sudman and Mary Spaeth (eds), *The Collection and Analysis of Economic and Consumer Behavior Data*. Urbana: University of Illinois.

Homem de Melo, Fernando

1983 *O Problema Alimentar no Brasil*. São Paulo: Paz e Terra.

Food and Agriculture Organization

1964 *Production Yearbook*, No. 18, FAO.

1972 *Production Yearbook*, No. 26, FAO.

1973 *Production Yearbook*, No. 27, FAO.

1981 *Production Yearbook*, No. 35, FAO.

1982 *Production Yearbook*, No. 36, FAO.

Inter-American Development Bank

1983 *Economic and Social Progress in Latin America. 1983 Report*. Washington, D.C.

Leff, Nathaniel

1984 "Dependency rates and savings: Another look." *American Economic Review* 74 (March).

Leonard, Jerry, David Franklin and Curtis Youngblood.

1984 "Consumption effects of agricultural policies: Peru. Evolution of food consumption patterns." Sigma One Corporation, Raleigh, N.C., February. Mimeographed.

Merrick, Thomas

1984 *Recent Fertility Declines in Brazil, Colombia and Mexico*. Working Papers in Demography. Washington, D.C.: Center for Population Research, Georgetown University.

Musgrove, Philip

1981 "The oil price increase and the alleviation of poverty: Income distribution in Caracas, Venezuela, in 1966 and 1975." *Journal of Development Economics* 9.

1984 "Welfare indicators and health." *Bulletin of the Pan American Health Organization* 18.

1985 "Food needs and absolute poverty in urban South America." *Review of Income and Wealth* 32.

Musgrove, Philip and Adele Shapanka

1982 *Income and Demographic Effects on the Structure of Consumer Expenditure in the U.S., 1975–2025*. Washington, D.C., Resources for the Future.

Musgrove, Philip 1986. *Que Los Pobres Coman Mejor. Evaluación de Programas Destinados a Mejorar el Consumo Alimenticio de Familias Pobres en el Brasil.* Washington, D.C.: Pan American Health Organization.

Pan American Health Organization
1980 *Health Conditions in the Americas, 1977–1980.* PAHO.

Pastore, José, Helio Zylberstajn and Carmen Silva Pagotto
1983 *Mudança Social e Pobreza no Brasil: 1970–1980.* São Paulo: Livraria Pioneira.

Peliano, Anna, Cláudio Castro, George Martine and Ronaldo García
1985 "O Problema Alimentar Brasileiro," in Castro, Cláudio and Marcos Coimbra, eds., *O Problema Alimentar no Brasil.* São Paulo: Editora Almed.

Pfeffermann, Guy and Richard Webb
1979 *The Distribution of Income in Brazil.* Working Paper No. 356. Washington, D.C.: World Bank, September.

Ram, Rati
1984 "Dependency rates and savings: Reply." *American Economic Review* 74 (March).

Reutlinger, Shlomo and Marcelo Selowsky
1976 *Malnutrition and Poverty: Magnitude and Policy Options.* World Bank Staff Occasional Paper No. 23. Baltimore: Johns Hopkins University Press.

Selowsky, Marcelo
1980 "Hacia la eliminación del déficit de satisfacción de necesidades básicas." In Economic Commission for Latin America and United Nations Development Program, *Se Puede Superar la Pobreza? Realidad y Perspectivas en América Latina.* Santiago: United Nations.

Sen, Amartya
1982 *Poverty and Famines: An Essay on Entitlement and Deprivation.* New York: Oxford University Press.

Webb, Richard
1977 *Government Policy and the Distribution of Income in Peru, 1963–1973.* Cambridge, Mass.: Harvard University Press.

World Bank
1979 *Brazil: Human Resources Special Report.* Washington, D.C.
1981 *Peru: Major Development Policy Issues and Recommendations.* Country Economic Report. Washington, D.C.
1984 *World Development Report*, Washington, D.C.

7

The Demographic Erosion of Development Efforts in Latin America, 1960–2000

RICHARD L. CLINTON

Pareciera haber un creciente conflicto entre la ilegalidad del robo y el derecho a comer.
BENJAMIN VIEL

As all who have made the effort are aware, establishing causality among sociopolitical phenomena is an uncertain undertaking, complicated by the interactions of an immense array of variables that frequently are mutually reinforcing but just as often cancel each other out. Merely endeavoring to measure the more important of these variables in a valid and reliable way invites frustration, the more so when temporal or cross-cultural comparisons are sought. Indeed, theorizing about probable causal chains and such seemingly simple matters as the direction in which causal arrows point can drive one to accept what unsympathetic wags have labeled the fundamental law of social science: "Some do, some don't."

To attempt such a problematic enterprise in the future tense necessarily compounds all these difficulties by orders of magnitude. It is with equal amounts of trepidation and humility, therefore, that I seek in this chapter to shed some light on the following questions: What can be said about the quality of life in Latin America during the two decades following 1960? How has the region's unprecedented rate of population growth influenced this changing quality of life? What is the outlook for these interactions during the last two decades of the century? What, in particular, does all this imply for the likelihood of social unrest in the area?

THE CHANGING QUALITY OF LIFE: A CLOSER LOOK

The first of these questions is most commonly addressed by making reference to the steady improvement in the region's gross domestic product (GDP) over the years (see Table 1). In constant terms, the GDP of Latin

TABLE 1
Percentage Change of Gross Domestic Product, 1961–1980 (calculated in constant terms)

Country	*1961–1970*	*1971–1975*	*1976–1980*	*1975*	*1976*	*1977*	*1978*	*1979*	*1980*
Argentina	4.4	2.8	1.6	−.9	−.2	6.0	−3.9	6.8	1.1
Bolivia	5.0	5.7	3.2	5.1	6.8	3.4	3.1	2.0	.8
Brazil	6.1	10.9	6.8	5.7	9.0	4.7	6.0	6.4	8.0
Chile	4.5	−.9	7.3	−14.3	3.8	9.7	8.3	8.2	6.5
Colombia	5.2	6.1	5.5	3.8	4.6	4.9	8.9	5.1	4.0
Costa Rica	6.0	6.1	5.2	2.1	5.5	8.9	6.3	3.3	1.9
Dominican Republic	5.4	9.1	4.9	5.2	6.7	5.0	2.2	4.8	5.6
Ecuador	5.5	8.9	5.7	5.0	7.1	6.0	5.3	5.3	4.6
El Salvador	5.7	5.7	3.7	5.6	4.0	6.1	3.9	−1.6	−8.7
Guatemala	5.5	5.6	5.7	1.9	7.4	7.8	5.0	4.5	4.0
Haiti	.3	3.7	4.1	−5.4	8.4	1.3	5.3	1.8	3.8
Honduras	5.2	2.1	6.6	−1.7	8.4	8.7	7.0	6.7	2.4
Mexico	7.0	5.7	5.6	4.1	2.1	3.3	7.3	8.0	7.4
Nicaragua	7.0	5.6	−1.3	2.2	5.0	.9	−5.4	−17.4	10.4
Panama	8.0	5.0	3.4	.6	−.3	3.4	3.7	4.9	5.5
Paraguay	4.5	6.7	10.3	6.3	7.0	12.8	10.9	10.7	10.0
Peru	5.1	4.6	1.6	4.5	2.0	−.1	−.7	3.4	3.4
Uruguay	1.6	1.4	5.1	4.8	4.2	1.8	6.2	8.6	4.5
Venezuela	6.1	4.9	3.5	5.9	8.4	6.8	3.2	.7	−1.6
Latin America[a]	5.7	6.6	5.2	3.8	5.3	4.7	4.6	5.8	5.4

[a] Includes Bahamas, Barbados, Guyana, and Trinidad and Tobago.
Source: Wilkie and Haber (1983:12).

America grew at a very respectable average rate of 5.7% during the 1961–1970 period and 5.9% between the years 1971 and 1980. Even when population growth is factored in, the per capita GDP expanded during the 1960s at an average rate of 3.8% per annum and at 4.0% throughout the 1970s (see Table 2). In an area undergoing one of the most rapid rates of population growth in human history, this was no mean accomplishment. It is not, though, a valid index of development, however often it may be adduced as such, for it obscures important variations not only between countries but within countries, a number of which actually experienced negative rates of GDP growth in some of the years under consideration: Argentina in 1975, 1976, and 1979; Chile from 1971 to 1975; Haiti and Honduras in 1975; Nicaragua from 1976 to 1980; Peru in 1977 and 1978; and even oil-rich Venezuela in 1980 (see Table 1).

If development is understood as involving improvement in the lives of all the people of a country, rather than merely in overall levels of economic performance, income-distribution figures provide a more revealing index

TABLE 2
Per Capita GDP, 1960–1980 (in constant dollars of 1978)

Country	*1960*	*1970*	*1975*	*1980*
Argentina	1371.2	1791.7	1904.8	1935.0
Bolivia	382.5	477.1	552.2	566.7
Brazil	669.9	929.6	1364.6	1664.2
Chile	1082.7	1413.4	1219.0	1590.5
Colombia	477.6	646.8	784.2	921.6
Costa Rica	838.1	1150.1	1353.2	1527.3
Dominican Rep.	513.0	673.0	927.3	1050.4
Ecuador	415.9	529.1	694.2	789.2
El Salvador	529.4	681.7	766.8	680.9
Guatemala	728.2	927.6	1051.3	1198.5
Haiti	251.6	217.5	239.0	267.4
Honduras	469.2	570.6	540.7	639.0
Mexico	878.6	1240.3	1381.5	1534.5
Nicaragua	618.8	950.3	1105.2	896.8
Panama	892.2	1564.3	1795.6	1917.6
Paraguay	525.6	637.8	783.0	1131.2
Peru	910.3	1142.0	1251.7	1137.3
Uruguay	1519.8	1671.5	1738.1	2163.9
Venezuela	1779.5	2295.6	2458.0	2457.5
Latin America[a]	824.0	1105.6	1334.5	1507.0

[a] Includes Bahamas, Barbados, Guyana, and Trinidad and Tobago.
Source: See Table 1.

than do GDP data. Thus, as Table 3 shows, despite the steady growth in GDP and GDP per capita that characterized 1960–1970, income shares remained remarkably stagnant, with 70% of the population receiving just over a quarter of the income and the remaining 30% garnering nearly three-quarters of the total. Another striking aspect of these data is that the income share of the poorest 20% actually declined by nearly a fifth in the 10 years. It should be also recalled that the distribution of wealth in a society tends to be far more skewed than the distribution of income.

Although the three indices—GDP, per capita GDP, and income distribution—provide some enlightenment, they ultimately raise the question: Whose quality of life are we talking about?

Some 30 years ago, Simon Kuznets (1955) and Gunnar Myrdal (1957) confronted the conventional wisdom of progress through growth with a jarring fact that Irma Adelman and Cynthia Taft Morris (1973) later found abundant evidence to substantiate, namely that rather than a trickle-down benefit to all, "development is accompanied by an absolute as well as a relative decline in the average income of the very poor" (Adelman and Morris, 1973:189). More recently and with specific reference to Latin America, David Felix echoed these findings: "The overriding conclusion I draw from the data and analysis . . . is that capitalistic economic growth in the Latin American institutional and cultural context is strongly biased toward income concentration and minimal rates of improvement in the quality of life of the lowest 60 percent" (1983:26). Table 3 indicates that a virtual stagnation in relative shares of income existed among the various levels of income recipients between 1960 and 1970, but in view of the consistently higher fertility of the lower-income groups, the deterioration that has occurred in the per capita income of the poorer 70% of Latin America is patent. This erosion of income share has, of course, been reinforced by the double- and triple-digit inflation rates that have become such a common feature of Latin America's economic landscape (see Table 4).

TABLE 3
Income Distribution: Latin American Average, 1960–1970

	Share (%)			
Stratum	*1960*		*1970*	
20% poorest	3.1	27.5	2.5	27.8
30% following	10.3		11.4	
20% following	14.1		13.9	
20% before highest 10%	24.6	72.5	28.0	72.2
10% highest	47.9		44.2	

Source: Wilkie and Haber (1983:187).

But what of the less material end of the development spectrum? Have not there been, for instance, significant strides in reducing the scourge of illiteracy in every Latin American country during the postwar period? Indeed, Table 5 confirms the very substantial achievement in each of the region's nations in lowering the proportion of illiterates. Yet, on closer inspection, in spite of the decline in the percentage of illiteracy in each society, one notes that in 12 (67%) of the 18 cases for which I could find data, the absolute number of illiterates is larger in the more recent period that it was in the earlier one. Moreover, in the other 6 nations, the absolute number of illiterates has remained almost constant. In other words, notwithstanding the very large proportion of their official budgets devoted to education (see Table 6), Latin American governments have been unable to reduce the absolute level of illiteracy among their citizens.

To point to the half-empty portion of this half-full glass is not to disparage the progress that has been achieved but to call attention to the tragedy that persists for many millions of Latin Americans, a tragedy all too often obscured by the way the data are normally presented. Moreover, a more clear-cut instance of the pernicious running-just-to-stay-in-the-same-place effect of rapid population growth can scarcely be imagined.

TABLE 4
Variations of the Consumer Price Index, 1960–1980 (average annual rates; domestic prices)

City	*1960–1965*	*1970–1975*	*1980*
Buenos Aires	23.3	64.0	100.8
La Paz	5.1	20.6	47.2
São Paulo	61.9	21.8	78.0
Bogotá	12.3	19.1	28.0
San José	2.3	13.7	18.1
Santiago	27.0	208.1	35.1
Quito	3.2	13.5	13.0
San Salvador	.3	8.6	17.4
Guatemala City	.1	—	10.4
Port-au-Prince	3.8	13.5	17.8
Tegucigalpa	2.7	6.2	18.1
Mexico City	1.9	12.1	26.5
Managua	—	—	35.3
Panama City	.8	7.2	13.8
Asunción	5.5	11.6	35.3
Lima-Callao	9.3	12.6	59.2
Santo Domingo	1.0	10.9	16.8
Montevideo	29.9	69.1	63.5
Caracas	.1	5.7	23.1

Source: Economic Commission for Latin America (1983a:152–153).

TABLE 5
Illiteracy by Country and Year

Country	*Year*	*Total Illiterates*	*Percentage of Population Over 15 Years of Age*
Argentina	1947	1,541,678	13.6
	1970	1,225,850	7.4
Bolivia	1950	1,109,385	67.9
	1960	1,278,000	61.2
Brazil	1950	15,272,632	50.6
	1970	18,146,977	33.8
Chile	1952	730,124	19.8
	1970	629,440	11.9
Colombia	1951	2,429,333	37.7
	1973	2,110,850	19.2
Costa Rica	1950	94,492	20.6
	1973	121,312	11.6
Dominican Republic	1950	677,293	57.1
	1970	678,910	32.8
Ecuador	1950	815,464	44.3
	1962	799,535	32.5
El Salvador	1950	644,514	60.6
	1971	816,716	42.9
Guatemala	1950	1,138,297	70.6
	1973	1,526,600	53.9
Haiti	1950	1,718,278	89.5
	1971	1,954,365	76.7
Honduras	1945	445,000	63.5
	1961	541,107	55.0
Mexico	1960	6,742,920	34.6
	1970	6,693,706	25.8
Nicaragua	1950	369,376	61.6
	1971	410,755	42.5
Panama	1950	132,978	30.1
	1970	175,152	21.7
Paraguay	1950	255,411	34.2
	1972	256,690	19.9
Peru	1961	2,185,646	38.9
	1972	2,070,294	27.6
Uruguay	1963	177,296	9.6
Venezuela	1950	1,365,888	47.8
	1971	1,313,561	23.5

Source: UNESCO (1977:158–183).

TABLE 6
Total Public Education Expenditure as Percentage of Total Public Expenditure (ca. 1976–1978)

Country	*Year*	*Percent*
Argentina	1977	10.7
Chile	1975	12.0
Colombia	1976	21.0
Costa Rica	1976	30.1
Dominican Republic	1977	12.6
El Salvador	1977	26.0
Guatemala	1976	13.2
Haiti	1976	7.9
Honduras	1978	15.2
Nicaragua	1978	12.8
Panama	1978	21.9
Uruguay	1970	26.1
Venezuela	1976	15.9

Source: Wilkie and Haber (1983:143).

A further example of the way rapid population growth has undermined efforts to advance educational goals can be seen in the student–teacher ratios of the various Latin American countries in the recent past (see Table 7). In spite of the phenomenal increases in the number of teachers at every level, rapid population growth and massive rural–urban migration have combined to bring ever larger proportions of young people into the school system. The flood of students has resulted in higher or essentially static (and generally very high) student–teacher ratios in 9 (45%) of the 20 republics for the primary grades, in 18 (90%) of them at the secondary level, and in 15 (75%) of them at the university level. Again, it would be soothing to focus on the increases in the numbers of young Latin Americans who are receiving some education today compared to a few decades ago, but the student–teacher ratios provide an approximate index of the probable quality of that education, and from this perspective, the situation is more vexing. Are these young people being prepared to function more effectively and productively in their rapidly changing societies, or are they merely having their expectations unrealistically heightened? If, indeed, their rote-learning experiences in overcrowded classrooms with few facilities, and ill-prepared and overworked instructors, have assured that their competencies are minimal, and the ever fiercer competition for employment throws increasing numbers of them into unrewarding and unremunerative jobs, *pluriempleo* (multiple jobs), or outright unemployment, will not their potential for disruptive social protest be far greater than that of their parents' more docile generation, for whom the advantages of their new urban existence had outweighed the disadvantages?

TABLE 7
Student–Teacher Ratios by Level, Over Time[a]

Country	Primary	Secondary	University
	Educational Level		
Argentina	22.0	7.4	20.2
	18.5 1977	7.5 1978	11.3 1978
Bolivia	28.6	7.0	7.2
	22.7 1975	18.2 1975	7.3 1965
Brazil	37.0	2.8	4.4
	18.2 1977	14.5 1977	11.7
Chile	56.1 1965	8.6	4.1
	33.7 1979	19.7 1979	13.1 1975
Colombia	37.6	11.4	4.8
	31.1 1979	21.9 1979	10.7 1978
Costa Rica	26.0	16.8	10.7
	26.7 1979	18.3 1979	11.7 1978
Cuba	38.0	17.7	10.7
	20.2 1979	14.3 1976	11.7 1978
Dominican Republic	57.7	12.3	23.8
	24.5 1975	24.5 1975	15.9 1965
Ecuador	37.1	11.3	8.2
	35.9 1979	17.0 1979	22.0 1978
El Salvador	39.1	7.0	4.8
	48.1 1975	18.0 1975	12.5 1978
Guatemala	28.5	7.5	11.1
	34.7 1979	18.6 1979	12.1 1978
Haiti	42.9	12.7	6.0
	41.3 1973	17.5 1975	8.5 1978
Honduras	31.8	9.9	16.1 1974
	40.8 1979	16.6 1975	15.6 1978
Mexico	44.0	13.1	7.8 1965
	40.4 1979	17.1 1979	12.1 1978
Nicaragua	35.3	12.6	7.7 1965
	35.1 1979	32.2 1979	15.5 1970
Panama	28.5	22.9	28.0
	24.8 1979	27.5 1979	14.2 1978
Paraguay	28.2	7.6	7.2
	27.7 1974	11.6 1977	11.3 1977
Peru	33.6	7.6	9.9
	14.2 1978	31.0 1978	17.3 1977
Uruguay	32.9	12.6	6.6 1974
	23.8 1979	11.8 1975	12.1 1977
Venezuela	35.2	6.5	8.6
	28.9 1978	16.6 1978	12.0 1978

[a] Data are for 1960 unless indicated otherwise.
Source: Economic Commission for Latin America (1983b:698–709).

LATIN AMERICA'S CAPITAL-GENERATING CAPACITY

Much of the foregoing scenario could perhaps be short-circuited were remunerative employment available, but with combined unemployment and underemployment levels hovering about 40% of the labor force in many Latin American countries, this escape route holds little promise. Moreover, the creation of modern-sector employment of the scale needed to satisfy the growth of the labor force would require huge quantities of capital. Not only is capital scarcity a perennial problem in Latin America, as in most less-developed areas, but the possibilities of generating capital are severely limited by another demographic constraint, the high dependency ratios that rapid population growth has produced.

The dependency ratio is simply the number of dependents in a given population per producer, the former usually taken to be those less than 15 or more than 65 years of age, and the latter those between these ages, that is,

$$\frac{\text{population less than 15 and over 65}}{\text{population between 15 and 65}} \times 100 = \begin{array}{l}\text{number of}\\ \text{dependents per}\\ \text{100 potential}\\ \text{producers}\end{array}$$

The dynamics of population growth dictate that a fast-growing population is also a young population (i.e., one with a low median age or a high percentage below the age of 15). As can be seen in Table 8, which takes only the youthful portion of the dependent age groups into account, the proportion of dependent young people in all the Latin American countries except Argentina, Uruguay, and possibly Chile will be quite high throughout the remainder of the century.

When dependency burdens are high, especially in conditions of widespread unemployment and underemployment, much of what is produced must go for immediate consumption, with little remaining for savings and investment. Thus it becomes impossible to generate the capital that might be creating more employment, a dilemma well described by Harvey Leibenstein's concept of a "low level equilibrium trap."

The situation is exacerbated when, because of skewed distribution of wealth, much of what is produced is exported, and significant proportions of the export earnings are either never repatriated (through false invoicing and the like) or are sent back out of the country. This capital-flight problem, moreover, can only worsen as prospects for stability dim, even though it will itself further contribute to the underlying causes of instability (i.e., less capital available for productive investment → insufficient employment opportunities → greater disaffection with the status quo).

TABLE 8

Total Population and Dependent Children, 1960–2000

Country	1960			1970			2000		
	Total Population (thousands)	*Age 0–14*		*Total Population (thousands)*	*Age 0–14*		*Total Population (thousands)*	*Age 0–14*	
		N (thousands)	%		*N* (thousands)	%		*N* (thousands)	%
Argentina	20,611	6,344	(30.8)	23,748	6,920	(29.1)	32,861	8,266	(25.0)
Bolivia	3,825	1,645	(43.0)	4,931	2,127	(43.1)	10,268	4,162	(40.5)
Brazil	69,797	30,396	(43.6)	93,387	39,844	(42.7)	212,507	79,269	(37.3)
Chile	7,585	2,970	(39.2)	9,369	3,568	(38.1)	15,355	4,348	(28.3)
Colombia	15,416	7,092	(46.0)	20,559	9,610	(46.7)	51,464	18,758	(36.5)
Costa Rica	1,236	588	(47.6)	1,732	790	(45.6)	3,695	1,258	(34.1)
Cuba	6,999	2,483	(35.5)	8,551	3,235	(37.8)	15,267	4,774	(31.3)
Dominican Republic	3,047	1,426	(46.8)	4,062	1,960	(48.3)	11,762	5,226	(44.4)
Ecuador	4,325	1,965	(45.5)	5,962	2,780	(46.6)	14,773	5,833	(39.5)
El Salvador	2,443	1,122	(45.9)	3,434	1,631	(47.5)	8,803	3,635	(41.3)
Guatemala	3,892	1,777	(45.7)	5,356	2,434	(45.4)	12,374	4,899	(39.6)
Haiti	3,623	1,426	(39.4)	4,235	1,763	(41.6)	7,045	2,511	(35.6)
Honduras	1,937	890	(46.0)	2,526	1,164	(46.1)	6,882	2,972	(43.2)
Mexico	36,003	16,433	(45.6)	50,417	23,431	(46.5)	132,244	55,905	(42.3)
Nicaragua	1,406	672	(47.8)	1,831	889	(48.6)	5,154	2,271	(44.1)
Panama	1,061	464	(43.7)	1,434	630	(43.9)	3,230	1,206	(37.3)
Paraguay	1,742	800	(45.9)	2,235	1,028	(46.0)	5,274	2,094	(39.7)
Peru	10,107	4,467	(44.2)	13,339	5,946	(44.6)	30,561	11,917	(39.0)
Uruguay	2,536	715	(28.2)	2,715	780	(28.7)	3,861	941	(24.4)
Venezuela	7,330	3,374	(46.0)	10,275	4,810	(46.8)	23,552	8,451	(35.9)
United States	180,667	56,072	(31.0)	204,880	57,858	(28.2)	264,430	59,693	(22.6)

Source: Wilkie and Haber (1983:83).

Beyond the certainty of continued high, albeit declining, dependency ratios (see Table 9) and the likelihood of increased capital flight, three further aspects of Latin America's economic–financial profile augur ill for the capital-generating capacity of the region between now and the year 2000.

In the first place, as the data displayed in Table 10 make clear, the manyfold increases in petroleum prices of the past decade have forced the 14 Latin American countries that are oil importers to dedicate an ever greater share of their scarce foreign exchange to oil imports, a trend that can only continue as world petroleum reserves are gradually depleted over the next 30 to 50 years.

Second, as can be seen in Table 11, by 1979 6 Latin American countries had dropped behind their 1969–1971 level of per capita food production, and 4 others had only barely managed to maintain that level. Thus, all but 2 (Panama and Peru) of the 15 Latin American countries reported on in the 1983 *Statistical Abstract of Latin America* more than doubled their food

TABLE 9
Population Under 15 Years and 65 Years or Over as a Percentage of Population Age 15–64 Years (Dependency Ratio), by Country, 1950–2000

Country	*1950*	*1960*	*1970*	*1980*	*1990*	*2000*
Argentina	53.2	57.0	57.0	58.2	58.4	55.1
Bolivia	81.9	85.1	85.3	85.5	84.1	78.7
Brazil	81.4	85.8	84.3	81.6	78.0	71.7
Chile	72.9	76.9	75.0	63.6	60.2	53.4
Colombia	89.1	95.9	98.0	89.4	79.2	67.1
Costa Rica	90.8	102.9	95.2	74.7	68.9	62.5
Cuba	69.8	64.9	76.6	73.9	67.8	61.7
Dominican Republic	90.1	98.9	103.8	101.0	96.5	88.7
Ecuador	88.1	92.2	97.0	92.1	83.9	74.9
El Salvador	88.6	96.3	102.4	93.8	89.5	81.2
Guatemala	86.0	94.2	93.5	87.7	83.0	76.4
Haiti	76.3	74.0	85.8	77.8	77.9	68.8
Honduras	89.7	93.8	95.2	99.2	93.2	87.1
Mexico	85.6	96.0	100.0	95.7	92.7	84.2
Nicaragua	89.0	101.4	104.0	101.8	96.0	86.9
Panama	85.0	91.2	91.0	83.8	79.9	72.4
Paraguay	85.6	97.1	97.1	91.5	86.2	76.9
Peru	94.5	92.4	90.7	87.1	80.7	73.8
Uruguay	53.4	55.3	59.8	59.3	57.9	56.6
Venezuela	84.4	94.9	98.9	83.0	78.0	67.6
United States	54.0	67.4	61.5	52.4	55.4	50.3

Source: PAHO (1978:4).

TABLE 10
Latin American Oil-Importing Countries: Imports of Crude Petroleum and Petroleum Products

Country	Millions of Dollars CIF (% of Total Imports CIF)						
	1970	*1973*	*1974*	*1978*	*1979*	*1980*	*1981*
Argentina	59	116	385	247	818	654	496
	(3.5)	(5.2)	(10.5)	(6.4)	(12.2)	(6.2)	(5.4)
Brazil	286	984	3,226	4,631	6,932	10,286	11,470
	(10.0)	(14.1)	(22.8)	(30.8)	(35.0)	(41.2)	(47.6)
Chile	54	69	246	479	889	960	930
	(5.8)	(6.3)	(12.9)	(16.0)	(21.1)	(15.7)	(12.6)
Colombia	9	4	14	206	349	532	620
	(1.1)	(.4)	(.3)	(7.3)	(10.8)	(11.2)	(11.9)
Costa Rica	12	30	63	116	186	199	170
	(3.8)	(6.6)	(8.8)	(9.8)	(12.9)	(13.0)	(14.0)
Dominican Republic	19	48	116	223	322	416	547
	(6.2)	(9.8)	(15.0)	(22.6)	(26.5)	(25.8)	(32.8)
El Salvador	5	21	52	80	95	159	155
	(2.3)	(5.6)	(9.3)	(7.8)	(9.4)	(16.3)	(15.1)
Guatemala	16	30	92	152	234	322	390
	(5.4)	(7.0)	(13.1)	(12.1)	(15.6)	(19.9)	(22.7)
Haiti	3	4	12	26	33	34	58
	(5.6)	(4.8)	(9.6)	(12.2)	(14.0)	(10.1)	(16.0)
Honduras	15	26	63	74	113	170	160
	(6.8)	(9.9)	(16.1)	(10.6)	(13.6)	(16.8)	(17.1)
Nicaragua	12	24	61	89	76	174	202
	(6.1)	(7.3)	(10.9)	(14.9)	(21.4)	(19.6)	(20.4)
Panama	66	89	274	228	334	421	382
	(18.5)	(18.2)	(34.3)	(24.2)	(27.8)	(28.0)	(25.2)
Paraguay	11	13	50	84	125	154	111
	(14.4)	(10.7)	(25.3)	(21.9)	(24.0)	(25.6)	(18.5)
Uruguay	33	48	151	230	282	455	503
	(14.2)	(16.1)	(30.3)	(32.1)	(24.0)	(27.0)	(31.5)

Source: Economic Commission for Latin America (1983a:40).

imports between 1971 and 1978 (Wilkie and Haber, 1983:456–1470). In Mexico, the value of food imports in those years soared by more than 500%, in Venezuela by more than 600%, and in Ecuador by 800%.

Incredible as it may seem in a region of such land area, no Latin American country has as much as 1 hectare (2.47 acres) of arable land per capita. In 12 cases there is already less than an acre per capita (Brazil, Colombia, Costa Rica, Dominican Republic, Ecuador, El Salvador, Guatemala, Haiti, Panama, Paraguay, Peru, Venezuela). Eight of these countries have less than one-half acre per capita (Colombia, Costa Rica, Dominican Republic, Ecuador, El Salvador, Guatemala, Haiti, Peru) (Wilkie and Haber, 1983:46).

TABLE 11
Index of per Capita Food Production, 1979 (1969–1971 = 100)

Country		*Country*	
Argentina	124	Haiti	94
Bolivia	110	Honduras	82
Brazil	109	Mexico	101
Chile	90	Nicaragua	112
Colombia	126	Panama	109
Costa Rica	116	Paraguay	108
Cuba	103	Peru	85
Dominican Republic	92	Uruguay	89
Ecuador	105	Venezuela	100
El Salvador	123	United States	118

Source: Wilkie and Haber (1983:9).

Given the low percentage of arable land in practically every Latin American country, the upward trend in food imports is unlikely to be reversed without a radically different approach to agriculture, land-tenure patterns, exports, and the myriad other aspects of these societies that are bound up in the present way of doing things.

The last of the three additional factors I have singled out as affecting Latin America's capital-generating capacity is the huge proportion of the region's export earnings being siphoned off by debt-servicing requirements (see Table 12), which between 1970 and 1982 soared from a reasonable 13% to an absurd 53% as the total Latin America foreign debt skyrocketed from less than $100 billion to more than $350 billion (World Bank, 1983:20–21).

This excessive burdening of future generations, especially in view of the few benefits they will receive (given the corruption, inefficiency, and poor planning that have accompanied the allocation of these massive influxes of funds), provides still more evidence of the failure of the currently accepted models of development in Latin America. Indeed, the bankruptcy of these unworkable models may well precipitate the bankruptcy of a number of Latin American countries, with untoward consequences for the entire international financial system.

THE QUALITY OF LIFE: THE BOTTOM LINE

Three further salient dimensions of the quality of life in Latin America merit brief discussion: nutrition, health care, and life expectancy.

As Table 13 indicates, in 9 (45%) of the 20 republics the average supply of calories in 1978–1980 was less than the recommended requirement. Appar-

TABLE 12
Debt Service Ratios, 1970–1982, for All Developing Countries (Debt Service Payments as a Ratio of Export Earnings)

Country Group	*1970*	*1982*
All developing countries	13.5	20.7
Low income		
Asia	13.3	10.1
Africa	6.5	28.3
Middle income		
Oil importers	14.0	23.0
East Asia	6.7	8.6
Latin America	13.0	53.2
Oil exporters	13.9	19.1

Source: World Bank (1983:21).

TABLE 13
Protein Consumption and Average Supply of Calories, 1978–1980.

Country	*Protein (average grams per day)*	*Calories (as % of average requirement)*
Argentina	111.9	127.8
Bolivia	52.7	87.3
Brazil	59.3	105.3
Chile	74.0	112.0
Colombia	—	—
Costa Rica	60.3	117.4
Cuba	71.1	117.6
Dominican Republic	46.6	94.4
Ecuador	48.7	91.4
El Salvador	57.6	94.5
Guatemala	55.9	94.2
Haiti	44.5	83.3
Honduras	51.5	96.2
Mexico	72.2	120.3
Nicaragua	64.7	101.5
Panama	55.9	99.1
Paraguay	81.3	125.6
Peru	56.3	92.2
Uruguay	86.8	107.4
Venezuela	70.8	107.2

Source: Economic Commission for Latin America (1983b:91).

ently protein requirements are less firmly established, but if the commonly used amount of 60 gm a day were the standard in Latin America, then average protein consumption in precisely half the countries was substandard at this reporting date. Again, this unsatisfactory nutritional level obtains even though there was some degree of improvement—often a very significant one—in both average daily calorie and protein intake in every Latin American country between 1965 and 1980 (see Table 14). Obviously, had population growth been more gradual during this period, the current deficits in nutrition would probably have long since been erased.

Table 15 records the number of people per hospital bed in 20 Latin American countries in recent decades, an important index of the level of health care available. In the more recent measurements, the number is larger in 11 (55%) of these countries and essentially unchanged in 1 other.

Another key indicator of the adequacy of health care, the number of physicians per 10,000 inhabitants (see Table 16), gradually inched upward in most of the 20 republics during 1950–1970, although in El Salvador, Nicaragua, Paraguay, and Uruguay the figure hardly changed, and in the Domini-

TABLE 14
Daily Caloric Intake and Protein Consumption, Percent Change, 1965–1980

Country	*Caloric Intake*	*Protein Consumption*
Argentina	7.0	11.2
Bolivia	22.6	23.3
Brazil	7.5	7.2
Chile	5.2	8.1
Colombia	.6	9.0
Costa Rica	11.2	17.1
Cuba	3.6	5.1
Dominican Republic	10.9	12.5
Ecuador	9.0	9.6
El Salvador	6.7	2.2
Guatemala	9.9	10.6
Haiti	.1	.4
Honduras	14.1	18.1
Mexico	2.9	1.4
Nicaragua	7.7	6.8
Panama	14.8	17.6
Paraguay	3.8	5.1
Peru	7.7	10.9
Uruguay	4.2	4.0

Source: Wilkie and Haber (1983b:7–8).

TABLE 15
Population per Hospital Bed, 1950–1970

Country	*1950*	*1960*	*1970*
Argentina	153	—	179
Bolivia	—	619	491
Brazil	320	—	262
Chile	97	—	102
Colombia	—	355	446
Costa Rica	198	—	254
Cuba	—	224	213
Dominican Republic	295	—	230
Ecuador	—	509	434
El Salvador	465	—	516
Guatemala	438	—	456
Haiti	1616	—	1374
Honduras	619	—	568
Mexico	1114	—	812
Nicaragua	411	—	409
Panama	245	—	319
Paraguay	—	398	624
Peru	502	—	474
Uruguay	162	—	176
Venezuela	276	—	316

Source: World Health Organization (1983:590).

can Republic it actually declined (I find it difficult to believe it declined in Cuba, as WHO data indicate).

Although not discernible from these data, the skewness of the distribution of physicians presents an even more serious problem for Latin American health-care coverage than does the inadequate number of physicians per 10,000 inhabitants. For entirely understandable reasons, the vast majority of Latin American physicians are concentrated in the region's major cities. For most of these doctors, living conditions for their families and especially education opportunities for their children, as well as adequate equipment and facilities for their work, are too lacking in the smaller provincial cities and towns for them to consider practicing there. Moreover, only a relatively small proportion of the patients they would have in these areas could afford to pay standard fees for their services. Thus, whereas the number of physicians per 10,000 inhabitants may be creeping upward in many Latin American countries, this does not translate into improved health-care services for the rural and small-town sectors of these societies. This reconfirms the inappropriateness of current market-oriented development models and provides a stinging indictment of the way Latin American governments have consistently favored their capitals and major cities at the expense of their hinterlands.

TABLE 16
Number of Physicians per 10,000 Inhabitants, 1950–1970

Argentina	11.7	18.9
Bolivia	2.4	4.4
Brazil	3.7	5.1
Chile	3.6	5.0
Colombia	3.1	4.6
Costa Rica	2.9	6.1
Cuba	9.7	8.7
Dominican Republic	1.9	1.6
Ecuador	2.6	3.4
El Salvador	2.0	2.5
Guatemala	3.2	5.2
Haiti	.9	.8
Honduras	1.6	2.7
Mexico	4.5	6.9
Nicaragua	4.1	4.9
Panama	2.9	6.5
Paraguay	3.6	4.3
Peru	2.4	5.2
Uruguay	10.0	10.6
Venezuela	4.4	9.1
United States	13.3	15.8

Source: World Health Organization (1983:482).

If a single statistic has to be selected as an index of development, with all the shortcomings inherent in such a reductionist approach, perhaps the most valid would be life expectancy at birth, for the average length of people's lives reflects the conditions under which they live and work, their nutrition, the medical care available to them, and all the other dimensions of their physical existence. This summary statistic has shown steady improvement over the years in Latin America, in large part for the same reason the region is undergoing a population explosion, namely, the success achieved, primarily through public health and sanitation measures, in reducing mortality. The major reductions in mortality rates have now been made, however, and consequently life expectancies will no longer show such dramatic increases. As can be seen in Table 17, Peru has actually suffered some erosion in life expectancy at birth in recent years.

Having years added to one's probable life span is by no means to be dismissed as of minor importance. Yet is there not more to life, particularly human life, then mere survival? What of the opportunities for personally satisfying work, for realizing one's human potential by expanding one's creative abilities and aesthetic sensitivities, and for deepening one's under-

TABLE 17
Life Expectancy, 1965–1970 and 1975–1980

Country	*1965–1970*	*1975–1980*
Argentina	68.1	69.4
Bolivia	45.5	48.6
Brazil	61.3	63.4
Chile	61.3	65.7
Colombia	57.9	61.0
Costa Rica	66.4	70.0
Cuba	66.8	—
Dominican Republic	52.0	55.4
Ecuador	57.7	—
El Salvador	55.4	59.0
Guatemala	51.9	57.8
Haiti	44.7	52.2
Honduras	48.3	55.5
Mexico	62.3	65.0
Nicaragua	50.3	55.2
Panama	63.3	69.1
Paraguay	60.7	65.1
Peru	58.0	57.2
Uruguay	69.4	72.0
Venezuela	64.0	66.4

Sources: For 1965–1970: Wilkie and Haber (1983:6). For 1975–1980: Economic Commission Latin America (1974).

standing and appreciation of the human past, the nature of the universe, and the enigmas and paradoxes of human existence? These personal growth dimensions of the quality of life are even more elusive of measurement than the elements we have been dealing with, but in my view they are of supreme relevance in any completely specified concept of development. Whereas few even among the affluent nations have made great strides in these areas for significant proportions of their populations, it is obvious that their very pursuit, as with Abraham Maslow's hierarchy of individual needs (Maslow, 1962), depends on adequate satisfaction of such prior necessities as food, clothing, housing, health care, and basic education. It is with supplying these basic prerequisites of survival that the development process has been primarily concerned and, by association, identified. What we have heretofore thought of as development, however, might better be understood as merely the first stage of a process. The project in its entirety consists of three stages: the initial one of laying the basis by providing for the general well-being of the population, the intermediate one of creating cultural and political mechanisms that will permit human groups to maintain themselves in harmony with the natural systems that sustain them (water purity, soil fertility, etc.), and ultimately the one that will actively promote and facilitate the sort of personal growth and fulfilment just alluded to. Obviously some people in any society will be in a position to pursue their personal growth, but I am referring here to the central thrust of social purpose around which a political system orients itself.

THE PREREQUISITES OF POPULATION GROWTH REDUCTION

For reasons I trust the foregoing pages have made clear, reducing rapid population growth is an essential element of the first stage of development. Zero population growth is equally intrinsic to the second stage, for, regardless of new scientific breakthroughs and technological advances, infinite growth of either population or material goods (much less both) in a system with finite capacities for reprocessing or absorbing wastes (heat, CO_2, ozone-destroying gases, toxic chemicals, etc.) is impossible (Daly 1977, 1980). So if the third and culminating, albeit unending, stage of development is to be reached, the sooner the planet's population growth is halted the better, for there is much else to be done.

As I and many others have spent good portions of our careers pointing out, however, effective programs of population growth limitation in Third World countries cannot be implemented on either a coercive or an exclusively family planning basis. Not even a medical model focusing on reducing infant mortality rates and providing maternal and child health assistance will suffice, although it is a very good way to begin. What many still need to recognize is that despite all the emotion, prejudice, cultural conditioning, and misinformation that unquestionably are involved in procreation among the world's poor, rationality is present as well. The people whose reproductive behavior is largely propelling the population explosion are primarily people submerged in poverty and ignorance, the product of exploitation and injustice; people who never know whether they will find work or, if they do, whether it will pay a living wage; people without access to decent health care or any kind of disability insurance or social security; people with no one else to rely on beyond their own extended family. These are people for whom it is entirely rational to have as many children as possible in the hope that several will survive to take care of their parents when they can no longer fend for themselves. Until the injustice and exploitation that characterize the political economies of Latin America cease and the poverty and ignorance and radical insecurity of the masses are eradicated, it will continue to be rational for these couples to have large families. Only when the unjust, exploitative, and repressive structures of Latin American societies are fundamentally altered in the direction of greater fairness in the distribution of social services, wealth, and opportunity can family planning programs be expected to bring population growth down to replacement level. Certainly such programs can help get the process started even in the absence of the necessary structural changes, as indeed they already are doing in many countries, for there is a large demand for access to contraception and sterilization on the part of millions of Latin American women who have already had the four to six children they wanted or did not know how to prevent. Many of these women are desperately concerned not to continue childbearing, as the very high abortion rates all over Latin America attest. Yet for enough couples to wish to limit their family size to only one or two children, sweeping structural changes are needed, not merely more family planning clinics.

THE WAY OUT OF THE MAZE

At this point in the analysis, pessimism threatens to take over, for structural changes of the magnitude required and in the time available (given the shortness of doubling times of most Latin American countries' populations) seem unlikely, especially in a region that has displayed such extraordinary continuity in its basic structural–institutional arrangements and culture over so many centuries (Mander, 1969; Morse, 1964; Veliz, 1965, 1967).

The outlook for the future, therefore, can only be described as impropitious. Even as fertility rates decline, the demographic momentum inherent in young populations will continue to assure high levels of population growth for many decades into the next century. The size of current populations means that the absolute numbers being added each year will be staggering, thus straining the resources, both natural and human, that must respond to them. Much of the margin for error (natural catastrophes, misallocations, planning fiascoes, etc.) and for adaptation has already been used up. It is difficult to imagine how megalopoli such as Mexico City, São Paulo, and Lima can continue to provide the basic services that make these crowded settings livable. Or are Latin American Calcuttas conceivable?

Alarming levels of street crime and vandalism have already become commonplace in many Latin American capitals, where such things were practically unknown a decade or two ago. As recent food riots in Brazil presage, the prospect of anomic violence on the part of desperate people with all too little to lose seems increasingly likely. The ever greater polarization of political groupings along class lines appears inevitable, as does the emergence of more fanatical and ultraviolent fringe groups such as Sendero Luminoso in Peru. More insidious and difficult to substantiate but nonetheless destructive are the alienation and *sálvase quien pueda* attitudes that increasingly pit each in a war against all.

As the defenders of the status quo increase their reliance on repression to combat the unraveling of social order, greater and greater numbers of disaffected citizens will shift their sympathies to those who are actively challenging the legitimacy of systems that are palpably incapable of—and uninterested in—creating minimal conditions for life, liberty, and the pursuit of happiness.

Perhaps the only antidote to the paralysis of pessimism prompted by such a dismal scenario is idealism. Yet, paradoxically, the utter bleakness of the outlook under business-as-usual assumptions is perhaps a source of justifiable hope. Just as an impossibility theorem in mathematics helps redirect efforts to solve a problem away from fruitless approaches, so a clearer vision of the inadequacy of past and present approaches to development might lead us toward more viable models of how to provide the basic needs for people long trapped in poverty and exploitation.

Seeing development as the three-stage process I have described is perhaps of some help in this regard. If we recall that "the perfect is the enemy of the good," we may better recognize that, by expecting too much of what is, in fact, only the initial stage of development, we have engendered unrealistic expectations that, in turn, have spawned the pessimism that now assails us. By generalizing the Western experience of Renaissance–Reformation–New World–Enlightenment–Industrial Revolution–Consumer Society into a universal theory of automatic progress through growth, we have overlooked the myriad unique and nonrepeatable conditions within which that experience occurred, not least of which were low rates of population growth and an unparalleled abundance of land and other resources.

If, on the other hand, we posit as the goal of the first stage of development the satisfaction of the basic needs of all the people rather than the creation of a full-blown consumer society such as ours, or levels of individual freedom similar to those we have come to enjoy, perhaps the goal would not be so unachievable (for instance, through a greater degree of centralized planning and organization and the adoption of a labor-intensive rural development approach focused initially on food production and rural infrastructure construction). Once we recognize that development is actually an evolving, open-ended process—one in which we ourselves have hardly completed the initial stage—perhaps we could focus our efforts domestically in a more concerted way on the emerging challenges of stages two and three as well as on assisting those less fortunate than we in their timing and resource base in meeting the challenges of stage one.

For this to occur, it is imperative that "charity begin at home." The obstacles to development in Latin America are not all to be found south of the border. We must recognize that the tragically limited and mistaken vision that currently guides our nation's role in the world compel us to support the opponents of needed changes in Latin America while threatening catastrophe on a global scale. Only through a more thorough understanding of all that is implied by the concept of development and through a deeper commitment to marshalling our resources more intelligently and compassionately in furtherance of the process can we begin to arrest and reverse the disintegration of our own society and prevent the decline of world order. If we cannot do these things, all efforts to assure our national security are but self-deluding exercises in the irrelevant.

CONCLUSION

At the aggregate level, a wide variety of indicators point to a fairly steady and, over time, substantial improvement in the quality of life for Latin Americans. Others have shown in specific contexts how misleading such aggregate figures can be because of the extremely skewed distribution patterns prevalent throughout Latin America (Durham, 1979:172–173). The data analyzed in this chapter demonstrate the significant degree to which rapid population growth and its demographic concomitants have diluted the often extraordinary advances that otherwise might have been translated into pronounced improvements in the quality of life of the average citizen of the region. Despite the positive values that have been registered in many categories of socioeconomic progress, therefore, the benefits of this progress have seldom trickled down to the worst-off 70% of Latin Americans.

Although fertility levels are edging downward in many Latin American countries, demographic inertia will continue to produce high growth rates and young populations in the region for many decades to come. Moreover, the size of Latin America's population after decades of rapid growth assures that the annual additions in coming decades will be large in terms of absolute numbers, thus continuing to complicate the development process in the various ways the present analysis revealed for 1960–1980.

Given the unjust and exploitative structures of Latin American societies, the deeply entrenched cultural values and institutions that sustain these structures, and the support the United States lavishes on the defenders of the status quo in the region, there does not seem to be great likelihood of the sort of radical and sweeping changes necessary to bring about significant betterment of the life chances and living conditions of the majority of Latin Americans. The outlook, therefore, is for spreading outbreaks of social unrest, spiraling levels of official repression, and increasing organized opposition, much of it violent, to the existing systems.

The only glimmer of hope lies paradoxically in the very grimness of this probable scenario coupled with the even grimmer prospects attendant on a continuation of the outmoded vision that guides and defines the U.S. role in world affairs (bastion of anticommunism, champion of the "free world," evangelist of free enterprise, crusader for consumerism, and defender of stability). If thermonuclear Armageddon or fascistic national security states in a global setting of biological, chemical, and nuclear terrorism are to be averted, a bold new vision of development must be kindled, a positive vision of such universality and power that it cuts through the cynicism of individuals and the shortsightedness of nations, enabling both to find renewal and unsuspected reservoirs of energy and imagination in its pursuit.

ACKNOWLEDGMENT

I am grateful to the Stanford–Berkeley Joint Center for Latin American Studies for the grant that made possible the writing of this paper.

REFERENCES

Adelman, Irma and Cynthia Taft Morris
1973 *Economic Growth and Social Equity in Developing Countries.* Stanford: Stanford University Press.

Daly, Herman E.
1977 *Steady-State Economics: The Economics of Biophysical Equilibrium and Moral Growth.* San Francisco: Freeman.
1980 *Economics, Ecology, Ethics: Essays toward a Steady-State Economy.* San Francisco: Freeman.

Durham, William H.
1979 *Scarcity and Survival in Central America: Ecological Origins of the Soccer War.* Stanford: Stanford University Press.

Economic Commission for Latin America (ECLA)
1974 *Statistical Yearbook for Latin America 1973.* Santiago.
1983a *Economic Survey of Latin America 1981.* Santiago.
1983b *Statistical Yearbook for Latin America 1981.* Santiago.

Felix, David
1983 "Income distribution and the quality of life in Latin America: Patterns, trends and policy implications." *Latin American Research Review 18*(2):3–11.

Kuznets, Simon
1955 "Economic growth and income inequality." *American Economic Review 45*:1–28.

Leibenstein, Harvey
1954 *A Theory of Economic–Demographic Development.* Princeton: Princeton University Press.

Mander, John
1969 *The Unrevolutionary Society: The Power of Latin American Conservatism in a Changing World.* New York: Knopf.

Maslow, Abraham
1962 *Toward a Psychology of Being.* Princeton: Van Nostrand.

Morse, Richard M.
1964 "The heritage of Latin America." Pp. 123–177 in Louis Hartz (ed.), *The Founding of New Societies*. New York: Harcourt, Brace, and World.

Myrdal, Gunnar
1957 *Economic Theory and Underdeveloped Regions*. London: Duckworth.

Panamerican Health Organization (PAHO)
1978 *Health Conditions in the Americas 1973–1976*. Washington, D.C.

United Nations Educational, Scientific, and Cultural Organization (UNESCO)
1977 *Statistics of Educational Attainment and Illiteracy 1945–1977*. Paris

Veliz, Claudio
1965 *Obstacles to Change in Latin America*. New York: Oxford University Press.
1967 *The Politics of Conformity in Latin America*. London: Royal Institute of International Affairs.

Wilkie, James W. and Stephen Haber
1983 *Statistical Abstract of Latin America*. Vol. 22. Los Angeles: UCLA Latin American Center Publications.

World Bank
1983 *World Development Report 1983*. Washington, D.C.

World Health Organization (WHO)
1983 *World Health Statistics 1983*. Geneva.

III

SECURITY DIMENSIONS

8

Population, Internal Unrest, and U.S. Security in Latin America

HOWARD J. WIARDA and IÊDA SIQUEIRA WIARDA

Population policy is a very controversial subject in the United States, and we are currently going through another one of those periodic, highly emotional, and deeply divisive debates about it that has raged over the past 25 years. Population policy is controversial not just because it relates closely to the abortion debate—about which feelings are very strong and politicians of all stripes would just as soon not tackle—but because it touches on deeply felt personal, ideological, and social science belief systems. It is also a political issue, not necessarily or always a moral or a technical one—a fact that is sometimes lost on population policy advocates.

Population policy has perhaps more "true believers"—that is, persons deeply committed to it to the extent of internalizing a whole way of thinking that has become something of a belief system and an ideology—than any other foreign public policy area. The population policy "true believers" think that once the demographic "facts" are presented, any right-thinking person will come to the same conclusions regarding the need for population policy; they are often bewildered, dumbfounded, and angered when politicians and others fail to draw same conclusions or see them in a different rank ordering of priorities. There are far more "true believers" in population policy, for example, than in agrarian reform, infrastructure growth, community development, basic human needs, or any of the other developmental panaceas that have been offered to the Third World in the last quarter-century. Perhaps that has something to do with dramatic book titles that command our attention, such as the *The Population Bomb*,[1] perhaps with the way statistics are high-

[1]Paul Ehrlich, *The Population Bomb* (New York: Ballantine, 1968).

lighted relating population growth to per capita income, perhaps with the universalist notions that are so often assumed in the fields of demography and sociology, perhaps with our own sense of urban blight and cramped space and the projection of these to other nations, perhaps even with the character and closely inbred nature of the population policy "establishment." Whatever the precise causes, the "true believer" syndrome is strongly present among population policy advocates.

The opposition has often been equally vehement, emotional, and ideological, condemning family planning and population-control programs in the harshest of terms. One suspects that the extremism of the one side plays on and reinforces the extremism on the other. Surely in all the heat and controversy that has been generated, there must be a middle ground, room for a prudent and realistic population policy program. That is at least the assumption on which the present discussion proceeds.

BACKGROUND: THE PROBLEM AND THE DEBATE

The Problem: Demographic Trends

Current demographic projections for the Western Hemisphere indicate that if the present population growth rates remain unchanged, the population of the Western Hemisphere will have increased by 42% between 1981 and 2001.[2] Translated into numbers of people, that means an increase of 263 million. Of this total, using current rates of increase, the United States and Canada will see an increase of 38 million by 2001, while the increase in Latin

[2]John V. D. Saunders, "Population Growth in Latin America—United States National Security" (Conference Proposal, Center for International Security and Strategic Studies, Mississippi State University, 1984; mimeographed. See also U.S. Department of Commerce, Bureau of the Census, *Illustrative Projections of World Populations to the Twenty-first Century* (Washington, D.C.: U.S. Bureau of the Census, 1979).

It should be noted that in the so-called middle-income countries of Latin America, birthrates have fallen more than death rates, which has slowed the rate of population growth somewhat. In Brazil, Mexico, Colombia, and Cuba the rate declines have been noticeable (from more than 2.5% to around or below 2% growth rate per year). Venezuela, probably the richest country per capita, has gone from a 5.8% growth between 1975 and 1980 to an estimated 3.3% growth for 1980–1981. The poorer countries, such as El Salvador, Guatemala, Honduras, and Nicaragua, still show growth rates of close to, or greater than, 3% per year. In Bolivia and Peru the growth rate is still 2.5%. The consequence is that, *overall*, the growth rate for Latin America is still above 2.5% and shows no sign of changing greatly in the short term— although there are considerable variations between countries. U.S. Department of Commerce, Bureau of the Census, *Demographic Estimates for Countries with a Population of Ten Million or More: 1981* (Washington, D.C.: U.S. Bureau of the Census, 1981).

America will be 225 million—six times larger. The most dramatic population increases during this period are projected in Mexico and Central America, the countries most proximate to the United States, the sources of most of the illegal migration to the United States, and the countries in the region currently of most concern to U.S. foreign policy. Put back into percentage increases, these figures indicate that while the U.S. population will increase by only 15% by the end of the century, that of Latin America will increase by over 60%. Table 1 shows these changes graphically.

By 2001 the population of Latin America will be approximately twice that of North America. Brazil will have a population of close to 200 million by the turn of the century, and Mexico will grow to 113 million—a population almost half that of the United States but on only one-fifth the national territory of the United States. The population of the Central American countries will be similarly burgeoning. Meanwhile, as Table 2 indicates, the relative percentage of the U.S. population globally, particularly with regard to Latin America, will have declined dramatically. By the year 2000, the U.S. population will be only 4.4% of the world's population, down from 5.3% in

TABLE 1
World Population and Average Annual Rates of Growth by Continent: 1950–2000

	Midyear Population (in millions)[a]								
Region	*1950*	*1960*	*1970*	*1975*	*1980*	*1985*	*1990*	*1995*	*2000*
World	2549	3035	3703	4082	4451	4845	5258	5702	6152
Africa	222	278	358	409	472	548	636	738	850
Asia	1410	1685	2111	2361	2591	2833	3081	3351	3620
Latin America	166	218	286	324	363	407	455	505	557
Northern America	166	199	226	239	252	264	277	287	297
Europe and Soviet Union	572	640	703	728	750	770	788	803	815
Oceania	12	16	19	21	23	24	26	28	30

	Average Annual Rate of Growth (percent)							
Region	*1950–1960*	*1960–1970*	*1970–1975*	*1975–1980*	*1980–1985*	*1985–1990*	*1990–1995*	*1995–2000*
World	1.7	2.0	1.9	1.7	1.7	1.6	1.6	1.5
Africa	2.2	2.5	2.7	2.9	3.0	3.0	3.0	2.8
Asia	1.8	2.3	2.2	1.9	1.8	1.7	1.7	1.5
Latin America	2.7	2.7	2.5	2.3	2.3	2.3	2.1	2.0
Northern America	1.8	1.3	1.1	1.1	1.0	.9	.8	.6
Europe and Soviet Union	1.1	.9	.7	.6	.5	.5	.4	.3
Oceania	2.3	2.1	1.9	1.3	1.5	1.4	1.3	1.2

[a] May not add to totals due to rounding.
Source: U.S. Department of Commerce (1984:2).

TABLE 2
Demographic Projections, 1950–2025: Relative Population Shares for Selected Countries and Regions in the World (in percent)

Country or Region	*1950*	*1975*	*2000*	*2025*
China	26.8	22.9	20.5	17.9
India	14.0	15.2	15.7	14.6
Africa	8.9	10.1	14.3	20.1
Latin America	6.6	7.9	9.0	9.6
Europe	15.6	11.6	8.4	6.4
USSR	7.2	6.2	5.1	4.5
United States	6.1	5.3	4.4	3.8
Rest of World	14.8	20.8	22.6	23.1
Total	100.0	100.0	100.0	100.0

Source: United Nations (1983).

1975 and from 6.1% in 1960. By 2025 the U.S. share will be only 3.8%. Meanwhile, Latin America's share will have increased from 6.6% in 1950 to 7.9% in 1975 to 9.0% in 2000 and 9.6% in 2025. At the same time, food output in Latin America has been going down.

Based on these kinds of projections, it can be surmised that population growth in Latin America will have serious political, economic, social, strategic, and other implications not just for that area but also for the United States. For example, the workforce in Latin America will double and in some countries triple without there being the remotest prospect that local industries or agriculture will produce the jobs to absorb the surplus manpower. Unemployment and underemployment, already severe throughout the hemisphere, will increase. Agricultural production will not be able to meet the food needs of the population. Pressures on utilities and basic services, especially in the area's mushrooming cities, which are almost unmanageable already, will dramatically increase. Pressures to emigrate will be immense in Central America, particularly toward the United States. Social unrest will surely grow. The level of tension, violence, and conflict will increase. Social and political systems are very likely to unravel under these pressures, and revolution and increased international conflict will result. All these prospective changes carry profound implications for the United States and for U.S. foreign policy.

U.S. Attitudes and Policy

Attitudes and policy in the United States with regard to Latin America's population increase have gone through various ups and downs since the

1960s. We began that decade with John F. Kennedy's Alliance for Progress. Almost no attention was paid in that program, or at any time earlier, to the dramatic increases in Latin America's population or to the implications of this for U.S. policy. By the mid to late 1960s, under Lyndon Johnson and with Robert McNamara's influence, the population problem in Latin America was being viewed in "crisis" terms. That perspective and orientation carried over into the 1970s, although the emphasis and commitment under the Nixon, Ford, and Carter administration was not quite so strong. And other concerns—basic human needs, human rights—were supplanting population control as new panaceas and preoccupations.[3]

Today we have returned, at least at the rhetorical level, almost to the posture of the 1950s. That is, Latin America is frequently viewed in the United States as still having vast empty spaces and as requiring larger internal markets for future economic growth. A larger population is seen as a plus not a negative, for economic development.[4] We are dealing with the population problem in Latin America by denying it exists; indeed, population growth is frequently viewed as advantageous rather than deleterious. The population "problem" in Latin America has thus been defined in almost exclusively economic terms. Practically no attention is being paid to the social, political, and strategic implications of unchecked population growth. Furthermore, almost no consideration is being given in the United States to Latin American ideas about population policy, which as we shall see have changed rather dramatically since the 1960s.[5]

The political climate in the United States and hence in Washington with regard to population policy has undergone a significant transformation. Few politicians at present want anything to do with population policy—and certainly not as sponsors of new bills dealing with the issue—because of the costs that will accrue electorally. The pro-life movement is stronger and more aggressive than it was before; the political tides in this country are running conservative, and the time does not seem to be propitious for new thrusts in the direction of larger and innovative programs. Yet, population policy goes on. In a subsequent section we shall have more to say on these themes.

Latin American Perspectives

Attitudes and the political winds in Latin America regarding population policy have followed an opposite trajectory. That is, in the 1960s the opposi-

[3]One of the best sources for the early history of U.S. involvement remains Phyllis T. Piotrow, *World Population Crisis: The United States Response* (New York: Praeger, 1973).

[4]Julian L. Simon, *The Ultimate Resource* (Princeton: Princeton University Press, 1981); Simon, *The Economies of Population Growth* (Princeton: Princeton University Press, 1977).

[5]J. Mayone Stycos, *Human Fertility in Latin America: Sociological Perspectives* (Ithaca, N.Y.: Cornell University Press, 1968).

tion to family planning was strong principally from nationalists, the military, the Church, the right, and the left.[6] Today, much of Latin America has gravitated to a position not unlike that of the United States in the 1960s, of support for family planning programs but with several modifications.

First, too-rapid population growth is now widely viewed in Latin America as aggravating the problems of development and putting severe strains on services and facilities: housing, land, health care, water resources, social services, and the political system. Second, all the surveys we have on Latin America show a growing preference for smaller families. This is especially true in the cities, where "more hands in the field" is not a compelling argument and where a point of diminishing returns has been reached in terms of numbers of children desired. The wish to limit family size is particularly strong among women. Third, both civilian and military elites in Latin America have come to the conclusion that unchecked population growth and hence an uneducated, alienated, unemployed "mass" in the area's capital cities spell disaster in the long run for the society and nation, and, likely, chaos in the short run in the form of food riots, mass protests, and general discontent that may produce the destabilization of the government in power at the moment.[7]

In general, the following may be said about developments in the population policy area in Latin America over the past 20 years: First, most countries of the area now have, more or less, an official statement that family planning should be available but that it should be voluntary. Second, most of the activities in the family planning area in Latin America are still carried out by private agencies, or by private groups now operating in and through public agencies. Third, in several countries, such as Colombia or Mexico, the government has become active in family planning, providing not just an official statement of support but also information and services. Colombia, known as "the most Catholic country in Latin America," not only has major research and training activities but a quite extensive program (albeit "nonofficial" and privately financed) for abortion services. Fourth, a few countries, such as Chile, have actually "regressed" in terms of family planning programs, going from a situation of well-run and extensive services before 1973 to a present situation of official denouncement by the regime of Augusto-Pinochet. Despite various *pronunciamientos* concerning family planning, other countries—for example, Bolivia—have changed little over 20 years.

[6]Ibid.; see also the essays on these groups in Terry McCoy, ed., *The Dynamics of Population Policy in Latin America* (Cambridge, Mass.: Ballinger, 1974).

[7]David K. Willis, "World Population," *Christian Science Monitor*, August 6–13, 1984; Bart McDowell and S. Maze, "Mexico City: An Alarming Giant," and Robert Fox, "The Urban Explosion," *National Geographic*, August 1984, pp. 138–186.

Fifth and overall, even in countries where an official statement has been made in favor of family planning and some limited services are available, family planning is not a major national priority. It ranks way down on the list and therefore seldom receives concerted governmental attention.[8]

Most Latin American groups remain divided on the population issue, but there has been change over time. The *military* in most countries has gone from a pronatalist position to one of concern for the "burden" of unchecked population growth and the instability that may result. The *Roman Catholic Church* is very divided on the issue. Many clerics are liberal on economic issues but quite conservative on family planning, although some priests and nuns have been supportive. Actually, what the Church says about the issue does not matter all that much because the demand to control family size is so great and most Latin Americans will decide to do what they have to do regardless of what the Church says. The Church's position has prevented some governments from doing more in an official way, and some already weak governments have decided they could do without a fight with another potential opposition force and hence have avoided the issue. But, by and large, the church has not been as vocal as might be expected on this issue, and some clever governments have learned they can go forward with family planning as long as they do not make a public issue out of it that needlessly antagonizes the Church.[9]

Leftist groups have been deeply divided. The Marxist argument is that the problem lies in the distribution of resources, not population; or in the notion—largely accepted, ironically, by the United States two decades ago—that larger numbers of starving babies and unemployed young people serve to fuel revolutionary fires later. But sometimes female Marxists see their male counterparts as excessively *macho* and complain that this is the real reason why their comrades are against family planning. The *traditional right* in Latin America has in the past been opposed to family planning programs but, like the military, has come to see the explosive and revolutionary potential of unchecked growth. Latin American *intellectuals* are divided on the issue, as are most *women's groups*, though the latter tend to argue that family planning services should be available as an option and that population is as much

[8]The best source on these changes for a number of years were the annual *Factbooks* written by Dorothy Nortman for the Population Council. The earlier positions of Latin American governments (up to 1970) are summarized by Vivian X. Epstein, "The Politics of Population in Latin America," in *Population Policies and Growth in Latin America*, ed. David Chaplin (Lexington, Mass.: Lexington Books, 1971), Chap 7.

[9]Howard J. Wiarda, "The Politics of Population Policy in the Dominican Republic: Public Policy and The Political Process," in McCoy, ed., *Dynamics*, Chap. 13. See also Pranay Gupte, *The Crowded Earth* (New York: Norton, 1984).

a woman's *personal* problem as any other.[10] A number of the private *family planning organizations* in Latin America have been discredited for providing insufficient medical back-up and inadequate health-care coverage, as well as for engaging in some questionable practices; *but* in many Latin American countries they are the only organizations providing family planning services.

Overall, deep divisions remain in Latin America over population policy, although the clear trend is toward greater acceptance of the need for voluntary family planning services closely attuned to the particular needs of individual countries. Moreover, the divisions are not always what one might expect. Some priests have been very active and vocal in supporting or calling for family planning services. The military in most countries has not been overly concerned with the issue except as its officers have come to understand the effects of unchecked population growth on internal security and stability. Women have tended to look at it in terms of *family* and personal health and the number of mouths to feed or hands to work—and not so much as a national issue. There are, in short, different perceptions by different groups in Latin America as well as distinct understandings of what the "population problem" is from country to country.[11]

POPULATION AND INTERNAL UNREST IN LATIN AMERICA

Our concern in this chapter is chiefly with the largely unexplored area of population and internal unrest in Latin America, and the implications of this for U.S. foreign policy. We concede the importance of other issues—the impact of population on family size, for example, or on economic growth, or the rights of families and mothers to choose. But our focus is the strategic and policy implications of unchecked population growth. In this exercise some of the issues noted in the preceding sentence will have relevance but only as they pertain to the internal unrest and security areas.

In focusing on population and internal unrest in Latin America we shall be treating the following topics: the relation between size, crowding, and internal tension; the changing age profile of Latin America and whether younger means more radical; the pressures on land and agriculture brought on by

[10]Iêda Siqueira Wiarda and Judith F. Helzner, *Women, Population and International Development in Latin America* (Amherst, Mass.: International Studies Program, University of Massachusetts, 1981).

[11]Iêda Siqueira Wiarda, "Approaches and Strategies of Population Policy-Making in a Democratic Context: The Case of Venezuela," in McCoy, ed., *Dynamics*, Chap. 14; Benjamin Viel, *The Demographic Explosion: The Latin American Experience* (New York: Irvington, 1976); Aaron L. Segal, ed., *Population Policy in the Caribbean* (Lexington, Mass.: Lexington Books, 1975).

increased population growth; the effects of urbanization and immigration and of cities that have grown beyond the size of livability or governability; the prospects for increased emigration and spiraling refugee problems; the prospects for economic growth or, alternatively, contraction and negative growth; rising social tensions, riots, and revolutionary activities; the unraveling of political systems; and, finally, war, both civil and international. The combined impact of these forces, we think, oblige us to consider more seriously than we have in the past the impact of Latin American population growth on security and stability issues in the hemisphere, and hence on U.S. foreign policy.

Size, Crowding, and Internal Tension

The relations between size, crowding, and internal tensions are complex and not entirely clear in the literature. Virtually all the scientific work that has been done relating crowding to tension and to increased levels of violence derives from studies of animal behavior. Those studies do show a close relationship between crowding and violence, but the relationship is usually indirect. That is, one cannot say that crowding *causes* violence in a direct way. But crowding does provide a set of conditions, a context, in which tension, violence, and various forms of aberrant behavior are more likely to occur.[12]

Of course, not all propositions need to be scientifically proven or provable for them to be valid. Common sense may be as valid a guide in this instance as the admittedly inadequate scientific evidence available. For example, we know that Latin America, like the United States, no longer has the virtually unlimited frontiers that it once had. There are no more vast empty spaces amenable to new settlements, an abundance of untapped lands on which the nation's discontents, or its excess population, can begin a new life.

Although the person-to-land ratio is not as high in Latin America as in India or China, for example, or even in Western Europe or the United States (see Table 3), that is often a misleading figure. Most of the unused land in Latin America is unusable, either so steeply mountainous or such dense tropical jungles with such meager topsoil (e.g., the Amazon Basin) that it cannot support even the most meager subsistence life. The frontiers that do exist in Latin America (Western Brazil, the Colombian and Venezuelan *llanos*) have been claimed and settled in the past 30 years, there is precious little new land left, and hence the "escape valve" of the frontier is virtually

[12]Good reviews of the literature on this subject may be found in Nazli Choucri, ed., *Multidisciplinary Perspectives on Population and Conflict* (Syracuse, N.Y.: Syracuse University Press, 1984).

TABLE 3
Population, Area, and Density for Selected Countries and Regions in the World

Country or Region	*Population*	*Area (sq. km)*	*Density*
United States	213,121,000 (1975)	9,363,353	24
South America	195,000,000 (1971)	17,834,000	11
India	547,367,926 (1971)	3,280,483	168
Europe	466,000,000 (1971)	4,936,000	94
China	853,000,000 (1976 est.)	9,560,990	89

Source: United Nations (1979).

nonexistent.[13] If there is a parallel in the United States, it is that we also can no longer advise anyone to "Go west, young man." The absence of any frontiers in our own nation has led to a certain sense of crowding and absence of escapes, as well as a new preoccupation with immigration to the United States and with securing our borders. Massive, uncontrolled immigration to the United States is giving rise to the same kinds of worries and problems as excess population growth is in Latin America: too many people, too little space, crowding, tension, high unemployment especially among the poor, few opportunities for release, and ultimately rising crime and violence.

These conditions are particularly acute in Latin America's teeming, exploding (and explosive) cities. Metropolises such as São Paulo or Mexico City have grown to 16 or 17 million population, almost twice the size of New York City, which once was the world's largest. Lima and Bogotá, cities that are not quite as large, have also seen their populations double in the past two or three decades. The same is true of capital cities in the smaller countries: Santo Domingo, with 300,000 people in 1950, now has over 1 million population, some of the most horrible slums anywhere in Latin America, and virtually unmanageable problems. In all the capitals of Latin America social services are breaking down, there is no water or sewage systems for over half the urban dwellers, unemployment and underemployment are rising, crime and violence are spreading, and food riots or other forms of rioting are frequent. The food riots in Santo Domingo in the spring of 1984 made national headlines in the United States, but the spreading riots and conditions of abysmal poverty in these other cities have not.[14]

[13]Alistair Hennessey, *The Frontier in Latin America* (Albuquerque: University of New Mexico Press, 1978); Jane M. Loy, *The Llanos in Colombian History: Some Implications of a Static Frontier* (Amherst, Mass.: Program in Latin American Studies, University of Massachusetts, 1976).

[14]For a perceptive account of deteriorating conditions in Lima, Peru, see *New York Times*, December 28, 1984.

No one knows or can define precisely what the upper limits of city size are. We do know that cities such as Bogotá, São Paulo, and, especially, Mexico City are breaking down, unraveling, becoming unlivable. Pollution, crime, disintegration, violence are becoming endemic. These cities are no longer, if they ever were, manageable. We read now of the phenomenon of "ungovernability" in the advanced industrial nations, but that is nothing compared with the increasing ungovernability of most Latin American capital cities. The relations between size, crowding, and domestic tension and violence may be indirect and all the evidence not yet in, but in Latin America it seems plain and visible for all to see.

Age: Does Younger Mean More Radical?

In virtually all the countries of Latin America, half the population is under 18 years of age (see Table 4). In some of the countries, half the population is under 15. The cause of these astounding figures is of course continued high birthrates accompanied by major improvements in infant and child care and in public health measures such as immunization. The implications for politics and foreign policy of these figures are enormous.

For one thing, in all countries there has been a quantum increase in what is called the dependency ratio. The dependency ratio is a figure that compares the economically active and productive population with the economically inactive, or "dependent," population. Throughout Latin America, this ratio has been increasing steadily in recent years—that is, fewer and fewer productive persons are being called on to support more and more nonproductive ones. The rising dependency ratio has created increased tensions in recent years, as an ever larger burden is being placed on governments and productive

TABLE 4
Percentage of Population Under Fifteen Years of Age, by Region, 1982

Region	*Percent*
Africa	45
Latin America	39
Asia	37
Oceania	29
North America	22
Europe	22
World	35

Source: United Nations (1982).

persons to carry on their shoulders an enormously large youth population.

There is mixed evidence on the relationship between youth and radicalism. What is certain is that in Latin America virtually an entire generation and more of university-trained young people is Marxist almost to a person. The figures we have indicate that whereas in the United States only 2–3% of the college-age population could be classified as "activist" in a political sense, in Latin America the figures may be 40–45%. Of course, the figures need to be broken down further: State universities tend to be more radical and politicized in Latin America than private ones; the law and arts and letters faculties tend to be more activist than engineering or other technical fields. Moreover, student politics in Latin America is way to the left of what it would be in the United States. Socialism occupies the middle of the political spectrum, with social democracy on the right; there are no what Americans would think of as conservative or middle-of-the-road groups on most Latin American campuses. Part of the ideology of these young persons is virulent anti-Americanism.[15]

The implications of these disaffected young persons coming to power are enormous. In some countries the age group that has grown up since the 1960s is already in low-level positions in the ministries and agencies. Within 5 or 10 years they will be in the cabinet or the presidency. And that is only the first wave. The generation that is at present under 15 is likely to be even more embittered, more radical, and more anti-American than their older brothers and sisters. Already, because of the suspicions and hostility, it is more difficult for American foreign service officers to work cooperatively with their Latin American counterparts than it was in the 1960s. In the future these problems will be multiplied, for among the younger generation the strong residue of trust, admiration, and goodwill that used to exist toward the United States is no longer present.

Illustrative of these themes is the Nicaraguan revolution. In our preoccupation with the political and ideological aspects of the revolution, we tend to forget that it also marked a sharp generational change. The Somoza regime and its more moderate opponents both represented one generation; the Sandinistas represent a whole new age group coming to power. In 1979 most of the *comandantes* were in their late 20s or early 30s; the revolution's strongest supporters are also to be found at the younger end of the age spectrum. That is why the Sandinistas lowered the voting age for the 1984 election from 18 to 16; they knew their vote margin would thereby be increased. If Nicaragua is at all indicative of what will happen politically when this younger generation rises to power (and many professional Latin

[15]S. M. Lipset, ed., *Rebellion in the University* (Chicago: University of Chicago Press, 1976).

Americanists think that it is), then the implications for U.S. foreign policy and security interests are enormous.[16]

It is not likely that there will soon be a wave of Nicaraguas sweeping over Latin America, although in quite a few countries radical change led by these new generations can be expected. What is more likely is that demagogic politicians and political movements will seize upon the aggravations, pent-up frustrations, and radicalism of the youth for their own purposes. The spectacle of high school and university students, or unemployed recent graduates, leading protest marches of recent migrants, or urging peasants to take the agrarian reform laws long on the books but often unimplemented into their own hands by seizing private landholdings, is now a common one in Latin America. These are, again, indirect effects of spiraling population growth rather than direct ones. To the governments in power where such "direct action" takes place, the culprit is not population growth per se but a malevolent opposition using the "marginals" (as the urban and rural unemployed are often called) as its shock troops. The predictable outcome is usually repression and overreaction on the part of the government and the reassertion of authoritarian controls rather than any consideration of the root causes of rebellion, which lie in overpopulation, poverty, marginality, unemployment, etc. In either case, if the revolution succeeds or if the government overreacts, U.S. foreign policy interests will be hurt.

Pressures on the Land and Agriculture

Latin America landholding has long been characterized by latifundia on the one hand (large, often unproductive estates) and minifundia on the other (small holdings that are too small to be economically viable). To these twin problems, which still exist in all countries of the region, have now been added some newer ones.

First, there is widespread abandonment of the land as people leave rural areas and flock to the cities. However awful the conditions are in the cities' slums, the possibilities and opportunities there are infinitely greater than in the countryside. Indeed, it is the most ambitious and energetic who tend to abandon the *campo*, leaving behind children, the infirm, and old people. Whole villages have been emptied of able workers and field hands, and agriculture has been neglected.

Second, and implied in the above, is the fact that food production in most Latin American countries has not kept up with population growth. In fact, population growth is considerably outstripping new agricultural production.

[16]Thomas Walker, ed., *Nicaragua in Revolution* (New York: Praeger, 1982).

Moreover, most of the new agricultural production created in Latin America has been oriented toward production for a world market, not home consumption. One can talk all one wishes about comparative advantage and the benefits of global divisions of labor, but the fact is that while foreign trade is increasing, most Latin American rural populations are becoming worse off rather than better off. Agricultural and once self-sufficient countries are being forced to import basic foodstuffs at, for them, very high prices that the poor cannot afford. Subsistence agriculture was not very profitable, but at least it enabled many to eke out a meager subsistence and to feed their own families. Today, these peasants are being forced off their lands and into the less fertile hillsides, often falling across that thin but deadly barrier separating subsistence from starvation. Under such conditions it is not unexpected that they would migrate massively to the cities—or that they might be lured by radical causes. The violent, destructive Mexican revolution of 1910 provides an early but instructive case in point.[17]

In the past, increases in food production in Latin America were mainly the result of bringing more unused lands under cultivation. Now, however, unused land is becoming more and more scarce. Furthermore, increased acreage has not provided a solution to the food problem. In part this is due to the orientation of that production toward a world market; in part also it is because land reclamation is often more costly than increasing production on existing land. The great expectation of the Amazon Basin, for example, becoming a breadbasket for all of South America has not been realized. More often than not, great efforts such as these have ended in equally spectacular failures. Other land areas are precluded from coming under production because of waterborne diseases; in still others the insecticides used to control flies and disease have had unacceptable environmental effects. Some Caribbean countries, such as Haiti, with its denuded hillsides and the topsoil washed away, have probably gone beyond the land-reclamation point; El Salvador and some other parts of Central America have also reached their limit. Overall, there is now widespread agreement that agrarian reform—if by that term is meant the division of larger landholdings—results in less production rather than more, thus compounding the problem. Agrarian reform may still be desirable for other reasons, but the case for its economic rationality seems awfully weak.

There is, derived from the U.S. experience, an argument for higher population densities that presumably would also assist agriculture.[18] By permitting economies of scale in the provision of infrastructure and services, it is agreed, population increases may also help induce improvements in agriculture. In

[17]John Womack, *Zapata and the Mexican Revolution* (New York: Knopf, 1968).
[18]World Bank, *World Development Report 1984*, p. 93.

the United States, rising population in the nineteenth century stimulated the development of transportation, which in turn aided agriculture to bring its products to markets more cheaply and at the same time raised the farmgate prices of agricultural products. These potential benefits to be gained from higher population density are not likely to be realized in the Latin American countries because *(a)* the landholding system is entirely different, with few medium-size family farms manned by risk-taking yeoman farmers; *(b)* the topography is entirely different, ruling out either mechanization or a nationwide grid of farm-to-market transportation; *(c)* Latin America's attitudes and perceptions toward agriculture are different (as much feudal as capitalist); and *(d)* several governments of the area (especially Brazil and Mexico) have decided to concentrate on production (soybean and other crops) for world markets rather than domestic use. Hence, even though Brazil is a thriving food producer and exporter, its people are literally starving to death. Governments of the area pay little attention to "poor people's food" because only by concentrating on export products will these countries be able to cope with their international debts. It is one more vicious circle on top of many others.

Thus, in key countries like Brazil, even if it were possible to keep food production ahead of population growth, there would be no guarantee that people could have a healthier diet. Where incomes are low, particularly in Latin America where the already meager per capita income is terribly unevenly distributed, *most* of the population may not be able to afford the food they need. Although the amount of labor used in agriculture has risen in most Latin American countries, most families have experienced little or no increase in real wages or nutritional levels. Hence most *campesino* families may actually be regressing, as shown in the figures for infant mortality that are rising everywhere throughout the region.

These complex pressures on the land and on agriculture are making living conditions for the rural poor more difficult rather than better, even in areas where "progress" is occurring in productivity and exports. And at the base of these pressures is the problem of still-spiraling population increase, unplanned, unchecked, and no longer rational either in terms of the wishes of people for smaller families, the capacities of economic or agricultural systems to absorb them, or for families to feed and take care of them. And if the problems now are intensifying, it needs to be recalled that the next generation of still greater problems has already been born.

Urbanization and Migration

There has been in the last 30 years a massive and unprecedented move toward the cities in *all* Latin American countries. Salaries may be low in the cities by U.S. standards, but for the marginal and landless peasant, the lure of

TABLE 5
Projected Total Population Growth Rates and Percentage Urban

Region	*Growth Rates, 1980–1985 (per thousand)*	*Percent Urban, 1985*
Latin America	23.9	66.05
Andean region	25.6	68.31
Bolivia	26.8	50.54
Colombia	21.4	69.50
Chile	16.7	80.31
Ecuador	31.2	47.49
Peru	27.9	65.88
Venezuela	32.5	78.04
Atlantic region	20.9	68.66
Argentina	11.9	82.96
Brazil	23.0	66.09
Paraguay	30.0	40.04
Uruguay	6.5	84.63
Central America	29.2	45.59
Costa Rica	23.1	49.20
El Salvador	29.2	46.66
Guatemala	29.1	37.78
Honduras	33.8	42.17
Nicaragua	32.6	57.24
Panama	22.0	58.89
Mexico and Caribbean	25.8	64.81
Cuba	6.2	70.39
Haiti	25.0	25.03
Mexico	28.6	68.54
Domincan Republic	24.3	50.83

Source: Centro Latinoamericano de Demografia (1981).

a job and a better education for his children overrides all other considerations. In Latin America, which is the most highly urbanized region in the Third World, over 65% of the population now lives in cities—and most live in the capital cities.

Mexico City is a case in point. Sometimes called "the capital of underdevelopment," it adds at least 350,000 immigrants from smaller towns and the countryside per year—this *in addition to* its natural annual increase by births of 2.5%—another 425,000. Estimates place the population of Mexico City by the year 2000 at 26 million. Even now, the city does not have the governmental infrastructure, economy, or social services to handle the present population—let alone that to come. It has one of the world's worst pollution problems, people spend about one-third of their day commuting to and from slums and jobs, and the traffic problems are legendary. The city is figuratively and literally sinking several inches per year as groundwater is progressively drawn from its swampy base. Conservative estimates put infant deaths at 30,000 a year from the effects of poor or no sewerage and air pollution alone.[19]

Mexico City is not unique in Latin America. Urban life requires a large and complex set of services—water, sewerage, electricity, to say nothing of schools and housing—that cannot easily or quickly be scaled up as population and migration accelerate. Cities are proverbially short of money, especially in Latin America where they have little or no taxing power and in most cases lack the administrative and technical capacity to cope with doubling of size in a single decade. The results are familiar: unemployment, underemployment, woefully inadequate housing (hence *millions* of persons, especially abandoned children, living in the streets), deteriorating public services, higher mortality and morbidity, congestion, pollution, crime, burning of buses, eventually protests and riots.

There are, of course, benefits to urbanization. These include economies of scale, more differentiated labor markets, and concentration of suppliers and consumers. People, by and large, move to towns and cities for higher incomes and greater opportunities. Once in the cities, three out of four migrants make economic gains. A move from the parched northeast of Brazil to Rio de Janeiro or São Paulo, or from the bleak Peruvian sierra to Lima, can easily triple the income of even unskilled workers. The higher costs of urban living may narrow rural–urban differences in real terms, but urban dwellers have better access to the limited services that do exist and, withal, their family income and possibilities are likely to be considerably higher. Women can also find employment more easily as factory workers, maids, or vendors in the cities than is possible in the rural areas.[20] While urbanization and migration may be beneficial in these ways, the sheer size and the uncontrolled nature of the cityward migration now threaten to produce such paralysis and chaos in Latin America as to rule out the potential for gains.

It should be noted that even though there has been extraordinarily rapid urbanization in Latin America, that has not so far had much of an impact on slowing population growth. It is usually assumed, based on the European and North American experiences, that urbanization helps stimulate the so-called demographic transition—that is, that as people become more urban, educated, and sophisticated, and as the arguments for "more hands in the field" becomes thus less rational—the population growth rate tends to drop. In some Latin American countries a form of this demographic transition seems already under way. But the evidence is also strong that as the *campesinos*

[19]"Mexico City: The Population Curse," lead article in *Time*, August 6, 1984.
[20]World Bank, *World Development Report 1984*, p. 97.

stream to the cities, they carry with them traditional attitudes and behavior regarding reproduction. That is, they tend still to desire large families, *machismo* remains strong, and few avail themselves of family planning services even where they are available. Hence the migrants move to the city but still contribute to population growth at the higher, more traditional rural rate than at the lower urban rate.[21]

Urbanization and internal migration are thus adding to the burdens of societies already woefully ill equipped to cope with present-day problems, let alone the more severe ones of the future. Urbanization and cityward migration are further ingredients in the trends toward fragmentation, paralysis, and breakdown that we have repeatedly seen as the disturbing prospects in Latin America's future. And at the root of these interlocking crises lies the population problem, the problem of unplanned, unchecked, uncontrolled growth and all the destabilizing potential associated with it. The security and foreign policy implications of these trends are immense; yet, as we shall see in a later section, it is doubtful if very much will or can be done about it.

Emigration and Refugee Problems

For a number of Latin American countries, especially Mexico, El Salvador, the Dominican Republic, Haiti, Colombia, now Cuba, and others in Central America and the Caribbean, the pattern of migration is not just from countryside to capital. It then goes on to the promised land of milk and honey, the United States. For many migrants cityward movement in their own countries is only a first step; the ultimate destination is the United States. In some instances, the flow from rural to urban areas and then to the United States is direct and rapid; in others, it may cover a span of years or even two or three generations.[22] Whether direct or drawn out, the result is that the United States has itself become a Caribbean–Central American nation: New York City has become the second-largest Puerto Rican, the second-largest Dominican, the second-largest Haitian, and the second-largest Colombian city; and Miami, Atlanta, Dallas, Houston, and Los Angeles—to name only the largest—have also become main centers of Latin American populations.

The motivation for most international migration is the same as for internal migration: higher wages and better opportunities. International migration can also be spurred by repressive and/or unsettled political situations, as is the case in Haiti, Guatemala, El Salvador, Nicaragua, and Cuba.

Emigration by the unskilled and those disaffected politically does not mean necessarily a loss of production in the countries of origin. In fact, the

[21]For good reviews of these matters, see Lorene Y. L. Yop, "The Attraction of Cities: A Review of Migration Literature," *Journal of Development Economies* 4 (1971):239–264.

[22]Glenn Hendricks, *Dominican Diaspora: From the Dominican Republic to New York City, Villagers in Transition* (New York: Teachers College Press of Colombia University, 1974).

emigrants may be encouraged to leave by their own governments. These countries have surplus populations anyway, so emigration to the United States serves as a "safety valve" for hard-pressed governments to relieve internal population pressures. Presidents from Colombia have openly told Colombians in New York that they should stay where they were—but continue sending their remittances back home! In other Central American–Caribbean capitals governments extensively assist (though neither they nor the local U.S. embassies can say so publicly) their "surplus populations" to leave.

This problem of extensive and, once again, virtually uncontrolled emigration to the United States will eventually have to be faced. The problem, even spectacle, of a porous border, and of American inability to control its own entryways—and the rising social, economic, and political problems to which it has given rise—must be dealt with. The situation is complicated by the fact that immigration is now a major U.S. domestic issue, with employers wanting to continue having available a large pool of cheap, nonunionized laborers and organized labor's argument that American jobs are being lost to illegal aliens. The burden on U.S. gateway cities for educating migrant children, providing housing and services, and in general dealing with the problems of recent migrants has also produced strains.[23]

The United States needs to get a handle on the problem of illegal immigration, needs to be able to control its own borders. In this light the Simpson–Mazzoli bill, with all its defects, was probably better than no action. But it must be remembered that as we begin to get a grip on our own border and illegal immigration problems, we thereby add to the explosive potential of various Latin American countries. For nations such as Mexico, the "safety valve" of allowing, even encouraging, emigration to the United States has been a lifesaver; should that outlet for surplus population be closed off, the possibilities for greater future instability in Latin America would be increased.

Economic Frustrations

The economic dilemmas facing Latin America are familiar and need not be analyzed in detail here.[24] These include incredible poverty, the world's

[23]Michael S. Teitelbaum, "Migration and United States–Latin American Relations in the 1980s," Working Paper No. 151 (Wilson Center Latin America Program, Washington, D.C., 1984).

[24]Recent analyses include Joseph Grunwald, "Perspectives on the Latin American Economic Crisis," in *The Crisis in Latin America: Strategic, Economic and Political Dimensions*, ed. Howard J. Wiarda (Washington, D.C.: American Enterprise Institute for Public Policy Research, 1984); William Glade, "Latin America: Options and Non-Options in Contemporary Development Strategy," in *The Alternative Futures of Latin America*, ed. Howard J. Wiarda (Washington, D.C.: American Enterprise Institute, 1985).

highest per capita debt, unemployment and underemployment that may reach 40–50% of the workforce, negative growth rates over the last 5 years, immense income inequalities, declining terms of trade, immense capital flight, very little new investment, little U.S. foreign assistance, increased protectionism on the part of countries with whom Latin America must trade, rising prices for the goods Latin America must import, and (in some countries) devastation of their economic infrastructure by guerrilla forces. The vicious circles of Latin America underdevelopment are such that it seems doubtful, even without being an undue pessimist, they will *ever* be resolved.

Governments of the area are thus caught in what might be called the "population-treadmill effect." For high-fertility countries that face a doubling or even tripling of the school-age population by the end of the century, that will require major increases in spending for education even if the objective is just to maintain the present, rather low, educational levels. The same population-treadmill effect applies to electric power, transportation, jobs, housing, health care, and other basic services. Given present and projected population growth, the Latin American economies must move ahead at unprecedented rates just to stay even. Nowhere, under present economic projections, is that likely to happen.

The population-treadmill effect means hard choices in a period of retrenchment. When the economic pie in Latin America was growing along with the population, it was easier to maintain at least the existing, albeit inadequate, level of services. Now, in a period of economic contraction, tough decisions must be made. For example, should scarce resources go to open up farm-to-market roads so that food crops do not spoil before they reach the cities, or should these limited resources provide schools, health service, or labor training programs for the new urban dwellers? These are difficult decisions; the case could reasonably be argued either way. As long as economic growth was going forward faster than population growth, as occurred in the 1950s, 1960s, and until the mid to late 1970s, Latin America had the luxury of time in making some of these decisions and could probably afford to do all or most of these things at once. Now, in conditions of economic downturn where population growth has not slowed apace, all decisions become zero-sum decisions: For every gain in one area, there must be losses in others.

It must also be recognized that deprivations incurred now will certainly have important effects later. It is clear that lack of, or insufficient spending on, education, for example, will mean a less skilled or nonskilled labor force in years to come. This at a time when the Latin American countries require a better and more technically trained population to diversify their economies, which is a key to economic growth. Additionally, there is mounting evidence that infant malnutrition or undernutrition means, to put it bluntly, less brainpower in years to come. Unchecked population growth also means the income inequalities that are already severe in Latin America will surely become worse. So will the poverty, the unemployment, the bitterness, and the frustration. One need not be a "bleeding heart" of the liberal or any other variety to recognize the immense implications for the Latin American economies of unchecked, uncontrolled population growth.

What concerns us here, however, are the implications for U.S. foreign policy and security in the area. All our aid programs, fashioned and passed into law with such difficulty, such as the Caribbean Basin Initiative and the Kissinger Commission recommendations, will have little or no effect in the face of unchecked population growth. Neither principal nor interest on the foreign debt will ever be paid if population growth continues unabated, and that spells disaster for our own banks as well as the international financial community. Social tension is sure to rise, as we shall see in the next section, and so will the likelihood of political breakdown. Precisely at the time when the United States is enormously preoccupied with internal stability, democracy, and the creation of viable economic and political systems in those nations on our southern border, unchecked and uncontrolled population growth threatens to wipe out all the gains made. The present rate of population growth is not only a root cause of the current endemic instability in the region but also threatens to have even more devastating and destabilizing effects in the future.

Rising Social Tensions

Unchecked population growth rates, in a time of economic downturn, have undoubtedly contributed to rising social tension in Latin America. In almost all countries of the region, petty and general crime rates are up, there is more wife beating and child beating, violence and violent behavior are on the increase, the incidence of abandoned children (10 million in Brazil alone) has reached epidemic proportions. Tension, frustration, and violence at the societal level is certain also to have an impact politically.[25]

Here we focus chiefly on unemployment and underemployment. Unemployment in most Latin American countries (depending in part on how one counts it) may reach 20–25% of the workforce. Underemployment, often referred to as "invisible unemployment," may add 20–25% more. Underemployment refers to the vendors who may sell a few single cigarettes and matches a day, the shoeshine boy who may have only two or three customers a day, the book and magazine salesmen who go all day without customers,

[25] *Recession Exposes Fragility of Latin American Social Progress* (Geneva: International Labor Organization, December 1984).

the vendors who deal in what Sol Tax long ago called "penny capitalism."[26] Taken together, underemployment and unemployment may total 40–50% of the workforce.

This *lumpenproletariat*, the residents of the urban slums surrounding all the Latin American capital cities, is a powder keg waiting to explode. Few if any social or city services ever reach their neighborhoods. The slums in which they live are God-awful, wretched, filthy, unhealthy, and increasingly victimized by crime, disease, and violence. Yet these are no longer isolated, diffused "sleepy" peasants, among whom we know from history revolution is unlikely to come. These are people who have been uprooted, who have ambition and raised expectations (which is why they moved to the capital cities), and among whom revolutionary and demagogic appeals are likely to find receptivity. We know that revolution does not occur among the most traditional and backward of people but among those who have been uprooted, whose expectations, once raised, have been dashed again.[27]

It takes relatively little—a change in bus fares, an increased tax on gasoline, rising prices for basic foodstuffs—to set off violent or anomic protests in the cities' teeming slums. An example is the spring 1984 food riots in the Dominican Republic, precipitated by increases in the costs for rice and beans as a result of an austerity program imposed by the government and the International Monetary Fund. Thousands of Dominicans spilled into the streets in protest, and several score were killed by the police. Fortunately, the Dominican government, which happens to be a democratic one, was able to survive.[28] Similar protests and food riots, although little noticed by the media, have recently occurred in Brazil, Colombia, Peru, Nicaragua, and Mexico.

These protests are generally unorganized; what social scientists call "anomic movements"—without leadership or clear political goals. The great danger in terms of U.S. interests and policy is that a more or less spontaneous movement of this sort may be captured by a disciplined Marxist–Leninist political movement with the potential to undermine, topple, and capture a government. The literature on these kinds of organized, usually carefully orchestrated protest movements in Latin America with their possibility for great violence, both physically and to the political fabric, is extensive.[29]

[26]Sol Tax, *Penny Capitalism: A Guatemalan Indian Economy* (Chicago: University of Chicago Press, 1963).

[27]Crane Brinton, *The Anatomy of Revolution* (New York: Random House, 1965); Ted Robert Gurr, *Why Men Rebel* (Princeton: Princeton University Press, 1970).

[28]Michael J. Kryzanek, "Dominican Republic," in *Latin America and Caribbean Contemporary Record*, ed. Jack Hopkins (New York: Holmes and Meier, 1985).

[29]See, especially, James Payne, "The Politics of Structured Violence," *Journal of Politics* 27 (May 1965): 362–373; Payne, *Labor and Politics in Peru: The System of Political Bargaining* (New Haven: Yale University Press, 1965).

Such movements, if they occur when other circumstances are propitious (the middle class is also feeling austerity's bite, the armed forces are divided, the government is weak and/or illegitimate), can produce revolutionary consequences.

The prime recruiting grounds for such movements are of course the big-city slums, the legions of unemployed or underemployed concentrated in the capital's downtown streets, the surplus population with nothing to do, the abandoned street children looking for adventure and diversion. It is usually but a short march from there to the national palace, where greater violence may be provoked or a minister or a government may be forced from office. These kinds of movements, arising from social tension and problems but carrying clear political overtones, derive directly from unchecked population growth; and we are likely to see more and more of them in the future.

The Unraveling of Political Systems

It sometimes surprises North Americans (and Latin Americans as well) to learn that there is a pattern, a *system*, of Latin American politics. We usually think, in our condescending and ethnocentric way, that a region as unstable as Latin American is characterized by the total absence of any form of systematic politics whatsoever.

In fact, Latin American politics is quite regular and systematic; the problem is not absence of system but that outside observors are unacquainted with what that system is and how it works. In other writings,[30] a more complete description of that system is given than can possibly be provided here. We should indicate, however, that the historic system of Latin American politics incorporates military as well as civilian regimes, and that the route to power often involves the kind of direct action outlined in the previous section (street movements, general strikes, marches on the national palace, carefully orchestrated political violence, coups and revolutions) as well as elections. The Latin American political process is more informal than formal, involving cliques, class, family, and patronage groups competing for power and spoils, as well as formal political parties, interest associations, and governmental institutions. Related to the informal nature of politics is the fact that the mandate of any political leader is tentative and indefinite and does not necessarily correspond to any given electoral timetable. As long as a political leader who comes to power, by whatever means, can legitimize his rule, and as long as he enjoys popular and corporate group support, he may stay in

[30]Kalman Silvert, *The Conflict Society: Reaction and Revolution in Latin America* (New York: American Universities Field Staff, 1966); Charles W. Anderson, *Politics and Economic Change in Latin America: The Governing of Restless Nations* (Princeton, N.J.: D. Van Nostrand, 1967); Howard J. Wiarda and Harvey F. Kline, eds., *Latin American Politics and Development* (Boulder, Colo.: Westview Press, 1985), Pt. 1.

office; but should he at any time lose legitimacy and support, he can quickly fall. The politics is hurly-burly and often unstable, but with well-understood rules of the game and persistent regularities.

Latin American politics has been not only more systematic than we usually think but it has also been quite accommodative—again contrary to much popular lore. The traditional *systems* of Latin American politics have been far more flexible and far less rigid ("closed," "oligarchic") than we ordinarily think. Two conditions must be met by a new and aspiring group seeking admission to "the system": It must demonstrate its power capability to disrupt or potentially take over the system; and it must not become excessively greedy or revolutionary, to the extent of seeking to destroy other, more traditional groups so as to monopolize power and privileges for itself.

In the 1930, 1940s, 1950s, and 1960s this process and system worked not entirely intolerably, inefficiently, or even undemocratically—although the meaning of the last term in Latin America was often different from that of the United States. First the rising business–commercial groups, then a sizable portion of the middle class, then some more accommodative labor groups were assimilated into the system. Pluralism increased, there was in most countries a certain rotation in power, progress occurred. The system worked, as we say.

But the system depended on an ever expanding economic pie to continue functioning at all democratically and well. As long as there were always more pieces to hand out, no group needed to be deprived. But with the negative growth rates of the last several years, chronicled earlier, the competition for the fewer pieces became more intense, violence and full-scale revolutionary challenges increased, and the existing political systems began to unravel—as in El Salvador, Nicaragua, Bolivia, Peru, and elsewhere. Additionally, it proved far more difficult to adapt the prevailing political systems to the new and mass challenges of the 1970s and 1980s than to the more traditional business and middle-class groups of the earlier era.

There is no doubt that the mass discontent and challenges to established ways and institutions that we see at present in Latin America have been fueled by the population and urbanization explosion explored earlier. Once more, the relationship is indirect rather than direct, but no less important for being so. The youthfulness of the Latin American populations, the absence of jobs and opportunities, the growing impatience, the economic downturn, and rising social tensions have all combined to make traditional accommodative politics in Latin America difficult at best and well-nigh impossible in certain countries. The *system* no longer works and in some countries is being superseded.

It bears emphasis that it is not just some particular regimes-of-the-moment that are being challenged in Latin America but an entire *system* (more or less accommodative and more or less democratic) of politics. The fact is not sufficiently understood in the higher echelon (or at any level) of the U.S. government. But it is safe to say that the implications of this political unraveling and of the undermining and destruction of a whole *system* of Latin American politics has immense destabilizing implications for not only the Latin American countries but U.S. policy as well. The transition to democracy that we have recently seen in Latin America will likely be halted or reversed. Not only can democracy not flourish in this context but *any* kind of moderate, middle-of-the-road government will be hard pressed to survive.

War

Although Latin America has been remarkably free of the international wars that periodically ravaged Western Europe over the past 500 years, the area is not without its flashpoints, its irredentism, and its *Realpolitik*.[31] There is potential for violence in Mexico's long-standing bitterness toward the United States for depriving her of half her former territory, tension on the Mexico–Guatemala border over streams of Guatemalan refugees flowing into Mexico, territorial disputes between Guatemala and Belize, civil war in El Salvador, barely submerged conflict between El Salvador and Honduras, and border problems between Honduras and Nicaragua as well as between Costa Rica and Nicaragua. Haiti and the Dominican Republic are rarely at peace on Hispaniola, the Caribbean (Cuba, Jamaica, Grenada, others) is torn by domestic and international conflicts, Nicaragua claims islands under Colombian control and is embroiled in conflicts on both its Honduran and Costa Rican borders, Panama wants complete control of the Canal before the year 2000 specified in the treaty, and Venezuela claims more than half the territory of Guyana. Farther south, Ecuador claims a large share of the Peruvian Amazon, landlocked Bolivia wants an outlet to the sea, Peru still smarts over Chile's depriving it a hundred years ago of its two richest southern provinces, Paraguay and Bolivia are not amicable neighbors, Brazil has imperial designs on all its surrounding neighbors, and Chile and Argentina will probably never get along well. Plus there is the dispute over the Falklands (Malvinas) Islands and another one over Antarctica. The potential for territorial and other forms of conflict is strong and increasing.

Not all these conflicts are directly related to population, but a goodly share of them are. At the root of the Haitian–Dominican conflict, for example, is the fact that, historically, Haiti has had twice the population of the Dominican Republic on half of the national territory. Mexico and El Salvador are similarly overpopulated, while Honduras and Nicaragua have lower popula-

[31] A useful overview is Mark Falcoff, "Arms and Politics Revisited: Latin America as a Military and Strategic Theater," in Wiarda, ed., *Crisis*.

tion densities and considerable open space for settlement. Brazil wants *Lebensraum*—breathing space for her great-power designs—and everyone who borders on it wants access to the near-empty Amazon Basin for population resettlement, mineral resources, and other purposes.

The war that could be most directly attributed to population pressures was the El Salvador–Honduran conflict of 1969, the so-called Soccer War.[32] The war had a long history and background; at its root was overpopulation in El Salvador (with the densest population in mainland Latin America) and the beckoning open spaces of Honduras. Over the years, thousands of Salvadorans had settled, often "informally" and without papers, across the border in Honduras. They had developed the land, built houses, had children, settled in. The tension between the more enterprising Salvadorans and the more easygoing Hondurans was always palpable, and eventually the Honduran government moved to force the Salvadoran settlers out. The forced exodus was sometimes bloody and traumatic. At a soccer game between the two countries the violence spilled over into a conflict between the two sets of fans, insults were traded, the armies of the two countries mobilized, and a short conflict ensued. More Salvadorans were forced out; the legacy of bitterness and tension between the two countries remains.

It is unlikely that all the geopolitics of Latin America will result in war, or that population will always be at the root cause of the conflict. Nevertheless, as Latin America also runs out of frontiers and open spaces, as population pressures mount inexorably, and as internal tension and conflict results, the need for external outlets will also increase. Some of these, and likely an increasing number, will produce conflict with neighboring countries that may not see the issue in quite the same way. The mass exodus of Guatemalans from their country and the nervousness of the Mexicans about this, including stepped-up border controls and real tension and conflict in Mexico's southernmost provinces, provides a case in point.[33] Similar population pressures with the potential for international conflict continue to be felt in Haiti, El Salvador, the Dominican Republic, and Mexico itself. When it reaches the level of war and international conflict, we then are able to see clearly the effect of unchecked population increase—albeit too late. It is likely we will begin to see more such population-induced conflicts in Latin America in the years ahead.[34]

[32]Thomas P. Anderson, *The War of the Dispossessed* (Lincoln, Neb.: University of Nebraska Press, 1981).

[33]Edward J. Williams, "Mexico's Central American Policy: National Security Implications," in *Rift and Revolution: The Central American Imbroglio*, ed. Howard J. Wiarda (Washington, D.C.: American Enterprise Institute, 1984), pp. 303–328.

[34]The astute observor of Latin America, Victor Alba, has predicted increased international conflict in the future between and among the Latin American countries; see his *The Latin Americans* (New York: Praeger, 1969).

POPULATION AND U.S. SECURITY

In this chapter an attempt has been made to link population growth in Latin America to internal unrest—economically, socially, politically, even militarily—and to draw out the implications of these trends for U.S. security policy. The evidence is overwhelming, we think, of both indirect and direct causal relations between unchecked population growth and the possibilities for rising social tension, violence, political upheaval, and breakdowns of entire national social and political systems. As yet, however, almost no one in the U.S. government—and certainly not at high decision-making levels—is paying attention to these issues. Nor, we predict, is anyone likely to in the near future. But if the problem is so severe, and the relationship so clear, why, one might ask, is nothing being done or likely to be done? The answer calls for some knowledge of Washington policymaking, and the place of population policymaking within that context.

U.S. Preoccupations in Latin America

The policy of the United States in Latin America has consistently been preoccupied with preserving stability and thus preventing another outside power (Britain, France, Spain, Germany, now the Soviet Union) from securing a beachhead there that might threaten U.S. security. That was the preoccupation of President James Monroe when he promulgated his famous doctrine, and it has consistently, albeit with sometimes differing emphases, been the policy of all American administrations since the United States first became a major power approximately 100 years ago. Economic investment by private U.S. firms was viewed as both a good in its own right and a means to help preserve the stability and independence of Latin America from other outside powers. The same goes for democracy, development, and human rights: The United States values these as laudable ends in themselves *and* as a means to help maintain friendly and stable governments. More recently, other concerns—the drug traffic, the debt issue, etc.—have come to the fore, but these are also viewed chiefly in terms of their potential for destabilizing the area and paving the way for Soviet–Cuban advances.[35]

Only rarely have population issues been considered part of this equation. When Lyndon Johnson issued his well-known statements on the population issue that were strongly lauded by the community of population policy activists, he did so largely because he had been convinced of the security dimensions of the problem. That is, unchecked population growth, he had been persuaded, may have profoundly destabilizing effects; it also serves to

[35]For further background, see Howard J. Wiarda, *In Search of Policy: The United States and Latin America* (Washington, D.C.: American Enterprise Institute, 1984).

undermine the U.S.-sponsored development projects aimed primarily at preventing such destabilization. That case, now elaborated to incorporate more recent trends in the areas of emigration, urbanization, and rising social and political pressures, has been presented in this chapter. But since the 1960s there has been less preoccupation with population issues in official Washington; indeed, the trend has been to de-link population issues from security issues—or to stay away from population policy altogether.

That helps explain the sudden popularity of the theories of economist Julian Simon. Simon holds that population increase can be strongly correlated with economic development, providing larger markets, economies of scale, etc. That is a nice model theoretically, but it has little relevance for the chaotic, unchecked population growth of Latin America. Nor does it pay sufficient attention to noneconomic arguments, such as the social, political, and security dimensions presented here or the fact that the Latin Americans themselves wish to limit family size. Simon's arguments are not convincing and do not hold up under close scrutiny or in the light of Latin American realities. But in political Washington they have been seized on as providing rationalizations for decisions already made. They provide a convenient set of arguments that politicians or governments can use to justify positions arrived at on other grounds.[36]

The question once more becomes: If the real facts are so obvious, if unchecked population growth is as potentially calamitous a problem as has been presented here, why are American policymakers so strongly opposed to doing anything about it? Or are they really that reluctant?

The Politics of Population Policy in Washington, D.C.

Several reasons may be adduced for the declining attention to population policy in the nation's capital. These reasons also make it clear why, despite the severity of the problem, we can expect little in the way of new or grand policy initiatives in this area in the near future.

First, the climate of the country has changed. Since Vietnam, Americans, especially American policymakers, are less inclined to get so deeply involved in the internal affairs of other nations; and population policy is no longer seen as the cure-all it once was. The country is also more conservative, and that means less inclination to legislate in this most intimate of private and family affairs: regulating births.

Second, Catholic, Protestant evangelical, and pro-life lobbies are far stronger than before. No congressman or presidential candidate is going to

[36]A scholarly and balanced review of Simon's work appears in "Review Symposium on *The Ultimate Resource*," *Population and Development Review* 8 (March 1982): 163–178.

risk political suicide by bucking these groups. If the primary concern of politicians is reelection, as the political science literature strongly suggests,[37] in the current climate they would have to be downright irrational to support population policy.

Third, population issues tend to be long-term and based on demographic projections rather than immediate and obvious. When demographers tell us that by the year 2025 Latin America's population will be umpteen millions, that causes the eyes of politicians, whose chief concern is the 1986 or 1988 election, to glaze over. If population issues become dramatic and immediate, in the form of food riots and collapsing governments, then politicians will become concerned; but not before.

Fourth, population policy has no constituency in this country. In this it is like foreign aid. Moreover, if support of population policy, or of foreign aid, is seen as costing votes in the politician's home district, as is now the case, he will stay away from it like the plague. Under the impact of unchecked immigration into Miami and the Southwest, this perception may be changing in some voting districts; but it is not yet perceived as a national problem requiring national attention. Population policy has a handful of dedicated and activist supporters located in Boston, New York, and Washington. But that is insufficient to force legislation or administrative action when so many other, seemingly more pressing issues demand attention.

Fifth, U.S. foreign aid generally is down since the late 1960s, and with it the emphasis on programs believed to have an impact on population, such as education, health, income generation, and agrarian reform. With continuing disputes within the Congress and the executive branch over the dollar amounts to be included in the foreign aid bill, how much of that would go to population versus other programs, and what kind of population policy to have, the U.S. Agency for International Development (AID) lacks determined financial handles to deal with population issues or to support stronger family planning efforts abroad.

Sixth, some of the U.S., United Nations, and private organizations responsible for carrying out population policy have acquired a quite spotty record. Some are losing U.S. financial support because of their activities in support of abortion. Quite a number have been accused of overbureaucratization and sinecures, of supporting bogus programs, doctoring statistics, providing misleading information about their programs, failing to provide adequate medical follow-up, and a host of other real sins of omission and commission. Some ostensibly private groups have simply become fronts for the U.S. government and have engaged in various deceptive practices. Others have

[37] David Mayhew, *Congress: The Electoral Connection* (New Haven: Yale University Press, 1974).

turned to "safe" projects, such as demographic studies, while ignoring action programs. Sometimes these actions can be justified, but overall the activities of the population agencies leave a lot to be desired. Their overzealous and ill-advised actions in far too many instances have helped poison the climate for the very programs they are charged with carrying out.

Seventh, there is presidential leadership. Neither Presidents Jimmy Carter nor Ronald Reagan have been convinced of the efficacy of population policy, or of its morality. Nor is it likely that the present administration will change its mind on this issue. This is an issue on which the president feels deeply, and it is unlikely that lobbying or the commissioning of polls showing most Americans to be pro-choice or indifferent will make much dent. Those groups that are lobbying to change Mr. Reagan's mind are likely wasting their time.

Eighth, when the president and the politicians feel this strongly on an issue, the bureaucracy also tends to be cautious. For example, U.S. AID, which administers population programs abroad, is likely to be very circumspect, at least for the duration of Mr. Reagan's second term. Its administrators do not wish to be put out to pasture if they espouse a policy contrary to the administration, as occurred in the 1984 debate over the U.S. position to be presented at the world population conference held in Mexico City; nor do they wish to be targeted by conservative or pro-life groups for being out of line. It seems likely that officially sponsored and sanctioned activities in the population field, short of any new directives from on high, will be very carefully implemented in the next several years.

And yet, and yet . . . population policy continues to be implemented, and the programs continue to grow. The rhetoric against some aspects of population policy (e.g., abortion programs) has sometimes been strong, but in actual practice not all that much has changed—or is likely to. The Congress continues to provide and even augment the funding, AID's population programs continue to expand, and the White House has generally, though quietly, gone along.[38] One could say that except for occasional blips, such as in the headlines generated over the Mexico City conference, which largely had to do with U.S. domestic politics, the trend line in population policy has been steadily upward since at least the 1960s. The lessons for population policy advocates (rather like those derived from the Latin American experience) seem to be as follows: *(a)* If we're going to support population policy, do so quietly rather than loudly; *(b)* don't do it in a way that antagonizes key domestic interest groups; *(c)* do it in a fashion that avoids embarrassing the White House or congressmen and thus gets them in trouble with their constituents; and *(d)* don't expect to be able to criticize some aspects of

[38]"Analysis and Commentary I and II: 1984 Developments, 1985 Implications," *Washington Memo*, January 9 and 11, 1985.

administration policy and still get funding for population programs, since politicians and their operatives tend to have long and detailed memories. In this context, and keeping these lessons in mind, a great deal can be done in the population policy area—not necessarily dramatically and with loud trumpets but quietly, incrementally, and with quite impressive results.

CONCLUSIONS AND IMPLICATIONS

There are both room and strong arguments for a sound and serious population policy as part of overall U.S. foreign policy in Latin America. Such a policy should be modest and restrained; unrealistic expectations should not be raised. Limits should be recognized on what population policy can produce, what can be expected. Population policy can be a useful component of a larger, overall development policy; it cannot be viewed as a panacea, a cure-all, or a substitute for a more broadly conceived developmental strategy. This is particularly true because most Latin Americans, including key decision-making elites, now support one or another form of family planning—a marked turnabout from the situation 20 years ago. The fact that Latin America's unchecked population growth is beginning to have, in the form of massive migration to the South and Southwest, an impact on the United States and on U.S. politicians and their constituencies, at least in certain regions, provides an added reason to pay serious attention to the issue.

If population policy is to receive serious attention in the United States, however, these concerns will have to be combined with national security concerns. That is how Robert McNamara "sold" population policy to Lyndon Johnson; national security was also the principal grounds for launching such notable programs as the Alliance for Progress and the Caribbean Basin Initiative.[39] "That's where the money is," as the notorious Willie Sutton said when asked why he robbed banks. National security is also "where the money is" in mobilizing the American public and, eventually, its politicians to support population policy.

In this chapter the national security implications of unchecked population growth in Latin America have been explored and analyzed. We have examined the relationships between population growth, crowding, and tension; the implications of a disproportionately young and dependent population and of this younger generation coming soon to power; the rising pressures caused by the population explosion throughout the hemisphere on the land and on agriculture; the effects of too-rapid urbanization and migration in

[39]For McNamara's most recent arguments, see his "Time Bomb or Myth: The Population Problem," *Foreign Affairs* 62 (Summer 1984): 1107–1131.

producing ungovernability; the strong effects of emigration and refugee problems; the worsening economic conditions of the area; the rising social tensions and potential for explosion, the unraveling of the region's political systems and the dimming of the prospects for democracy; and, finally, the potential for war and international conflict. These *facts* and trends add up, we think, to a compelling case for population policy on U.S. national security grounds. They also suggest a strategy for advocating a stronger U.S. role in the population area.

And yet, at least in the near to intermediate term, for all the reasons already given, little of a dramatic sort is likely to happen. The climate is not propitious. Too many strong interests are opposed. Politicians do not wish to touch it for fear of being burned. The population agencies have not always acted responsibly, and there are a lot of old skeletons and scandals out there. For these reasons and others, it will likely require a real crisis for population policy to get much further off the ground and for the United States to begin implementing an effective program. That is, after all, how U.S. foreign policy in Latin America most often is initiated: in response to crisis. That crisis would have to take the form of really massive (if El Salvador or Guatemala, for example, begin to disintegrate, or if Mexico is destabilized) emigration from Latin American to the United States and an equally massive clamoring that something be done about it. Or perhaps policy action would be precipitated by the collapse and takeover by the revolutionary left of one or more Central American governments in ways that pointed dramatically to unchecked population growth as a major contributing factor. Neither of these two things is likely to happen soon or in the manner described. That also helps explain why any new, let alone dramatic, initiatives in the population policy area are unlikely soon to be forthcoming. Meanwhile, at lower and less dramatic levels, and keeping in mind the lessons suggested, quite a bit continues quietly to be accomplished.

9 Population Growth and the Struggle for the Hearts and Minds of Rural Populations in Central America

T. DAVID MASON

One perceived source of threat to U.S. security interests in Latin America is the intermittent emergence of rural insurgencies intent on, first, overthrowing an existing regime that is supportive of (and supported by) U.S. interests in the region and, second, replacing it with a revolutionary regime that is, in any of several ways, hostile to the United States and its regional interests. Indeed, disagreement over how to prevent such movements from emerging in the first place (as with Honduras), how to subdue them once they have escalated to threatening proportions (as in Guatemala and El Salvador), and how to deal with them once they have succeeded in establishing a revolutionary regime (as in Nicaragua) has come to dominate both the public and official debate over U.S. policy and interests in Latin America. Our policies toward Central American instability are of considerable moment today because their outcomes will not only affect direct U.S. interests in Central American but will reverberate throughout the entire complex of our political and economic relations with other Latin American nations, since those nations too have interests at stake (directly or indirectly) in the outcome of what Howard Wiarda has aptly termed "the Central American imbroglio."

This chapter represents an attempt to enhance (however slightly) our understanding of the nature and preconditions of these rural insurgencies and the threat they pose to current regimes in these nations, the strategies those regimes employ to prevent insurgent victory, and the problems that U.S. policies in the region should address if they are to secure U.S. interests by bringing about greater stability in the region. In particular, the chapter presents, in broad terms, a model of the way in which population growth catalyzes the erosion of political, social, and economic stability in the countryside and thereby creates a vacuum in which rural insurgencies frequently arise. Within this framework, I derive some predictions regarding the likely impact of regime-sponsored programs of both reform and repression on the level of peasant support for these movements. The model is applied in brief analyses of reform, repression, and revolution in El Salvador and Guatemala, since in these two nations the level of insurgent violence presents the most immediate threat to regime stability and U.S. interests. Finally, I derive from these case studies an assessment of the policy options facing the United States and the groups it supports in these nations in their attempts to preempt revolutionary victory, restore political stability and, in so doing, enhance the prospects for U.S. security interests in the region.

THE CALCULUS OF PEASANT POLITICAL SUPPORT

My initial task is to describe the decision calculus by which the typical peasant decides whether to remain loyal to the existing regime or lend his support (in whatever degree) to an insurgent organization. One social scientific paradigm that has been applied in the analysis of peasant political behavior is the clientelist model of politics in rural agrarian societies. This paradigm would seem to be potentially applicable in this study because in both of the nations with which I am concerned here—El Salvador and Guatemala—rural insurgencies have emerged amid conditions typical of a clientelist system in transition: the predominance of the agricultural sector in the economy, the concentration of landownership (and wealth generally) in the hands of a small oligarchy, the enforcement of the political status quo through an authoritarian state controlled by the landed oligarchy in alliance with the military, and the emergence of rural insurgencies amid the erosion of clientelist stability that is catalyzed by the pressures of economic change and demographic transition.

The basic elements and structure of the clientelist paradigm have been elaborated extensively in a number of studies concerned with political change—both evolutionary and revolutionary—in transitional societies.[1] Of relevance to the present study is that paradigm's depiction of the decision calculus of peasant political behavior. For the peasant existing at or near the margins of subsistence, the legitimacy of elites, collectively and individually, is a function of both the balance of goods and services transferred ("the terms

[1]Portions of this chapter are derived from a paper entitled "Land Reform and the Breakdown of Clientelist Politics in El Salvador", presented by the author at the 1984 meeting of the American Political Science Association. See, for instance, Migdal (1974), Popkin (1979), Scott (1976), and Scott and Kerkvliet (1976).

of trade") between patron and client and the distribution of the economic risks of agriculture that is inherent in the terms of trade that prevail between the peasant and patron at any given time (Scott and Kerkvliet, 1976:441). This exchange relationship is highly asymmetric, with the patron providing clients with access to the basic means of subsistence and the clients reciprocating with a combinations of economic goods and services (e.g., rent, labor, portions of crops) and social acts of deference and loyalty (including their votes if elections take place).[2]

The asymmetry in the economic terms of trade translates into a corresponding asymmetry in the distribution of political power between the small oligarchy of landed patrons and the large (and growing) population of rural tenants, laborers, and smallholders. More specifically, the landed oligarchy is able to establish and control the institutional machinery of an authoritarian state that effectively excludes the client population from political power. Therefore, if the level of stability necessary for the preservation of the status quo cannot be purchased through clientelist exchanges, it can usually be enforced through the oligarchy's monopoly over the state's characteristically well endowed coercive capacities.

The source of the patrons' disproportionate control of economic wealth and political power is their monopoly (or near monopoly) over access to land, which is vital to the peasant not just for his economic livelihood but for the subsistence of himself and his family. In an economy where farming is the only means by which most of the rural population is able to avoid subsistence crises, demand for land will be highly inelastic, with increases in its effective price not appreciably diminishing demand for it (Scott and Kerkvliet, 1976: 442). Thus, control over land translates not only into economic wealth but into political power as well.[3]

Because the loss of access to land would result in a subsistence crisis for a

[2]This characterization of the exchange relationship seems to be common to all treatments of patron–client politics and indeed is the definitive characteristic of such systems. A diverse array of political implications is derived from this fundamental dynamic. See, for instance, Eisenstadt and Roniger (1981), Lemarchand (1981), Migdal (1974), Powell (1970), Scott (1972, 1976), and Scott and Kerkvliet (1976), among others. For a comprehensive bibliography of political clientelism, see Roniger (1981).

[3]Other resources of the patrons can include their monopoly or near monopoly (often by default) of skill and knowledge (i.e., human capital, including the organizational skills necessary to mobilize communities for public works and other collective goods), their control over other economic resources (e.g., credit, seed, equipment, marketing services, and alternative employment opportunities) and their control over "indirect, office-based property" (e.g., patronage jobs, the distribution of corvée labor requirements and tax burdens for the community, and their provision of brokerage services between the local population and the national government). See Powell (1970), Scott (1972, 1976), and Scott and Kerkvliet (1976), among others, for discussion of the nature of the respective resource bases of patrons and clients.

client, the patron can unilaterally affect the terms of trade that prevail between him and his clients at a given time. His ability to manipulate the terms of trade will vary according to the size of the client population, the availability of migration opportunities (where there are unused lands, patrons offering better terms of trade, or occupational alternatives to farming), and the extent to which the patron can coerce compliance with the terms of trade he dictates. Thus, the patron's bargaining position improves with increases in the size of the client population and with decreases in the size of the patron population; conversely, the peasant's bargaining position improves with the availability of "escape valves", such as unused lands, emigration opportunities, and the availability of occupational alternatives. While the availability of escape valves improves the bargaining position of the client in "negotiating" the terms of trade with the patron, however, it will always be the case that, no matter what the extent of their availability, the individual client's ability to influence the terms of trade unilaterally will remain insignificant compared to that of the patron.

In assessing the stability of a given clientelist exchange network, it is important to determine not only the distribution of goods and services that results from the exchange but also the distribution of the risks of agriculture that is implicit in the terms of that exchange. The economic risks of agriculture include those unpredictable events in weather and/or market conditions that are beyond the control of the farmer but can severely alter the size and value of his annual production and thereby jeopardize the assets that define his status in the national or local economy.

For peasants whose assets leave them on the margins of subsistence, the distribution of the risks between him and his patron may be more salient a factor in his behavioral calculus than the average annual income he can expect from the terms of trade between him and his patron. If weather-related disasters or potentially crippling market fluctuations are a significant (to the peasant) possibility, then the client may be willing to accept a lower average income over several years from a patron who offers some disaster insurance (in the form of emergency food, reduced or delayed rent) in bad years. Indeed, Scott (1976:29–32) has argued that under certain conditions, a client may be willing to accept a variable rent that keeps his income relatively low and constant, even in good years, if he is also provided with subsidies that amount to a subsistence floor in the years when his income falls short of subsistence requirements. We would expect that a peasant's willingness to submit to such an arrangement, which amounts to virtual serfdom, will vary positively with the frequency with which climatic or market disasters are expected to occur and negatively with the size of the expected margin above subsistence he can expect in good years.

Variations in the terms of trade and distribution of the risks of agriculture are largely a function of variations in the land tenure arrangements that prevail in different local economies. Likewise, changes in the terms of trade and distribution of risks in a locality are to a large extent the result of changes in the land tenure arrangements. Whether a local patron also provides subsistence insurance, public goods and services (e.g., education and health care), and brokerage between the local population and the various agencies of the state will vary according to whether the clients exist as individual smallholders, permanent year-round employees on large estates, renters or sharecroppers on small plots of land, seasonal wage laborers, or temporary squatters on unused land.

While smallholders are not directly dependent on the local patron for access to land, they often depend on him for such things as credit, seed, marketing services, legal and political brokerage, and whatever public goods and services the patron can make available. Those public goods and services are the only insurance that a smallholder has against the risks of agriculture, since he is otherwise on his own as an actor in the marketplace. Thus, for the smallholder, terms of trade are a function of the price he can command for his crop and the price the patron can extract from that income for the services he provides.

Tenancy arrangements can be based on a fixed amount of rent or on a proportion of the harvest. With the former arrangement, the client assumes most of the risk, since his debt to the landlord is the same regardless of the size of his income from the harvest. It is his income and not the landlord's that fluctuates with variations in the yield, variations that are themselves a function of the risks of agriculture. In the latter arrangement, the landlord is assuming more of the risks, since his income, as a share of the harvest, will vary with the size of the harvest. If, additionally, the landlord provides a subsistence floor in disastrous crop years, then a disproportionately larger share of the client's risks has been relieved, since the client is now insured against subsistence crises while the landlord has risked only a marginal reduction in his total income from all his clients.

For those in the third kind of land tenure arrangement (agricultural employees), employment may be seasonal and temporary, with employees receiving a fixed wage and few additional services; or employment may be more permanent, with employees receiving housing and perhaps a small plot of land on the estate to cultivate in subsistence crops for their own consumption. Thus, while their actual income may be low and unlikely to rise with the fortunes of the estate on which they work, they are to some extent insured against subsistence crises by the assurance of some income, low though it may be, and by their access to land on which to grow some if not all of their own food. For seasonal wage laborers, their income will vary with the supply and demand for labor, and there is usually little or no subsistence insurance available to them through the patron–client network. Unless such services are provided by the state or some agency outside the local clientelist system, seasonal wage laborers are at the mercy of fluctuations in the market for farms products and farm labor: When harvest are bad, fewer workers will be hired; and when labor is plentiful, they will earn a lower wage. In effect, they exist outside the clientelist system as such, since their status is dependent on market conditions at not on the informal diffuse exchange networks of the clientelist system.

Changes in the terms of trade and distribution of risks that prevail in a locality at a given time occur with changes in the supply and demand for the resources that the client brings to the exchange. The client's resources consist primarily of labor services, rents (in the forms of cash or crops), and various services (including political support) that he can provide to a patron on demand. To the extent that the amount of arable land is fixed and agricultural technology remains constant, however, demand for these client resources will be relatively constant, and therefore the price that a client can extract for them will be highly sensitive to changes in the supply of such resources in the local economy. In short, as population increases, the price that a client can demand for the resources he brings to the exchange will decline. His bargaining position in the negotiation of the terms of trade and distribution of risk will deterioriate as increases in the size of the client population intensify competition for a fixed supply of land and jobs. Thus wages will decrease and rents will increase.

I turn now to an analysis of such changes in an effort to explain the dynamics by which growth in the rural population and commercialization of the agricultural economy catalyze the erosion of clientelist structures and thereby create conditions that are favorable for the emergence of rural insurgencies intent upon overthrowing the existing regime.

POPULATION GROWTH AND THE BREAKDOWN OF THE CLIENTELIST STATE

Changes in the terms of trade and the distribution of risks that prevail at any given time can be catalyzed by changes in any of several dimensions of the political economy of the clientelist state. Among the processes of change that are most corrosive to the legitimacy and stability of the clientelist state are the commercialization of the agricultural economy and the expansion of the rural population.[4] Given the fact that such economic and demographic transfor-

[4]For discussions of the impact of these changes on clientelist structures, see Migdal (1974), Powell (1970), Scott (1972, 1976), and Scott and Kerkvliet (1976).

mations have accompanied, if not caused, the long-term erosion of political stability in Central America, it would seem that an elaboration of the relationship between these changes and political stability would be a useful framework within which to analyze the threats to U.S. security interests that are created by instability in Central America and the likely impact on these nations of U.S. policy initiatives intended to protect those interests.

I begin by examining the effects of agricultural commercialization on the terms of trade and distribution of risks underlying the clientelist system. As the clientelist state's political economy is penetrated by and integrated into the modern international political economy, the opportunity structure facing landed patrons is altered, inducing them to initiate unilateral changes in the terms of trade and distribution of risks that prevail between them and their clients. Specifically, the nation's entry into the world political economy is usually characterized by a shift in the agricultural economy from the production of subsistence crops for domestic consumption to the production of cash crops for export markets.

This shift in land use instigates shifts in the distribution of the peasant population among the various types of land tenure arrangements. As the market price of the export crops that could be raised on a given unit of land comes to exceed the market value of the goods and services a local client can pay in exchange for the use of the land, the local patron will have an incentive to displace peasant clients from the land and convert that land to the production of export crops. Tenants can simply be evicted, and smallholders can be pressured through indirect means (e.g., more stringent credit terms) to sell off their land to export producers. Thus, there is usually an increase in both the numbers and proportion of the client population existing as landless laborers devoid of any insurance against subsistence crisis.

The displacement of peasants from the land begins the erosion of clientelist bonds and, eventually, of clientelist legitimacy. The range of goods and services exchanged between patron and client is reduced as the "density" of the clientelist network declines. Relations between peasant and patron become more nearly contractual, more generally instrumental and impersonal, and less dependent on the face-to-face ties between patron and client that characterize the precommercial rural economy. In effect, the clientelist system as such is being dismantled as more and more peasants are displaced into economic situations that leave them effectively outside the network of formal and informal exchanges that characterize the precommercial clientelist order (Scott, 1972:106–107; Scott and Kerkvliet, 1976:451). As this trend accelerates, the local price of subsistence goods will increase, since, assuming the amount of arable land is fixed, the displacement of subsistence crop production by cash crop production will reduce the local supply of subsistence goods and thereby raise their price.

These unfavorable (for the client) shifts in the terms of trade and distribution of risks are compounded by the similar effects of rapid population growth in the countryside. To the extent that the amount of arable land is fixed and its use saturated, population growth increases demand for land and therefore generates upward pressures on the sale and rental prices of that land. Concomitantly, population growth exerts downward pressures on agricultural wages as labor supply increases. Thus the patron is faced with a situation in which he can extract more favorable (to him) terms of trade: He can lower wages, raise rents, and/or reduce the range of additional goods and services he provides his clients in return for a given amount of rent, labor, or other client resources. Finally, unless there is an increase in subsistence-crop production, which is unlikely, the terms of trade for the peasant will deteriorate further as population increases exert upward pressures on the price of a constant or declining supply of subsistence goods.

Population growth can also instigate deterioration in the economic status of peasants by altering the distribution of land tenure arrangements in such a way as to shift more peasants into those arrangements that provide little or no insurance against subsistence crisis. Specifically, the shift in the distribution of population from smallholding, tenancy, and *colonos* arrangements to landless wage-labor arrangements is accelerated by population growth.

In the first place, population growth increases competition among peasants for a limited (and perhaps shrinking) supply of tenancy arrangements. This competition will result (obviously) in increasing rents and (less obviously) in an increase in the portion of the risks of agriculture assumed by the tenant. In particular, with the growth in demand for tenancy arrangements, landlords can shift more easily from rental arrangements based on a proportion of the tenant's crop (in which the landlord assumes more risk) to arrangements based on a fixed (and high) rent (in which the tenant assumes more of the risk). If a particular tenant objects, he can easily be replaced by one of the increasing group of peasants who would prefer even this more risky tenancy arrangement to the uncertainties (and declining wage rates) of seasonal labor.

Second, population growth often leads to the displacement of *colonos* into the landless population. As the value of land increases and wages decrease, a point is reached at which, for the patron, the costs of hiring temporary seasonal wage labor drops below the cost of maintaining the marginal permanent employee on a large estate. At this point, large commercial estates will begin reducing the size of their permanent workforce to the minimum needed at the least active point in the production cycle, replacing marginal *colonos* with seasonal wage laborers as required during the production cycle. In this manner, the landlord reduces his labor costs, releases for cash crop production those lands previously devoted to subsistence cultivation by the *colonos*, and reduces the total cost of the other services he provides to his permanent workforce. In this shift the patron is reducing the number of peasant households to whom he must provide some insurance against subsistence crisis (in the form of a steady income, access to a small plot of land for personal cultivation, and perhaps other services) by replacing them with landless laborers to whom he provides only seasonal wages. In the aggregate, this trend further accelerates the growth in the landless population and thereby compounds the downward pressure on agricultural wages while expanding the number and proportion of the population that is devoid of protection against the high risk of subsistence crises inherent in seasonal agricultural labor.

Finally, it would appear that the increase in land values that accompanies population growth would represent an economic boon to the smallholder segment of the peasant population. After all, it means that the value of their assets is increasing. To the extent that their economic viability is dependent on credit and other services available only through the local patron, however, they are subject to pressures by that patron to sell off their increasingly valuable land, preferably to him. Through his control of credit, crop-marketing services, and access to transportation and other public goods, the local patron is able to alter the terms of trade for smallholders and shift greater risks on to them in hopes that the smallholders will be forced by fluctuations in markets and climate to sell their land in order to pay their debts. Thus, smallholders too are vulnerable to displacement into the landless population.

THE POLITICAL IMPACT OF THE EROSION OF CLIENTELIST STRUCTURES

As clientelist bonds dissolve, clientelist networks erode, and the risks of subsistence crises increase for the growing population of displaced peasants, the legitimacy of the clientelist state itself will begin to erode unless there are adequate escape valves available to the growing landless population. The choices available to displaced peasants consist of *(a)* migration, either to a region where better terms of trade, unused lands, or alternative occupations are available; *(b)* attempting through coercion to extract better terms from their current patron; *(c)* accepting the status quo despite its unfavorable and inexorably declining terms; or *(d)* withdrawing from the system and obtaining subsistence through means other than those available in the local or national economy (e.g., squatting or crime) (Scott, 1972:93–94).

Nevertheless, the very trends that led to this erosion of clientelist bonds (i.e., the transition to export-oriented agriculture and the rapid growth of the rural population) also serve to restrict if not foreclose even these limited options for the displaced peasant population. In the first place, as population grows, export markets expand, and export prices remain high, the resulting robust demand for land will lead to saturation of land use. Previously idle lands will be brought under cultivation for export crops by those with the resources to do so. Even if some lands remain idle, population growth will eventually saturate its use with displaced peasant squatters. Thus, internal migration to regions with unused lands will eventually be foreclosed as an option.

Second, to the extent that export production is concentrated in only a few major crops, the terms of trade offered by different patrons will be rather uniform, thereby limiting the option of migration to regions where better terms of trade are available from other patrons. Uniformity in the terms of trade is greater where the size of the landowning oligarchy is smaller (Scott and Kerkvliet, 1976:451).

Migration to urban areas in search of nonagricultural employment is also restricted in several ways by the aggregate effects of rapid population growth. Rapid population growth alters the age structure of the population in such a way as to increase the dependency ratio. As life expectancy increases and the number of women of childbearing age increases, the nation as a whole is faced with growing numbers and proportions of the population who are either too young or too old to contribute to economic production. A larger share of the national income must be devoted to consumption by this dependent population, leaving less income for investment in enterprises that will generate the jobs needed to relieve the economic distress of the displaced peasant population. Thus, even if growth in the production of food crops outpaces population growth, there still may be a decrease in per capita consumption among the displaced peasant population, as the high rates of unemployment or underemployment leave many of them lacking the effective demand to buy these food crops despite their relative abundance.

This shift in the age structure of the population has further implications for the stability of the regime in that it has been demonstrated in a number of contexts that, under certain circumstances, increases in the size of the young male population are associated with increases in the frequency and intensity of civil disorders (Moller, 1968). More specifically, increases in the numbers of *politically disaffected* young males is associated with an increase in civil disorders. Displaced and disaffected young males are more susceptible to the appeals of revolutionary groups than their older counterparts because the expected benefits of revolutionary change are greater and the expected costs of supporting revolutionary movements are less for them than for older age cohorts. Expected benefits of revolutionary change (i.e., the value of the benefits × the probability of their being produced) are greater for younger as opposed to older males because the benefits of change will be compounded over the longer remaining life span of the younger age cohorts. Similarly, expected costs of supporting insurgents (i.e., the value of the sanctions imposed on those apprehended for supporting the rebels × the probability of apprehension) will be lower for younger as opposed to older males because these costs will be discounted over a longer time for younger cohorts. It should be apparent from the discussion to this point that rapid population growth and its accompanying economic and political dislocations create precisely those conditions under which large numbers of young males become economically displaced, politically disaffected, and therefore willing to participate in civil disorders. As the numbers of such youths increase further with continued population growth, the probability of civil violence increases as well.

In the absence of an organized opposition movement, withdrawal from the system or resignation to the current terms of trade become the most likely alternatives to joining a revolutionary insurgency. Peasant coercion of the landed oligarchy, in the form of spontaneous collective acts such as food riots, may occur sporadically; however, the effects of these collective actions will typically be short-term and localized, with the underlying terms of trade and distribution of risks facing the displaced peasant population being little altered in any permanent or significant degree. Instead, the most likely response of the state to such actions is to increase the use of its coercive power to enforce the stability and persistence of the status quo (Scott, 1972:100). For this reason, joining or otherwise supporting a rural insurgency organization is an extremely risky undertaking for the typical peasant, and only under the most extreme of circumstances will he assume those risks. If the level of state coercion is great enough and its application arbitrary enough, however, the risks of violent death become more nearly equal for the peasant regardless of whether he withholds or contributes his support to the insurgents. As such a point is approached, one's decision to support the existing regime (tacitly or actively) or to cast one's lot with the revolutionary elite becomes more nearly a matter of the terms of trade and distribution of risks promised by the revolutionary elites once they attain their goal (Scott and Kerkvliet, 1976).

When revolutionary organizations do come to challenge the viability of the existing regime, that regime is faced with two broad options in order to maintain a minimally required level of popular support in the countryside. It can increase its reliance on coercion against not only the displaced peasants but also the revolutionary organizations, or it can attempt to reform its political and economic institutions and secure their effective penetration into the countryside in order to restore to minimally acceptable levels the flow of goods and services and the availability of subsistence insurance to the displaced peasant population. Within this broad framework of the erosion of clientelist legitimacy and stability, I now analyze the policy options available to regimes in their efforts to reverse these trends, secure their popular support in the countryside, and thereby preempt the success of rural insurgents. This analysis should be of direct relevance to an assessment of U.S. interests in Central America, since current U.S. policies are generally predicated on the success of existing regimes in winning the struggle with rebels for the hearts and minds of rural populations.

POLICY OPTIONS FOR "WINNING THE HEARTS AND MINDS" OF RURAL POPULATIONS

In its efforts to secure its stability and continuity in the face of the threat posed by a rural insurgency, the clientelist state can pursue any number of policies aimed at restoring its popular support in the countryside. It can increase its level of coercive activity in the countryside in hopes of inducing displaced peasants, whose conditions would otherwise leave them susceptible to rebel promises, to refrain from supporting the rebels for fear of coercive sanctions. It can take actions to induce new investments (be they indigenous or foreign) that will create jobs and other economic opportunities for displaced peasants. It can initiate a redistribution of land that shifts the terms of trade and distribution of agricultural risks in a direction more favorable to the client population. I discuss these options in broad terms, with special attention to the impact of population growth on the likelihood that each initiative will succeed in "winning the hearts and minds" of displaced peasants and reducing the ability of insurgent organizations to persuade displaced peasants to join their movement.

Coercion

The almost reflexive response of most clientelist states to the challenge of peasant unrest and rural insurgencies is to increase the level of coercion in the countryside. This is not surprising for a number of reasons. First, given the character of clientelist authoritarianism—a landed oligarchy maintaining its monopoly over political and economic power through an alliance with the military in an authoritarian state—coercion is the one policy response for which the institutional machinery already exists in the state apparatus. Indeed, the coercive machinery of the state is typically the most extensive, long-standing, and highly sophisticated of political institutions in the clientelist system, since other functions that in other systems would fall within the purview of the formal state are typically left for the informal machinery of local clientelist networks to manage, while official coercion in the support of the status quo remains almost the sole *raison d'être* of the authoritarian state.

Although coercion may be the lowest-cost alternative in the short term, its effectiveness in securing peasant support for the regime and precluding peasant support for the rebels is limited, largely because of the nature of guerrilla warfare. The successful application of a coercive strategy requires that its application be relatively surgical, in the sense that the typical peasant must be certain that if he withholds his support from the revolutionaries, he has no need to fear coercive sanctions from the state. In other words, coercion must be targeted on the rebel organization and their known supporters and not on the rural population in general. The difficulty here is obviously in distinguishing the guerrilla irregular from the remainder of the peasant population. If coercion is applied too harshly and too indiscriminately, the regime risks the possibility of converting previously indifferent peasants into active supporters of the rebels.

Any shift in peasant loyalty from the regime to the rebels is a gradual process, constrained by the conservative risk-aversive decision calculus of individuals living on the margins of subsistence (Migdal 1974; Scott 1976). Peasant support for insurgents first appears as a relatively tacit form of support, whereby they simply do not provide officials of the regime with any information about rebels or rebel operations in their area. Such support is most likely among peasants whose deteriorating economic conditions have left them essentially indifferent to the regime but whose vulnerability to subsistence crises has left them unwilling to risk further threats to their survival by actively supporting the rebels. A landless peasant faced with rising land prices, a shrinking labor market, and declining agricultural wages is still not likely to lend support overtly or covertly to the rebels unless they can provide him with benefits in sufficient amounts to offset the added risk of severe coercive sanctions by the state if his support of the rebels is discovered. The expected costs of such support for the peasant would be the value of the sanctions multiplied by the probability of apprehension. The probability of apprehension would vary according to the level and frequency of the peasant's supportive acts, given a constant level of detection capability by the regime. If the level of regime coercion increases and the pattern of its application becomes more arbitrary, however, then the peasant's expected costs from aiding the rebels becomes less correlated with the level of support he provides, since the probability of receiving coercive sanctions becomes more arbitrary and less dependent on anything that he does. Under these circumstances, the rebels can offer a better deal by simply providing the individual with the means (whatever they may be) to avoid regime coercion. Landless peasants would be especially susceptible to this kind of conversion, since they are able to relocate in areas controlled by the rebels and therefore secure from regime coercion.

With high rates of population growth, the costs to the regime of a coercive strategy will rise, while the ability of the regime to target its coercion effectively will decline. In the first place, the shift in the age structure of the population that occurs with high growth rates implies that the number of young males will increase, perhaps at a rate greater than the aggregate growth rate for the population as a whole. Since the vast majority of these young males will be added to the landless portion of the population, it follows that the number of politically disaffected youths (i.e., potential rebel recruits) will be increasing, as will the probability of civil disorders among them. Therefore, the regime will be faced with the necessity of constantly increasing its level of coercive activity in the countryside in order to contain these building pressures.

However, the effectiveness of these constantly growing coercive forces is likely to decline for several reasons. First, it will become more difficult to identify insurgents from among the large and growing population of likely insurgents (i.e., young males). Second, the regime's financial resources will obviously be strained at some point. Third, the need for a constant buildup in forces combined with the limited financial resources of the regime means that the quality of the added troops is likely to begin declining at some point. The new troops will be less well trained and therefore less skilled in applying coercion discriminately. As raw trainees are unleashed on the countryside, their blunt, undisciplined application of force will exacerbate the process by which the displaced peasant is induced to turn to the rebels for protection. Thus the size and proportion of the rural population that actively or tacitly supports the insurgents are likely to increase with rapid increases in regime coercive sanctions, and the exclusive reliance on a coercive strategy will eventually begin to contribute to, rather than retard, the erosion of support for the regime among the peasant population.

Reform

Facing a legitimacy crisis in the countryside, clientelist states often attempt the implementation of democratic reforms as a means of regaining the tacit, if not active, support of the rural population. Land reform has been the centerpiece of many democratic reform strategies. By redistributing land to large segments of the rural population, the regime hopes to "inoculate" this population against the revolutionary appeals of insurgent organizations. Land redistribution obviously alters the terms of trade facing the individual peasant and therefore must alter his willingness to provide support to the rebels. Land reform is perhaps the most crucial element in any reform program, since it is the one element that can reduce significantly the risk of subsistence crisis that faces the landless peasant and make him more susceptible to the appeals of the regime's revolutionary rivals.

The extent to which a land reform program does in fact increase support for the regime among the rural population will depend on specific terms of the redistribution formula adopted and implemented by the regime. The extent to which (and ways in which) the terms of trade and distribution of risks facing the individual peasant are improved, and the distribution of improvements across the peasant population, will vary according the how much land is redistributed to how many peasant families (and how many are unaffected) and what pattern of land tenure arrangements is created by the particular formula implemented. In particular, if large estates are redistributed as smallholdings among individual peasant families, the terms of trade and distribution of risks inherent in the resulting land tenure pattern will differ significantly from those that would prevail if the same amount of land were to be converted into multifamily communes or cooperatives.

If the redistribution formula provides land for individual smallholders, then the terms of trade for the affected families will be improved, but they will still be assuming most of the risks of agriculture unless the regime also establishes a network of rural development agencies whose services would amount to a certain level of risk insurance for the smallholders. Such services would include credit programs, extension services, transportation infrastructure, marketing services, investment capital, and perhaps price supports in times of crisis. In the absence of such support programs, the smallholder faces a greater risk of losing his assets (especially his land) because of the exigencies of weather and markets over which he has no control.

The smallholder's ability to weather such crises will also depend on certain specifics of the redistribution formula, such as the amount of land redistributed relative to the number of families receiving land and the amount of compensation they must pay the former landlord in order to receive title to the land. The larger the population-to-land, ratio, the less effective a "land to the tiller" redistribution formula of this type will be. As this ratio rises, the regime is faced with the choice of reducing the size of the plots made available to each family or reducing the number of families eligible for land under the program. The smaller the plot of land available to each family, the more nearly their expected income from it will approach the level that represents the minimum needed for subsistence and/or financial solvency. Similarly, the greater the compensation each family is required to pay the former landlord, the lower will be their income and the greater the probability that a given climatic or market fluctuation will result in a crisis of subsistence or solvency. Unless the regime's reform package also includes development agencies whose services provide some insurance against such crises, then, over time, we would expect a gradual redistribution of families from the smallholder category back into the landless population, as intermittent financial crises compel them to sell their land.

The alternative to reducing the size of the individual plots is to reduce the proportion of the rural population that is eligible for land under the program. Obviously, in this manner the regime is able to offer better terms of trade to those peasants who do benefit from the program, since they can receive a larger plot of land and therefore earn a larger income. Families that receive land should be more economically viable than would be the case if more families received smaller plots; for this reason, we would expect families to be forced back into the landless population with less frequency. Of course, the tradeoff that the regime is making here is that the total landless population will be reduced by a smaller amount than if the land were divided into smaller plots, and therefore the size of the peasant population that is still vulnerable to subsistence crises and still susceptible to rebel appeals will remain larger than if the formula mandated smaller plots for more families. Unless the creation of the new group of smallholders significantly improves the demand-to-supply ratio for agricultural labor, then the program will do little to relieve the economic distress of the remaining landless population. And, it should be noted, this landless population will continue to increase with population growth, thereby continuing to depress agricultural wages and probably offsetting any benefits for the landless that could be generated by the creation of a new group of relatively prosperous smallholders.

From this we can see that, regardless of what formula is used, the success of any land to the tiller program can easily be undermined by rapid population growth. Population growth increases the population-to-land ratio and therefore reduces the extent to which the regime can improve the terms of trade for the individual peasant household. Even if a redistribution formula is successful initially, population growth can undermine its success over time as the continued growth in the landless population generates pressures to reduce the size of the average holding. Even if those who receive land remain economically viable over an extended period—after all, increases in the landless population will increase the value of the smallholder's land and therefore his credit line and reduce the wages he has to pay for seasonal workers—the size of the segment that is unaffected by the reforms and therefore still vulnerable to subsistence crisis will increase (as will their proportion of the total population.).

The alternative to the "land to the tiller" distribution formula is one that creates larger multifamily cooperative or communal farms. This can be effected by the conversion of existing privately owned large estates into peasant-owned cooperatives, or by the consolidation of a number of smallholdings into a single unit. This sort of redistribution formula differs from the land-to-the-tiller formula in that the risks of agriculture are shared among all the families in the unit rather than being borne individually. There is the possibility with this arrangement of achieving certain economies of scale; assets can be pooled, labor can be used more efficiently with greater specialization, and projects that require the cooperation of several families can be undertaken. Likewise, production can be diversified to a greater extent, thereby reducing the risks of economic disaster inherent in a monocrop operation. Additionally, a larger operation is more able to undertake the production of certain cash crops (e.g., coffee) that require larger initial investments, longer gestation periods, and higher levels of production in order to recover fixed costs.

A further advantage is that larger communes are less vulnerable than isolated smallholders or tenants to intimidation by both rebels and the regime. Intimidation may be by elements of the regime seeking to force the peasants to abandon their land in favor of the former landlord, or it may be by the rebels seeking to undermine the success of the reform program and, therefore, of the regime's efforts to increase its level of support among the peasant population.

The pattern of relationships between reform, repression, and peasant support for the regime (as opposed to the rebels) can be summarized schematically, as in Figure 1. Since the major motivation for land reform is the desire

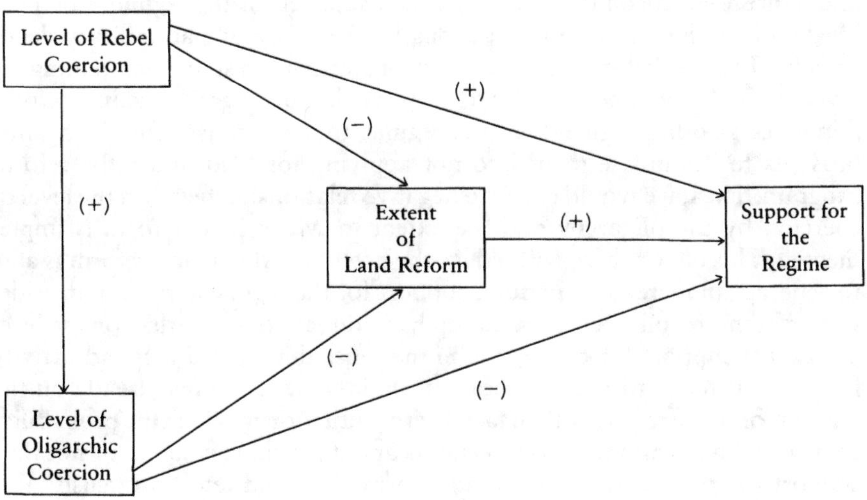

FIGURE 1. **Relationships between reform, repression, revolution, and support for the regime.**

to enhance peasant support for the regime and preempt the growth of popular support for the rebels, I begin by examining that portion of the model that depicts this relationship. We would expect that, in the short term, there should be a positive relationship between the number of families benefiting from a land reform program and the level of support for the regime in the countryside. We would also expect the strength of this relationship to decline over time, however, as accelerating population pressures continue to expand the size of the landless population despite the efforts of the regime to redistribute land. This decline should be more rapid where the redistributive formula is one that distributes land in small parcels to individual peasants rather than one that creates larger, multifamily cooperatives. Land to the tiller programs should be more vulnerable to the deteriorating effects of continued population growth because the individual smallholders must assume the risks of agriculture individually, and unless the regime provides some insurance against these risks, smallholders will eventually be faced with a short-term crisis that renders them insolvent and thereby displaces them back into the landless segment. Reform programs that create larger, multifamily cooperatives should be less subject to the erosion of support levels, since larger units will be more able to insure themselves against the risks of agriculture. Still, population growth will continue to exert pressures on the political success of such reforms, first, by continuing the growth of the landless population unaffected by the reform and, second, by creating pressures to increase the number of families on the cooperative.

Levels of coercion by both the rebels and the oligarchy have both direct and indirect effects on the level of peasant support for the regime. Coercion by the oligarchy can occur as actions by the army or paramilitary death squads. The landed oligarchy has an obvious interest in maintaining its ownership of land, and in order to preserve that prerogative against reform initiatives of other segments of the regime, they often use violence against peasants to intimidate them into not applying for land under the reform program. Thus, we would expect a negative relationship between the level of coercion by the oligarchy and the extent to which land reform is implemented. This effect, then, will reduce the extent to which land reform is able to generate an increase in popular support for the regime in the countryside.

Furthermore, oligarchic repression has a direct negative effect on the level of peasant support for the regime in the sense that as death squad activity increases, it tends to become more indiscriminate. Peasants already on the margins of subsistence are then faced with a situation in which the probability of their falling victim to such violence is about the same whether or not they support the rebels. Again, population growth would tend to intensify this effect by increasing the number of young landless peasants that the oligarchy has to control through coercive intimidation. The more extensive the coercive machinery needed, the more indiscriminate that machinery will become in its application of violence, and therefore the more extensive will be the shift of peasant loyalty from the regime to the rebels.

Finally, the model depicts the relationships between rebel violence and both the success of land reform and the level of peasant support for the regime. Insurgents have an obvious interest in the failure of the land reform program, since to the extent that it succeeds, they will be less able to win the hearts and minds of the beneficiaries of that program. Therefore, we would expect that insurgent violence would also be aimed at undermining the success of the land reform program by intimidating peasants into refraining from applying for land and by inducing the government and the oligarchy to increase its level of coercion against the peasants.

The direct relationship between the level of insurgent violence and the level of support for the regime is more ambiguous. To the extent that such violence is directed against the peasants themselves, we would expect a positive relationship between rebel coercion and peasant support for the regime. If insurgent violence is directed at the oligarchy or the government, however, the level of such violence may not be positively correlated with peasant support for the regime. Indeed, high levels of rebel activity in a region can in a sense be seen as an indicator of the low level of support for the regime there, since such violence may indicate that a large number of peasants in that area have shifted their loyalty rather completely from the regime to the rebels. We would expect such a relationship to hold in those regions in which the rebels have succeeded to the point of having virtually replaced the regime as the de facto political authority in the region. In these rebel strongholds, high levels of violence occur as skirmishes between insurgents and forces of the regime rather than as rebel coercive activity directed against local peasants.

With this rather extensive theoretical elaboration of the effects of population growth on reform, repression, and support for the regime, I now present a brief analysis of how the dynamics of this process are manifest in the instability of El Salvador and Guatemala. Following that, I conclude with a brief discussion of the implication of this analysis for U.S. policies and interests in the region.

REFORM, REPRESSION, AND REVOLUTION IN EL SALVADOR

The historical roots of the crisis in El Salvador have been traced in considerable detail by a number of scholars (Baloyra, 1982; Montgomery, 1982; Shulz, 1984) and need not be recounted in great depth here. Nevertheless, it does appear that the evolution of this crisis fits the pattern of the erosion of clientelist politics brought on by the commercialization of the agricultural economy and the expansion of the rural population. I examine this pattern briefly in order to gain some insights into the implications of current reform strategies for the legitimacy of the current regime and for the security of U.S. interests that, at least officially, remain clearly tied to the survival of that regime.

The transformation of El Salvador's rural political economy can be traced to the advent of coffee cultivation in the nineteenth century. Before this, land tenure in El Salvador was typically clientelist in its distribution of peasants as *colonos* on large haciendas, as smallholders and tenants on surrounding minifundia, or as landless laborers and squatters (Baloyra, 1982:5; Montgomery, 1982:27–42). The peasant's bargaining position in these arrangements was enhanced by the existence of a relatively stable population size and the fact that a plurality of the land was owned not by the oligarchy but by *mestizos* who farmed it communally. To an extent, the *ejidal* lands of the *mestizos* represented an escape valve for peasants dissatisfied with their current terms of trade, and as long as population remained fairly stable, intermittent pressures could be relieved by internal migration.

The shift to coffee production catalyzed a number of changes that drastically altered these patterns of land tenure and thereby gave rise to the crisis of legitimacy that has plagued the Salvadoran state for much of this century. Most of the lands best suited for coffee production were in fact the *ejidal* lands; the oligarchy, through its control of the state, managed to pass several laws in the latter half of the nineteenth century that made it possible for them to displace the *mestizos* from this land and convert it to their own ownership for the production of coffee. First, in 1856, the state mandated that two-thirds of the *ejidal* lands had to be planted in coffee, or they would revert to the state. Later, in 1881, the state decreed that all communally owned lands be divided into individual smallholdings, or they would revert to the state. With the breakup of communal lands into minifundia, individual *mestizo* households were soon forced into financial insolvency, as their individual plots were not large enough to be economically viable as coffee-producing farms. Nor were these households able to acquire the credit or capital needed for the high start-up costs of coffee farming. Thus the formerly *ejidal* lands eventually were taken over by the oligarchy and consolidated into large coffee plantations (Baloyra, 1982:5; Montgomery 1982:40–42).

The displacement of these peasants into the landless segment of the population began to build pressures in the countryside that culminated in the abortive peasant revolt of 1932. The *matanza* was suppressed brutally by the regime, resulting in the death of 10,000 to 20,000 peasants and committing the state, from that point on, to a heavy reliance on both official coercion by the army and unofficial coercion by paramilitary death squads as the primary means by which stability in the countryside would be maintained (Shulz, 1984:194–196).

This system "worked" in the sense that the Salvadoran regime survived until the 1970s. During the intervening decades, however, demographic and economic transformations in the countryside began to generate pressures that the coercive machinery of the oligarchy could no longer control. For instance, landownership became increasingly concentrated in a small number of estates owned by the "fourteen families," with the rapidly growing peasant population becoming increasingly concentrated in the smallholder, tenant farmer, and (especially) landless segments of the population. As Table 1 demonstrates, by 1975 less than 1% of all property owners controlled 40% of the land (Baloyra, 1982:25; Montgomery, 1982:27–28), and 2% of the population controlled 60% of the land, all in plantations of 100 hectares or more (Shulz, 1984:190). As the size of the rural population increased dramatically, the result was an increasing concentration of this population in the landless segment, with between 40% and 65% of all households having no access to farmland as of 1975. Of those who were not landless, 49% had less than a hectare and 94% had less than 10 hectares (Montgomery, 1982: 27–28; Shulz, 1984:191; Simon and Stephens, 1981:160–161).

This concentration of landownership and displacement of peasants into landlessness contributed to a deterioration in the terms of trade and distribution of risks available to peasants, a process accelerated by the rapid growth in the peasant population. Coffee, cotton, and cattle production on large estates has grown at the expense of subsistence production, indicating the decline in access to land for peasants and resulting in upward pressures on the price of subsistence goods. More of El Salvador's land resources are devoted to cattle grazing than to food crop production, and the amount of pastureland has remained unchanged despite rapid increases in the size of the peasant population (Simon and Stephens, 1981:160). Between 1960 and 1975, El

TABLE 1
Landowners and Landholdings, El Salvador, 1979

Number of Hectares	*Number of Proprietors*[a]	*Percent*	*Total Hectares*	*Percent*	*Average Farm Size (hectares)*
Less than 1	86,798	37.20	28,126	2.55	.32
1–10	144,516	61.95	222,399	20.15	1.54
100–999	1,894	.81	636,166	57.65	335.88
1000 or more	82	.04	216,796	19.65	2643.85
Total	233,290	100.00	1,103,487	100.00	

[a] The Departments of San Miguel, Morazán and La Unión are excluded from these data.

Source: Salvador Arias Peñate, "Las Perspectivas del Desarrollo Agropecuario en Relación con la Tenencia de la Tierra" *Estudios Centroamericanos* (ECA), no. 379 (May 1980): 462. Reproduced from Montgomery (1982:29).

Salvador's population grew from 2.5 million to 4.1 million, resulting in an average annual decline of .1% in calories per capita per diem (Taylor and Jodice, 1983:143, 92). And, it should be noted, this decline in per capita consumption does not take into consideration maldistribution of available food, which we would expect to contribute to an even more severe decline in the consumption patterns of peasants, given the highly skewed distribution of wealth, income, and landownership in El Salvador. Indeed, it has been reported by the United Nations that between 1970 and 1977, the consumer price index in El Salvador rose by 182% (Montgomery, 1982:30–31), indicating the dramatic acceleration of demand relative to supply for subsistence goods that has been generated by population growth and the shift of more lands to export crop production.

The shift in land use and landownership patterns has served to alter the distribution of the peasant population among the major classes of land tenure arrangements; as a result, a greater proportion of the peasant population was shifted into those arrangements that carry the greatest risk of subsistence crisis. With coffee, cotton, and cattle production coming to dominate export production, the peasant population has been faced with a situation where not only is there less land available to them for subsistence cultivation but the opportunities for wage labor positions is also affected negatively by the shift to these particular crops. Coffee production is rather less labor intensive (except perhaps at harvest) than many other crops and is increasingly subject to mechanization. The same is true of cotton and cattle production. Therefore, as more lands are shifted into production of these commodities, the availability of jobs on the estates is less than what it would be were they producing other crops, such as sugar.

Additionally, these production shifts combined with the decreasing agricultural wages brought on by the growth in the landless population have induced many plantations to reduce the size of their *colonos* workforce to the minimum needed at the slowest time in the production cycle, with temporary wage laborers hired and laid off as needed. This practice not only reduces labor costs for the plantation but frees up for cash crop production those plots of land previously devoted to subsistence cultivation by the *colonos*. Additionally, many of those who do remain on the estate are now being required to pay rent on the plots of land they cultivate for household consumption. Thus, between 1961 and 1970, the number of *colonos* households has declined from 55,000 to 17,000, with most of the displaced households relegated to the more risky status of landless seasonal laborers (Simon and Stephens, 1981). Between 1960 and 1975, the proportion of the population that was landless grew from 12% to 40% because of the displacement of *colonos*, smallholders, and tenants, and the dramatic increase in the total size of the rural population (Montgomery, 1982:70–80; Simon and Stephens,

TABLE 2
Use of Agricultural Land in El Salvador

Crop	*Hectares*	*Percent*
Basic grains		
Corn, beans, rice, sorghum	455,000	31
Export Crops		
Coffee, cotton, sugar cane	285,000	20
Minor crops	40,000	3
Pasturelands	410,000	28
Forest lands	260,000	18
Total in Agriculture	1,450,000	100

Source: Strasma *et al.* (1983:41).

1981:161–162). During this period, the addition of 1.5 million people to a population of 2.6 million resulted in an increase of 34.4 persons per square kilometer of arable land in a country that already had one of the highest agricultural densities in the world (Taylor and Jodice, 1983).

Similarly, the economic situation of smallholders has deteriorated amid the demographic and economic transformation of the countryside, leaving them more vulnerable to crises that would leave them financially insolvent and would force them to relinquish their land. Traditionally, the smallholder in El Salvador has been able to insure himself against economic disaster by hiring on as a seasonal worker on nearby plantations. The differing production cycles of subsistence crops and export crops make this feasible (Dorner and Quiros, 1973). With the rapid growth of the landless population, smallholders have come to face increasing competition for these seasonal jobs, the supply of which has been declining because of automation and shifts to less labor-intensive crops, as was noted earlier. Thus, the smallholder's ability to supplement his income has been reduced by increases in the supply of labor, leaving him increasingly dependent on scarce credit for financing production costs on his own farm and for carrying him through bad crop years. To a large extent the smallholder is crowded out of the limited credit market by the credit demands of the larger estates and by the fact that those who control credit institutions are closely tied to, if not synonymous with, the plantation oligarchy (Baloyra, 1982). As a result, the size of the smallholder population has steadily declined as constraints on their financial solvency have become more stringent. Their land has either been absorbed by the neighboring plantations or converted into tenancy plots, with the tenants facing the same sorts of economic risks as the smallholder but with the additional burden of high demand for tenancy opportunities forcing up rents.

Finally, the economic and demographic transformation of the Salvadoran countryside has resulted in a dramatic increase in the number of tenancy arrangements, while at the same time the average size of the tenant's plot has decreased. The number of tenancy arrangements increased by more than 100% between 1950 and 1971, yet today 98% of the tenancy plots are less than 5 hectares and 70% are less than 2 hectares (Simon and Stephens 1981; Shiras 1981a; Wheaton 1980).[5] The rapid expansion of the rural population during this period has raised the market price of tenant plots to the point that many large estates that are not suitable for coffee production have simply been subdivided by their owners into minifundia of tenant plots (Simon and Stephens, 1981). In addition, as was noted above, the reduction in the size of the *colonos* population on large estates has allowed those estates to rent out lands previously given over to subsistence cultivation by the estate's permanent workforce. This shift in land use was further exacerbated by the 1965 minimum wage law, in response to which many estates not only reduced the size of their permanent workforce but also began charging rent—either to their own permanent employees or to independent renters—on plots that *colonos* had previously been allowed to cultivate in subsistence crops as a condition of their employment on the estate (Simon and Stephens, 1981).

In general, then, the erosion of precommercial clientelist politics in El Salvador has resulted in a dramatic displacement of peasant population from the smallholding and *colonos* classes into the landless and tenant classes, which leaves these displaced peasants in a weaker bargaining position and more vulnerable to subsistence crises. The overwhelming majority of the peasant population today is not only landless but completely lacking in any security against fluctuations in the market prices of both the subsistence goods they must purchase and the labor services they must sell. Population growth has accelerated this deterioration in the economic situation of the peasantry by swelling the ranks of the landless even further, lowering the wage rate for agricultural labor, and raising the price of subsistence goods and tenancy plots.

The Salvadoran state, controlled by an authoritarian coalition of the landed oligarchy and the military, has lacked the institutional capacity and the political will to take the steps needed to generate occupational alternatives for the rapidly increasing portion of the population that is vulnerable to subsistence crisis. Indeed, since the peasant revolts of 1932, authoritarian coercion has been by far the dominant strategy for securing the state against the threat of peasant insurgency.[6] El Salvador's population density has

[5]It has been estimated (and widely cited) that 9 hectares is the minimum farm size necessary to support a family of six (Shulz, 1984:191). Prosterman (1981) disputes this figure, claiming that far less is needed for subsistence requirements.

[6]That the fundamental character of the Salvadoran state consists of an authoritarian alliance between the landed oligarchy and the military is discussed by Anderson (1984), by Baloyra

contributed to a situation where land use is virtually saturated. There are no regions where unused lands exist and to which displaced peasants can migrate to improve their economic situation and relieve local population pressures. Migration to neighboring countries had served as an outlet during the 1960s, but the Soccer War with Honduras in 1969 foreclosed that option (Montgomery, 1982:80–81).

Given its reluctance to undertake reforms, the regime has instigated increases in its levels of coercion in order to preserve the economic and political status quo. The erosion of the state's legitimacy in the eyes of the growing population of displaced peasants is evidenced in the emergence of the Faribundo Marti National Liberation Front (FMLN), a coalition of insurgent organizations, and the Democratic Revolutionary Front (FDR), a coalition of corresponding political organizations, both of which are intent on overthrowing the Salvadoran regime and establishing a new one.[7] Their competition with the regime for the loyalty of the rural population is based upon their promises of "deep-going agrarian reform, which will put the land that is now in the hands of the big landlords at the disposal of the broad masses who work it." Additionally, they promise other institutional reforms that, in terms of our model, are designed to insure the rural population, especially the "great majority of the poor and middle peasants and agricultural workers," against subsistence crises and to offer them a wider range of alternative means of livelihood.[8]

Before 1980, the regime's strategy for competing with the insurgents for peasant loyalty had relied almost exclusively on increasing the level of its coercive activity in the countryside. However, as the level of regime coercion has increased, its application has become less discriminating and more arbitrary, with targets now including not just those peasants suspected of supporting the rebels but also those who have resisted (in any of several ways) unilateral actions by the oligarchs (e.g., wage reductions, rent increases, and layoffs) (Amnesty International, 1981). As such violence has increased and become less selective, its deterrent effects on peasant support for the rebels appears to have declined, as evidenced by the further deterioration of the situation in the countryside in the late 1970s.

Eventually, a struggle emerged within the Salvadoran regime between, on the one hand, the traditional oligarchy and their allies in the military who

---

(1982), Hoeffel (1984), Montgomery (1982), McDonald (1984), and Wiarda (1984). See also Leiken (1984) and Millet (1984) for discussions of civil–military relations in El Salvador.

[7]The FMLN and FDR are the major umbrella organizations of the opposition military and political organizatons, respectively. For discussions of their composition and evolution, see Baloyra (1982), Evans (1984), Leiken (1984), Montgomery (1982), Shulz (1984).

[8]The Revolutionary Manifesto of May 1980 was released by the Unified Revolutionary Directorate (DRU). An abridged version of it is presented in Gettleman *et al.* (1981: 120–127).

were intent on preserving the status quo through increased coercion and, on the other hand, reformist elements in the Christian Democratic party and some younger members of the army officer corps who had come to the realization that coercion alone would not stem the tide of eroding support in the countryside. The coup of 1979 brought to power a junta dominated by these reformist elements, and after several false starts, marked by the defection of key members who were not satisfied with the extensiveness of the reforms being discussed, the reconstituted junta announced a three-phased land reform program and a return to civilian government under a new constitution written by a Constituent Assembly chosen in competitive elections (Baloyra, 1982:73–74; Montgomery, 1982:7–24; Shulz, 1984:259).

Since the purpose of the land reform program was clearly to win the hearts and minds of displaced peasants and thereby to prevent the further erosion of popular support in the countryside, we should analyze its elements briefly in terms of how its redistribution formula alters the terms of trade and distribution of risks and, therefore, how likely it is to succeed in its purpose of restoring support for the regime in the countryside. Land reform was to proceed in three phases. The first phase called for the conversion of estates larger than 500 hectares into peasant cooperatives. Phase II would affect farms between 100 and 500 hectares, which includes most of the coffee plantations. Phase III was termed the "land to the tiller" program, and it called for the transfer of title on tenant plots from the landlord to the current tenant. In Phases I and III, the former landowner would be compensated with 25% payment in cash and 75% in bonds redeemable only through investment in the commercial or industrial sector of the Salvadoran economy.[9]

If analyzed in terms of the model presented earlier, it becomes apparent that this program is flawed by a number of problems in both conception and implementation. To begin with, 69% of the land redistributed under Phase I had been used for cattle grazing (which is indicative of the poor quality of the soil for crop production), and only 9% of the coffee acreage was subject to the Phase I redistribution (Wheaton, 1980). There is also evidence that many of the landlords affected by Phase I removed equipment, slaughtered herds, and even dismantled fences in an effort to liquidate as much of their assets as possible before the reforms took effect, leaving the postreform cooperatives seriously lacking in the basic equipment necessary to make them economically viable (Shiras, 1981a; Wheaton, 1980).

More important, however, the potential political benefits of Phase I were

[9]The elements, intent, and implementation of these reforms are discussed in depth by Prosterman (1981) Prosterman and Temple (1980), Simon and Stephens (1981), Strasma *et al.* (1983), and Wheaton (1980). The merits and demerits of the reforms are also discussed in Baloyra (1982), Bonner (1981), Gomez (1981), Montgomery (1982), Shiras (1981a, 1981b), and Shulz (1984).

seriously undermined by aspects of both the way in which the reform was implemented and the restrictions on the pool of peasants who qualified as potential beneficiaries. (Similar limitations have continued to plague the other phases as well.) The implementation of Phase I was effected by what has been termed a "state of seige" imposed on the estates by the military. Ostensibly, the military was sent to the affected estates in order to overcome possible resistance to the reforms by both the landlords and the rebels. However, it appears that this strategy was intended also (if not primarily) to intimidate peasants into abandoning the cooperatives or not applying for title to them.[10] During the first year of the reform, over 500 peasant leaders, dozens of ISTA officials and land reform workers (including Rodolpho Viera, the head of ISTA, the Salvadoran Institute of Agrarian Transformation), and thousands of members of peasant unions and cooperatives were assassinated by various military and paramilitary units (Shiras, 1981a; Shulz, 1984: 213–214). The success of these efforts in discouraging peasant participation in Phase I is reflected in the fact that by 1982, 45 of the Phase I cooperatives had reverted to their former owners under a legally dubious "Plan of Devolution," and 28 cooperatives totaling 10,764 hectares had been completely abandoned because of violence—by the rebels as well as by the oligarchy—directed against the cooperatives (Strasma *et al.*, 1983).

The political impact of the reform was diluted perhaps most critically by the fact that only those peasants already employed as permanent workers on the estates were allowed to enter the Phase I cooperatives. The vast and growing landless population remained unaffected by Phase I and therefore was still very much susceptible to rebel appeals. Given the prereform trend toward reductions in the size of the permanent labor force on large estates, this provision of Phase I probably severely underutilized the potential political benefits of land reform by restricting the pool of beneficiaries to a number far less than could reasonably be supported by the amount of land that was redistributed. Therefore, unless the new cooperatives shifted production to more labor intensive crops (thereby increasing demand for the labor of the landless), it is doubtful that Phase I would contribute very much toward defusing the revolutionary potential of the landless population.

The implementation of Phase II, which would have included most of the coffee lands, was postponed indefinitely, reflecting the still-powerful influence of the coffee oligarchy in the Salvadoran regime (Armstrong and Shenk,

[10]A widely cited example of this kind of intimidation through violence is the account of an ISTA (Salvadoran Institute of Agrarian Transformation) official: "The troops came and told the workers the land was theirs now. They could elect their own leaders and run it themselves. The peasants couldn't believe their ears, but they held elections that very night. The next morning the troops came back, and I watched as they shot every one of the elected leaders." See Armstrong and Shenk (1980:17).

1981). It was not until the December 1983 promulgation of the new Salvadoran constitution that the specific provisions of Phase II were spelled out. The most important provision was that within 3 years, affected landowners must sell to peasants or peasant organizations all land in excess of 245 hectares or face expropriation of that land by the government without prior compensation. This ceiling would free 20,000 to 70,000 acres of land for redistribution, according to a State Department report (1984). To date, no evidence could be found of the extent to which Phase II's implementation has in fact proceeded.

Following the delay of Phase II, the Phase III "Land to the Tiller" program was announced, and its implementation begun under the auspices of FINATA, a totally new administrative agency established specifically to implement this phase. However, as with Phase I, limitations in the pool of eligible peasants and in the size of the plots they were eligible to receive, as well as high levels of military and paramilitary coercion that accompanied its implementation, served to undermine its capacity to generate the desired political effects. The volume of administrative work involved in the transfer of title on the estimated 100,000 parcels of land included in Phase III created a deluge of administrative overload for FINATA (Strasma *et al.*, 1983: 135–142). Furthermore, only those peasants who were currently renting land were eligible to apply for title under Phase III, and they were restricted to no more than 7 hectares. Thus, as with Phase I, the landless population remained unaffected by this new phase and therefore were rendered no less susceptible to rebel appeals. Finally, the level of coercion directed against peasant beneficiaries remained high, and, given their relative isolation as individual farmers, they were much more vulnerable to intimidation aimed at reducing their willingness to apply for land than were the groups of peasant families on the Phase I communes.

In summary, it seems that the Salvadoran land reform program is severely limited in its ability to "inoculate" the countryside against rebel appeals. The major limitations of the program are that it does not yet offer any improvement in the terms of trade or distribution of risks facing the most vulnerable (and most rapidly growing) segment of the rural population: the landless peasants. Additionally, the failure of the regime to control the activities of both its own military and the paramilitary death squads means that these economically vulnerable peasants remain subject to high levels of rebel and regime coercion, which, as I have argued theoretically, makes them especially susceptible to rebel appeals.

The policy of the United States toward El Salvador should be based on an awareness of these limits to the Salvadoran reforms and should be directed toward remedying some of their major inadequacies. In the first place, land reform by itself can never completely defuse the situation in the countryside because the population density there is too high to allow the conversion of all the landless peasants into either smallholders or members of cooperatives. Instead, policy should be directed toward creating occupational alternatives for the landless, which means encouraging investment in new enterprises at a level sufficient to relieve the population pressures in the countryside. Otherwise, the alternatives facing the displaced peasant will be to join the rebels or emigrate to another country. The former option obviously works against U.S. interests in El Salvador by increasing the threat to regime stability. The latter alternative would have the effect of simply moving the problem geographically and perhaps contributing to instability in neighboring countries. The question for the United States is one of cost effectiveness: At what point is it more efficient to invest a dollar in creating jobs in El Salvador as opposed to spending that dollar on additional military equipment or personnel, on supporting a neighboring regime being destabilized by a wave of Salvadoran immigrants, or on increasing our own ability to control the flow of economic and political refugees into our own country? We can invest in job-creating enterprises in the Salvadoran economy and thereby reduce the base of support for the rebels there and eventually reduce the level of military spending needed to secure the Salvadoran regime against rebel threat. It already appears that the pressures created by population growth have begun to outpace the ability of the Salvadoran regime to control them through strictly military means. If population pressures are not relieved through the creation of economic alternatives for displaced peasants, then we may be faced with the much more costly alternative of providing assistance to neighboring regimes facing a crisis of stability or with a victorious revolutionary regime that is hostile to the United States and its interests in the region.

GUATEMALA: INSTITUTIONALIZED COERCION

The transformation of the Guatemalan countryside follows much the same pattern as that presented earlier in my model, with the additional variables of a greater degree of foreign involvement in the agricultural economy and a significant ethnic (i.e., *mestizo*) factor in the definition of the segment of the rural population that has faced the most serious deterioration in both their economic conditions and their security from regime-sponsored coercion. In recent decades agricultural production for export has grown dramatically, while subsistence crop production has remained relatively stagnant (Bowen, 1984:272). With rapid population growth accompanying this transformation of the rural economy, the result has been serious inflationary pressures on the price of food. Guatemala's 2.9% annual population growth between 1960 and 1975 has resulted in a 50% increase in total population (from 3.9 million to 6.1 million). Like El Salvador, Guatemala is beset by rural insurgencies that threaten the stability of the current regime. In this section I trace briefly the origins of these movements amid the economic and demographic transformation of the Guatemalan countryside.

Guatemala's rural economy was transformed by the coffee boom of the late 1800s. The shift to coffee production was facilitated by the "reforms" of Justo Rufino Barrios, who nationalized all lands belonging to the Church and the monasteries, most smallholdings, and *ejidal* lands and encouraged their consolidation into latifundia large enough for the production of coffee (Brown, 1983:240). The resulting concentration of landownership displaced the Indian population on to smallholdings or tenancy plots on lands that were so marginal that their inhabitants were compelled to seek seasonal employment on the coffee estates in order to supplement their production from these plots, since that in itself was not sufficient to prevent subsistence crises.

This latifundia–minifundia system proved to be a profitable arrangement for the landed oligarchy and has been the basis for their persistent resistance to any attempts at agrarian reform. As long as the minifundia exist, the plantations do not have to support large populations of permanent employees in order to ensure a sufficient labor force at harvest time. And as long as the minifundia plots are not sufficient to ensure the subsistence of the peasant household, then that family will have little choice but to seek seasonal work on the plantations in order to avoid subsistence crises. Thus the oligarchy's labor costs are minimized.

This system has survived several attempts at reform, the most notable of which was by the ill-fated Arbenz administration of 1951–1954. Jacobo Arbenz promulgated a land-reform decree in 1952 that called for the expropriation of holdings over 233 acres and the redistribution of those lands to peasants in plots of up to 42.5 acres. Beneficiaries would pay for the land at a rate of 3–5% of their annual production, with the former owners being compensated with 25-year government bonds earning 3% annual interest (Brown, 1983:243). In the terms of the model presented earlier, it should be noted that this formula would provide peasant beneficiaries with enough land to be economically viable private farmers, while the compensation formula's reliance on percentages of output rather than fixed-amount payments relieves the peasants of some of the economic risks of farming.

In 1952 a total of 107 state-owned *fincas nationales* were converted into peasant cooperatives, and by 1954 all or parts of 1002 plantations had been expropriated and distributed to about 100,000 peasant families (Brown, 1983:242). However, the American-owned United Fruit Company, the largest landowner in Guatemala, objected to the government's offer of $1.2 million for the 387,000 acres of its land that was then idle and therefore targeted for expropriation. United Fruit claimed the land was worth $16 million, even though the Arbenz government had determined its value in the same manner it had for all other lands: by using the amount that the owner had declared as its value in the previous year's tax assessment (Brown, 1983:243). This dispute brought to a head the conflict between the Arbenz government and the United States, which through its State Department had backed the claims of United Fruit. Finally, in 1954 a coup backed by the Central Intelligence Agency (CIA) brought down the Arbenz government in favor of Castillo Armas, who proceeded to dismantle the Arbenz land reform, displacing the beneficiaries of the reforms from their land, returning it to the former owners, and suppressing the grass-roots peasant organizations that had emerged and briefly thrived as a result of the land reform (Bowen, 1984:273–275).

Over the next two decades, reform became little more than an intermittent promise that was never fulfilled, as the dominant change in the Guatemalan regime was the institutionalization of its authoritarian character along with a dramatic increase—with U.S. assistance—in its coercive capacity. Discontent over unfulfilled land reform promises erupted into riots in 1960, and urban unrest in 1962 contributed to the abortion by a military coup of planned elections in 1963 (Bowen, 1984:278). Increasingly, the level of regime coercion (supported by large infusions of U.S. military assistance) was intensified as the primary if not sole strategy for dealing with disaffection in the countryside and in the city. Elections in 1966 brought a civilian president, but no change in this strategy. Peasant unrest intensified into a small guerrilla insurgency in the late 1960s, but this movement was never able to gain the numbers or the momentum to overcome the overwhelming coercive capacity of the army and its paramilitary allies in the countryside. Between 3000 and 8000 noncombatants died at the hands of the army and various death squads, and for a time this intimidated most of the peasant population into refraining from overtly or even covertly supporting the rebels (Bowen, 1984:281).

During the 1970s, however, a number of over-time trends and short-term catalysts converged to generate new pressures that could not be so effectively suppressed with simply additional increments of regime coercion. High population growth rates were undoubtedly the underlying force of change that acted as a catalyst for the other problems for the regime. As noted, an additional 2.1 million people had been added to the 1960 population of 3.99 million (Taylor and Jodice, 1983:92). Amidst two decades of aggregate economic growth, new developments in oil production and nickel mining served to create at least some occupational alternatives for displaced peasants. The development of the transportion infrastructure necessary to exploit these resources served to displace additional peasants, however, as many of the richest mineral deposits were in the highland regions that had been given over to *mestizo* minifundia because of the marginal agricultural value of the land. Most new investment was flowing into nonagricultural sectors of the economy, and there was a corresponding shift in the workforce to the industrial and (especially) service sectors. While these occupational alternatives were not being created at a rate sufficient to offset population growth, there does appear to have been an improvement in the bargaining position of some peasants, as evidenced by the rise of missionary-sponsored rural development programs, peasant cooperatives, and even urban labor unions.

The earthquake of 1976 led to a drastic reversal of this trend toward peasant organization, for the Laugerud government seized the opportunity created by the earthquake to mount a "counterinsurgency" operation targeted more at peasant organizations than at any rebel insurgents. By 1980 one-half of all rural development projects had been terminated or substantially reduced (Bowen, 1984:286).

The postquake insurgency that has faced the regime has been more substantial and persistent than previous ones, largely because of the greater involvement of displaced *mestizos* in the current insurgent organizations. Coercion by the army and paramilitary units has been directed at the Indians to a greater degree than before because, as noted, the poor agricultural lands they lived on were now highly valued for their mineral deposits. Death squad activity, in the guise of counterinsurgency, has in effect removed the last escape valve available to Indians and other peasants living on the margins of subsistence, as coercion has been directed at displacing Indians from lands that previous were of little interest to the oligarchy. Thus, Indian participation in the Guerrilla Army of the Poor (EGP) and the Organization of the People in Arms (ORPA) is greater than was the case with any previous insurgencies (Bowen, 1984).

The persistence of the current insurgency is reflected in the fact that despite increases in the already high level of counterinsurgency operations and death squad terror in the highlands, the regime has been unable to eliminate the guerrillas and establish its control over those regions. As a result, a military coup in 1982 overthrew General Lucas Garcia, replacing him with General Rios Montt, who was overthrown in August of 1983 by General Oscar Humberto Meija. Regime-sponsored coercion has increased to the point that it is apparently perceived by peasants as being relatively indiscriminate. Therefore, in the absence of any positive inducements (e.g., reforms) to support the regime, Guatemalan peasants are increasingly faced with a situation in which their chances of falling victim to this terror are less a function of whether or not they actually provide support of any kind to the rebels. Thus the number of peasants willing to lend support of varying degrees to the rebels seems to be on the increase, as evidenced by the persistence of the rebel movements despite considerable loss of lives at the hands of intensified government and paramilitary counterinsurgency operations.

IMPLICATIONS FOR U.S. SECURITY INTERESTS IN CENTRAL AMERICA

The purpose of this analysis has been to describe the broad socioeconomic context in which rural insurgencies arise and, within that context, to analyze the corresponding historical developments in El Salvador and Guatemala that gave rise to the current insurgent challenges to their respective regimes. The Reagan administration (and, for that matter, all its predecessors) have made it clear that they believe U.S. security interests in the region are dependent upon the restoration of the political stability of the existing regimes in these two nations. This being the case, it follows that U.S. policy toward the region should be predicated on enhancing those governments' ability to restore their support in the countryside and thereby preempt the popular support of the rebels. This chapter has described the pressures that induce peasants to shift their loyalty from the regime to the insurgencies. The question that remains is how to shape policies that can relieve these pressures.

It seems to me that the major failure of U.S. policy toward Central America has been its lack of awareness of, and attention to, the impact of population growth on both the problems that face these regimes and the policies intended to remedy these problems. No one has ever denied that these nations are poor. What seems to be ignored is that they also have rapidly growing populations and that therefore any program intended to relieve this poverty must be predicated on the expectation that the number of poor people will most likely continue to increase while that program is being implemented. No one would deny that there are gross inequalities of wealth and income, as well as political power, in these countries. What is often ignored is that simply redistributing what resources are there can, under the best of circumstances, serve as only a temporary palliative. The size of the populations will continue to increase into the next century, even if policies are initiated now to induce reductions in fertility rates. Therefore, any programs intended to restore the stability of the current regime, whether those policies rely on a coercive strategy or a reform strategy or some combination of the two, must be shaped with an awareness of the impact of population growth on the problems they seek to address and, therefore, on the likely outcome of the policy initiatives themselves.

Support by the United States of the regimes in Central America has traditionally tended to emphasize increasing the coercive capacity of those regimes to deal with any insurgent challenges to their stability and legitimacy. But there seems to be some threshold of population size (or perhaps population-to-land ratios) beyond which a strictly coercive strategy of controlling the countryside becomes counterproductive. As population pressures go beyond this threshold, the number of peasants facing serious risks of subsistence crises becomes so large and continues to grow so rapidly that the regime's ability to augment its coercive capacity is overwhelmed. Indeed, as I argued earlier, there seems to be a point beyond which the costs begin to approach prohibitive levels for the regime, and the addition of more troops or paramilitary units actually serves to accelerate the shift in peasant loyalty away from the regime. Additional troops are less well trained, and the ability of the regime to control the actions of these raw recruits, as well as the paramilitary death squads, begins to deteriorate. The application of force becomes more indiscriminate, and peasants on the margins of subsistence come to see the regime as posing a threat to their life regardless of whether or not they actually have provided support in any degree to the rebels. Under those circumstances, the ability of the insurgents to persuade peasants to join them becomes easier.

This aspect of the model would seem to have some general implications for the extent and nature of U.S. military assistance to the regimes in Central America. Specifically, U.S. efforts should concentrate on training programs intended to reduce the indiscriminate application of force by indigenous units. While I can by no means presume to prescribe the tactics that should be involved, they should be devised and taught with an awareness of the ways in which regime-sponsored coercion can in fact work to the detriment of the regime's level of support in the countryside.

The United States should also urge the regimes in these countries to outlaw and disband all paramilitary units and to devote considerable resources to enforcing this measure. This would have a number of potential benefits to the regime. To the extent that these units are outside the formal command structure of the regime's own military, their activities are less subject to regime control, even though it is the regime that will pay the political price of the erosion of popular support in the countryside that is often catalyzed by the actions of these units. These units are the least well trained and disciplined and therefore are most likely to engage in the sorts of indiscriminate terror that serve to erode peasant confidence in the positive benefits of remaining loyal to the regime. Outlawing them would thus enhance the regime's ability to control the application of coercive sanctions in the countryside by eliminating elements that are the most indiscriminate in their use of violence.

In addition, I have presented an argument that, given the acceleration of population growth, a strictly coercive strategy is no longer sufficient and that regimes must also undertake measures to improve the terms of trade and distribution of risks facing the large and growing population of landless peasants. Eliminating paramilitary units would also serve to facilitate the implementation of such reforms, whatever they may be, and therefore would enhance the chances of such reforms generating the desired political payoffs in increased support among the peasants. It is clear, especially in El Salvador, that paramilitary activities have quite frequently been directed at intimidating peasants into not participating in reform programs initiated by the regime. The examples from the land reform program in El Salvador are numerous. Death squad activity directed at peasant leaders, land reform workers, and potential beneficiaries of the reforms among the general populace have served to undermine the effectiveness of the reforms and thereby to reduce the expected benefits to the regime in terms of enhanced popular support. This type of violence is indicative of the struggle that exists within the regimes in the countries, between the landed oligarchy intent upon preserving their economic and political dominance and the reformist elements of the regime intent upon changing the economic and political structure of the regime in order to preempt the victory of the insurgents. Given the urgency of the crisis in the countryside, it would seem that a wise course for U.S. policy would be to lend active support to the reformist elements in their efforts to implement and enforce a prohibition against the existence and operation of paramilitary units.

This brings us to the question of U.S. support of reforms in these countries. I have argued in this chapter that the pressures created by population growth necessitate reforms that will provide opportunities that reduce the risk of subsistence crises facing the large and growing numbers of peasants displaced by economic and demographic changes. What is also evident from the preceding discussion is that population growth in most of these countries has gone beyond the point that this problem can be solved with a redistribution of land. Land reform is a legitimate element of any reform package, but the size of the population that is facing severe economic crises is too large for their conditions to be relieved strictly through the redistribution of a fixed amount of land. The Salvadoran land reform program is indicative of the limits of such reforms in securing the legitimacy of the regime among those whose support for it is rendered so fragile by their deteriorating economic conditions. The Salvadoran program redistributes land only to those who were already tenants or permanent employees of large estates. Estimates are that 40–60% of the rural population is now landless and therefore is unaffected by these reforms. Yet they are the very ones who face the greatest risk of subsistence crisis and therefore are the most susceptible to rebel appeals. Reforms must address their conditions as well, and indeed should arguably concentrate most intensely on relieving their distress.

The land reform programs that are implemented must go beyond a mere redistribution of land. "Land to the Tiller" programs, for instance, should be devised in such a way that the typical beneficiary will have enough land to become and remain financially solvent. Phase III of the Salvadoran land reform program set a ceiling of 7 hectares on the amount of land that any one family could receive. Yet various international agencies have estimated that 9 hectares is the minimum needed for subsistence in El Salvador. Debates have raged over the validity of these competing estimates of the minimum plot size, but the point that should be stressed is that plots need to be large enough, not just for subsistence, but for viability as a commercial farmer. This will require not just sufficient land for each farmer but the creation of a complex of support institutions and infrastructure including credit institutions, extension services, transportation infrastructure, and administrative agencies that can assist groups of farmers in cooperating in the acquisition of seed, fertilizer, and equipment, as well as in the marketing of their crops. Assisting in the construction of these support institutions and in the training of indigenous personnel to manage them would seem to be a wise investment of U.S. aid to these countries. Otherwise, the newly created population of smallholders will eventually begin to fall victim to fluctuations in markets and weather and be forced back into the landless population.

This chapter's description of the political economy of land reform also contained some implications about the relative benefits of various distribution formulas. I argued that the redistribution of land into larger cooperative enterprises had certain advantages over "land to the tiller" formulas. In general, these larger units are more able to insure themselves and their members against the risks of agriculture inherent in commodity markets and the weather. Such considerations should be kept in mind when regimes are designing land reform programs, as the stability of the redistribution is essential to the long-term maintenance of popular support in the countryside. These larger units, too, will require the support institutions mentioned above; in addition, they will require an immediate infusion of managerial and administrative expertise. U.S. policies could be directed toward providing this through training programs. Otherwise, the cooperatives will be forced to turn for such assistance to the only indigenous sources of managerial experience: the staffs of the former *latifundistas*. The experience of other nations that have used such a strategy does not recommend it to the Central American situation. Assistance by the United States in the form of direct infusions of technical personnel and longer-term training programs of indigenous personnel would enhance the economic viability of each unit, the stability of the land redistribution, and therefore the security of whatever increases in popular support for the regime result from the land reform.

Still, land reform in and of itself will not relieve the economic distress of the vast majority of the rural population, and steps must be taken to generate occupational alternatives for families that cannot be absorbed into the agricultural economy. This will require investment in new enterprises, and given the limited resources of the indigenous regimes and the drain on those resources imposed by large investments in internal security, the United States seems to be the likely source of such investment capital. Proposing an economic development strategy for these regimes is obviously beyond the scope of this chapter and my expertise. Nevertheless, the goal of that program should obviously be to provide jobs and some measure of economic security to the large numbers of displaced peasants who otherwise are threatened by subsistence crises. Given the fact that population growth will continue for the foreseeable future, the question that must be addressed is how to create enough jobs, and continue to create them at a high enough rate to absorb the current unemployed and underemployed as well as the future entrants into the job market. There is no easy answer to this dilemma, but a few suggestions can be offered. In the first place, policies should be shaped to encourage indigenous investors, since they are more likely than foreign investors to reinvest profits in the local economy. Second, it would probably be wise for policies to encourage some geographic dispersion of new enterprises, since overconcentration of them will impose greater public service infrastructure requirements on a regime already short of resources. Third, government investment in infrastructure, education, and health care will be necessary to enhance the productivity of domestic enterprises and make them competitive with foreign counterparts.

These and other elements of any development program will obviously require infusions of outside financial and technical assistance, and the United States should consider the value to its interests of making such a commitment. It should be clear from the demographic picture of Central America that any such commitment will have to be long term as well. If occupational alternatives are not created for the displaced rural population, then the ability of the regimes in the countries to prevent a loss of popular support in the countryside will erode with further increases in the size of that displaced population. Creating these opportunities will be expensive, and its is clear that the indigenous regimes do not have the required resources. The question for the United States, then, is which is more expensive: making the commitment to the development of these societies or dealing with the security threat and immigration problems that the collapse of these regimes will entail.

REFERENCES

Amnesty International

1981 *Amnesty International Report.* London: Amnesty International.

Anderson, Thomas P.

1984 "The roots of revolution in Central America. In Howard Wiarda (ed.), *Rift and Revolution: The Central American Imbroglio.* Washington, D.C.: American Enterprise Institute.

Armstrong, Robert

1980 "El Salvador: Why revolution?" *NACLA Report on the Americas* 14(2) (March–April).

Amstrong, Robert and Janet Shenk
1980 "El Salvador: A revolution brews." *NACLA Report on the Americas* 14(4) (July–August).
Arnson, Cynthia
1981 "The *Frente's* opposition: The security forces of El Salvador." In M. E. Gettleman *et al.* (eds.), *El Salvador: Central American in the New Cold War.* New York: Grove Press.
Baloyra, Enrique
1982 *El Salvador in Transition.* Chapel Hill: University of North Carolina Press.
Bonner, Raymond
1981 "Salvador land program aids few." In M. E. Gettleman et al. (eds.), *El Salvador: Central America in the New Cold War.* New York: Grove Press.
Bowen, G. L.
1984 "Guatemala: The origins and development of state terrorism." In D. E. Shulz and D. H. Graham (eds.), *Revolution and Counterrevolution in Central America and the Caribbean.* Boulder, Colo.: Westview Press.
Brown, Andrea
1983 "Land of the few: Rural land ownership in Guatemala." In Stanford Central American Action Network (eds.), *Revolution in Central America.* Boulder, Colo.: Westview Press.
Dorner, Peter and Rodolpho Quiros
1973 "Institutional dualism in Central America's agricultural development." *Journal of Latin American Studies* 5(2):217–232.
Eisenstadt, S. N. and Luis Roniger
1981 "The study of patron–client relations and recent developments in sociological theory." In S. N. Eisenstadt and R. Lemarchand (eds.), *Political Clientelism, Patronage and Development.* Beverly Hills, Calif.: Sage.
Evans, Ernest
1984 "Revolutionary movements in Central America: The development of a new strategy." In Howard Wiarda (ed.), *Rift and Revolution: The Central American Imbroglio.* Washington, D.C.: American Enterprise Institute.
Gettleman, M. E., P. Lacefield, L. Manashe, D. Mermelstein, and R. Radosh (eds.)
1981 *El Salvador: Central America in the New Cold War.* New York: Grove Press.
Gomez, Leonel
1981 "El Salvador's land reform: A real promise, but a final failure." *Food Monitor,* No. 22 (July–August). Excerpted in M. E. Gettleman *et al.* (eds.), *El Salvador: Central America in the New Cold War.* New York: Grove Press.
Hoeffel, Paul H.
1984 "Twilight of the oligarchs." In Donald E. Shulz and Douglas H. Graham (eds.), *Revolution and Counterrevolution in Central America and the Carribbean.* Boulder, Colo.: Westview Press.
Leiken, Robert S.
1984 "The Salvadoran left." In Robert S. Leiken (ed.), *Central America: Anatomy of a Conflict.* New York: Pergamon.
Lemarchand, Rene
1981 "Comparative political clientelism: Structure, process and optic." In S. N. Eisenstadt and R. Lemarchand (eds.), *Political Clientelism, Patronage and Development.* Beverly Hills, Calif.: Sage.
McDonald, Ronald
1984 "Civil–Military relations in Central America: The dilemmas of political institution-

alization." In Howard Wiarda (ed.), *Rift and Revolution: The Central American Imbroglio*. Washington, D.C.: American Enterprise Institute.

Migdal, Joel S.
1974 *Peasants, Politics and Revolution: Pressures toward Political Change in the Third World*. Princeton: Princeton University Press.

Millett, Richard
1984 "Praetorians or patriots? The Central American military." In Robert S. Leiken (ed.), *Central America: Anatomy of a Conflict*. New York: Pergamon.

Moller, H.
1968 "Youth as a force in the modern world." *Comparative Studies in History and Society* 10:237–260.

Montgomery, Tommie Sue
1982 *Revolution in El Salvador: Origins and Evolution*. Boulder, Colo.: Westview Press.

Popkin, Samuel L.
1979 *The Rational Peasant: The Political Economy of Rural Society in Vietnam*. Berkeley: University of California Press.

Powell, John Duncan
1970 "Peasant society and clientelist politics." *American Political Science Review* 64(2) (June):411–425.

Prosterman, Roy L.
1981 "El Salvador's land reform: The real facts and the true alternatives." *Food Monitor*, No. 22 (July–August). Excerpted in M. E. Gettleman *et al.* (eds.), *El Salvador: Central American in the New Cold War*. New York: Grove Press.

Prosterman, Roy L. and Mary Temple
1980 "Agrarian reform in El Salvador." *AFL–CIO Bulletin*.

Roniger, Luis
1981 "Clientelism and patron–client relations: A bibliography." In S. N. Eisenstadt and R. Lemarchand (eds.), *Political Clientelism, Patronage and Development*. Beverly Hills, Calif.: Sage.

Scott, James C.
1972 "Patron–client politics and political change in Southeast Asia." *American Political Science Review* 66(1) (March):91–113.
1976 *The Moral Economy of the Peasant: Rebellion and Subsistence in Southeast Asia*. New Haven: Yale University Press.

Scott, James C. and Benedict J. Kerkvliet
1976 "How traditional rural patrons lose legitimacy—A theory with special reference in Southeast Asia." In S. W. Schmidt *et al.* (eds.), *Friends, Followers, and Factions: A Reader in Political Clientelism*. Berkeley: University of California Press.

Shiras, Peter
1981a "The false promise—and real violence—of land reform in El Salvador." *Food Monitor*, No. 20 (January–February). Excerpted in M. E. Gettleman *et al.* (eds.), *El Salvador: Central American in the New Cold War*. New York: Grove Press.
1981b "El Salvador's land reform: The relationship of reform to repression." *Food Monitor*, No. 22 (July–August). Excerpted in M. E. Gettleman *et al.* (eds.), *El Salvador: Central American in the New Cold War*. New York: Grove Press.

Shulz, Donald E.
1984 "El Salvador: Revolution and counterrevolution in the living museum." In Donald E. Shulz and Douglas H. Graham (eds.), *Revolution and Counterrevolution in Central America and the Carribbean*. Boulder, Colo.: Westview Press.

Simon, Laurence R. and James C. Stephens, Jr.
1981 *El Salvador Land Reform: 1980–1981—Impact Audit* OXFAM–America. Excerpted in M. E. Gettleman *et al.* (eds.), *El Salvador: Central America in the New Cold War* New York: Grove Press.

Strasma, John, *et al.*
1983 *Agrarian Reform in El Salvador.* Washington, D.C.: Agency for International Development.

Taylor, Charles L. and David A. Jodice
1983 *World Handbook of Political and Social Indicators*, 3rd Ed. New Haven, CT.: Yale University Press.

U.S. State Department
1984 "Report on El Salvador." Mimeographed.

Wheaton, Philip
1980 *Agrarian Reform in El Salvador: A Program for Rural Pacification.* Washington, D.C.: EPICA Task Force.

Wiarda, Howard
1984 "The origins of the crisis in Central America." In Howard Wiarda (ed.), *Rift and Revolution: The Central American Imbroglio.* Washington, D.C.: American Enterprise Institute.

10

U.S. Security, Labor-Force Absorption, and Food Supply in Latin America

DANIEL S. PAPP

This chapter's purpose is straightforward and simply defined: to examine the impact that the level of labor-force absorption and food supply in Latin America have and may be expected to have on U.S. security interests. Unfortunately, defining the purpose is the only simple task in this chapter.

Complexities begin with the subject of the study: Is there in fact a linkage between U.S. security, on the one hand, and labor-force absorption and food supply, on the other? If so, what is that linkage? The answers to these questions in turn are related to the answers to other questions: How is U.S. national security defined? What specific conditions exist and may be expected to exist in the issue areas of labor-force absorption and food supply? What are the internal social, political, economic, and other dynamics within the states under discussion that may be affected by labor-force absorption and food supply? What external factors may be expected to play roles, and how? Only when these questions have been examined may we reasonably and logically explore the original inquiry; even then, any conclusions reached must be tentative and open to debate and discussion. Given the speculative nature of much of the present and all of the future "data" on labor absorption and food supply, as well as the uncertainty that exists about the dynamics of the relationships between key variables used herein, greater certitude would be misleading and, in a policy sense, dangerous.

U.S. NATIONAL SECURITY IN THE CONTEXTS OF LABOR-FORCE ABSORPTION, FOOD SUPPLY, AND LATIN AMERICA

National security is a comprehensive concept that includes not only the defense of a state's people, territories, and properties against physical attack but also the "protection, through a variety of means, of vital economic and political interests, the loss of which could threaten fundamental values and the vitality of the state" (Jordan and Taylor, 1981:3). Defined in this way, U.S. national security interests imply certain broad goals for U.S. policies toward developing states, including those in Latin America. These goals include:

1. Maintain world peace and avoid and prevent large-scale warfare. Thus, the United States maintains extensive military forces and seeks to solve disputes peacefully.
2. Prevent the expansion of influence of states opposed to U.S. values. This implies the need to maintain or strengthen the political and economic stability of U.S. friends and allies in the developing world and nonaligned states.
3. Maintain an open global economy and protect U.S. access to foreign markets and resource needs.
4. Encourage other states to adopt principles of self-determination, human rights, and other concepts that are the basis of the U.S. political system (Sewell and Mathieson, 1981:148–168).

An Overview of U.S. Security Interests in Latin America

These general goals can be given specific meaning in the context of different developing regions—for our purposes, Latin America. The national security interests of the United States in Latin America include prevention of the establishment of any military presence in the Western Hemisphere that presents a threat to the U.S. homeland or to the homelands of U.S. friends and allies in the hemisphere. National security interests also include preventing the expansion of influence of dictatorships, whether they be politically on the left or the right. Indeed, under certain circumstances, reduction or elimination of the influence of left- and right-wing dictatorships in Latin America, eventually leading to the establishment of freely elected governments, may even become a security objective.

Economic interests of the United States in Latin America are also considerable, and their protection must be considered a security goal. Of all U.S. private investment in the developing world, 62% is in Latin America alone (Kissinger *et al.*, 1984:8). Fifteen percent of all U.S. trade is with Latin America (Kissinger *et al.*, 1948:8) and as much as two-thirds of all U.S. seaborne foreign trade passes through the Caribbean, the Gulf of Mexico, and the Panama Canal (Anonymous, 1984:1). Three-fourths of all imported U.S. oil and over half of U.S. imported strategic minerals transit Caribbean waters alone (Anonymous, 1984:1).

In a certain sense, social and cultural linkages between the United States and Latin America also create U.S. security interests in Latin America. Even as a cultural kinship has existed for centuries between the United States and Europe, U.S. cultural connections with Latin America have in recent decades become increasingly important. While this cultural identity may be of arguable merit in national security terms, it cannot be dismissed.

Finally, geography dictates that Latin America, or at least Central America and the Caribbean, be a security interest of the United States, not only because of the possibility of hostile military presence but also because of legal and illegal immigration from the region. Only residents of Central America and the Caribbean have the possibility in large numbers of reaching the United States without governmental approval. Ronald Reagan expressed his own fears of a possible Central American refugee problem in 1983, arguing in a speech in Jackson, Mississippi, that if the United States accepted a "string of anti-American Marxist dictatorships" there, then "the result could be a tidal wave of refugees—and this time they'll be feet people not boat people—swarming into our country seeking a safe haven from Communist repression to our south." The overstated alarmism of Reagan's rhetoric should not obscure the fact that in a very real sense, the ability to control immigration from Central America and the Caribbean is a security interest of the United States.

These diverse and extensive U.S. goals and interests in Latin America may be threatened by a variety of factors (Dominquez, 1980). In this study, however, I restrict myself to the threats that might be posed by inadequate labor-absorption rates and inadequate food-supply and distribution systems. Both labor-absorption rates and food-supply and distribution systems play significant roles in determining an individual state's overall economic condition, a factor that in American eyes has often played a major role in furthering or hindering U.S. efforts to promote and defend national security interests. Thus, before I examine the roles that labor absorption and food supplies have in national economies, I first explore the role that the United States has assigned to the economic conditions of foreign states in its overall national security policy.

Economic Conditions and National Security: The American Perspective

That economic conditions within certain foreign states are closely linked to U.S. national security interests has been a fundamental assumption of our foreign policy and national security policy since at least 1947. Indeed, part of the original impetus for the Marshall Plan in that year was the belief that Europe's disastrous economic condition, including high unemployment and food shortages, provided fertile ground for the growth of communism, fascism, and other extreme political–social–economic philosophies deemed antithetical to U.S. values and traditions (Jones, 1955; Spanier, 1983: 38–40). In part, this belief stemmed from the German and Italian experiences of the 1920s and 1930s; in part, it flowed from the growth of communist and other radical political influence in Western Europe following World War II. Additionally, of course, any growth of communist influence following World War II was interpreted as expanded Soviet influence as well. Thus, the economic–security linkage became even more credible.

Gradually, the argument that economic conditions within certain foreign states were closely linked to U.S. security interests was expanded to apply to regions beyond Europe. The U.S. economic assistance programs to developing states, originally articulated in the Point Four program, the Food for Peace program, and related foreign assistance efforts, were therefore to a considerable extent implemented because of their perceived contribution to U.S. national security. Insofar as Latin America was concerned, much of the rationale behind the Alliance for Progress was tied to security. John Kennedy's 10-year plan to develop stable economies and growing middle classes sought specifically to prevent more Castro-style revolutions in Latin America. The United States promised Latin American states about $20 billion in aid and sought internal tax and land reforms in turn from the recipient states (Schlesinger, 1965:185–205).

More recent U.S. administrations have also used this logic and linked U.S. security interests in Latin America to economic conditions there. Some linked security and economics implicitly; some linked the two explicitly; none have been more vocal than the Reagan administration. Reagan's Assistant Secretary of State for Inter-American Affairs Langhorne A. Motley has been particularly articulate about the linkage in Central America:

> In Central America, communism, violence, and dictatorship feed on misery and a dismal history of injustice. . . . This destructive dynamism must end. But it cannot be broken without immediate and persistent action in support of democratic self-determination, economic and social development that fairly benefits all, and cooperation in meeting threats to the security of the region. . . . The U.S. interests involved . . . are both moral and strategic. They are threatened by

> human rights abuse and economic misery and by Cuban and Soviet intervention. (Motley, 1984b:77)

Elsewhere, Motley observed that throughout Latin America, left-wing and right-wing extremism is weakened by economic development (Motley, 1984: 4). Reagan himself acknowledged his acceptance of this linkage both in the Caribbean Basin Initiative (CBI) proposal of February 24, 1982, and the Central American Initiative legislation of February 17, 1984. The former initiative, signed into law on August 5, 1983, as the Caribbean Basin Economic Recovery Act, created a one-way free trade area for 12 years for Caribbean exports to the United States and provided tax incentives for convention tourism to the Caribbean. A year later, the Central American Initiative provided $400 million for fiscal year 1984 for emergency economic stabilization, and another $5.9 billion in appropriated funds and $2 billion in insurance and guarantees for fiscal years 1985 to 1989. For fiscal year 1985, $1.1 billion in appropriations and $600 million in insurance was originally requested, with appropriated monies being divided between El Salvador ($341 million), Costa Rica ($208 million), Honduras ($139 million) and Guatemala ($96 million). Monies were requested for balance-of-payments support for imports ($550 million), Food for Peace purchases under U.S. Public Law 480 ($120 million), commercial agriculture ("major funding"), and "labor intensive construction of infrastructure and housing" (Reagan, 1984a:75).

Obviously, then, past and present U.S. policymakers have linked internal economic conditions in certain developing states with U.S. national security interests, and they have done so within the context of Latin America. Although current concern is riveted on Central America and the Caribbean, the economics–security linkage extends throughout Latin America.

Labor-Force Absorption and Food Supply as Economic Inputs

Having explored U.S. security interests in Latin America and the economic–security linkages as seen by U.S. policymakers, I now turn to the role that labor-force-absorption rates and food-supply levels play within national economies. The political impact of both factors is also examined; indeed, insofar as American security interests are concerned, political impacts of labor-force-absorption rates and food-supply levels may be more important than their economic impacts.

Labor-force absorption may be roughly defined as the degree to which available labor assets are utilized. Both the demand for labor and supply of labor must be known or estimated before labor-force-absorption rates can be determined. These rates may differ significantly from county to county within a region; within a country, they may differ significantly between rural and urban locations, and even between rural locations in different parts of one country and urban locations in different parts of the same country.

Labor-force-absorption rates are particularly difficult to calculate in many developing countries because of the uncertainty and paucity of available data. Further complicating the question is the combination of underemployment statistics within labor-force absorption. Nevertheless, despite these difficulties in ascertaining these rates, the economic impacts of unutilized labor are considerable: poverty for unemployed and underemployed workers, loss of potential national output, increased propensity to emigrate to countries where employment possibilities are better, higher crime rates, and the probability of heightened political unrest (Gendell, 1985:1).

The last point deserves additional commentary. The extent to which unemployment and underemployment lead to political unrest depends on a number of factors, including a government's ability and willingness to suspend a "safety net" under unfortunate laborers; the degree of politicization of the unemployed and underemployed; the degree of equity in the distribution of wealth; the availability of food, housing, medical assistance, and other "basic needs"; and other quality-of-life considerations. Perhaps the most significant factor influencing the degree to which unemployment and underemployment may lead to political unrest is yet another factor: expectations. The greater the level of expectations held by those unemployed and underemployed, the greater the likelihood that political unrest will eventuate. Indeed, at least according to the U.S. Central Intelligence Agency (CIA), one of the central failings of the Alliance for Progress was that is promised too much and then failed to deliver on its promises. Since Latin American publics allegedly blamed "governments for most evils and failures," the "hazards of governing [in Latin America] may be increasing rather than lessening," according to the CIA research. The security interests of the United States were also increasingly jeopardized, since Latin American "governments and peoples look abroad for convenient scapegoats (Central Intelligence Agency, quoted in La Feher, 1984:60).

Food-supply uncertainties in many respects parallel labor-force-absorption uncertainties. Both demand for food and supply of food must be known or reliably estimated before meaningful conclusions can be drawn; even then, extensive difficulties remain. Food supply and demand may differ significantly from country to country within a region, and within a country, between rural and urban locations. Food supply and demand are also difficult to calculate in many countries because of the uncertainty and paucity of available data. These points are further complicated by the realization that even though a country in the aggregate may have sufficient food supplies, some people may not be getting enough to eat. Thus the distribution of available food becomes an issue at least as important as absolute food levels. And inadequate food consumption, regardless of whether it is caused by absolute food deficits or maldistribution of food, has both human and economic costs. Hunger yields human misery and health problems, and prevents the fullest realization of human capabilities. All in turn reduce economic output.

But what about the political fallout of food issues? Here, a concept similar to the "expectations" formulation used earlier in the discussion of labor-force absorption may prove useful; the concept of "entitlements" to food consists of individuals' own production of food for domestic consumption; incomes earned in any activity; and/or enrollment in programs that give away food or make it available in other ways outside market structures (Musgrove, 1985:17; Sen, 1982). Entitlement implies that one has a right to a particular item, whether it is food or something else (Musgrove, 1985: 32–33). In a political sense, then, food shortages, again regardless of whether they result from absolute shortages or maldistribution, are more likely to lead to political unrest when food is viewed as an entitlement. Even as the political impact of the rate of labor-force absorption may be most usefully interpreted in the light of the expectations of the labor force, the political impact of the level of food availability may be most usefully interpreted in the light of the degree to which disparate populations view food as an entitlement. None of this makes analysis easier, but perhaps it will make conclusions more meaningful.

Low rates of labor-force absorption and low levels of food availability have the potential to cause political unrest, and political unrest has the potential to lead to outcomes that could adversely impact U.S. security interests in Latin America and beyond. Any conclusions that may be reached must be based on the specifics of labor-force absorption and food availability in Latin America, and it is to those issues that I now turn.

LABOR-FORCE ABSORPTION AND FOOD SUPPLY IN LATIN AMERICA: ECONOMIC AND POLITICAL IMPLICATIONS

What forecasts may be made about the near term and midterm future situations in Latin America concerning labor-force absorption and food supply? Recognizing all the shortcomings and difficulties inherent both in present data and future projections, two noted experts, Murray Gendell (1985) and Philip Musgrove (1985), have hazarded the following predictions and estimates of, respectively, the Latin American labor-force-absorption situation and the Latin American food-supply situation to the year 2000.

Except where otherwise noted, all statistical information in this section comes from these two sources.

Labor-Force Absorption

The labor force in Latin America has grown extremely rapidly in recent decades, but is projected to grow at somewhat slower rates during the rest of the century.[1] Even so, the labor force will more than double between 1970 and 2000, and will increase by 70% between 1980 and 2000. Extensive country-to-country variation is probable, with Argentina's labor force expected to grow by as little as 44% between 1970 and 2000 and Mexico's expected to almost triple during the same period.

This growth will differ immensely between rural and urban regions in most countries; in urban areas in some states, labor-force growth will be differentiated between sexes as well. Table 1 presents the comparative sizes of the urban and rural labor forces in selected Latin American countries and the region as a while for 1970 and 2000, as well as the percentage growth for the respective labor forces over the period. Table 2 shows the different growth

TABLE 1
Urban and Rural Labor-Force Growth in Latin America, 1970–2000 (in millions of workers)

	Argentina		*Brazil*		*Columbia*		*Mexico*	
Year	*Rural*	*Urban*	*Rural*	*Urban*	*Rural*	*Urban*	*Rural*	*Urban*
1970	1.8	27.5	13.2	16.8	2.5	3.9	5.7	8.0
2000	1.6	11.9	15.7	51.2	3.0	11.5	8.4	30.4
Percentage growth, 1970–2000	89	159	119	305	120	295	147	380

Source: Gendell (1985:Tables 3 and 4).

TABLE 2
Male and Female Labor-Force Growth in Latin America, 1970–2000 (in millions of workers)

	Argentina		*Brazil*		*Columbia*		*Mexico*	
Year	*Male*	*Female*	*Male*	*Female*	*Male*	*Female*	*Male*	*Female*
1970	5.4	2.1	12.3	4.5	2.7	1.2	6.3	1.7
2000	8.1	3.8	36.2	15.0	7.9	3.6	22.7	7.7
Percentage growth, 1970–2000	150	181	294	333	293	300	360	453

Source: See Table 1.

[1]Gendell (1984:2) estimates labor-force growth in Latin America as 34% in the 1970s, 32% in the 1980s, and 29% in the 1990s.

rates for male and female segments of the urban labor force over the same 30 years; again, percentage growth rates are also included.

The key question, of course, is whether these new laborers will be able of find jobs. Despite differences between different projections of growth of labor demand, most projections conclude that the economies of most Latin American states will not expand rapidly enough to absorb all the new laborers. This will be true at least through the 1980s; during the 1990s, if Latin American economies can expand as rapidly as they did during the 1960s and 1970s, labor-force absorption could keep pace with labor-force growth. Because of declining fertility rates, the unemployment and underemployment situation improves somewhat after the turn of the century, although a lag of about 15 years exists before a drop in fertility rate effects labor supply.

Food Supply

In the aggregate, Latin America's overall food situation improved between 1960 and 1981. Sixteen of 22 countries showed either constancy or a net increase in per capita caloric intake per day, and 12 of 22 countries increased the quality of food produced. Nineteen of 21 countries imported more cereal grains in 1982 than in 1960, thus accounting for much of the increased caloric intake. In some cases, increased cereal imports were paid for with proceeds from nonfood agricultural exports; indeed, 16 of 21 Latin American states showed overall increases in agricultural production between 1960 and 1982 (i.e., foodstuffs plus nonfood agricultural products).

These 22 states may be further subdivided into six major groups.[2] The first two groups include those states where caloric input went down. Three states—Haiti, Nicaragua, and Peru—had decreased food production and constitute the first group. Three more states—Panama, Brazil, and Uraguay—enjoyed greater food production but nevertheless experienced lower caloric intakes per person per day. The third and fourth groups had caloric intakes per person per day that remained constant or increased by 10% or less between 1960 and 1981. Group 3, consisting of Honduras, the Dominican Republic, Ecuador, and Cuba, had decreased food production despite constant or slightly increased consumption, while group 4—Bolivia, Guatemala, and Columbia—increased their food production. Finally, the fifth and sixth groups of states all enjoyed per person per day caloric increases of over 10%. The fifth group—Jamaica, Chile, and Trinidad and Tobago—produced less food; the sixth group—El Salvador, Costa Rica, Paraguay,

[2]This division is significantly different from the one put forward in Musgrove (1985:6, 7). The following categories were compiled from Musgrove (1985:Table 1).

Mexico, Argentina, and Venezuela—produced more. Interestingly enough, only Paraguay and Uraguay decreased their cereal grain imports; Argentina never imported any.

These categorizations are useful for informational purposes, but they do not approach what may be a more meaningful parameter of measurement: internal distribution of food. Nor do they address the entitlement question: To what extent do people believe that they rightfully should have more food than they do?

But what of the future? With Latin America's population estimated to grow by between 1.62% and 2.08% per year between now and the end of the century (Musgrove, 1985:12–13), food supply must grow by at least that level to keep current average caloric intakes constant. Can it? Musgrove (1985:13) concludes not only that it can but also that indigenous Latin American food output by itself can, exclusive of imports.

Once again, this optimistic assessment tells only part of the story. It is "optimistic" in that supply keeps pace with demand, but it is insufficient in that demand may not keep pace with need; low income or no income in many cases artificially depresses demand below the point where basic needs are satisfied. In the aggregate, then, all factors taken together lead to "requirement of a 58 percent increase [in food production by the end of the century] for the 22 countries, with much variation among them" (Musgrove, 1985:15). Caloric intake in Bolivia, Honduras, El Salvador, Nicaragua, Guatemala, Ecuador, and Venezuela would have to rise by 80% to eliminate malnutrition and keep pace with demographic and income growth (Musgrove, 1985:15–16). Other states would need less sizable increases, but all would need more.

Economic and Political Implications

In both relative and absolute terms, Gendell and Musgrove do not see the aggregate Latin American labor-force-absorption picture or the overall food-supply picture getting much worse than it currently is before the end of the century. Some countries will fare better than others, and labor underemployment will probably increase. Even so, this is not the picture of economic armageddon and famine that is sometimes painted.

Neither is there room for complacency. More people than ever before will have barely enough income and food to scrape by at the subsistence level, if Gendell and Musgrove are correct; neither envisions significant changes in the internal distribution of income or food throughout Latin America. And as the World Bank (1984) data displayed in Table 3 indicates, income distribution in Latin America is extremely uneven.

TABLE 3
Income Distribution in Latin America

Country	Year	Percentage Share of Household Income By Percentile Groups of Households: Lowest 20%	Second Quintile	Third Quintile	Fourth Quintile	Highest 20%
Argentina	1970	4.4	9.7	14.1	21.5	50.3
Brazil	1972	2.0	5.0	9.4	17.0	66.6
Chile	1968	4.4	9.0	13.8	21.4	51.4
Costa Rica	1971	3.3	8.7	13.3	19.9	54.8
Mexico	1977	2.9	7.0	12.0	20.4	57.7
Panama	1970	2.0	5.2	11.0	20.0	61.8
Peru	1972	1.9	5.1	11.0	21.0	61.0
Trinidad and Tobago	1975–1976	4.2	9.1	13.9	22.8	50.0
Venezuela	1970	3.0	7.3	12.9	22.8	54.0

Source: World Bank (1984:272).

Equally foreboding, more and more of Latin America's population will be in urban locales. This was reflected earlier in the discussion of the growth of the urban labor force as compared to the rural labor force. Total population percentages are equally surprising. By 2000, 75.4% of Latin America's population is expected to be urbanized, compared to 65.3% in 1980 and 41.4% in 1950 (World Bank, 1984:67). Estimates for city sizes in Latin America by 2000 are, in several cases, nothing short of staggering. Mexico City will be the world's largest city with 31 million people, and São Paulo will be the second-largest city in the world in 2000, with a population of 19 million. Latin America will also have two other cities among the 20 largest in 2000: Buenos Aires in sixteenth place with 12.1 million people and Bogota in twentieth place with 11.7. By way of comparison, Mexico City in 1975 was the world's third-largest city with 11.9 million people (World Bank, 1984: 68).

These observations, when viewed in the context of earlier labor-force-absorption and food-supply summations, lead to several inescapable conclusions. First, Latin American governments must devote increasing amounts of time, money, and effort to service delivery and job creation in the cities. More service delivery is necessary simply because of the crush of people, and more urban jobs are needed because of the growth of the urban labor force. From both economic and political perspectives, logic dictates that new jobs, whether created by public or private efforts, must be labor intensive.

Second, unless internal income distribution is improved or absolute levels of income are raised significantly, urban political activism and in some cases radical activism are likely to increase. Here it is assumed that uneven income distribution becomes less of a political factor as absolute levels of income of all sectors of the population increase. This assumption must be qualified by the previously discussed concepts of expectations and entitlements. To the extent that the Latin American public comes to expect more and better jobs, food, and standards of living, but does not receive them, political activism will rise; and to the extent that the Latin America public comes to believe that they are entitled to more and better jobs, food, and standards of living, political activism will rise. This activism will be increasingly radical the more that activists feel their expectations and entitlements are not being met. Activism and radicalism will probably span the political spectrum from extreme left to extreme right. And the more that radicals can make their case credible that shortfalls in expectations or entitlements are the result of governments in power or systems in being, the greater will be the likelihood of large-scale opposition to those governments and systems.

Third, the above chain of logic is likely to hold true under most circumstances if only because the absolute numbers of those who expect more or feel themselves entitled to more are likely to increase. Even if the percentages of underemployed hold relatively constant, more people will be in these categories. Additionally, political philosophies such as revolutionary communism and elitist fascism present explanations for existent problems and prescribe solutions to those problems, and may well find increased followings among Latin America's poorer millions. In a somewhat similar vein, "liberation theology" (Cone, 1981; Conn, 1982; Krauthammer, 1981; Sidu, 1980; Wall, 1982) may play a larger role than either communism or fascism in politicizing the poor in Latin America because of the Catholic church. The church is seriously divided by liberation theology's assault on traditionalism. Nevertheless, even if the percentage of unemployed and underemployed holds relatively constant, a greater percentage of them will probably be politicized. To repeat the words of the CIA's 1964 assessment of the Alliance for Progress, the "hazards of governing may be increasing rather than lessening" (cited in La Feber, 1984:60).

Fourth, although it is far from certain, constancy in rates of labor-force absorption and availability of food therefore imply that democratically elected governments in many Latin American states and even governments that are not democratically elected but may be described as moderate will, by the end of the century, be increasingly hard pressed to remain democratic and moderate. This pessimism is in stark contrast to the current optimism, in Latin America and beyond, generated by the wave of democratic reforms and free elections in the mid 1980s that has swept Latin America. Indeed, by 1985 many Latin American states either had or were moving toward democratically elected governments.

Obviously, factors additional to labor-force-absorption rates and food-supply levels affect these economic and political trends. But labor-force absorption and food supply play central roles in all of them. With this in mind, I now turn to the central theme of the chapter: the implications of labor-force-absorption rates and food supply in Latin America for U.S. national security.

LABOR-FORCE ABSORPTION AND FOOD SUPPLY: CHALLENGES FOR U.S. SECURITY

The challenges that labor-force-absorption shortfalls and food-supply problems in Latin America could present to U.S. security interests may be usefully grouped into three different categories. The first form of challenge stems immediately from labor and food questions; these challenges may be termed first-order challenges because they present direct threats to U.S. security interests. The second form of challenge is more the result of forces that inadequate labor-force-absorption rates and insufficient food availability unleash; they are thus second-order challenges. The final form of challenge may result from governmental changes that second-order challenges bring about; this final challenge is then a third-order challenge, since it is neither direct nor the immediate result of forces unleased by inadequate labor-force-absorption rates or inadequate food availability.

First-Order Challenges

There are very few ways in which inadequate labor-force-absorption rates and shortfalls in food availability could present immediate and direct challenges to U.S. security interests either in Latin America or elsewhere, and it is perhaps because of this fact that unemployment, underemployment, and hunger often rank relatively low on the list of threats to U.S. security. Nevertheless, two first-order challenges to U.S. security exist that may, under certain circumstances, be linked to inadequate labor-absorption rates and food availability. These first-order challenges are attacks on American properties and lives and uncontrollable immigration to the United States. The first challenge exists throughout Latin America; the second is important primarily in Central America and the Caribbean.

The link between inadequate labor-absorption rates and inadequate food-supply and distribution systems, on the one hand, and attacks on American property and personnel, on the other, flows from a simple assumption: People who have little, people who believe that they have too little, and people who see themselves as champions of those who have little frequently see those who have much as the cause of poverty and inadequate satisfaction of basic needs. Whether out of resentment or a desire to "change the system," they lash out at properties and persons that represent "the rich." In some respects, then, terrorism and other attacks on U.S. property and citizens is linked to inadequate labor-absorption rates and food availability.

Unfortunately, the number of attacks on American property and citizens may be more closely related to the absolute numbers of dispossessed people who see themselves as dispossessed, and to people who believe they represent the dispossessed, than to the percentage of the population that is in, or sees itself as being in, these categories. Thus, simply raising the labor-absorption rate and increasing the availability of food, as desirable as they are as objectives, may do little to curb attacks on American property and citizens unless population growth is slowed as well. Even in the most favorable circumstances, however, such attacks probably could not be eliminated short of instituting draconian methods of societal control that are opposed to other U.S. values.

Anticapitalism and anti-Americanism, whether they stem from ideological or nationalist extremism, are probably unavoidable. Nevertheless, improving labor-absorption rates and improving adequacy of food-supply and food-distribution systems, even in the absence of additional slowdowns in population growth, could curtail the growth in frequency of terrorism and attacks directed against U.S. property and citizens in Latin America. This in itself would be a step in the right direction, although probably not as far as security interests under ideal circumstances would demand.

Illegal immigration presents another first-order challenge to American security. Here, the challenge is not to the safety of American property and citizens overseas but to the U.S. social fabric and economic structure at home.[3] The issue here is not immigration per se but the extent to which the United States can control illegal immigration. And during the last decade and more, the United States has been unable to control it borders.

That illegal immigration to the United States from Central America and

[3]Considerable clarification is needed here. The United States has "imported" low-price labor from Mexico and the Caribbean for some time, most noticeably in the case of Mexico under the *bracero* program that formally continued until 1964. Since then, illegal immigration has provided an economic stimulus to the U.S. economy as Central American, particularly Mexican, and Caribbean residents made their way to the United States to take low-paying jobs that, quite often, U.S. laborers refused to touch. At some point, however—and this observation does not render judgment on whether that point has been reached—the number of illegal immigrants seeking low-paying jobs will surpass the number of available jobs. From that time on, each additional illegal immigrant will detract from U.S. economic well-being rather than contribute to it. These observations, it should be stressed, are made without categorizing the low-paid illegal immigrant system as good or bad.

the Caribbean is at least in part tied to labor absorption, and possibly to food supply and availability as well, seems to be beyond dispute. Other factors are of course involved, but the availability of jobs in the United States, even if they are low paying by American standards, serves as a undeniable magnet to draw unemployed and underemployed Central Americans and Caribbean residents to the United States. Raising the labor-absorption rate in Central America and the Caribbean would undoubtedly slow the tide of illegal immigration to the United States; it would not stop it—wage differentials, unless eliminated or greatly reduced, would continue to attract some illegal immigration. But, again, any reduction in the rate of illegal immigration would be a step toward meeting the challenge, and a higher labor-absorption rate and greater availability of food would be movement in that direction.

Second-Order Challenges

Terrorism and illegal immigration are first-order challenges to American security interests because they present immediate and direct challenges to U.S. objectives. Second-order challenges are somewhat less immediate and direct; gradually, over time, inadequate rates of labor-force absorption and inadequate food-supply and food-distribution systems may lead to festering resentment in some Latin American states that results in revolutionary violence, warfare, and governmental changes. Revolutionary violence and warfare may not be directly targeted against U.S. interests, and in some cases, governmental change from the U.S. perspective may even be desirable. Espousal of violence and warfare, however, is not in the alleged American political tradition, and in some cases, leftist or rightist governments that espouse values and systems alien to those that the United States prefers could come to power. In either case, while U.S. property and lives may not be harmed and the U.S. social fabric and economic well-being may not be weakened, U.S. security objectives are challenged.

These are defined as second-order challenges because they need not present immediate and direct threats to U.S. property, lives, social structure, or economic well-being; but they have the potential to weaken U.S. friends and allies and undermine those political traditions that the United States allegedly prefers. These threats may emanate from either the political left or political right, and in some cases may be tied directly to low labor-absorption rates and inadequate food supplies or food distribution systems.

That certain hemisphere and extrahemisphere states, namely Cuba and the Soviet Union, work to exacerbate whatever resentments emanate from inadequate labor-force-absorption rates, food supplies, and food-distribution systems is beyond doubt. Soviet sources regularly accuse U.S. multinational corporations of being the cause of Latin American economic problems, including unemployment and underemployment (*Selskaya Zhizn*, 1982). The Soviets also change that multinational corporations are major contributors to food shortages and food-distribution problems in Latin America (Zhuravleve, 1982:41–44). Soviet commentators also tie low rural wages in Latin America to high profits for American agrobusinesses, noting specifically that cattle is produced in Mexico, Brazil, Nicaragua, Costa Rica, and Guatemala for American markets, and that strawberries are imported to the United States from Mexico (Bagramov, 1982:52–53). Radio Moscow and Radio Havana both make frequent broadcasts to Latin America stressing that the United States and capitalism are at the roots of unemployment, underdevelopment, and food problems in Latin America.

The point must be made that Cuban and Soviet efforts to foment upheaval and revolution in the hemisphere add to, but rarely create, the domestic climates that lead to revolutionary violence and warfare. Soviet and Cuban efforts build on resentments and animosities that already exist and that in some cases are caused by low labor-absorption rates and food-supply and distribution problems. This is also true of right-wing support for revolutionary violence. Neither of these observation implies that threats to U.S. interests are any smaller if they are from the left or the right; both observations imply that remedies additional to coping with left-wing and right-wing extremists are required before the dangers of extremist political revolutions can be meaningfully lessened. It is doubtful that such dangers can ever be eliminated; as argued earlier, at least some revolutionaries base their actions on ideology and nationality rather than objective realities such as unemployment, underemployment, and hunger.

Additionally, it should be noted that with increasing urbanization in Latin America, and with labor-force growth in urban areas being much more rapid than in rural areas, political unrest arising from underemployment, unemployment, and hunger has a greater likelihood to begin in urban areas. Thus, while land reform and other rural rich–poor inequities remain issues that must be dealt with, urban political unrest in Latin America is likely to become more important than rural political unrest by the end of this century. Again, this observation carries major policy implications: Reforms and job creation must become increasingly urban oriented.

It also may carry implications for the speed with which revolutions are accomplished. Although empirical evidence is sparse, it may be argued that "true" urban revolutions (as opposed to government coups) have transformed societies, altered governmental policies, and changed international allegiances more rapidly than rural-based revolutions. If this is true, then the rapidity of change brought about by political unrest in Latin America may be expected to increase as that unrest becomes more urban oriented.

Third-Order Challenges

A final form of challenge to U.S. security interests in Latin America could result from policy decisions made and implemented by governments that come to power on a tide of political unrest fueled by underemployment, unemployment, and hunger. These decisions could mean that U.S. access to needed markets and resources would be limited or eliminated; sea and air lanes of communication could be jeopardized; property could be nationalized; and under extreme circumstances, U.S. friends and allies and even the United States itself could by physically endangered.

It is difficult to link any of these threats directly to inadequate labor-force-absorption rates or inadequate food supplies or distribution systems. Yet a link does exist, if only because such problems lend potent fuel to arguments advanced by extreme left-wing and right-wing political movements; if they came to power, they would be more likely to implement such policies. This is not to say that left-wing or right-wing governments are the only ones that could effect policies adverse to U.S. interests; only that they are more likely to do so. Given this fact, it is reasonable to conclude that the policies of some states, ruled by governments that came to power as a result of political upheavals fueled in part by underdevelopment, unemployment, and hunger, could adversely affect U.S. security interests in Latin America. And to the extent that more jobs and more food could lessen the possibilities that that chain of events would occur, U.S. security interests would be served by responding to their needs.

IMPLICATIONS FOR U.S. POLICY

The challenges that inadequate labor-absorption rates and inadequate food-supply and food-distribution systems present to U.S. security interests in Latin America vary significantly in immediacy and degree of threat. Only two threats, terrorism and illegal immigration, currently present direct dangers to U.S. interests. Arguments can be made that the causes of terrorism are alien value systems, inequitable land and property distributions, foreign intervention, and the "violent nature" of Latin societies; terrorism need not necessarily be linked to underemployment, unemployment, and hunger. In a conceptual sense, policy recommendations to combat terrorism by combating shortfalls in the issue areas under discussion in this chapter are likely to make little headway. Too many possible causes for terrorist activity exist to point to remedies for inadequate labor-absorption rates and inadequate food supplies and food-distribution systems as remedies for this first-order challenge. Thus, in most cases, U.S. policy to combat terrorism will more likely than not continue to be tied to penetrating terrorist networks and reducing the vulnerability of targets rather than approaching the job and food factors that may contribute to the proliferation of terrorist activity.

Illegal immigration is another story. Although the 1984 fate of the Simpson–Mazzoli immigration reform bill highlighted the difficulties inherent in any political approaches to illegal immigration, other American efforts to limit illegal immigration—and not coincidentally to improve Central American and Caribbean living standards—have stressed economics. Both the August 1983 Caribbean Basin Economic Recovery Act and the February 1984 Central American Initiative legislation had as one of their objectives the creation of more jobs in Central America and the Caribbean. Ronald Reagan (1984b:1) lauded the CBI in a July 1984 speech to Caribbean leaders at the University of South Carolina because it "encourages *job-creating* business investment." Reagan's July 1984 Presidential Food Aid Initiative also indicated that the president is cognizant of the food–security as well as the food–humanitarianism link, although the initiative itself was not directed toward Latin America (McPherson, 1984:31). Thus, while one may debate whether present emphasis on labor-absorption shortfalls and food-supply and distribution questions is adequate to address the scope of the problem, it is evident that the Reagan administration is cognizant of the problem and has taken some steps to address it in Central America and the Caribbean. Ignoring the debate over the degree of emphasis placed on job creation, it is nevertheless clear that U.S. concerns and responses are targeted to Central America and the Caribbean. Beyond these subregions, elsewhere in Latin America, where illegal immigration presents little or no threat to American security interests, the United States has only peripherally addressed the job-creation question.

Job creation in Central America and the Caribbean is also, of course, closely tied to the second-order challenge of festering resentment leading to violence, warfare, and governmental change. While the impetus for American programs in Central America and the Caribbean was probably Reagan's expressed fear of a "string of anti-American dictatorships" in Central America, the president's conceptual awareness of the relationship between economic issues and security was expressed in a May 1984 message to Mexico's President Miguel de la Madrid Hurtado on the eve of the International Conference on Population: "Recognizing the seriousness of environmental and economic problems and their relationship to social realities, the United States places a priority upon technological advancement and economic expansion which holds out the hope of prosperity and stability for a rapidly changing world."

Again, however, U.S. policy initiatives clearly indicate that U.S. concern about revolutionary violence, warfare, and government coups, as well as their relationship to underemployment, unemployment, and hunger, is directed primarily toward Central America and the Caribbean. This is understandable, given both the level of violence there and both subregions' proximity to the United States. Nevertheless, future years may find it necessary for the United States to expand its interest beyond Central America and the Caribbean. More urbanization and more population may heighten second-order challenges to U.S. security beyond Central America and the Caribbean, even if labor-force-absorption rates and food-supply and distribution situations remain constant in percentage terms. Thus, for American policy, some "preventive medicine" may be in order.

Unfortunately, preventive medicine is difficult to administer, given the American political system. Preventing future problems is difficult even when those problems are foreseeable simply because they are future, rather than current, problems. As a result, the causes of many foreseeable difficulties are not dealt with before those difficulties arrive; then, quite frequently, they must be dealt with in crisis or near-crisis conditions. The Truman Doctrine, the Marshall Plan, and the Caribbean Basin Initiative all support the point.

Another point must be made that presents problems for U.S. security interests; it also discomforts many Americans. While the United States often advocates that domestic reforms be undertaken by Latin governments or that equity issues present less potential for revolutionary violence, warfare, and government change, the United States has certain equity-related questions that have not been resolved successfully. Thus, many of the more conservative governments that have been favorably disposed toward the United States regard U.S. pressures for, and support of, land reform, graduated tax structures, and other equity-inducing policies as disingenuous, as a case of the pot calling the kettle black. Indeed, when the United States advocates programs that will, from U.S. perspectives, lead to more equitable internal distributions of wealth within Latin America in the hope of reducing political extremism, conservative Latin American governments may respond that the American distribution of wealth is scarcely different from that of many Latin countries.[4] The credibility of U.S. arguments is thus reduced. Of course, what is overlooked is that America's greater wealth permits even the "have nots" in the United States to have much more than the "have nots" in Latin

[4]U.S. wealth distribution figures, taken from World Bank (1984:272–273), are as follows:

Year	*Lowest 20%*	*Second Quintile*	*Third Quintile*	*Fourth Quintile*	*Highest 20%*	*Highest 10%*
1978	4.6	8.9	14.1	22.1	50.3	33.4

For Latin American figures, see Table 3.

America; the assumption is made here that absolute deprivation is a more powerful motivator of revolutionary sentiment than relative deprivation accompanied by some degree of potential for economic advancement. Given this assumption, and assuming that no radical redistribution of wealth will take place within the United States, logic dictates that U.S. economic policies be directed more toward increasing the total wealth of Latin societies rather than redistributing wealth, with most of the new wealth being received by the poor. This, clearly, relates directly to labor-force absorption and food availability; both must be improved.

Additionally, as stated earlier, with more and more people living in cities, more newly created jobs must be urban. Urban food-distribution systems must also be improved, probably at rates greater than the urban population growth rates. This is true because of the accelerated rate of political change that urban life appears to bring, as opposed to the rate of rural political change.

The major thrusts of needed U.S. programs to prevent second-order challenges rising from labor-absorption and food-supply and distribution situations from becoming full-blown threats to U.S. security seem relatively clear: Basic human needs must be met, urban jobs must be created, food distribution systems must be improved, existent democratic institutions and reforms must be nurtured, and economic growth must be accelerated. All this takes money. Within the context of Central America and the Caribbean, the Reagan administration realizes this; indeed, between 1980 and 1983, U.S. economic assistance to Central America tripled (Dam, 1984:80). While the scope, total, and geographical distribution of economic assistance may be issues of debate, few would deny that the overall trend is propitious. Beyond Central America and the Caribbean, it is less clear that the United States is cognizant of a potential problem.

What about third-order problems? To a considerable extent, successfully meeting second-order challenges will eliminate third-order problems. Without a radical government to implement them, radical policies will rarely be implemented.

The key question, then, is whether significant enough political support can be won within the United States to allocate sufficient funds to help improve inadequate labor-absorption rates and inadequate food supplies and distribution systems in Latin America. Job creation will be at least as crucial in the future as it is now, and the same may be said for problems of food supply and distribution. Will American policymakers have the foresight to realize that unemployment, underemployment, and hunger present current and future challenges to U.S. security interests throughout Latin America? Happily, there is some room for optimism here. In 1947, U.S. policymakers realized that unemployment, underemployment, and hunger presented challenges to

U.S. interests in Europe and responded with the Marshall Plan; in 1983 and 1984, they realized it in Central America and the Caribbean and responded with two different initiatives. One hopes that, in regard to Latin America as a whole, U.S. policymakers will come to the same realization about Latin America. Unfortunately, both in Europe in 1947 and in Central America in the early 1980s, crises were needed before responses were initiated. The precedent of tardy, crisis-initiated response seems well ingrained.

Nevertheless, in international security affairs and domestic law alike, precedents are made to be overturned. Timely response is still possible. The challenges to U.S. security stemming from inadequate labor-absorption rates and inadequate food-supplies and food distribution are there; whether adequate U.S. policy will be there is another question.

REFERENCES

Anonymous
1984 "The U.S. and the Caribbean: Partners in economic development." *AID Highlights* 1(3).

Bagramov, L.
1982 "Food and superprofits." *International Affairs*, No. 2 (February):52–53.

Central Intelligence Agency
1964 "Survey of Latin America, April 1, 1964." *NSC Country File, Latin America.* Container No. 1, Lydon B. Johnson Library, Austin, Texas.

Cone, J. H.
1981 "Gospel and the liberation of the poor." *Christian Century* 98 (February):162–166.

Conn, C. P.
1982 "Where the World Council of Churches went wrong." *Saturday Evening Post.* 254(May–June):12.

Dam, Kenneth W.
1984 Remarks. Quoted in *Department of State Bulletin* 84(2082):80.

Dominquez, Jorge I.
1980 "U.S. and its regional security interests." *Daedalus* 109(Fall).

Gendell, Murray
1985 "Population growth and labor absorption in Latin America, 1970–2000." Paper presented at the Conference on Population Growth in Latin America and U.S. National Security, Center for International Security and Strategic Studies, Mississippi State University, February 21–22.

Jones, Joseph M.
1955 *The Fifteen Weeks.* New York: Viking.

Jordan, Amos A. and William J. Taylor, Jr.
1981 *American National Security: Policy and Process.* Baltimore: Johns Hopkins University Press.

Kissinger, Henry A., *et al.*
1984 *Report of the National Bipartisan Commission on Central America.* Washington, D.C.

La Feber, Walter

1984 "The burdens of the past." (In Robert S. Leiken (ed.), *Central America: Anatomy of Conflict*. New York: Pergamon.

McPherson, Peter
1984 Statement before the House Foreign Affairs Committee. *Department of State Bulletin* 84(2091):31.

Motley, Langhorne A.
1984a "Democracy in Latin America and the Caribbean." *Department of State Bulletin* 84(2091):4.
1984b "A national response to the crisis in Central America." *Department of State Bulletin* 84:77.

Musgrove, Philip
1985 "Food supply and Latin American population growth: Is this the right question?" Paper prepared for the Conference on Population Growth in Latin America and U.S. National Security, Center for International Security and Strategic Studies, Mississippi State University, February 21–22.

Reagan, Ronald
1984a Text of speech on Central American Initiative. *Department of State Bulletin* 84(2085):75.
1984b Text of speech delivered at the University of South Carolina, July 19. *Department of State Bulletin* 84(2090).

Schlesinger, Arthur M., Jr.
1965 *A Thousand Days: John F. Kennedy in the White House*. Boston: Houghton Mifflin.

Selskaya Zhizn
1982 News story, March 6.

Sen, Amartya
1982 *Poverty and Famines: An Essay on Entitlement and Deprivation*. New York: Oxford University Press.

Sewell, John W. and John A. Mathieson
1983 "The Third World: Exploring U.S. interests." Pp. 148–168 in Charles W. Kegley, Jr., and Eugene R. Wittkopf (eds.), *Perspectives on American Foreign Policy*. New York: St. Martin's.

Sider, R. J.
1980 "Evangelical theology of liberation." *Christian Century* 97:314–318.

Spanier, John
1983 *American Foreign Policy Since World War II*. New York: Holt, Rinehart and Winston.

Wall, J. M.
1982 "Liberation ethics: Insisting on equality." *Christian Century* 99(November).

World Bank
1984 *World Development Report 1984*. Washington, D.C.

11

U.S. Security, Economic Growth, and the Population Problem in Latin America

MARGARET DALY HAYES

SECURITY IN LATIN AMERICA

Security is a dimension of U.S. relations with Latin America that is little understood and frequently maligned.[1] Different studies of U.S. security interests yield many different and often noncomplementary understandings of what security is. There seems to be no agreed-upon definition of security, security interest, or what might constitute threats to security.

A chief cause of confusion in the discussion of national security interests is that there is no good and accepted definition of security itself. Dictionary definitions of security include concepts such as "free from fear, care, doubt, anxiety, or danger" and "safe, sure, certain, confident, or undisturbed." The international relations literature is replete with studies of perceptions of *threat* to security, but does not define what constitutes a state of security.

Hans Morgenthau, dean of the traditionalist school of foreign policy studies, does not define "security." In Morgenthau (1973), security is mentioned only in the context of "collective security," "disarmament," or "policing." A recent text entitled *American National Security* suggests that

> clearly [national security] signifies protection of the nation's people and territories against physical assault and in that narrow sense, is roughly equivalent to the traditionally used term, *defense*. National security, however, has a more extensive meaning than protection from physical harm; it also implies protection, through a variety of means, of vital economic and political interests, the loss of which could threaten fundamental values and the vitality of the state. (Jordan and Taylor, 1981:3)

[1]This section draws on arguments prsented in Hayes (1986a).

Former Secretary of Defense Harold Brown defines national security as "the ability to preserve the nation's physical integrity and territory; to maintain its economic relations with the rest of the world on reasonable terms; to protect its nature, institutions and governance from disruption from outside and to control its borders." In Brown's view, the Soviet Union's pursuit of its national security goals poses the greatest threat to the United States, but domestic international economic problems, regional instability, and terrorism also figure prominently. Brown observes that while a Soviet nuclear threat is real, a much more likely threat to U.S. security is "military intimidation of, or conventional (non-nuclear) attack on, U.S. allies and friends. If such tactics were successful, the world military and political balance would tilt dangerously against the United States" (Brown, 1983:4, 5).

Security is not an absolute but a matter of degree. National security is defined only in its most simplistic form as freedom from physical (i.e., military) threat. National security also entails defense of economic interests and promotion of a world order that is compatible with national interests and goals and accepting of national values and ideology. Security implies confidence, opportunity, and capability in dealing with events. It is the end result of a nation's successful coping with its political, economic, and geographic environment. Threats, challenges, crises, and routine change all influence the degree of security that a nation perceives itself to enjoy. The more supportive a nation's environment is, the more secure the nation is. The more the environment challenges the nation's physical or managerial capabilities, or is hostile to national goals and interests, the more insecure the nation is. Except in situations of direct military threat, security is a state of mind.

In defining U.S. security interests in Latin America, a broad definition of national interest is appropriate. Such a focus gives greater emphasis to the nonmilitary dimensions of security—to the things that contribute to security in the long term rather than those that threaten security. This is not the usual way of considering security. In his "Inquiry into the American National Interest," Henry Kissinger noted that Americans have historically shied away from addressing

> the essence of our national interest and the premises of our foreign policy. . . . A mature conception of our interest in the world would . . . take into account the widespread interest in stability and peaceful change. It would deal with two fundamental questions: What is it in our interest to prevent? and What should we seek to accomplish? (Kissinger, 1973:91–92)

U.S. INTERESTS AND CONCERNS IN LATIN AMERICA

In conceptualizing the U.S. national interest in Latin America, I have suggested an even more precise definition of U.S. interests. The definition includes the following considerations:

> It is in the United States national interest that there exist in the hemisphere friendly, prosperous states, with stable responsive governments that permit the free movement of goods and services through the region, that respect the political integrity of their neighbors and that offer no support to the United States global political rivals. (Hayes, 1986b)

It is in the U.S. interest that such conditions exist in the hemisphere, and it is the goal of U.S. policy to see that they obtain. There are things we would prevent in the hemisphere and things we would promote, and U.S. security is enhanced to the extent that these goals are achieved.

In establishing policy by which one can pursue the national interest, it is necessary to establish priorities. Any nation's most fundamental interest is in securing its borders against hostile enemies. No Latin American country is likely to attack the United States; that much is clear. However, it has been the historical concern of the United States to prevent powers from outside the hemisphere from establishing a base of power or influence within the region. The Monroe Doctrine, the Spanish-American War, contingency planning for defense of the Panama Canal and the development of the Inter-American security system in the post–World War II climate were all predicated on the goal of preventing powers from outside the hemisphere from establishing a base of power or influence. In the 40 years since World War II, concern that revolutionary Marxism associated with the Soviet Union (or Marxism–Leninism) might establish a hostile, ideological foothold in the region has been the key factor influencing U.S. policy in the hemisphere.

Increasingly it is recognized that preventing what is politically and militarily unacceptable—the hostile foreign ideological base—may well depend on the success with which the United States identifies and pursues policies that strengthen the capabilities of other nations to prevent that unacceptable outcome. The challenge, as Kissinger noted in the essay cited above, is that the United States is

> no longer in a position to operate programs globally. It has to encourage them. It can no longer impose its preferred solution; it must seek to evoke it. . . . Our designs can be meaningful only if they generate willing cooperation. We can continue to contribute to defense and positive programs, but we must seek to encourage and not stifle a sense of local responsibility. Our contribution should not be the sole or principal effort, but it should make the difference between success and failure. (Kissinger, 1973:94)

It is also in the U.S. interest to promote friendly, prosperous states that enjoy stable and responsible governments. Elsewhere (Hayes 1986b) I have discussed the reasons why the United States should cultivate friends in the hemisphere; what is meant by stable and responsible government, and why it in our interest to promote them. The current discussion concerns prosperity and economic growth.

It is in the U.S. national interest that countries of the Western Hemisphere be prosperous. The U.S. public generally wishes prosperity and well-being for its neighbors. Assistance programs are supported in the U.S. Congress because of lawmakers' sense of responsibility for assisting the poor of other nations. Increasingly it is recognized that regional economic prosperity is a key interest of the United States. Regional poverty and income inequality have direct consequences for the United States. The large-scale, uncontrolled migrations from Central America and the Caribbean region (see Pastor, 1985, for a review of Caribbean migration to the United States). The political factors that cause migrations complicate U.S. domestic and foreign policy.

The economic consequences of Latin America's poverty are also direct. Latin America's economic recession of the early 1980s resulted in hundreds of thousands of lost income dollars and employment in the United States as purchases from Mexico, Brazil, and other large market countries were cut back. More urgently, regional poverty and income inequality have created fertile ground for the development of political instability.

It should be stressed that prosperity does not mean economic activity dominated by U.S. multinational corporations. Latin American governments long ago learned to regulate and control foreign investors for their own purposes.[2] Nor does economic prosperity mean simply growth measured by an expanding gross domestic product (GDP). It also means distribution of the benefits of growth across the population and the involvement of that population in the development process. Stable economic growth requires not only access to external markets and sources of hard currency but also broad-based domestic consumption.

We now recognize that fundamental changes in the domestic economic policies of our neighbors must be undertaken in order to end the cyclical and structural causes of the severe economic problems they face. In the past, the United States has regarded issues of economic management as the responsibility and concern of national governments. Because of the direct effects that Latin America's economic management and mismanagement have on the U.S. economy, the U.S. government now is pressing economic reform and adjustment aggressively. Economic growth is even more imperative today because of the unavoidable pressures of burgeoning population in Latin America.

[2]Latin American governments have been so successful in regulating the activities of multinationals that the region has ceased to be an especially desirable place for investment. See Council of the Americas (1984).

THE CHALLENGE OF GROWTH IN LATIN AMERICA

The chief threats to the United States from Latin America stem from the inability to date of governments in the region to deal adequately with complex political and economic problems. As a consequence, those economic problems have become more and more serious and more politicized over time. The recent and continuing "debt crisis" has been the most severe manifestation of this inability to cope. Compromises worked out between governments and the commercial banks, forced on both by the International Monetary Fund (IMF), have resulted in momentary stabilization of the crisis for large countries such as Mexico, Brazil, Argentina, and Venezuela, but smaller countries in Central America, Jamaica, Peru, and Ecuador, not to mention Bolivia, will have to work out their own solutions with considerably less international support.

Latin American governments will be sorely challenged to show political astuteness and leadership in their efforts to meet the challenge of adjustment. South America today is an area of new democratic governments that have come to power as a consequence of the exhaustion of military governments and the determination of democratic political forces. The prospects for these new governments are bleak. Pent-up demands for social reforms are tremendous. The economic wherewithal to respond is often lacking. Most countries in the region owe 30–60% of their foreign exchange earnings to foreign lenders. Optimum growth rates are estimated to be 5% and are dependent on developed-world growth of 3–4% and expanded trade opportunities (DeLarosiere, 1985). That 5% growth in the developing world may yield only 2% real growth once population expansion is factored out.

In the 1970s, developed-world growth and internal expansion contributed to GNP growth rates in Latin America that ranged from 4% to over 11%. No country was not favored by the pull factors of economic expansion as the effects of world growth trickled down and through even the poorest economies. In the post-1974 oil shock, extreme and unprecedented international liquidity provided foreign exchange for further investment. In the recession brought on by the second oil shock (1979), however, Latin America found itself overexpanded. Growth ground to a halt. Most Latin American countries posted zero to negative growth rates in 1982 and 1983.

Optimistic forecasts indicate that the losses in momentum that have occurred in the region in the past several years will not be overcome easily. In many cases, the GDP levels achieved between 1970 and 1980 will not be reached again until 1990.

Several powerful constraints make it difficult for Latin America to achieve economic growth sufficient to support the region's growing population. The first set of constraints stems from the region's population growth rate, from the parallel growth of its labor force, from rural to urban migration, and from high levels of existing underemployment and unemployment. The second set of constraints stems from the levels of investment needed to promote development.

THE POPULATION CHALLENGE

Although figures for individual countries vary, Latin America's population is presently growing at an average of approximately 2.7% per year, down from over 3% a decade ago. Table 1 demonstrates that in certain countries the rate of population increase has taken a downward turn in recent years because of a decline in birthrates (see the average annual population growth rates in Table 1). The World Bank estimates an average annual

TABLE 1
Latin American Population Growth, 1983–2000

Region or Country	*Population 1983 (millions)*	*Population 2000 (millions)*	*Average Annual Growth (%)* 1965–1973	1973–1983	1983–2000
Caribbean					
Dom. Republic	6	6	2.9	2.4	2.2
Jamaica	2	3	1.5	1.3	1.4
Haiti	5	5	1.5	1.8	1.8
Central America and Mexico					
Mexico	75	109	3.3	2.9	2.3
Costa Rica	2	3	3.0	2.4	2.1
El Salvador	5	8	3.4	3.0	2.6
Guatemala	8	12	3.0	3.1	2.6
Honduras	4	7	2.9	3.5	3.0
Nicaragua	3	5	2.9	3.9	3.0
Panama	2	3	2.7	2.3	1.9
South America					
Argentina	30	37	1.5	1.6	1.3
Bolivia	6	9	2.4	2.6	2.4
Brazil	130	179	2.5	2.3	1.9
Chile	12	15	1.9	1.7	1.5
Colombia	28	37	2.6	1.9	1.8
Ecuador	8	13	2.7	2.6	2.5
Paraguay	3	5	2.7	2.5	2.2
Peru	18	26	2.8	2.4	2.2
Uruguay	3	3	.6	.5	.7
Venezuela	17	26	3.6	3.5	2.6

Source: World Bank (1985).

population growth rate from 1973 to 1983 of 2.4%, compared with 2.5% from 1965 to 1973. Individual country growth rates have changed more dramatically. For example, Mexico, which posted population growth rates well over 3% for most of the 1960s and 1970s, began to experience a sharp drop in birthrates in the mid 1970s. Overall population growth is now measured at 2.5% per annum instead of 3.3% (Inter-American Development Bank, 1984).[3]

The cumulative momentum of population growth and the youthful age of the existing Latin American population all conspire to make any different pattern of population growth very difficult to orchestrate. Indeed, the recent turndown in growth can be deceiving, for the lower rate of growth is taking place on a still rapidly expanding base; thus, despite declining rates of growth (based on lower birthrates), Latin America's population will continue to grow well into the next century. Life expectancy is high and increasing, and the children of the years of high birthrates—the 1950s and 1960s—are now having children of their own. The World Bank cautions that

> a population tends to grow even after fertility has declined to replacement level because past high growth rates will have produced an age distribution with a relatively high proportion of women in, or still to enter, the reproductive ages. . . . A population takes 50–75 years, depending on the initial conditions, before its age distribution fully adjusts to the changed fertility rates. (World Bank, 1984:281)

United Nations' statistics predict that Latin America's population will increase by about 130% between 1980 and 2025 (Inter-American Development Bank, 1983) with overall population rising from 390 million to about 800 million in 45 years. Because of progressive migration to urban areas, the urban population will grow substantially faster; the rural population will either stagnate or decline. Total labor-force participation will grow disproportionately because of the youthful structure of the population.

Latin America's labor force was about 55 million in 1950; it reached 99 million in 1975. By 2000 it will be about 197 million and about 300 million by 2025 (Fox, 1984). Labor-force growth through 2000 is known because it is based on a population already born. Reliable estimates of labor-force participation, population growth, and work habits of different population age groups permit fairly accurate estimates of labor-force size to 2025.

World Bank projections of population growth, under assumptions of

[3]These figures are slightly higher than those reported by the World Bank (1984). Such discrepancies are common in reported population data and underscore the severe measurement problems that demographers and policymakers face in assessing the impact of population growth on development.

declining population growth rates, give some idea of the dimension of the burgeoning population-expansion problem. Table 1 gives figures for Latin American countries included in the World Bank's annual *World Development Report*. Most Latin American countries will increase in population size by more than 50% between now and the year 2000—only 15 years away. Even under assumptions of sharply declining birthrates, no country will achieve stable population growth until well into the twenty-first century.

THE UNDEREMPLOYMENT PROBLEM

Statisticians tend to calculate labor-force entry as occurring at ages 15–18 years. Labor-force growth tends to occur with a generational lag. Thus the population born from 1950 to 1970 is just entering the peak years of activity in the labor force. They will remain active for 30–50 years. This means that the problems of Latin American population growth and labor-force utilization are just beginning to be felt. Figure 1 demonstrates the effect of both generation lag and increasing urban population growth and life expectancy. The graph demonstrates the relative stagnation of rural labor-force growth and the increasing bunching of employable persons, especially males in the 20–50 age group.

Latin America's population growth rate and its impact on labor-force participation is not all of the story. To meet the challenge of pressures of population growth, Latin American policymakers will be required not only to generate employment opportunities for the growing labor force but also to occupy more efficiently and more productively its large population of underemployed and unemployed.

Unemployment in Latin America has always been high, but it has been rising since the economic downturn of the 1980s. Official statistics put absolute unemployment in various countries of the region at anywhere from 10% to 20%. Absolute unemployment in Latin America is certainly a cause of concern, but not the major cause. Recently an official of the Mexican government cited 8% as the level of unemployment in his country.[4] Others put unemployment at 15% and underemployment at 25% for a total unemployment and underemployment of 40% of the working-age population (Volman, 1984:4).

Given the nature of economic participation in the various countries, the often unrecognized and generally uncounted levels of underemployment are, or ought to be, of much greater concern than they now are. Underemploy-

[4]Communication to the author reported to the Senate Foreign Relations Committee in memorandum of July 30, 1983, "U.S.–Mexican Relations: Effects of the Economic Crisis."

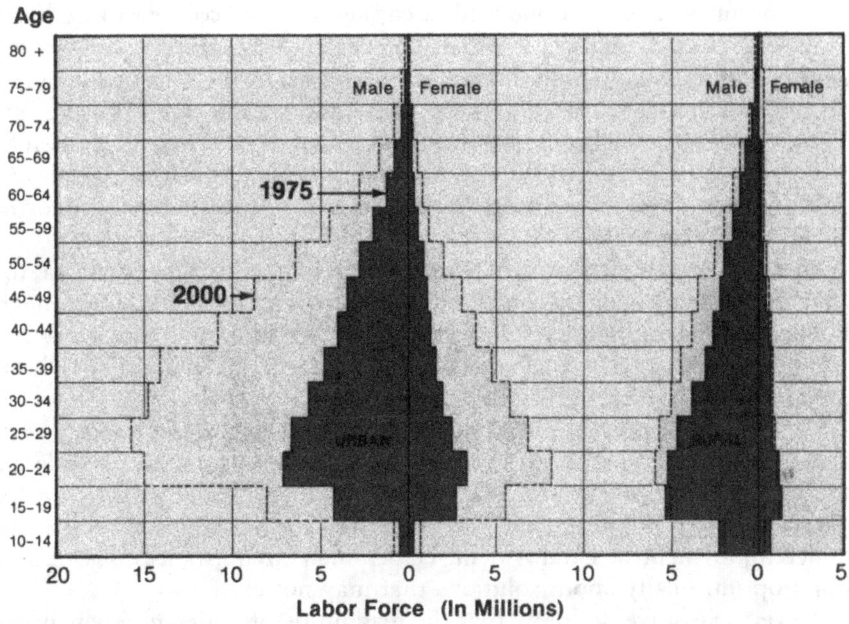

FIGURE 1. **Latin America, urban and rural labor force, 1975 and 2000 as projected, by age and sex. (*Source:* Centro Latinoamericano de Demografia, 1982. This CELADE report was prepared prior to the availability of 1980 census returns from Latin American countries. A cursory review of several census documents now shows that even the modest labor-force gains projected for the rural sector may not be attained. Brazil, for example, was projected to experience a 3 million total population increase in rural areas during the 1970s. The 1980 census revealed that in fact total rural population dropped by 2 million. Reprinted from Inter-American Development Bank, 1984:183.)**

ment has been a way of life in rural Latin America for generations. Underemployment reaches levels of 60–70% in countries like Peru, where it results primarily from the extreme low productivity of rural agriculture. In the last two generations, a good portion of the redundant rural labor force has migrated to urban areas, raising unemployment and underemployment in urban Latin America to levels of 20–40%.

No country is immune from the chronic effects of underemployment, although the levels of underemployment again vary greatly as a function of the productivity of economic activities in the country and the age structure of the population. Where the population's age structure is relatively mature, as in Argentina or Uruguay, there are fewer pressures than in countries in which the population's age structure is young, as in Mexico, El Salvador, and Brazil.

Economists have not done well in coping with the concept of underemployment.[5] Conceptually it is difficult to describe. Moreover, few countries have continuous household sample surveys by which they can document the problem or measure trends. Where household sample surveys have been conducted, they have been done mostly in urban areas. There they often fail to tap the realities of extended-family support mechanisms whereby a household group supports its members rather than a single breadwinner supporting himself and his family.

In rural areas, employment surveys fail to tap two phenomena that characterize work: unpaid contributions that women make to supporting the family, and the multiple-job phenomenon whereby a farmer may work only 15 hours a week at his principal occupation of farming but another 60 hours in various other jobs.

As a result of these measurement differences, there is no good baseline against which to measure rising underemployment, especially as underemployment has become an urban as well as a rural problem. Because of lack of data, there are no reasonably accurate trend lines for projecting future underemployment or employment. Under such circumstances, it is easy to think optimistically about solutions that may not exist.

Nevertheless, we do know that the magnitude of underemployment and unemployment or, in more technical terms, "labor force underutilization," is increasing. Because of high inflation, underemployment accelerated in the 1970s. During times of inflation, underemployment increases because worker hours diminish, wages decline, and support systems fail to function.

THE EMPLOYMENT TASK

Latin America as a whole must create approximately 4 million jobs per year for the remainder of this decade and well into the twenty-first century just to provide employment for young persons entering the job market for the first time. However, Latin America's employment problem is not only one of providing jobs for new entrants into the labor force. The region must also provide increasingly large numbers of jobs for persons already in the labor force, but unemployed, and for the 20–40% underemployed, who also compete for newly created jobs. Given the decreasing mortality rates and longer life expectancies demonstrated in Figure 1, each age group is growing in size and demanding employment.

Table 2 illustrates that the demand for jobs in Latin America is increasing at an alarming rate. To give a vivid example, in 1979, then Planning Minister

[5]I am especially indebted to Robert W. Fox, formerly of the Inter-American Development Bank, for raising these issues with me.

TABLE 2

Growth of Latin America's Labor Force, 1983–2000

Region or Country	*Population 1983 (millions)*	*Labor Force 1983 (millions)*	*Average Annual Growth (%)*			*Projected Labor Force, 2000 (millions)*
			1965–1973	*1973–1983*	*1983–2000*	
Caribbean						
Dom. Republic	6	3.3(55)[a]	2.7	3.2	2.8	5.42
Jamaica	2	1.1(56)	.7	2.6	2.6	1.70
Haiti	5	2.7(55)	.7	1.5	2.0	3.85
Central America and Mexico						
Mexico	75	39.7(53)	3.1	3.1	3.2	67.90
Costa Rica	2	1.2(59)	3.6	3.6	2.8	1.89
El Salvador	5	2.6(52)	3.2	2.8	3.4	4.59
Guatemala	8	4.3(54)	2.9	3.0	2.9	7.02
Honduras	4	2.0(50)	2.4	3.3	3.5	3.59
Nicaragua	3	1.5(51)	2.8	4.0	3.8	2.88
Panama	2	1.1(57)	3.1	2.6	2.4	1.71
South America						
Argentina	30	18.3(61)	1.4	1.0	1.4	23.18
Bolivia	6	3.2(53)	1.8	2.5	2.8	5.09
Brazil	130	76.7(59)	2.5	3.1	2.4	114.79
Chile	12	7.6(63)	1.3	2.6	2.0	10.59
Colombia	28	16.5(59)	3.1	2.8	2.0	25.56
Ecuador	8	4.2(53)	2.6	2.6	3.3	7.36
Paraguay	3	1.6(55)	2.6	3.3	3.0	2.73
Peru	18	10.1(56)	2.4	2.9	3.0	16.66
Uruguay	3	1.9(63)	.3	.5	.9	2.20
Venezuela	17	9.5(56)	3.7	4.1	3.4	16.81
Industrial market economies		(67)	1.2	1.2	.5	
East European nonmarket economies		(66)	.9	1.0	.5	

[a] Numbers in parentheses indicate labor force as a percentage of the population.

Source: Inter-American Development bank (1984); World Bank (1984); author's calculations.

of Brazil Dr. Mario Henrique Simonsen indicated in a speech at the Center of Brazilian Studies at The Johns Hopkins School of Advanced International Studies that the Brazilian economy needed to generate 1.2 million jobs per year in order to accommodate new entrants into the labor market. In 1984 Brazilian economists were saying that Brazil needed to generate 1.5 million new jobs per year to accommodate new entrants, and up to 1.8 million jobs to absorb persons displaced by the profound recession and inflation of the early 1980s. Unemployment in the city of São Paulo, Brazil's most industrialized and urbanized state, was estimated to be 20% in early 1985. Idle capacity in the industrial sector was estimated at 20–40%, depending on the industry, and full employment would yield only an additional few hundred thousand jobs. Thus, even the half-million jobs needed to accommodate persons displaced by the recession, much less the 1.3 million new jobs needed to provide employment for new entrants, will be hard to achieve.

The phenomenon that confronts Latin America (and many other developing regions) today is something new under the sun. There are no precedents, and there is no experience to suggest how to manage the problem. The phenomenon has occurred as a result of the massive fall in mortality, especially infant mortality, in the Third World that began in the 1950s and the consequent population explosion that accompanied the decline. Development, especially rural-sector development, did not accompany population growth, so the rural sector has become stagnant, both in terms of population growth and economic productivity. In urban areas, the factors of productivity, labor-force skills, application of capital and technology, and even the availability of natural resources have been deficient. Indeed, whereas job creation requires the application of foreign or domestic capital, Latin America historically has been an exporter of capital. The exodus of domestic capital reached flood proportions in the 1970s and 1980s, as economic difficulties mounted. Many Latin American countries have a scant resource base with which to develop their economies anyway. The Caribbean countries are particularly vulnerable on this measure, but so also are Central America and Peru, Chile, Uruguay, Paraguay, and others.

The models of development that have been and are being applied in Latin America are simply inadequate to stimulate jobs for the growing labor force. Import substituting industrialization has tended to focus on capital-intensive industries such as steel, autos, and petrochemicals. The more recent emphasis on export production in both industry and agriculture also tends to yield capital-intensive activity. Exports to the developed world have to be tooled and tailored to developed-country tastes, or they will not be competitive. To promote precision production, specialized machinery, often imported from the developed countries, is needed. Export agriculture also tends to require machinery applied over large tracts of land. Fertilizers and pesticides are imported to yield the large-volume harvests that will satisfy fickle world commodity traders. Peasant agriculture simply cannot yield the volume at the same cost. But, in the process, as peasants are pushed off the best lands so that those lands can be employed more intensively for export, domestic food production has slacked off dramatically. Latin America as a whole now imports a substantial and often increasing portion of its food needs. Even the continent's recent emphasis on indigenously developed technology tends to result in more capital-intensive activities. Technology is almost by definition capital and not labor intensive. A new model is needed.

Some critics of the Latin American development experience have argued that the region should do an about-face and pursue a policy that would maximize labor-force employment. This would entail greater emphasis on small-plot farming and production for domestic consumption. In industry it would mean emphasis on low-technology assembly production and, probably, large applications of government money to create jobs. The fallacy of this model is that domestic savings in the less developed countries are not adequate to generate the capital necessary to permit the model to work. Even with indigenous production techniques, the country would need to import the fertilizers and pesticides necessary to make small-plot farming productive or the machines at which people might work in labor-intensive jobs.

THE DEVELOPMENT PROBLEM

With 2 million new jobs required every year and a commensurate $47 billion in new investment needed each year to obtain 5% growth (Inter-American Development Bank, 1984a), the current level of investment in Latin America has a gap of millions of dollars that are not to be found. At present growth rates of 3–4%, or even at historical (7%) growth rates, Latin America's growing population simply cannot be absorbed into the market economy as it is currently structured.

According to the World Bank (1984), population growth affects economic growth in three dimensions: through the influence on gross domestic savings per person; on the amount of capital invested per person, and on the efficiency with which the economy operates. In the high-population-growth developing countries, savings per capita tend to be low because of the large number of persons outside the monetized economy. That low level of savings must be employed to educate a large and more youthful population (frequently 30–40% percent of the population may be of school age). World Bank studies show a strong trend toward budgetary downgrading of education in developing countries. One study reported in the Bank's 1984 *World Development Report* "showed that in Latin America public spending per primary student fell by almost 45 percent in real terms between 1970 and 1978. As a share of educational budgets, spending on non-wage items—chalk, maps, textbooks, and so on—fell in eight out of ten Latin American countries" (World Bank, 1984:84).

Finally, a growing labor force requires continually increasing capital investment (both human and physical) just to maintain present levels of production. Unless capital increases, productivity will decrease; wages will fall and income inequalities will be exacerbated. For incomes to rise, investment must increase faster than the labor force is increasing, or more than 2.7% per year, the estimated average annual rate of labor-force growth between now and the end of the century (see Table 2). For low per capita income countries especially, this is a difficult goal to achieve. Data displayed in Table 3 show that while the investment ratio (investment as a percentage of GDP) is only 18% in the United States, this yielded investment per new worker on the order of $189,000 in 1983. In Korea, with an investment ratio of 31% (high), new investment per worker was only $30,000 because of the relatively larger increment to the Korean labor force. Brazil, whose leaders claim that they must find 1.3 million new jobs per year, has an investment ratio of only 22, and can afford only $28,780 per worker.[6] Colombia, a smaller developing economy with a similar investment ratio (22) has only $20,300[7] to invest per new worker. Except for Nicaragua and Panama, the Central American countries show investment ratios in the low teens. Bolivia has an investment ratio of only 5 and only $1870 per worker of investment capital. Even more alarming statistics are those that project the percentage increase in working-age population over the 20 years from 1980 to 2000. In both Brazil and Colombia the working-age population will increase by about 65%, whereas the working-age population will increase by only 1% in West Germany and 15% in the United States. The World Bank notes:

> Just to maintain the current small amount of investment per potential new workers [countries with the lowest absolute levels of investment per potential new worker] will have to increase their investment rapidly. In contrast, developed countries can increase the capital available to each potential new worker in 2000 even if investment grows by less than 1 percent a year. (World Bank, 1984:87)

[6]The *World Development Report 1984* shows in Table 5.4 that Brazil's gross domestic investment per potential new worker in 1980 was $40,360 and the increase in working population 1979–1980 was 1.3 millions. The calculations in Table 3, based on World Bank figures for size of labor force and average annual growth in labor force, and Inter-American Development Bank data for population, gross domestic investment, and GDP, yield the substantially larger figures for 1982 that are seen. I cannot reconcile the differences in estimated size of new labor-force entrants (1.5. million) claimed by Brazilian economists more recently.

[7]Again, the figures for Colombia differ substantially from those presented for 1980 in the *World Development Report 1984*.

TABLE 3

Investment Ratio, Gross Domestic Investment, and Increase in the Labor Force and Working-Age Population, 1983–2000

Region or Country	*Investment Ratio*	*Gross Domestic Investment (GDI) (millions)*	*Increase in Labor Force, 1982–1983 (thousands)*	*GDI per Worker, 1982 (thousands)*	*Increase in Working-age Population, 1980–2000 (%)*
Caribbean					
Dom. Republic	20	1413.4	93.7	15.08	64
Jamaica	14	537.1	27.9	15.94	55
Haiti	17	274.5	55.12	4.98	43
Central America and Mexico					
Mexico	22	35281.6	1206.7	29.24	71
Costa Rica	10	359.0	38.3	9.37	57
El Salvador	12	394.8	92.95	4.25	76
Guatemala	11	1009.4	114.58	8.81	63
Honduras	12	324.9	69.21	4.69	79
Nicaragua	17	455.9	49.5	9.21	92
Panama	23	1011.1	27.81	36.36	55
South America					
Argentina	18	10174.0	236.46	43.03	27
Bolivia	5	170.0	90.93	1.87	59
Brazil	23	51469.0	1788.5	28.78	50
Chile	10	1820.0	149.56	12.17	39
Colombia	23	6493.0	319.54	20.32	55
Ecuador	22	2236.0	149.98	14.91	75
Paraguay	28	1274.5	53.27	23.93	71
Peru	19	3928.0	285.55	13.76	65
Uruguay	14	909.6	166.87	5.45	16
Venezuela	42	18158.9	266.68	68.09	77
Industrialized Countries					
Japan	32	332800.0	620.0	535.04	11
Australia	24	35530.0	160.0	219.35	19
France	23	149940.0	330.0	461.34	13
West Germany	25	204790.0	430.0	481.33	1
United States	18	465680.0	2460.0	188.99	15

Source: Author's calculations based on World Bank and Inter-American Development Bank data. This table is modeled after Table 5.4 in World Bank (1984).

For income to rise, investment must increase faster than labor force. This demands new sources of investable income. One accepted ratio of capital to output is 3:1 (i.e., $3 of new investment can be expected to yield a continuing flow of $1 in additional income). Given the constraints on investment that heavy debt-service burdens portend, low domestic private investment, diminished prospects for external investment and low prospects for additional large-scale lending, it is difficult to imagine from where the investment capital needed to achieve continuing growth will come. This is indeed the dilemma confronting policymakers in Latin America and the United States and the multilateral lending institutions.

SOME PRESCRIPTIONS

The preceding description sounds like a prescription for imminent disaster in Latin America. If job creation and economic growth cannot keep up with population increase, what will occur? What can be done?

One immediate solution to Latin America's problems, and one used by Latin Americans in the past, is migration to the United States. In the near term, it is clear that the U.S. economy can continue to absorb at least the volume of immigrants that has occurred to date. Immigration has come principally from Mexico, but also from the Caribbean and increasingly from Central America and even South America. All studies of recent developments in migration trends suggest that the rate and volume of migration to the United States is on the increase and, in difficult economic circumstances, could reach flood proportions.

For example, a recent study of migration from the Caribbean states (not including Central America) to the United States shows that documented Caribbean immigration to the United States average less than 5000 per year in the 1940s. That level tripled in the 1950s, was four times the 1950s' rate during the 1960s, and doubled again in the 1970s. Between 1965 and 1979, immigration from Jamaica and Trinidad and Tobago increased tenfold. The figures reported do not include the large and increasing volume of illegal immigrants. Estimates suggest that as of 1981, 3 to 6 million undocumented Mexican workers, more than 500,000 El Salvadorans (long the second-largest illegal immigrant group), and about 1 million Caribbean islanders were in the United States illegally (Pastor, 1985:6–9).

Experiences such as Jamaica's in the tumultuous later Manley years and El Salvador's from 1979 to the present document that political instability contributes to rapid increases in migration. But lack of development also contributes a steady, increasing, but less noticeable, push of migrants to the heretofore seemingly limitless opportunities of the United States.

The United States cannot absorb the redundant labor force of all of Latin America. The drain on local revenues would be cumulative and, increasingly, resisted by taxpayers. Political backlash could occur on a wide scale, especially in times of economic downturn. This has already been seen in border states such as California, Texas, and Florida. In the near future, massive immigration to the United States must be stemmed.

One approach to halting emigration from Latin American to the United States lies in promoting regional development to a level that can better support its growing population. Rapid economic development with increased distribution of incomes and enhanced creation of domestic wealth is the only route by which Latin American societies can hope to avoid turmoil and/or debilitating poverty in the long term. There is no single approach to development or magic policy solution that will resolve Latin America's economic problems overnight. Instead, a number of adaptations of policy might relieve pressure and stimulate growth sufficiently to maintain certain equilibrium.

One of the first adjustments that Latin America must pursue is to reestablish equilibrium between its rural and urban sectors. Latin America's most efficient agricultural production (sugar, soya, wheat, cotton) is increasingly capital intensive and export oriented. Traditional crops like sugar and cotton are also available in abundance in the world and frequently cost more to produce than they will bring in the market. As noted above, Latin America's food imports have increased dramatically in the past decade. Policies must be devised that will permit the foreign-exchange-generating export of agricultural products and at the same time generate enough production for the domestic market so that foreign exchange is not wasted unnecessarily on basic food imports. If export agriculture must often be capital intensive, domestic food production need not be so. The problem with the domestic market, historically, has been lack of money and credit. Governments must find ways to entice capital into rural areas and into increased food production. Prices must be realistic in rural areas. Governments must find ways to improve the efficiency of production of the peasant farm family, thereby generating investable savings and, one hopes, stemming the exodus from rural to urban areas.

A second area of policy initiatives available to Latin American policymakers is the more effective incorporation of nonmonetary economic activity (of the informal sector) into the market and national economy. Recent investigations in Peru suggest that as much as 60% of economic activity in that country occurs in the "informal" sector, that is, in an unregistered, untaxed, and unregulated economic activity. Hernando de Soto of the Institute of Liberty and Democracy of Lima argues that state regulation has caused the emergence of the informal sector because of the costly and time-consuming requirements that the state bureaucracy imposes for entry into legal economic activity. He argues that bureaucratic roadblocks represent a systematic (and, in Peru, possibly racist) bias against the popular classes. Such regulation has resulted in "massive inefficiencies and . . . perverse distributional effects—enriching the powerful and the corrupt at the expense of the poor" (*El Comercio*, 1984). Others argue that the informal sector did not emerge as the result of legal barriers but as a consequence of the economic development process, particularly the inability of the formal sector to absorb unemployed population, and of a development model that has given preferential treatment to the city to the detriment of the rural sector.

Regardless of what has generated the informal sector, the fact that it exists in every country in Latin America is undisputed. Moreover, the effects of its existence on government tax revenues are recognized as increasingly profound. Brazil recently took action aimed at better incorporating the informal sector into national economic life. Its Microenterprise Law, passed by the Congress in the fall of 1984, recognizes the economic fragility of small, informal enterprises. The new law excuses a variety of taxes for very small businesses. It is anticipated that several hundred thousand businesses could be registered under the new law. Registration will give entrepreneurs access to credit and will assure a minimal safety net for employees.

Despite constraints on budgets, and the austerity imposed by the IMF, governments throughout Latin America must also give renewed attention to the quality of human resource development. Primary school education in particular has nearly always lacked the attention of national governments eager to emulate developed countries by investing heavily in universities. Frequently, the quality of university education has been low because of lack of adequately trained professors. The quality of public primary education has been low historically and has suffered profoundly in the belt tightening of the 1970s and 1980s. It will take a generation of effort to amend that situation. It is time to start.

Latin American governments must also give new and creative attention to all manner of calculations that will increase income and income equality in Latin societies. The continued small size of the Latin American domestic market is in itself a constraint on growth.

Finally, Latin American governments must commit themselves to consistent and far-reaching population programs aimed at reducing fertility at a rapid rate. Targets must be set and pursued. The economic growth performance of countries that have adopted population programs—the World Bank cites both Colombia and Mexico as examples—has been remarkably positive. Forecasts of new jobs needed for 15 and 20 years from now are encouraging and permit reasonable calculations of the investment needed.

The security concerns of the United States in Latin America are enhanced by the increased prosperity and development of the region. The U.S. government can enhance its security in a variety of ways as well. First and foremost, the United States must again accept responsibility for providing assistance to population planning programs. The present U.S. administration's contention that economic growth will solve the population problem is partially true. It will do so in the long run, if circumstances are fortuitous. But the population problem in Latin America has become so severe that even the most concerted efforts at promoting growth will be frustrated. Efforts to stimulate growth and population planning support must go hand in hand.

The United States can also support economic growth efforts by continuing a large-scale, creative, and efficiently applied foreign assistance program that includes encouragement of private-sector initiative. Shortages of capital for investment make economic assistance a necessity in the least developed countries (LDCs). Most LDCs receive a minimum of U.S. bilateral assistance, however. The bulk of U.S. aid is targeted politically at Israel and Egypt. Israel will receive some $1.9 billion in fiscal year 1986; Egypt will receive slightly less. All of Latin America will receive less than $1.5 billion.

The United States must also take a positive attitude toward the resource needs of multilateral institutions that support economic development assistance and family planning efforts. Large-scale aid to the multilateral banks, especially to their soft loan windows, is increasingly difficult to sell to a Congress exasperated with the seeming lack of success in the programs of such institutions. Congressional frustration is understandable, but acquiescence to that frustration is not acceptable. Administrations must promote and endorse aid to the multilateral banks actively. At the same time, it is fair to question the effectiveness and efficiency of multilateral programs.

Finally, the United States must encourage, even insist on, new thinking about the means to develop Latin American countries.

REFERENCES

Brown, Harold

1983 *Thinking about National Security: Defense and Foreign Policy in a Dangerous World.* Boulder, Colo. Westview Press.

Council of the Americas

1984 "Debt, economic crisis and United States corporations in Latin America." Mimeographed.

DeLarosiere, Jacques

1985 "Interrelationships between protectionism and the debt crisis." Address by the Managing Director of the IMF before a Symposium organized by the Federation of Swedish Industries, Stockholm, February 6.

Fox, Robert W.

1983 "The challenge of numbers." *IDB News* (December):6–7.

Hayes, Margaret Daly
1984 *Latin America and the U.S. National Interest: A Basis for U.S. Foreign Policy.* Boulder, Colo. Westview Press.
1986a "Security in the Western Hemisphere". In K. Middlebrook and C. Rico (eds.), *The United States and Latin America in the 1980's.* Pittsburgh, University of Pittsburgh Press.
1986b "Understanding United States policy toward Latin America and the Central American crisis." In *Conflict in Central America: Approaches to Peace and Security.* New York: St. Martin's Press for C. Hurst & Company, London (forthcoming).

Inter-American Development Bank
1984 *Economic and Social Progress in Latin America: 1984 Report.* Washington D.C.

Jordan, Amos A. and Taylor, William J., Jr.
1981 *American National Security: Policy and Process.* Baltimore: Johns Hopkins University Press.

Kissinger, Henry A.
1973 "On the national interest." In *American Foreign Policy.* Expanded ed. New York: Norton.

Morgenthau, Hans J.
1973 *Politics among Nations: The Struggle for Power and Peace.* Fifth ed. New York: Knopf.

Pastor, Robert
1985 "Migration and development in the Caribbean: The policy challenge." Paper presented to Conference on Migration and Development in the Caribbean, sponsored by the School of Public Affairs, University of Maryland, September.

Volman, Dennis
1984 "Would freer economy aid or hurt Mexico? *Christian Science Monitor* (August 21):9.

World Bank
1984 *World Development Report 1984.* Washington, D.C.

12

U.S. Security and Latin America: Arms Transfers and Military Doctrine

WILLIAM J. TAYLOR, JR.

The literature on military arms and arms transfers to developing nations, including Latin America, has grown rapidly over the past two decades—almost as fast as the burgeoning military arsenals in the Third World. In 1980 the nations of Latin America spent over $9 billion on their military establishments (Sivard, 1983:33). Deliveries of military goods from foreign sources cost $215.5 million in 1984 (U.S. Department of Defense, 1984:15). That the Soviet Union, the United States, and many industrialized democracies have been in the forefront as arms suppliers is not disputed, although many would argue numbers at the margin.

Depending on the source, the rationale for supplying arms to Third World and developing countries include one or more of the following:

- Support "wars of liberation."
- Provide for the safety, security, and welfare of the citizens of an allied or friendly state.
- Support a coup d'etat.
- Support endangered political systems or regimes.
- Protect national interests.
- Provide regional balance or stability.
- Enforce international obligations.
- Fill a demand (whether or not rational) from Third World countries.
- Compete commercially with the defense industries of other nations who will supply arms.
- Maximize commercial profit.

Anxieties in the West are caused in large part by devotion to the liberal ethic that arms transfers are out of control, and that whatever the rationale for providing arms, such sales adversely affect the safety, security, and welfare of the people of Latin America. In brief, some argue that modern weapons lead to more conflict, increase the danger of escalation, kill more people, and sap economic resources from vital economic and social development efforts. In this regard, much attention has been focused on increasing arms transfers to Latin America.

THE UNITED STATES AND LATIN AMERICA

James Reston observed that Americans will do anything for Latin America except read about it. Thus it is no surprise that it was not until the 1980s that Latin America began to receive increased attention from U.S. policymakers. Another reason for this is that countries in the region, unless assisted by an outside power, have been unable to project a significant threat to U.S. interests. Historically, when U.S. interests in Latin America were challenged by regional powers, the United States responded with overwhelming military force in order to remove even a perceived threat. Recently, the U.S. incursion into Grenada, although only a rescue operation, caused many observers to recall the Monroe Doctrine. At one time, this doctrine provided justification for the United States to intervene anywhere in the Western Hemisphere in order to exclude the influence of nonhemispheric powers. The doctrine was broadened under President Theodore Roosevelt to justify U.S. intervention to deal with a threat to *any* U.S. interest. American diplomacy, including security and economic assistance to Latin America, therefore labors under a somewhat dubious historical legacy. For example, U.S. support for authoritarian regimes and the image of U.S. parochialism continue to constitute *causes célèbres* for moderate and extreme leftists. When the United States could resolve hemispheric disputes unilaterally, our policy could be simple and relatively unnuanced. Those days, if not over, are clearly numbered.

Consistent with the first term, the second Reagan administration places Latin America high among U.S. diplomatic priorities. The threat of low-intensity conflict in Latin America is accurately perceived as a significant threat to regional stability. The goal of U.S. policy is to contain the threat of Soviet-supported terrorism, insurgency, proxy war, and psychological warfare while addressing the root causes of instability that facilitate Soviet intrusions. The President's National Bipartisan Commission on Central America (1984:61) stresses the critical need to deal with the root causes of unrest: social conditions, inequitable distribution of wealth and land, and weak economies. However, the commission report places primary emphasis on the "elimination of the climate of violence and civil strife" before satisfactory programs to cure social and economic ills can be carried out. The report emphasizes that the welfare and security of the populace cannot be served by economic assistance alone. A critical problem, which prevents the reduction of violence and civil strife, is the capability of armed, disenfranchised elements in various countries to terrorize existing governments and hold the civilian population hostage to radical ideologies. Powerful external forces help aggravate conditions that cause existing governments to resort to military force to preserve the status quo. Pope John Paul II, for instance, has focused on this problem and is trying to reduce the credibility that left- and right-wing extremist ideologies now have among Latin America's youth (*Washington Post*, 1985:A1)

The United States has many interests in Latin America. It is important to review these interests, for, unlike Europe, Asia, and Africa to an extent, even specialists sometimes become confused over the strategic importance of America's "backyard."

U.S. Interests in Latin America

Historically, Latin America has been a low priority in U.S. foreign policy, in large part because of its relative isolation from the geostrategic competition among the superpowers of today and the European powers of yesterday. The U.S. interest has been insufficiently motivated to warrant deep, sustained involvement in Latin American affairs. The Monroe Doctrine, warning external powers to stay away from the region, essentially emphasized a traditional interest in minimizing strategic costs and risks in America's backyard. Apart from Fidel Castro's Cuba, the United States has been content to concentrate on economic rather then military concerns.

In the 1980s, relations between the United States and Latin America are being redefined. Regional developments have had an impact on U.S. interests, posing a variety of challenges and at the same time offering large opportunities. Among these are the Soviet–Cuban potential for causing instability in the region; the increase in Marxist-inspired regimes in Central America; and the growing regional rivalries between Brazil and Argentina, and Chile and Argentina. Each has an expanding military capability, a nascent nuclear capacity, and all seek world-power status. The humiliation of Argentina by Britain in the Falkland Islands may eventually exacerbate Argentina's traditional need for regional "status."

Traditional discussions of U.S. interests have always included the role of Latin America in U.S. security and will continue to do so in the future, mainly because southern-flank security is becoming increasingly important. A clear U.S. interest, therefore, is to prevent historic rivalries among South American nations from being fanned by outside forces into full-scale military conflicts that would divert U.S. attention and resources from European, Middle Eastern, and Asian theaters or from trouble spots elsewhere. Conflict of this type could increase the tendency any Latin American nation might have to establish a closer relationship with the Soviet Union (Jordan and Taylor, 1984: 444–445). This would be intolerable. The United States, since the Monroe Doctrine, has seen the exclusion of foreign powers, particularly hostile ones, as crucial to the stability of Latin America and the security of the United States (Hayes, 1984:7).

For reasons that are well known, the southern flank can no longer be regarded as completely secure. Neither is it reasonable to conclude that the United States could return to the days of "gunboat diplomacy" if we only "had the will" to do so. It would be a grave error to look at the Latin America of the 1980s as if it were the Latin America of the 1880s. The relationship between the United States and Latin America has changed, and continues to do so. Latin American security has been severely eroded in the face of increased levels of inter- and intrastate violence and instability. Thus, the U.S. interest in maintaining a stable and secure southern flank is being challenged (Jordan and Taylor 1984:459–461). The maintenance of a secure flank involves three main factors: limiting interstate violence; restricting the influence of external powers; and supporting the development of democratic government and the evolution of the political culture of the region (Gonzalez *et al.*, 1984:v). Meeting the challenge of these three security mandates will occupy an ever increasing portion of U.S. policymakers' time.

The interests of the United States are served by promoting political stability and regional harmony in Latin America. The United States is dependent on the assurance of friendly and stable nations to the south. Certain developments are jeopardizing the certainty of this relationship (Hayes, 1984:4).

In the late 1980s Central America will be the most unstable and volatile region in the Western Hemisphere. The battle between traditional regimes and the ideologically motivated opposition will be fueled by endemic domestic problems such as widespread poverty, starvation, and economic crisis (Taylor, 1983:45). Central America will remain the prime focus of, and challenge to, U.S. policy in the Western Hemisphere because of its proximity to U.S. territory and the involvement of the Soviet Union and its allies in fomenting instability. Regional conflict will occur between conservative or right-wing groups, in some cases supported by the United States, and left-wing Marxist–Leninists. The extent of Soviet and Cuban support for leftist elements in the region is no longer speculative. Soviet- and Cuban-sponsored violence will continue in countries now plagued by it—El Salvador, Nicaragua, and Guatemala—and it is likely to spread into neighboring nations—Costa Rica, Honduras, and Mexico—in the near future.

In some cases, U.S. analysts have been slow to identify, and politicians reluctant to accept, the reality of Soviet–Cuban support for insurgents. This reluctance has sometimes given minor insurgencies time to germinate into a substantial threat. It took something as unambiguous as the construction of a 10,000-ft runway on Grenada to demonstrate that the Soviet Union, directly and through its Cuban proxies, was moving to challenge U.S. interests. Grenada has been dealt with for the time being.

The primary U.S. interest in Latin America is the commitment to encourage the evolution of democratic governments. Human rights, the guiding principle for foreign policy during the Carter years, continues to play a significant role in shaping U.S. policy. According to the Reagan administration, "in the last five years, nine countries of the [Western] hemisphere have moved to democracy from dictatorship and zero countries have gone from democracy to dictatorship" (Bruske, 1985:A1). Human rights violations play an important role in the U.S. critique of the Sandinista government in Nicaragua.

While political and social unrest constitutes a threat to U.S. interests in Latin America, a more pervasive and direct threat comes from illegal immigration. The borders of the United States have been proven porous by millions of Mexicans, Cubans, and Haitians (U.S. General Accounting Office, 1984:33). If nations in Central America and the Caribbean continue to generate the wholesale migration of their peoples, whether intentionally (as in the case of the Cuban boatlift) or unintentionally (by natural disaster), immigration will present the United States with serious problems (Taylor, 1983:46).

The economic links between the United States and Latin America are important to U.S. interests and contribute to the economic well-being of both regions. Economically, Central America's relationship to the United States in the 1980s will remain about what it is at present—more important for Central America than for the United States. Nevertheless, the viability of U.S. economic ties with Central America will continue to be of great importance. For example, U.S. access to petroleum in the region (Mexico's oil potential and the Caribbean refinery capacity) would be strategically and economically important in the event of a cutoff of normal supplies. Although current U.S. trade and investment in South America is relatively small, the region could become one of the larger U.S. trading areas. This trade will include imports of increasingly large quantities of raw materials, strategic minerals such as manganese and aluminum, and a growing variety and quantity of manufactured goods. In turn, U.S. industries will export greater volumes of goods to a rapidly growing South American market. The U.S. private capital investment, already substantial, continues to flow into this region as well. And South American states, notably Brazil, are gaining additional global economic status day by day.

Aside from the obvious macroeconomic benefits of the economic ties that exist between Latin America and the United States, such as the protection of the U.S. investments and general growth, other benefits accrue from a sound economic relationship. A sound regional economy promoted by U.S. investments and trade creates conditions that allow an increase in the standard of living for the people of Latin America. This acts as an impediment to wholesale emigration and revolutionary conflict, which are fostered by social unrest. Thus economic security for Latin America translates into physical security for the United States by removing the catalysts for instability and stimulating acceptance of the current system (Hayes, 1984:13).

Certain developments are increasingly affecting economic relations between Latin America and the United States. The flow of raw materials, access to resources and markets, and free transit for trade through the Caribbean Basin are critical for U.S. business. Trade with Latin America has grown dramatically in the past decade; imports of petroleum and natural gas from Venezuela and Mexico account for much of this growth (Gonzalez *et al.*, 1984:v). Yet most Latin American countries have grown uncomfortable because the United States plays such a dominant role in the economic fortunes of the region, even though they would be unable to continue their development without U.S. capital, technology, and expertise (Jordan and Taylor, 1984:446). This growing resentment could impact adversely on the economic and political relationship that exists between the United States and Latin America.

Another U.S. interest on the southern flank, one that is directly linked to the economic and physical security of the Western Hemisphere, is the protection of strategic sealanes of communication and transportation routes in the 1400-mile-wide South Atlantic Narrows (Natal, Brazil to Dakar, Senegal). Persian Gulf oil imports to the United States pass through this area daily. In addition, the Caribbean Basin is also a key transit zone for oil imported to the United States from Mexico, Venezuela, Africa, and the Middle East and is currently the route for half these imports. The U.S. government has forecast that imported raw materials will rise from a current 20% to almost 50% of total U.S. raw material consumption by the year 2000. Most of these materials will enter the United States via the Caribbean. In NATO contingency planning the Caribbean Basin is also the prospective passage for U.S. wartime reinforcements for Western Europe.

The Panama Canal, once the centerpiece of U.S. interests in Latin America, is no longer considered the vital national security interest it once was—as evidenced by the Panama Canal Treaty, which gradually transfers the canal to Panamanian control by the year 2000. Although still important for ship deployment in wartime and commercially relevant in recent years because of high fuel costs, which rendered South American routes prohibitively expensive, the canal has lost its primary emphasis in U.S. national security debates. A proposed second Panama Canal could become of major interest to the United States if it were constructed to permit passage of the larger U.S. warships.

The primary U.S. interests concerning Latin America, as previously detailed, are (*a*) the creation of a stable political environment that promotes the evolution of democratic governments and addresses the problems and sources of social unrest in the region; (*b*) a strong economic relationship, which benefits both the United States and Latin America; (*c*) measures to halt indigenous and foreign-induced revolutionary violence and terrorism in the region; and (*d*) the protection of vital sealanes.

Unlike the situation in the nineteenth and early twentieth centuries, Latin America today is not isolated, and the United States can no longer insulate it from the influence of nonhemispheric powers. This influence should not be underestimated. The structure and traditions of the military forces in Latin America have been shaped to a considerable extent by outside forces, even though domestic traditions do play an important role.

THE ROLE OF THE MILITARY IN LATIN AMERICA

The military establishments in Latin America and their relationships with their publics differ markedly from the situation in the United States. These differences have a profound impact on the people of Latin America and the ability of the various regional military establishments to accomplish their national security missions.

An important difference between Latin American military establishments and recent U.S. military traditions is that there is very little commonality between the officer corps and the enlisted ranks in Latin America. Traditionally, officers came from the landed aristocracy. More recently, officers tend to come from the aspiring middle class—those in the middle of the socioeconomic spectrum who are aspiring for more wealth and prestige—and from the offspring of career military officers and civil servants. The enlisted ranks, in contrast, have historically been composed of people from the working classes who are short-term conscripts (6 months to 1 year). This difference creates a schism between the professional officers and the short-term, poorly trained soldiers.

The U.S. experience has been very different over the last generation. Increasingly the officer corps have been filled from the families of blue-collar workers or career soldiers. This has been true whether the source of commission was a U.S. military academy, Reserve Officers Training Corps (ROTC), or Officer Candidate School (OCS).

The point here is that the commonality in background that exists for officers and enlisted men of the U.S. armed forces, in addition to other factors, tends to foster the "unit cohesion" that is instrumental in forging effective military fighting organizations. Some would argue this point in the U.S. case, citing contrary examples from the Vietnam war. The comparison is relative, however, and one need refer only to the predictable results of the Argentine Army's performance in the Falkland Islands, where unit cohesion and morale disintegrated rapidly, leading to abandonment of weapons and equipment and mass surrenders. It seems as difficult for Latin American military leaders to identify with their men as it is for them to identify with the plight of the working class form whom the soldiers are drawn. This has implications for the approach Latin American officers take in quelling local insurgencies or reacting to terrorism or psychological warfare aimed at local populations.

There is a distinct tactical similarity in the Latin American and U.S. military establishments' approach toward low-intensity conflict. They simply are not well prepared to deal with it,. Many Latin American officers have been and are now being trained along the lines of U.S. professional military schools. Most Latin American military school curricula are patterned after U.S. military schools. Thus Latin American officers are taught the doctrine, tactics, and force structure of "divisions," "brigades," "battalions," and "companies," along the lines of the U.S. model. This training prepares them to fight the large, conventional, European-style wars in which conventional maneuvers and massive firepower are keys to success on a battlefield. Like U.S. forces (who have only very recently begun to focus on low-intensity conflict), the Latin Americans do not understand the necessity of "staying power" to establish security at the village level. They do not understand that they must establish an identity with the villagers, which means identifying with their hopes, fears, ideals, and aspirations. They do not understand that the first priority is to establish local security and communal freedom from the fear of terrorism, which is a lead element of insurgency. This means nothing short of a major shift in the priority of conventional tactics. It means defending something valuable *in locus rei sitae* (the freedom from fear in the lives of those whose hearts and minds both sides seek), rather than "carrying the battle to the enemy." Local security comes first, and this requires living, day *and night*, among the people, regardless of the creature comforts foregone. With the exception of the U.S. Marine Civic Action Platoons (CAPs) and some U.S. Special Forces Units in Vietnam, this is something U.S. ground forces have yet to learn—or at least to demonstrate—in combat or combat training. Living with and protecting local populations, and inducing and training them to provide for their own security, is a difficult mission and one that Western and Western-trained military organizations generally neither like to perform nor perform well. In this environment, "unit maneuver" and "application of massive firepower" are almost irrelevant.

Latin American military leaders generally seek the most modern, most lethal military equipment they can acquire. In most cases the equipment they want most is the equipment currently used by the U.S. forces, both because of the "prestige factor" and the expectation that ammunition and spare parts will be in production and available. For example, many Latin American military leaders seek "helicopter gunships," which can find and fix the enemy and transport firepower and troops to destroy his units wherever they assemble (which, by tactical design, is seldom). The problem is that insurgents, terrorists, and psychological warfare experts seek to stay close to local populations, and the application of massive firepower tends to overlook the distinction between friend and foe. Innocent people die; local populations learn to fear both insurgents and counterinsurgents; some manipulate both sides and others become refugees out of sheer desperation and the instinct for survival.

The essential point here is that Western (primarily U.S.) models for doctrine, training, and force structure among Latin American military establishments generally are ineffective as responses to low-intensity conflict in their own countries.

To reiterate, in Latin America: (*a*) There is little identification between the officer corps and the increasingly hard-pressed, leveraged, working classes that serve as enlisted soldiers and are at the same time from families that are the targets of insurgency, terrorism, and psychological operations by radical, dissident groups; (*b*) Western-trained Latin American officers push to acquire the most sophisticated and lethal modern weapons available; (*c*) training experience is largely irrelevant at best and often counterproductive in advocating massive firepower against low-intensity conflict threats; and (*d*) the use of massive firepower is relatively indiscriminate, which creates insecurities for local populations. Added to threats posed by insurgents, this creates refugees who flee to avoid being caught between insurgent and government military forces.

ARMS PRODUCTION IN LATIN AMERICA

The effort by developing nations to expand their market prospects for manufactured goods is a major element of their plans for economic development. The export of manufactured goods is an important source of income and a clear imperative for a majority of developing nations faced with overwhelming balance-of-payments deficits and foreign-debt burdens. As more developing countries emphasize the industrial sector of their national economies, the military hardware sector frequently emerges at the forefront.

The two leading suppliers of arms in the world, the United States and the Soviet Union, can no longer afford to sell military hardware at prices below the wholesale cost. This led at least a decade ago to a highly competitive international arms market, which is increasingly a buyer's market (Cahn *et al.*, 1977:8). This competition has allowed growing numbers of smaller nations to work effectively in the arms market by undercutting the two largest producers. The production and sale of military hardware has a multiplier effect for developing nations because it helps to create jobs, allows some independence from the traditional suppliers, and reduces the unit cost of systems for the national military.

The accumulation of capital necessary to acquire the machinery to build modern weapon systems is a difficult problem for developing nations. The extension of export licenses or joint-venture agreements is the traditional method nations use to establish indigenous production, but arriving at these arrangements is problematic and sometimes dampens enthusiasm to compete in more sophisticated systems. But there is a tremendous market, particularly among other developing nations, for relatively simple military hardware. Armored personnel carriers and small propeller aircraft are items that are well within the technological reach of developing industry in several countries, and the extension of coproduction and licensing arrangements for these systems is common.

Latin American nations have been eager to cash in on the benefits of national armaments production. Brazil is an example of an enthusiastic, reliable arms supplier. Many other countries in Latin America are at various stages in developing a manufacturing capability for military hardware. It is difficult to establish the value of indigenous production, but it is estimated that the amount of arms production in Latin America reached $450 million (1970 dollars) in 1980 (Leontif and Duchin, 1983:87). The majority of these weapons are produced under license or in some coproduction arrangement with one of the Western industrialized nations. Licensing and coproduction arrangements usually do not allow further marketing of the products beyond the country of manufacture, so most of the arms produced are for the domestic market. Despite these restrictions, the export of arms from Latin America has taken an impressive leap in the past 3 years. In 1982, Latin American nations exported $705 million worth of military goods. Although this still represents only a small fraction (.7%) of total exports from the region, there are obvious political benefits from this trade. It reduces dependence on foreign suppliers, facilitates more nationalistic foreign policy, and creates a significant industrial sector in the country (U.S. Arms Control and Disarmament Agency, 1984:55).

Brazil has enjoyed real success in the arms market and has essentially thwarted the historic dilemma faced by nations that buy arms from the superpowers. By developing its own arms industry, Brazil has been able to reduce its dependence on the superpowers and capture an impressive share of the global arms market. As a direct consequence, the share of Brazil's GNP devoted to its own military expenditures has steadily decreased since 1975. (U.S. Arms Control and Disarmament Agency, 1984:19). In 1980 Brazil spent only .6% of its GNP on the military, which is one of the lowest in the hemisphere (Sivard,1985:33). The value of arms imports has decreased ninefold since 1978, and arms exports have almost quintupled (U.S. Arms Control and Development Agency, 1984:61). The Brazilian arms industry had a humble beginning, dealing mostly in trucks and armored vehicles, but it has developed into an ambitious array of companies that offer a wide range of products. Brazilian firms sell subsonic jet aircraft and trainers, naval patrol aircraft, patrol boats, and heavy and light tanks (Martin, 1985:18).

Cuba and Peru are the only other Latin American countries that export significant amounts of arms. In 1982 Cuba exported arms and military equipment valued at $20 million. In the same period, Peru exported $60 million worth of miliary equipment (U.S. Arms Control and Development Agency, 1984:65,83). In Cuba's case it is doubtful whether military exports represent a significant commercial asset. Military exports accounted for only .3% of Cuba's total exports in 1982. It is more likely a politically motivated program with marginal monetary benefits. Considering the vast amount of arms sent to Cuba from the Soviet Union ($2.6 billion between 1972 and 1982), arms sent from Cuba to other nations and groups (which are largely undocumented) represent a meager fraction. Peruvian arms exports are also limited in the size and level of their sophistication. There is a potential for increased exports in the aircraft market, as Peru intends to begin production of a military training aircraft to replace its own Cessna T-37s.

There are also a number of arms-producing nations in Latin America that have not gone beyond satisfying their own national requirements or are just taking their first tentative steps in the international market. A number of states have turned to indigenous production when foreign suppliers have refused them sales because of their concern over poor records in human rights. Argentina and Chile are two examples of this reluctance on the part of suppliers, and they have responded with spirited efforts to build their own equipment. Argentina has one of the oldest arms industries on the continent and continues to place heavy emphasis on the production of arms. Military hardware produced by Argentina includes light and medium tanks, armored personnel carriers, training aircraft, a few small naval vessels, and a variety of ordnance (Anonymous, 1981:20). The clear emphasis of the Argentine arms industry is on self-reliance, although the majority of the work is done under license. Argentina has yet to develop any prototypes on its own. Pakistan and the Peoples Republic of China have expressed an interest in acquiring an

Argentinian-built medium tank, but no actual sales of military equipment are known to have been arranged.

The Chilean government spends an impressive amount on military expenditures, approximately 5.3% of its GNP in 1980 (Sivard, 1983:33). Chile has yet to develop arms exports to any extent, but it has increased its production of military hardware by fashioning coproduction and licensing agreements with U.S. and European companies. A serious barrier to Chilean exports will be the same political problems that afflict Chile as an arms importer. Nevertheless, Chile may be able to sell its products to other developing nations that have less concern about the politics of their trading partners.

Surprising progress has been achieved by efforts to establish an industrial base for arms in Guatemala. A fledgling attempt to construct an ammunition manufacturing plant is a good illustration of a country taking the first steps toward constructing an indigenous capacity to supply its national army. Using technology thought to have been provided by Austria, the Guatemalan Army should have just recently finished a plant to produce 5.56 mm and 9 mm ammunition (Lewis, 1983).

Mexico's arms industry, in contrast to other Latin American countries, is not fundamentally motivated by economic concerns and the desire to export. The primary rationale for Mexico's arms industry is military self-sufficiency and the accomplishment of national security objectives. This is in a sense the inverse of countries that establish an arms industry for economic reasons; desiring to build and export arms in order to bolster their industrial base (Katz, 1984:252–255). The types of systems produced, the majority of them under U.S. or European license, are specifically designed for the Mexican armed forces and there is currently no plan to market these systems internationally.

ARMS TRANSFERS TO LATIN AMERICA

Arms sales to Latin America have grown dramatically since 1945. The United States and the Soviet Union are the undisputed leaders in the global arms market and receive significant returns on their sales of arms. Arms sales have become a major source of Soviet hard-currency earnings. The essential logic of arms transfers is based on a combination of political, strategic, and economic imperatives. In the post–1945 era, and at the height of the cold war, the distribution of weapon systems was an important link in a political and strategic struggle for global influence. More recently, financial considerations have played a more determinant role in the export of arms.

The transfer of U.S. or Soviet military equipment, especially to developing nations, was once a political imperative during the cold-war years because it symbolized an ideological affinity between the donor and the recipient or defined areas of interest. Hindsight suggests that the significance of this linkage was either lost on many recipient nations or became a cause for resentment. The use of arms exports to symbolize tenuous links of political unity, although understandable in cold-war logic, was clearly not a sound rationale for the granting of dangerous technology to increasing numbers of unstable governments.

There is specific military utility behind the transfer of arms to allied or friendly nations. In preparing for low-intensity conflict contingencies, a superpower would find it extraordinarily useful to have indigenous armies in certain regions trained to its standards and equipped with its hardware. The United States has gone a step farther and has considered prepositioning supplies and equipment, not just for indigenous troops, but for the use of U.S. troops. Linking the forces with the equipment has been problematic, however, because it is difficult to predict the location of future crises or to negotiate with host nations.

These political and strategic concerns, while still important, are now accompanied by the financial lure of the arms market. From 1980 to 1983, the USSR sold military goods worth $40.7 billion to the countries of the Third World. In the same period, the United States delivered arms totaling $38.4 billion to the Third World (Grimmett, 1984:16).

Latin American countries have many arms suppliers, among which the communist bloc, Western Europe, and the United States are the largest. From 1980 to 1983, the Soviet Union was the primary supplier to Latin America with one-third of the market. French firms accounted for 14.6% of the deliveries of arms, and West Germany ranked third with 10.4% of the market (Grimmett, 1984:11). In addition, there are large, unrecorded transfers of military goods for which there can only be speculative estimates. The best known of these covert supply operations is the supply to guerrillas in El Salvador by Cuba and Nicaragua. The existence of this supply line has been well documented by the U.S. Defense and State Departments (1984:18–23).

Soviet arms transfers to the Third World reflect the strategic objectives of the USSR and help meet the needs of the long-suffering Soviet economy. Soviet strategy in Latin America, carried out principally through Cuban proxies, focuses on the Caribbean Basin, where major U.S. interests tend to concentrate. These interests are free access to air routes and waterways (including the Panama Canal), access to Venezuelan and Mexican oil, defense of island dependencies, and the containment or reversal of Soviet–Cuban ideological expansion. The Soviet–Cuban strategic objective appears to be to erode U.S. leadership in the region, acquire the capability to interdict the supply of raw material, threaten the lines of communication, and divert U.S. resources and attention from higher-priority Soviet threats in Europe and Asia (Taylor *et al.*, 1984:492–493).

A relatively recent element of Soviet strategy has been the marketing of arms on a commercial basis. The defense industry is the single largest portion of the USSR's industrial base, and the export of arms allows the Soviets to produce more efficiently and at lower cost. The return of hard currency is an obvious benefit for the Soviets because it helps them address their chronic balance-of-payments problem (Cooper and Papp, 1983:60).

From 1980 to 1983, the Soviet Union agreed to send $3.4 billion worth of military equipment to Latin America (Grimmett, 1984:19). The primary recipients of this supply were Cuba, Nicaragua, and Peru. The majority of the equipment is sent to Cuba, with approximately 20% going to Peru and 3% to Nicaragua. The level of Soviet exports to Cuba is deceptive because Cuba acts as a staging area for the transport of military equipment to other places in Central America, just as Libya does for other Third World regions. The flow of arms from Cuba within the region is even more difficult to estimate, but its existence is unquestioned. The destinations are also clear: Nicaragua, El Salvador, Guatemala, Jamaica, and until the U.S. rescue mission, Grenada.

Western Europe

France and the Federal Republic of Germany are significant suppliers of military hardware to Latin America. The major countries of Western Europe delivered $3.6 billion in military equipment to Latin America from 1980 to 1983. This equipment included 38 surface naval vessels and 290 aircraft and helicopters (Grimmett, 1984:25, 31). The distribution of this equipment appears to be driven by a market attitude, bound by nothing but the broadest sort of political restraint. No Western European country has sold a significant amount of arms to Cuba, but it is questionable whether they would refuse if Cuba offered to buy them. The technological level of armaments supplied seems to be constrained only by the purses of recipient nations. There is some technology that is regulated by the Coordinating Committee for Multilateral Export Controls, but this has not prevented Latin American nations from purchasing surprisingly sophisticated weapons. The Argentine purchase of the French-made Exocet proved to have devastating consequences for the British, and this sort of development will not be uncommon if the current trend in arms transfers continues.

United States

The remaining portion of arms sales in Latin America is dominated by the United States. In 1983 the United States was the primary supplier of arms to the Third World. Sales of $9.68 billion outpaced Soviet deliveries of $8.83 billion and put the United States above the Soviet Union for the first time since 1977. Latin America has drawn considerably more attention from the United

States recently, and the number of agreements for arms sales, as well as the magnitude of arms deliveries, have increased dramatically, although the percentage of U.S. exports to Latin America, 3.2% in 1983, is still a small fraction of total U.S. exports. In the early 1980s, the percentage of U.S. arms sales with Latin America increased as a proportion of all U.S. arms sales to the Third World (Grimmett, 1984:2). The primary recipients of U.S. equipment in Latin America—Brazil, Dominican Republic, Ecuador, El Salvador, Honduras, and Venezuela—are either traditional allies of the United States in the region or are involved in internal struggles with Soviet and Cuban-supported elements. Obviously, it is in the U.S. interest to bolster the strength of traditional allies and assist those countries that are battling insurgents supported by Soviets and Cubans.

The United States has traditionally linked the sale of military hardware in Latin America to cooperative training and use agreements with recipient nations. The extent of these arrangements has been somewhat restricted under the 1976 Military Assistance Act, which prohibits U.S. forces from involvement with civilian police agencies, but the relationship between U.S. military elements and the military services of recipient nations continues. Training, support, and logistics management are probably the most widely distributed U.S. support in the region. Under the International Military Education and Training Program, the United States expended just over $10 million in 1984 in Latin America (Defense Security Assistance Agency, 1985). The U.S. Army Corps of Engineers' support for building roads, bridges, dams, and other construction projects accounts for another significant portion of U.S. involvement in the region.

Arms transfers by the United States are either heavily subsidized through the use of credits and loan guarantees or outright grants. As mentioned, deliveries to Latin America from the United States do not yet amount to a significant portion of U.S. arms exports, but they are a major source of supply in the region. There does not appear to be any serious movement on the part of U.S. industry to expand the Latin American market because of its limited resources and tendencies for political instability. For all Latin American nations in 1984, the United States sold $235 million in military equipment and services. As of January 1985, the United States still had $752.9 million of undelivered equipment outstanding for the region (Defense Security Assistance Agency, 1985:79).

CONFLICT IN LATIN AMERICA

The history of Latin America is punctuated by wars, revolutions, and political oppression. From the Spanish enslavement of the Aztec Indians in the fifteenth and sixteenth centuries to the conflicts raging in El Salvador and Nicaragua today, violence has been a significant ingredient in Latin American political life. Despite the progress in development achieved by some Latin American nations, general social conditions remain volatile. The distribution of "wealth" remains inequitable, and a "revolution of rising expectations" is constantly in progress. The consequences of victory or defeat in Latin America are no longer limited to regional actors. For many reasons, events in the region have become part of the international security concerns of the superpowers, some medium powers, and and a large portion of the developing world.

The conflicts in Latin America vary, but they are founded on a core set of problems that have evaded simple solutions—problems that are generally common to all developing nations. A single, overwhelming similarity of conflict in Latin America is the effect it has on the populations of the countries afflicted by it. The citizens of many Latin American nations have found themselves embroiled in the struggle between those in power and those who seek to usurp government power. The ideological preferences of populations at large, hard to measure in any case, are the first casualties in conflict. In many instances, the only recourse available has been for people to leave their homes and seek refuge in other areas.

The flow of refugees from conflict areas in Central America has grown to truly monumental proportions. The problem of overpopulation has been worsened in some areas by the large-scale, mass migration of displaced persons to neighboring countries in 1984. A full one-third of these refugees are Guatemalans, Salvadorans, and Nicaraguans. Their wholesale migration to Honduras and Mexico has exacerbated existing tensions in these countries and others that have provided havens for them.

Granting asylum to those who have fled their homes in the face of political oppression or chronic violence has been a tradition in Central America, but in recent years the question of asylum for thousands of homeless has become a major irritant. Since the Cuban Revolution in 1960, the massive flow of refugees has dwarfed any possible capacity to accommodate it. The policies of individual nations with regard to refugees vary in the region, but this influx of humanity presents a unique threat to any nation that opens its borders. The question of assimilating refugees into the indigenous culture is no longer a reasonable option. The size and diversity of the refugees are just too great. Most of the asylum nations in Central America—Honduras, Guatemala, Costa Rica, and Mexico—have isolated refugee camps from the general population and have prohibited the refugees from integrating into the existing society. The individual governments of the region differ in the degree to which they enforce this isolation. Costa Rica allows refugees a great deal more freedom than Mexico does, but concerns about opening their economic system and culture to an overwhelming foreign influence are commonly held. This policy seems cruel and unjust, but the government must be primarily concerned with raising the standard of living of its own citizens. As a rule, the indigenous population is not a great deal better off than the refugees in the camps. Sometimes, because of the assistance provided to the refugees by national and international organizations, they are worse off.

Large numbers of these refugees will wind up trying to enter the United States illegally to look for employment (Fauriol, 1984:5–14). The United States has not yet granted any special immigration status to the Salvadorans, Guatemalans, and other nationalities who are flocking to its borders. A large number will elude the border police and the Immigration and Naturalization Service, and the impact of these immigrants on the southwestern states will be acute. Localities are required by law to provide illegal aliens with health services and public education, and the increasing number of Central Americans using community services is a decided drain on municipal treasuries (U.S. General Accounting Office, 1984:30–36). Failing a reversal of restrictive immigration policies by the countries in Central America, the flow of illiterate, nonskilled refugees to the United States will not decrease. Although the United States contributed $11 million in 1984 to refugee assistance in Central America, national policy will continue to focus on removing the root causes of this emigration rather than providing alternative areas for resettlement (U.S. General Accounting Office, 1984:11).

The primary form of conflict in the Caribbean Basin will continue to be *low intensity conflict* (defined in the next section) in a number of the Central American nations: Nicaragua, El Salvador, Honduras, and Guatemala. The potential for interstate, overt "war" is relatively low. There is a potential "external" threat from Cuba and Nicaragua; the strategy preferred by guerrillas, however, capitalizes not on overt aggression but on unconventional means that democratic nations are least prepared to counter. Of course, if Soviet involvement in Central America begins to constitute a clear threat to vital U.S. interests, this could lead to U.S. military intervention (Moorer and Fauriol, 1984).

The conflicts in Nicaragua and El Salvador capture the most attention, but these countries are by no means the only ones afflicted. Honduras, Guatemala, and Costa Rica are all threatened by nascent insurgencies. The island nations are the loci of a series of internal conflicts. The Mexican security environment is becoming increasingly fragile and is potentially the greatest threat in the region to U.S. security interests. The refugee problem, mentioned above, is only part of the problem.

Mexico today faces problems of an unprecedented magnitude. Economic, social, and political developments, both within Mexico and in its international environment, have thrust it into a new era of uncertainty. The chronic tendency of policymakers and opinion leaders to ignore Mexico has obscured the fact that Mexico's problems are severe and immediate. The stakes involved in its future are great, not just for Mexico but for the region as a whole, especially the United States. Though the nation remains a reservoir of potential, resolution of its multifaceted crisis will require the support and participation of others. But a murky grasp of these matters and an attitude of benign neglect toward them by leaders in the United States are real impediments to meaningful assistance.

The economic dimensions of Mexico's crisis have been the first to percolate into the international consciousness. Mexico's near default on its $80 billion foreign debt in 1982 focused worldwide attention on its ailing economy. The investment climate has grown increasingly uncertain, the pace of capital flight has proceeded, and the promise of the Mexican oil industry has become less obvious. This has profound implications for the character of long-term Mexican economic prosperity. These problems are aggravated by endemic corruption, rapid population growth, and the continued failure of the agricultural sector to fill basic needs (Levy and Szekel, 1983; Needler, 1982).

These economic problems have critical social implications. The middle class is growing increasingly impoverished, with a concomitant diminution in its historic role as a buffer between the extremes of wealth and poverty. Discontent among peasant and labor sectors is on a dramatic upswing. President Miguel de la Madrid acknowledged in his inaugural address that there is the potential for even more profound fissures in the fabric of Mexican society.

Realistic economic policy options are quite limited for Mexico, however. The state's long-dominant role in the economy affords important leverage, and this could be a critical asset. But there is great controversy about both the limits of that leverage and the means by which it should be applied—a controversy sharpened by recent nationalizations of large portions of the private sector, especially the banking system. The present course of enforced austerity holds real risks, particularly if those elements in society whose acquiescence is crucial to the success of this approach become alienated. If the domestic costs of the current approach grow too high, Mexican policy might shift in another direction—toward default. This policy has substantial risks: economic dislocation, financial chaos, a further weakening of the Mexican private sector, and political upheaval.

The political dimensions of Mexico's crisis are less widely appreciated outside Mexico, but they are no less severe and immediate. The prospect for significant domestic political change in Mexico over the next 4 years is great. They relate primarily to critical changes in the long-standing political institutions. The long-ruling Institutional Revolutionary party (PRI) faces a very uncertain future as the labor–peasant–middle-class coalition, which has formed the core of its support, further unravels. Many believe that the PRI will be increasingly tempted to resort to tactics of fraud and repression to preserve its dominant role. Opposition parties of the left and right are gaining strength and may constitute a serious challenge to the PRI in the next national election (U.S. Department of State, 1984). The roles of the Confederation of Mexican Workers, the Confederation of Popular Organizations, the National Confederation of Peasants, and other political and labor organizations are in considerable flux.

These complex forces are counterbalanced by important stabilizing factors. The army endures in its role as an ultimate guarantor of Mexican stability, although it too is experiencing vulnerability to disruptive pressures within the society. The presidency remains an institution of great importance and stability and is currently occupied by someone who commands considerable respect for his grasp of Mexico's problems and his commitment to their resolution. Public fear of a Second Revolution, parallel to the revolution of 1910–1920, also dampens the passions that might be invoked by the prospect of turbulent political change.

The dynamic and volatile character of domestic change in Mexico has significant international ramifications and is rendered more complex by the international environment. Mexico is not alone in attempting to grapple with a burdensome international debt, declining growth rates, and politically, unpopular austerity measures. Its kinship with other troubled nations on these problems adds a complicating layer of highly politicized diplomatic bargaining. In the last decade, Mexican prosperity has become increasingly intertwined with regional prosperity, and its trade relations and production capabilities have been diversified. Changes in its domestic polity accompany transformations in the political cultures of many neighbors, and the regional struggle for broadened political liberty and enhanced economic well-being show many signs of growing more internationalized. Clearly, the way in which Mexico weathers its crises will have great regional impact. A worsening domestic situation will contribute to a deepening of regional economic, political, and security problems. An improvement will contribute to international peace and prosperity.

These factors suggest that the comfortable historical circumstances that have allowed the United States largely to ignore Mexico no longer exist. The tendency to take Mexico for granted and view it as a low priority national interest for the United States is no longer acceptable, if it ever was. The stakes are simply too high.

The stability and relatively even development of the nations on the northern coast of the South American continent, coupled with the essentially nonstrategic character of their geography, have muted potential conflict situations in the region. Mineral wealth has enabled the national economies to develop beyond the single-cash-crop tradition and has largely insulated these countries from the feast-or-famine cycle in global economic markets. There is some potential for conflict, both intra- and interstate. There have been some attempts by Cuba to foment domestic insurgencies, most notably in Colombia (Fauriol and Perry, 1984:300). Colombia has endured a succession of insurgencies, which have caused control of the government to alternate between civilian and military authorities, prohibiting either from sufficiently addressing the sources of popular unrest. But domestic insurgents have been unable to establish enough popular support to challenge seriously the government. In 1979 Colombia returned to democratic government after a period of military rule, and a democratic government was recently installed in Ecuador (Stephan, 1981). The precise role of the Soviets and the Cubans is difficult to determine, but their involvement is an acknowledged fact. Yet, so far, governments of the region have successfully combatted terrorism without outside help.

Irridentist claims of some nations will increase the risk of conflict. Present international borders have been accepted by only some of the regional nations; an accord that stipulated acceptance of these borders has been disallowed, but there have been no direct consequences. The Andean Pact nations of Venezuela, Ecuador, Peru, Colombia, and Bolivia should be able to manage tensions over borders at below-crisis levels.

The recent crisis over the Falkland (Malvinas) Islands is an indication of the volatility of the southern cone, but it is unlikely that such a confrontation will recur in the foreseeable future (Anonymous, 1984b). The nations in this region have enjoyed a period of relative calm in their relations, and the probability of interstate conflict is very low.[1] The definition of some of the borders in this region also remains subject to interpretation, but the likelihood of violent alterations of the status quo is remote.

The nations of Paraguay, Uruguay, and Bolivia all harbor some fear of Brazil's role in the region. These countries are not powerful enough to deny concerted efforts to displace them from areas in dispute. But the incentives for Brazil, or any other nation, to attempt revision of existing boundaries by military force are low (Perry and Schneider, 1985). Peru remains an active recipient of Soviet military and economic assistance, but it has yet to develop a foreign policy that would cause its neighbors in the region concern.

[1] Chile and Argentina signed a friendship agreement at the Vatican in January 1984 that resolved the long-standing Beagle Channel dispute (Anonymous, 1984a:A3).

ARMS TRANSFERS AND LOW-INTENSITY CONFLICT

As stated in the preceding section, the potential for conventional, interstate conflict is low in comparison to the level of low-intensity conflict that is becoming endemic to the region. *Low-intensity conflict* can be described as "situations ranging from terrorism, crises, and small wars to revolutions and counterrevolutions which require tailored, limited responses short of national mobilization and often in conjunction with host regimes and third countries. These responses are likely to be military or paramilitary for short situations, but of mixed political–economic–military–other actions for revolutionary and protracted conflicts" (Dean, 1985:46). As in most developing regions of the world, political instability and unrest are chronic problems in Latin America. Civil disorder and local wars spawned indigenously, without foreign influence, by social inequities and political instabilities challenge the security of the region. Also, the potential for expanded Soviet and Cuban involvement in the domestic political affairs of Latin American nations presents a serious set of challenges for U.S. interests in the region. Since the mid 1970s, the Soviet Union has recognized that peaceful means are not sufficient to carry the socialist revolution to Latin America (Leiken, 1982:34–35). A policy of active reinforcement of existing underground armies and guerrilla groups has introduced revolutionary elements into the Latin American political milieu that are decisively stronger and better organized than their predecessors.

Many existing governments are inadequately prepared to respond to any form of insurgent movement, particularly the range of activities guerrilla forces are capable of carrying out. On the one hand, the acquisition of relatively sophisticated Warsaw Pact weaponry, including small arms, machine guns, mortars, grenades, and other explosives, allows guerrillas to deliver unexpected and devastating blows to critical areas of the national infrastructure, such as electric power grids, water supplies, and industry.

On the other hand, government military forces tend to respond (when they can detect guerrilla formations) with increasingly sophisticated and lethal weapons, such as high-performance fighter aircraft capable of delivering iron bombs, multiple rockets, and napalm; helicopter gunships mounted with machine guns and rockets; artillery with high-explosives, white phosphorus or "beehive" rounds; and other lethal weapons capable of "massive firepower." But rarely do guerrillas mass their forces, preferring instead to hit and run. When they blend into the population, but are detected by government military units, the guerrillas invite the kind of retaliation that kills innocent civilians.

The insurgent's agenda goes beyond attacks on vulnerable points of the society. Low-intensity conflict is primarily a psychological struggle, and the most important battles are those that cause the general population to become alienated from an existing government and lend support to the revolutionary cause (Robert H. Kupperman Associates, 1983:12). The guerrilla movement cannot survive without some support from the population at large. Therefore the emphasis of low-intensity conflict is not on militarily decisive battles with government forces. The propaganda campaign is a primary concern of the revolution. Through guerrilla acts of terror and violence, the government is portrayed as weak and ineffective, or, in response to guerrilla actions, as brutally repressive. Either way, the eventual objective of the guerrilla movement is to supplant the political system with its own form of government.

Attempting to measure the importance of armaments to low-intensity conflict begs the question of the significance of the military component of the struggle. Low intensity conflict is primarily a sociopolitical, not a military or technological phenomenon. The level of military weaponry possessed by guerrilla forces will affect their military strategy but will not determine the existence of a revolutionary force. Advanced military hardware increases the user's mobility and firepower. But even less than state-of-the-art systems allow great mobility and the ability to strike with overwhelming force. Each of the participants in a low intensity conflict will seek to utilize sophisticated military hardware to meet an objective, and although insurgent groups benefit by the acquisition of modern, destructive weaponry, they will continue to rely on light weapons that are easily transportable on foot, by pack animal or water craft.

The main objective of guerrillas is far different from that of the military. Guerrillas do not need to secure territory, nor are they concerned at first with the outright defeat of the military. Initially, they desire only to disrupt the normal routine of political life and force the government to take measures that will alienate the population. Only in the latter stages of a revolution will the guerrilla be ready to confront the military directly.

Military leaders schooled in the European and U.S. regular army traditions have had difficulty adapting to the different tactics needed to fight a guerrilla war. The army tends to stay in its garrisons and venture out against guerrilla forces only in large formations during daylight. The military often does not have an opportunity to use its advanced weapons because of the difficulty in locating verifiable targets (Robert H. Kupperman Associates, 1983:12). Some exceptions, such as advanced communication equipment, modern helicopter gunships, and certain intelligence apparatus, have been used with success.

With the exception of "individual weapons" (rifles and pistols), military weapons are designed to produce mass casualties by concentrating massive firepower. The pace of modern technology for conventional military weapons constantly increases their lethality. The issue, from the government—military perspective, is control and discipline of the application of firepower. Resolution of that issue resides in command, control, leadership, and training. Without discipline, military units are most often motivated to respond to guerrilla attacks with massed firepower that tends to be indiscriminate. Often, the response will be motivated by fear and anger. The Vietnam case of Lieutenant Calley and his superior officer, Captain Medina, is instructive in this respect.

Military firepower applied without discipline can kill and wound innocent civilians, creating resentment and hatred of government forces, which is precisely the guerrilla's objective. The greatest anguish for a military commander is to sustain casualties in his unit without the capability to respond. In addition to hit-and-run tactics, the war in Vietnam demonstrated the guerrilla's propensity to hit and then take refuge in local hamlets where disciplined U.S. military leaders would refuse to permit their troops to fire. This dilemma can be resolved only by the disciplined command and sound leadership that makes the application of firepower discriminate and proportional.

Although it does not necessarily occur if the guerrilla's psychological and political efforts are successful, often the guerrilla forces grow in number over the years, and they are eventually forced to conduct operations on a large scale and to act more like a regular army. This makes them more vulnerable to government efforts to engage them in a decisive battle. But the existence of a revolutionary core of extremists will always allow for guerrilla forces to recoup from anything but a total loss. The level of violence and the manner in which it is applied changes as the movement grows in popularity or is curtailed by government actions, but while the political spirit remains, the conflict will continue.

In concert with necessary political and economic measures, the only real tactical solution to low-intensity conflict is the refinement of government and military strategy and tactics. The government troops in El Salvador only very recently have been effective because smaller groups of soldiers have been allowed to make sweeps through guerrilla territory and take the battle to the countryside (Mallin, 1984:1).

The most effective strategy against insurgent movements combines political, economic, and psychological measures with judicious and surgical application of military force. Low intensity conflict truly is a battle for "the hearts and minds of the people" (Robert H. Kupperman Associates, 1983:12). The level of armaments used in this battle is not inherently a factor in the political outcome of the conflict. Without other measures, the introduction of modern, highly lethal military hardware on both sides will only make the conflict more costly in terms of lives and property.

Local political leaders and the local populations over which they exercise authority must believe that they have a stake in preserving the national government. First and foremost, together with the government's military, paramilitary, and police activities, they must be able to provide for the security of the population. Against an insurgency, weapons alone do not provide security. Equally critical is doctrine, training, tactics, and the coordination of command, control, communication, and intelligence. Second, local populations must believe in the government's cause. This requires not only an acceptable social agenda but communication including physical presence and public relations (or "propaganda"). Third, a decent or visibly improving standard of living must prevail. Under the best of policies and circumstances, this will take time in most Latin American countries.

Well-trained guerrilla leaders will understand all this. They will seek to undermine local security by night raids and terror tactics. They will exploit all means to cut communications between the central government and local populations by mining roads, blowing up bridges, cutting telecommunications, and using other measures of psychological warfare, such as local indoctrination sessions. They will impose their own means of taxation on the transport of local produce. In brief, they will seek to remove all instruments of effective governance except for the application of massive firepower.

Another issue in this analysis is the effect of arms transfers on the political and economic development of the nation. Expenditures on military equipment and forces divert scarce resources from social programs (Sivard, 1983: 22–25). There may be no direct relationship between the sale of arms to developing nations and political stability, but emphasis on the military sector clearly has a negative effect on the public sector. If the government does not apply a realistic sense of limits to its arms purchases, the economic health of its nation can be impaired. Argentina is a useful example. The government of Argentina continued an ambitious program of military spending beyond the need to meet any realistic contingency of external threat. Overconfident of its military capability and miscalculating British resolve, the government of Argentina bought itself political humiliation in the Falkland Islands. Argentina is now left with some $2 billion in debts from that war. The groundswell of popular opinion, which initially supported the occupation of the islands, turned against the government, and the war rapidly turned against the Argentine forces.

Arms transfers do not create low-intensity conflict, although overinvestmentin arms can erode public support and bankrupt a small treasury and thereby help create those conditions that foster low-intensity conflict. Nor does the transfer of arms provide a simple solution to conflict. The clear message in relation to low-intensity conflict is that it must be addressed at the most basic levels of political action. There is some evidence indicating that the premature militarization of a low-intensity conflict leads to escalation instead of overcoming it. The U.S. experience in Honduras in the late 1970s and early 1980s has shown that while some level of aid and economic assistance is helpful, U.S. intervention on a large scale serves only to alienate the population and provides for more substantive criticism of the government. A U.S. presence in Honduras served to highlight its importance to the Soviets and Cubans and thus ensured its inclusion in Soviet plans for the region.

It is now beyond the capacity of a single supplier to affect the decisions of a recipient government if that government is insistent on purchasing a specific kind of weaponry. Often, a major criterion in the decision to purchase is the "prestige factor" associated with the systems currently in use with U.S. armed forces. Because of the variety of alternative suppliers in the present world market, however, unilateral restraints on any arms sales are becoming less and less effective.

Restraints placed on a government that is in the midst of a low-intensity conflict and in clear need of military equipment will not restrain the conflict. If restraints are applied on the government, and no such restraints are placed on the guerrillas, the potential for calamity is high. If mutual restraint is a viable option in a low-intensity conflict situation, it certainly should be pursued with enthusiasm. But these opportunities are rare indeed.

U.S. INTERESTS AND SECURITY ASSISTANCE: GUIDELINES FOR THE FUTURE

In its November 1983 report, the Commission on Security and Economic Assistance, chaired by Frank Carlucci, emphasized that security and economic development are two sides of the same coin. Neither can be assured over the long term without the other. For this reason, U.S. interests in allied and friendly nations of the developing world are best served when these two aspects of national well-being are supported in a balanced fashion. Over the past 35 years there have been some notable swings in arms transfer policy, but the United States keeps coming back to the common-sense concept reaffirmed by the Carlucci Commission.

The wisdom of an integrated approach was again confirmed by the findings of the National Bipartisan Committee on Central America, issued on January 10, 1984. This commission recognized that "neither the military nor the political nor the economic nor the social aspects of the crisis (in Latin America) can be considered independently of the others" (pp. 4–5) Security assistance, while essential for countering insurgencies, must be considered in the broader context of regional unrest; a holistic approach must be adapted to redress the conditions that lead to indigenous and foreign-supported revolutions. Finally, the commission accepted the necessity of cooperation between the United States and Latin America in assessing the requirements of each country individually and the need for agreement on a strategy to meet these requirements.

Any U.S. security assistance program should consider this multitude of factors. While it is axiomatic that economic assistance is essential to the success of security assistance, the following focuses solely on U.S. security assistance efforts. It is beyond the scope of this chapter to address specific economic measures.

Since World War II, the United States has supplied over $150 billion in arms to allied and friendly governments. This program has been a major factor in preserving the security of our allies and of the United States itself. But there have been notable instances when it did not succeed and may even have contributed to instability and conflict. In some cases, U.S. arms served security in the short term. But, over time, as economic conditions failed to improve or even declined, the political situation deteriorated, and U.S. interests suffered severely. This exemplifies the problem with an arms transfer policy that ignores other factors.

The experience in Latin America illustrates the vicissitudes of U.S. arms transfer policy. During World War II, we included Latin American allies in the lend-lease program with the aim of securing our southern flank against Axis threats to our overseas lines of communication and in order to add to allied strength in the European and Pacific theaters of war. After the war, successive U.S. administrations adopted the position that the countries of Central and South America did not face any serious military threats and that major arms imports into the region would encourage military adventures and divert local efforts from economic development. Unfortunately, neither the Soviet Union nor the Western European suppliers exercised the same restraint. The Soviets employed arms transfers to gain influence, and the Western Europeans exploited them for commercial profit. The result was that the tenuous U.S. influence in the region was diminished further.

In addition to the emphasis given to the need to treat military and economic assistance in an integrated way, the Carlucci Commission also noted that the design of an assistance program should begin with the needs of the recipient countries. This admonition is particularly applicable for the countries of Latin America, many of which face security threats that are quite different from those posed to countries in Asia and the Middle East. The U.S. awareness of threats posed by Cuban and Soviet adventurism in Latin America has become much keener with ongoing developments in Central America. This awareness was highlighted by the Grenada intervention.

R. Bruce McColm summarized the Soviet–Cuban threat in the Central American–Caribbean region as follows:

> The fixation of the American debate on El Salvador obscures the broader outlines of a Soviet–Cuban strategy convergence in the Central American–Caribbean region following the triumph of the Sandinistas in Nicaragua. The unified strategy is still geared to the accelerated export of revolution into the area, capitalizing upon an extensive and sophisticated regional infrastructure of arms flows and training that is now tied into the global logistical network of Soviet, surrogate and terrorist forces. Looming in the background of this immediate conflict strategy, however, is a huge stockpiling of modernized conventional weapons systems in Cuba, spilling over increasingly into Nicaragua. The short-range purpose of this buildup clearly is the fashioning of a regional conventional deterrent for shielding revolutionary forces once they have seized power. The ultimate goal, from Moscow's vantage point, is to mount the kind of power projection into the area that, by squarely threatening vital U.S. interests and lifelines, would in effect hold America's global strategy hostage in the event of a larger conflict. (1983:28)

Some would argue that the scenario painted by McColm grants too much to Soviet–Cuban ingenuity and capability. These detractors argue that the United States must recognize long-standing human rights abuses and endemic poverty as the root causes of social upheaval in the region. They add that the oft-cited Soviet–Cuban strategic threat is a phony argument used by various regimes in the region to help maintain their power.

To be sure, there exists a complex web of motives operating within the region, but many would recognize that the United States can scarcely countenance the establishment of a multitude of hostile pro-Soviet regimes in its backyard. Measures must be taken to ensure that Soviet- and Cuban-supported insurgencies are not able to capitalize successfully on legitimate local aspirations for political freedom and economic dignity. President Reagan articulated U.S. policy for Central America with these concerns in mind in his April 27, 1983, address to Congress:

> We will support democracy, reform, and human freedom. This means using our assistance, our powers of persuasion, and our legitimate "leverage" to bolster humane democratic systems where they already exist and to help countries on their way to that goal as quickly as human institutions can be changed.

In quoting the president, Deputy Secretary of State Kenneth Dam noted that the United States is using military assistance as a shield to help countries of the region defend themselves and to give diplomacy and democracy a chance to work. In particular he noted that this shield should "foreclose a military victory by antidemocratic forces supported through Nicaragua by Cuba and the Soviet Union (Dam, 1982).

In recent years the bulk of U.S. security assistance in Latin America has gone to countries that are now threatened or potentially threatened by Cuban and USSR supported insurgencies (e.g., countries of Central

America and the Caribbean Basin). In fiscal year 1984, $9.14 million in grant military aid (MAP), or 93% of total MAP expenditures in Latin America, went to Central America and the Caribbean; and 52% of the 2253 Latin American students under the International Military Education and Training (IMET) program were from the Central American–Caribbean region (U.S. Department of Defense, 1984:61).

It is widely recognized that a carefully articulated and administered security assistance program can enhance the achievement of U.S. political, economic, and security objectives. One aspect of this security assistance is arms transfers. This reality was given added emphasis when President Reagan recast U.S. arms transfer policy in July 1981. That directive noted the utility of arms transfers to achieve the following:

- Help deter aggression.
- Improve the effectiveness of U.S. forces.
- Improve the deployability of U.S. forces.
- Demonstrate U.S. support for its friends.
- Foster regional and internal stability.
- Enhance U.S. defense production capabilities.

As noted, however, the transfer of arms with a high-firepower capability is not a reasonable response to the security challenges of low-intensity conflict. In fact, high-technology weapons with their greater capacity for lethality can act as a destabilizing influence by wreaking more havoc on noncombatants than on guerrilla forces. The transfer of arms is only one facet of security assistance, and it must be executed judiciously. Not only are high-technology weapons often incongruous with the cultures of Latin America, but they can also be applied as tools of repression, which only compounds the root problems of insurgency.

The use of security assistance to foster regional and internal stability is a particularly noteworthy objective that is clearly applicable in Latin America. Nevertheless, many would argue that the United States has not been particularly successful in its own counterinsurgency programs, and the assistance we are apt to offer in regions threatened by insurgencies, such as Central America, will undoubtedly fail. This expectation of the failure of U.S. security assistance policy in Central America is rooted in the Vietnam syndrome. Many point to our Vietnam experience as an example of the inability of the United States effectively to influence internal events in other countries. Some question whether the United States ought to attempt to interfere in the internal affairs of other sovereign states.

Clearly, the prospect of successful insurgencies in Central America and the Caribbean poses a challenge to U.S. ingenuity and policy. Ideally, the United

States must strive to achieve its objectives of democracy, diplomacy, development, and deterrence without being heavy-handed. Nevertheless, the potentially disastrous circumstances that could result from a failed policy for the region must be recognized. The United States has a vital interest in limiting the growth of Soviet–Cuban influence in the region.

An appropriate security assistance policy for the region must be properly integrated with an economic assistance program and with diplomatic efforts. In this context, a number of potential improvements to U.S. security assistance policy and techniques are suggested.

The training component of security assistance offers a unique opportunity to have an impact on the security and stability of recipient countries. The IMET program should be in the vanguard of U.S. security assistance. Through the application of the IMET program, the United States instructs foreign military personnel on the use of U.S. weaponry and tactics. Thus the IMET program can heavily influence the military establishments of Latin America by training military professionals in the modern approach to low-intensity conflict. The military establishments of Latin America are instructed in modern forms of counterinsurgency warfare, such as the surgical application of firepower, so that the general populations are spared from indiscriminate violence at the hands of those who claim to act as their benefactors. The active participation of the military in civic projects such as road and bridge construction, food distribution, and health care through the use of paramedics is also emphasized. The IMET students are exposed to U.S. political and social values, and enduring personal relationships are formed between U.S. and IMET individuals. The impact of exposure to U.S. values and personal friendships cannot be measured easily, but should not be discounted. Much more than professional and tactical competence of recipient cadres are at stake. Through IMET, it is hoped that leaders of indigenous military forces can be influenced in ways that will promote the disciplined, discriminant, and judicious use of military force when force must be employed in proximity to noncombatants. New initiatives on the subject of low-intensity warfare in the U.S. professional military education and training schools augur well in this respect.

In addition to the benefits of a well-designed training program, the development of an accurate, real-time intelligence apparatus is essential in conterinsurgency operations. It is impossible to apply surgical firepower to combat insurgency, even with sophisticated weaponry, without the proper intelligence assets to locate insurgents and deliver munitions accurately. These capabilities are particularly relevant to a guerrilla warfare environment, where much of the guerrilla's success depends on his ability to avoid contact with government forces when he chooses to do so. The surgical use of violence implies the coordination of highly developed intelligence assets with the selective application of low-intensity firepower. To ignore this important link in the war against insurgency invites the civilian casualties that are contrary to the interests of the forces in power. The ability to impart this kind of sophistication rests, to a large extent, on the use of U.S. advisory personnel. Our reluctance to use them will make it that much more difficult.

The umbilical cord attached to the transfer of hardware must be recognized. In the same way that the U.S. military attempts to ensure that the cutting edge of our forces is enhanced, or at least maintained, we must be careful that the transfer of U.S. arms does not degrade the capabilities of the recipient countries by overtaxing their logistical capabilities.

Finally, care should be exercised that military-to-military contacts between U.S. and recipient country personnel do not undermine civilian authority in the recipient countries. A precise program for implementing this and the preceding concerns is beyond the scope of this chapter.

The United States has indisputable, vital national interests in Latin America, and the security of the Western Hemisphere depends on a concerted effort to define and protect these interests. A central threat to these interests is low-intensity conflict waged by insurgent forces trying to implement political goals through violent means. Insurgencies do not arise from a vacuum. Economic, social, and political conditions, along with foreign interference, can act as catalysts for insurgent movements and undermine the credibility of existing governments. The unique nature and origin of low-intensity conflict demand an equally unique solution. Ignorance of this fact results in unnecessary deaths and inadvertently assists insurgent movements in the attainment of their goals. Armaments, both those that are indigenously produced and foreign imports, can either contribute to or detract from stability in Latin America—depending on their type and their application. Guerrilla forces will continue to use light, mobile weapons to foment instability and further their political goals. Government forces friendly to the United States need the proper security assistance and economic measures that embrace and address the true complexity of the problem, to thwart these attempts.

ACKNOWLEDGMENT

The assistance of Roger Merritt in research and draft revision for this chapter is gratefully acknowledged.

REFERENCES

Anonymous

1981 "Latin wings: South America's burgeoning aviation industry." *Defense and Foreign Affairs* (July).

1984a "Argentina signs accord with Chile." *New York Times* (January 24).
1984b "Escaping from a dismal history: Trevor Fishlock on a new mood in Argentina which may produce peace in the Falklands." *Times* (London) (February 20).

Bruske, Ed
1985 "U.S. sees democracy rising in Latin American nations." *Washington Post* (February 14).

Cahn, Ann Hessing, *et al.*
1977 *Controlling Future Arms Trade*. New York: McGraw-Hill.

Cooper, John F. and Daniel S. Papp
1983 *Communist Nations Military Assistance*. Boulder, Colo.: Westview Press.

Dam, Kenneth
1982 "Economic growth and U.S. policy in Central America." *Current Policy*, No. 509.

Dean, David J.
1985 "The USAF in low-intensity conflict: The Special Air Warfare Center." *Air University Review* 36(2):46.

Defense Security Assistance Agency
1985 "Foreign military sales: Status of purchase and deliveries." January 18.

Fauriol, Georges
1984 "U.S. immigration policy and the national interest." *Humanist* (May/June).

Fauriol, Georges and William Perry
1984 "The Americas." In Robert H. Kupperman and William J. Taylor, Jr. (eds.), *Strategic Requirements for the Army to the Year 2000*. Lexington, Mass.: Lexington Books.

Gonzalez, Edward, Brian Michael Jenkins, David Ronfeldt and Caesar Sereseres
1984 *U.S. Policy for Central America: A Briefing*. Santa Monica, Calif.: Rand Corporation.

Grimmett, Richard F.
1984 *Trends in Conventional Arms Transfers to the Third World by Major Supplier, 1976–1983*. Washington, D.C.: Congressional Research Service.

Hayes, Margaret Daly
1984 *Latin America and the U.S. National Interest*. Boulder, Colo.: Westview Press.

Jordan, Amos A. and William J. Taylor, Jr.
1984 *American National Security: Policy and Process*. Rev ed. Baltimore: Johns Hopkins University Press.

Katz, James Everett
1984 *Arms Production in Developing Countries*. Lexington, Mass.: Lexington Books.

Robert H. Kupperman Associates
1983 *Low Intensity Conflict*. Prepared for U.S. Army Training and Doctrine Command, July 30.

Leiken, Robert S.
1982 "Soviet strategy in Latin America." *The Washington Papers*, No. 93. Washington, D.C.: Praeger and the Georgetown Center for Strategic and International Studies.

Leontif, Wassily and Faye Duchin
1983 *Military Spending*. New York: Oxford University Press.

Levy, Daniel and Gabriel Szekely
1983 *Mexico Paradoxes of Stability and Change*. Boulder, CO: Westview Press.

Lewis, Mark P. (Ed.)
1983 "South America/Australasia." *DMS: Foreign Military Markets* (February).

McColm, R. Bruce
1983 "Central America and the Caribbean: The larger view." *Strategic Review* (Summer).

Mallin, Jay, Sr.
1984 "Salvadoran army now seeks destruction of guerrillas." *Washington Times* (August 30).
Martin, Everett C.
1985 "Brazil's fledgling arms industry making a hit with weapons-hungry Third World armies." *Wall Street Journal* (January 4).
Moorer, Thomas H. and Georges Fauriol
1984 "Caribbean Basin security." *The Washington Papers*, No. 104. Washington, D.C.: Praeger and the Georgetown Center for Strategic and International Studies.
Needler, Martin C.
1982 *Mexican Politics: The Containment of Conflict.* New York: Praeger Press.
Perry, William and Ronald Schneider
1985 *Brazilian Political Report.* Washington, D.C.: Georgetown Center for Strategic and International Studies.
President's National Bipartisan Commission on Central America
1984 *Report of the President's National Bipartisan Commission on Central America.* New York: Macmillan.
Sivard, Ruth Leger
1983 *World Military and Social Expenditures, 1983.* Washington, D.C.: World Priorities.
Stephan, Alfred
1981 "The United States and Latin America: Vital interests and instruments of power." Pp. 19–38 in Elizabeth G. Ferris and Jennie K. Lincoln (eds.), *Latin American Foreign Policies.* Boulder, Colo.: Westview Press.
Taylor, William J., Jr.
1983 *The Future of Conflict: U.S. Interests.* Washington, D.C.: Praeger and the Georgetown Center for Strategic and International Studies.
Taylor, William J., Jr., *et al.*
1984 *Strategic Responses to Conflict in the 1980s.* Lexington, Mass.: Lexington Books.
U.S. Arms Control and Disarmament Agency
1984 *World Military Expenditures and Arms Transfers 1972–1982.* Publication No. 117. Washington, D.C.
U.S. Department of Defense
1984 *Foreign Military Sales, Foreign Military Construction Sales, and Military Assistance Facts.* Washington, D.C.: Data Management Division, DSAA. September 30.
U.S. Department of State, Bureau of Public Affairs
1984 "Democracy in Latin America and the Caribbean." *Current Policy*, No. 605 (August).
U.S. Department of State and Defense
1984 *Background Paper: Nicaragua's Military Build-Up and Support for Central America Subversion.* Washington, D.C. July 18.
U.S. General Accounting Office, Office of the Comptroller General
1984 *Central American Refugees: Regional Conditions and Prospects and Potential Impact on the United States.* NSIAD–84–106. Washington, D.C. July.
Washington Post
1985 News story, February 3.

Index

www.ingramcontent.com/pod-product-compliance
Lightning Source LLC
LaVergne TN
LVHW010621300926
849162LV00001B/21